POP CULTURE
ARAB WORLD!

Upcoming titles in ABC-CLIO's series

Popular Culture in the Contemporary World

POP CULTURE
ARAB WORLD!

Media, Arts, and Lifestyle

Andrew Hammond

A B C · C L I O

Santa Barbara, California   Denver, Colorado   Oxford, England

Library of Congress Cataloging-in-Publication Data
Hammond, Andrew, 1970–
  Pop culture Arab world! : media, arts, and lifestyle / Andrew Hammond.
    p. cm. — (Popular culture in the contemporary world)
  Includes bibliographical references and index.
  ISBN 1-85109-449-0 (hardback : alk. paper) — ISBN 1-85109-454-7 (e-book)
1. Civilization, Arab—21st century. 2. Popular culture—Arab countries. 3. Mass media—Arab countries. I. Title. II. Series: Contemporary world issues.
DS36.88.H357   2005
306'.0917'4927—dc22
200402260808

09 08 07 06 05 | 10 9 8 7 6 5 4 3 2 1

This book is also available on the World Wide Web as an eBook.
Visit abc-clio.com for details.

ABC-CLIO, Inc.
130 Cremona Drive, P.O. Box 1911
Santa Barbara, California 93116-1911

Text design by Jane Raese

This book is printed on acid-free paper.
Manufactured in the United States of America

Contents

Preface

This book is intended as an easy reference tool, as well as a discussion of many of the political and cultural issues raging in Arab societies. Chapters cover television and radio, the press, cinema, music, theater, popular religion, belly dancing, Western consumerism, sports, and the Arabic language. Each chapter is followed by a list of books, articles, and Web sites that I've found useful, though most of the material throughout the book is based on my own research.

Perhaps a few words are in order on why I consider there is a need for such a book. Many works that cover this territory are either focused on one specific issue and extremely specialized, or they are too vague and lack up-to-date details. There are, for example, studies of Arab cinema, academic and journalistic works on the region's politics, a few works that focus on singing stars, and a number of general anthropological works and ethnographies. At the same time, there are thousands of titles dealing with Arab politics. Here I hope to have put a bit of the politics into culture and the culture into politics, in an attempt to present the region as the Arabs see it. Despite the region's ethnic, linguistic, and religious diversity, this book focuses on the greater Arab-Islamic tradition and the vibrant contemporary culture that refers to itself as Arab.

In no particular order, I'd like to offer thanks to the following people who have helped in various ways with this book: Simon Mason, Rola Mahmoud, Diana Digges, Elijah Zarwan, Hanan Samaha, Mahmoud Kassem, Steve Negus, Hisham Kassem, Martha Whitt, Sharon Daugherty, Norbert Schiller, and Claude Stemmelin.

A Note on the Spelling of Arabic Words

There are academic conventions for transliterating Arabic, using diacritical marks and symbols for letters to indicate exactly how the words should be pronounced, since Arabic is a phonetic language. But not wanting to tax the reader, I've kept to standard formats for many names and terms as they have tended to appear in the media over the years, and in other cases I have written them in a manner that closely resembles the way they are heard when pronounced by Arabic speakers, usually in the relevant dialect. I've used the spelling "Gaddafi," instead of Qaddafi and other variants, and the spelling "Mohammed" in most cases since it is the most common form one comes across, although "Muhammad" would be more phonetically correct. The definite article is rendered with the conventional English "al" in most cases, or "el" where the person referred to normally spells the name in that fashion or if it has tended to appear that way in the media. This is despite the fact that both "al" and "el" mislead a reader in pronunciation, since the definite article is actually the single letter "l," preceded by an "i" sound. Either way, in the case of certain letters the article is elided with the first letter of the following defined word. For example, Egyptian theologian Ahmed al-Tayeb's name would sound like "ahmad it-tayyib" in pronunciation and that would also be the proper phonetic rendering of the name. In general, a long vowel in English transliteration is a key that the vowel should be emphasized. For example, I have referred to a popular program on the al-Jazeera satellite channel as *al-Ittijaah al-Mu'aakis*, indicating that emphasis in both words is on the long "*aa.*"

Chronology of Some Key Cultural and Political Events

1945	As World War II ends, Arab League is established in Egypt.
1948	Fighting following the British withdrawal from Palestine leads to the creation of the State of Israel and the Palestinian refugee problem.
1952	Military coup in Egypt ends the monarchy, bringing Gamal Abdel Nasser to power and spurring a new era of cultural flourishing.
1956	Nasser emerges victorious from the Suez crisis, becoming a heroic figure around the Arab world.
1958–1961	The merging of Egypt and Syria into the United Arab Republic.
1962	Algeria gains independence after a seven-year war against the French, resulting in the takeover of the Arab nationalist regime.
	Omar Sharif makes his shift from Egyptian cinema to Hollywood, scoring global success in *Lawrence of Arabia*.
1963	The Baath Party takes power in Syria, restricting the press and other elements of civil society and cultural life.
1964	Palestinian Liberation Organization (PLO) established.
1967	The Arab-Israeli war, resulting in Israel's occupation of the West Bank, including East Jerusalem, Gaza Strip, Sinai, and Golan Heights.
1968	The Baath Party takes power in Iraq, bringing Saddam Hussein into government.
1969	Release of director Shadi Abdel-Salam's *The Mummy (al-Mumyaa')*, seen as the high point of Egyptian cinema.

1970   Nasser dies, succeeded by Anwar Sadat, who takes Egypt into the Western orbit.

1973   Shaabi singer Ahmed Adawiya releases the seminal pop song *Zahma*, a sign of the times as consumer culture spreads in post-Nasser Egypt.

The October war, led by Egypt and Syria against Israel; OPEC hikes oil prices.

1975   The Lebanese civil war begins.

Arab nationalist singer Umm Kalthoum dies.

Success for Algerian post-independence cinema when director Mohamed Lakhdar Hamina's *The Chronicle of the Years of Embers* wins the Palme d'Or at the Cannes Film Festival.

Saudi Arabia's King Faisal assassinated by a royal disgruntled with modernization.

1977   Sadat makes a sudden trip to Jerusalem, where he addresses the Knesset with a call for a comprehensive Arab-Israeli peace.

Egyptian heartthrob singer Abdel-Halim Hafez, a kind of Arab Elvis figure, dies.

Belly-dancing clubs are attacked during riots in Cairo.

1979   Egypt and Israel sign a peace treaty, leading to Egypt's expulsion from the Arab League.

Edward Said publishes his seminal study, *Orientalism*.

Egyptian belly dancer Fifi Abdo first comes to public attention.

Iranian revolution, spurring Islamist politics around the Arab world.

1980   The eight-year-long Iran-Iraq war begins.

Berbers stage protests against political marginalization and cultural repression in Algeria.

1981   Egyptian president Anwar Sadat assassinated; succeeded by Hosni Mubarak.

1982   Israel besieges Yasser Arafat and the PLO in Beirut.

1983   Southern Sudanese launch civil war against northern domination.

1984   Moroccan athletes take two golds at the Los Angeles Olympic Games.

1987   First Palestinian Intifada against Israeli
occupation begins.

Zein al-Abidine Ben Ali takes power in Tunisia,
bringing in a new wave of Arabization.

Murder in London of dissident Palestinian
cartoonist Naji al-Ali.

1988   Algeria allows political liberalization.

Launch of revamped *al-Hayat* newspaper in
London under Saudi ownership.

Developing genre of Arabpop finds its stride with
huge hit *Law Leki*.

Egypt sets up the annual Cairo International
Festival for Experimental Theater.

Egyptian novelist Naguib Mahfouz wins the Nobel
Prize for literature.

1990   Iraq invades Kuwait; UN sanctions on Iraq begin.

End of Lebanese civil war officially declared.

1991   U.S.-led coalition ousts Iraqi forces from Kuwait,
Iraqi regime survives rebellion.

1992   Algerian military cancels parliamentary elections;
Islamist revolt begins.

Radical Islamist groups in Egypt begin insurgency
against the Egyptian government.

Algerian *rai* music makes it big in Europe with
Cheb Khaled's *Didi*.

Work begins on rebuilding Beirut's gutted city
center.

Algerian Hassiba Boulmerka wins gold in the
women's 1,500-meter race at the Barcelona
Olympics, breathing life into Arab sport.

1993   Oslo peace accords between Israel and the PLO.

1994   Jordan signs a peace treaty with Israel.

1996   Israeli right wing comes to power under
Netanyahu.

1996   Qatar sets up al-Jazeera satellite television channel.

Lebanese entertainment channel LBC launches around the region.

1997   The film *Ismailiya Rayih Gayy* reinvigorates Egyptian cinema.

1998   Algerian Berber dissident singer Matoub Lounes is murdered.

Influential Egyptian television preacher Sheikh Shaarawi dies.

Morocco and Saudi Arabia make it to the second round of the World Cup finals.

2000   Mauritania establishes diplomatic relations with Israel.

Second Palestinian Intifada begins.

Hafez al-Assad dies; his son Bashar takes over, raising hopes of political reform and cultural revival.

Israel ends twenty-two-year occupation of south Lebanon.

Algerian Nouria Merah-Benida wins gold in women's 1,500-meter race at the Sydney Olympics

2001   Right-wing Israeli government led by former general Ariel Sharon comes to power.

Launch of Arabic version of TV quiz *Who Wants to Be a Millionaire?* marks the rise in popularity of the quiz show genre in the Arab world.

Golden Age cinema actress Soad Hosni commits suicide in London.

September 11 attacks in the United States; new war on Islamic extremism begins, resonating throughout the Arab world.

2003   A U.S.-led invasion topples the regime of Saddam Hussein; UN sanctions end.

2003   Islamists claiming links to al-Qa'ida launch fight against the Saudi monarchy and proliferate in Iraq.

2004   Reality TV debuts in the Arab world to a mixed reception: shows like *'Al Hawa Sawa* (Together on Air) win big audiences but protests force an Arab version of *Big Brother* off the air.

1

Overview:
The Arab World Today

The Middle East has undergone immense changes over the last century, and in the last fifty years alone the region's demographic profile has changed beyond all recognition. Egypt contains around 70 million people, when twenty years ago its population was only just over 40 million. Sudan, Algeria, and Morocco each house around 30 million, while Qatar barely manages 500,000—hardly enough to fill a five-star Cairo hotel, as one Egyptian newspaper editor sniped several years ago during a tiff with the tiny Gulf state. The comment was telling: The desert states are wealthy from oil, while the nations with ancient urban traditions are poor and very resentful of the fact. Despite the presence of oil in a region of the world that produced the world's most stunning early human civilizations, the Arab world today is for the most part ridden with poverty, illiteracy, and political instability, while untold wealth is enjoyed by a privileged minority. Virtually all of the accoutrements of modern life have come in a short span of time. Print and visual media developed within decades of each other in the Arab world, as opposed to developing through centuries in Western Europe. This is just one clue to the many diverse influences, lifestyles, and ideologies fighting for space in the Arab world today.

When, why, and in what ways did this culture perceive itself as Arab? Given the size and complexity of the region, one might well ask whether it is possible to write about something called contemporary Arab culture at all. With the end of World War II and the emergence of newly independent Arab nation-states, a self-aware, homogenous, but richly diverse Arab culture emerged. Today, over five decades later, pop culture has finally succeeded in bringing the peoples of the region together, where fifty years of politics failed. Culture and ideology have worked in tandem to complete a process of Arabization that began 1,400 years ago with the Arab conquests of the Middle East and North Africa, and the postcolonial era has witnessed a process that could be termed the "Arabization of Arab culture." This might seem tautologous: the Arab world is surely Arab by definition. Yes and no; for, while the saying goes that if you scratch a Russian you'll find a Tartar, if you scratch an Arab you might find a Berber, an ancient Egyptian, or a Nubian—in fact, a whole range of non-Arabic-speaking ethnicities. Today's Moroccan Arab culture is informed by Berber culture, Egypt's culture is informed by ancient Egyptian culture, and Iraq's culture is informed by a number of influences, including Bedouin, Semitic, Persian, Kurd, and even Sumerian cultures (Sumer was the first civilization to settle in Mesopotamia and its words have found their way into modern Arabic). But, since independence, cultural reaffirmation has transpired among countries of the region and also between individual countries and the rest of the world, emphasizing similarity, homogeneity, and a greater sense of something, identified as Arabness or Arab identity (*al-huwiyya al-arabiyya*), or, with more political overtones, Arabism (*al-'uruuba*). The widespread sense of defeat at the fall of Baghdad to the invading Westerners in 2003 ("the biggest modern disaster for the Arabs since 1948," said Egyptian commentator Hamdy Kandil, Dream TV, August 2003) suggested that rather than dying from the crushing defeat to Israel in 1967, Arab nationalism is very much alive and well—perhaps more than Westerners, obsessed with Islamism, have realized. Modern media and communications have increased the sheer volume of those shared cultural elements and further marginalized those aspects of the region's cultural profile that don't fit into the wider picture.

In today's Arab world there is a greater tradition influencing all areas of the region, and even many of the local traditions have taken on an Arab worldwide status. Anthropologists concerned with religion, mu-

sic, and other cultural forms all over the world have heavily borrowed from the idea of "greater" and "lesser" traditions, first posited by American anthropologist Robert Redfield in his 1973 ethnography, *The Little Community and Peasant Society and Culture*. Basing his ideas on a study of rural communities in Middle America, Redfield talked of a "great tradition," which is literary, formal, and urban, coexisting with a "little tradition," which is oral, informal, and community-based. Experts in the field of cultural studies saw an immediate application of the paradigm in the Islamic world, where an all-encompassing "official" form of Islam exists alongside and negotiates space with a myriad of smaller, local traditions of diverse origins, some of which assume an Islamic legitimacy, some of which are frowned upon. Similarly, there is a greater tradition of Arab identity that exists alongside ancient, little traditions of local, non-Arab identities. But the last fifty years have witnessed a process whereby more and more of these smaller traditions are assuming the lofty title "Arab," as the historic process of Arabization of the Middle East, begun with the Arab conquests in the seventh century C.E., reaches some point of cultural closure.

Yet while Arab identity has gelled, fears of its disintegration are high, and many Arab intellectuals and politicians wonder whether these are destined to become nothing more than a group of nations that happen to speak similar languages—there are constituencies in the region that would be happy to see that happen. Both trends can be observed in the way that Western policymakers and institutions deal with the region today and have dealt with it in the past: there are trends that treat the Arabs as a whole and trends that intentionally or

The Arab Human Development Report Stirs Controversy

The contents of the first United Nations Arab Human Development (UNDP) Report in 2002, and a follow-up report in 2003, provoked a huge debate both inside and outside the Arab world over defining the problems of the region, sparking discussion about who sets the agenda in tackling those problems. Released post–September 11, the first report in 2002 was seized on by politicians and media in the West as a bold acknowledgment by Arabs of their problems of political and economic dysfunction, which had become issues of public debate for Western politicians and commentators. But Arab critics such as Palestinian American writer Edward Said and Egyptian economist Galal Amin argued that the report failed to give sufficient weight to the Arab-Israeli conflict as a major obstacle to human development in the region and that it essentially told the U.S. administration and supporters of an anti-Arab agenda what they wanted to hear: that Arabs were only good for making babies and turning them into illiterate adults. The *New York Times* columnist Thomas Friedman, for example, wrote that "getting rid of the Bin Ladens, Saddams and Arafats is necessary, but is hardly sufficient. Americans also need to roll up their sleeves and help the Arabs address all the problems out back" (4 July 2002).

The second report in 2003 was stronger on the fundamental, underlying issue ruining Arab chances for harmonious societies—the Arab-Israeli conflict—and addressed head-on the debate over the first report. In the foreword, Rima Khalaf Hunaidi, assistant secretary-general and regional director of the Regional Bureau for Arab States (RBAS) at UNDP, wrote, "At this precarious juncture, some observers questioned the wisdom of issuing further reports, while others worried that special interest groups might exploit their outspoken approach, to the detriment of Arabs. Indeed, the authors are well aware that their work might be misused or misinterpreted to serve the purposes of parties—outside as well as inside the Arab world—whose interests run counter to an Arab awakening. . . . Turning a blind eye to the weaknesses and shortfalls of the region, instead of decisively identifying and overcoming them, can only increase its vulnerability and leave it more exposed" ("Foreword," Arab Human Development Report 2003. www.undp.org/rbas/ahdr/).

The 2003 report said the "war on terror" had radicalized Arabs who were angry with both the West and autocratic rulers bent on curbing their political rights. It said that Arab countries lagged behind other regions in dissemination of knowledge, that readership of books was relatively limited, that education dictated submission rather than critical thought, and that the Arabic language was in crisis. The report blamed an absence of "effective and peaceful channels for dealing with injustices" as the reason that radical political groups seek change by violence. It cited wider censorship, from restricting Internet access to suppressing publication of material deemed encouraging to "terrorism." Even a best-selling novel sells on average only 5,000 copies compared to hundreds of thousands elsewhere in the world. Official educational curricula in Arab countries "bred submission, obedience, subordination and compliance rather than free critical thinking" (Arab Human Development Report 2003. www.undp.org/rbas/ahdr/). The report said that Arab universities are overcrowded wth old laboratories and poor libraries, and research and development in the Arab world does not exceed 0.2 percent of the Gross National Product (GNP). Fewer than one in twenty Arab university students pursue scientific disciplines, compared to one in five in South Korea, while the number of telephone lines in

(*continues*)

The Arab Human Development Report Stirs Controversy (*continued*)

Arab countries is barely one-fifth of that in developed countries. Access to digital media is also among the lowest in the world. The report said there are 18 computers per 1,000 people (compared to a global average of 78), and only 1.6 percent of over 270 million Arabs have Internet access, one of the lowest ratios in the world.

The Arab Intelligentsia

The postcolonial era in the Arab world saw deep rifts emerge among the intellectual class (*al-mufakkirun*), rifts that deepened the crisis left after the Gulf War in 1991. The apologists were "with" the autocratic, undemocratic systems that came into being after World War II. Of those who were "against," many of them chose life in the West. But the invasion of one Arab country by another, which also cited Arab nationalism as one of its motives, and the subsequent U.S.-led intervention to undo the invasion ripped Arab politics apart. While governments sided with the international alliance, intellectuals of all persuasions roundly opposed the Western-imposed solution, a position that Iraqi writer Kanan Makiya (a.k.a. Samir Khalil) damned as moral bankruptcy, given the brutal nature of Saddam Hussein's regime. Lebanese intellectual Fouad Ajami pursued this line of argument in his book *The Dream Palace of the Arabs:* Arab nationalism and its obsessions with Israel, he said, had blinded Arab thinkers to the horrors inflicted on their peoples by regimes they had accepted too easily. Ajami directed special venom toward Egyptian thinkers, whom he despises as the strongest force in the Arab nationalist political constellation. Ajami and Makiya were loud supporters of the 2003 invasion of Iraq, which again met with rejection among the vast majority of the intellectual community throughout the Arab world. The American adventure in Iraq, which

cited human rights as one of the reasons for the removal of a leader who had made those rights subordinate to pan-Arab causes, has thrown down the gauntlet to Arab intellectuals and ruling elites: Is it not time for individual rights to come before concepts of national rights and principles concerning Palestine, the wider Arab nation, and the community of Islam? At heart is the question of the strength of the nation-state and whether individual countries, prodded by Washington, should ditch the grand concerns of Arab nationalism. An attitude of "Iraq first" is now on the rise in Iraq, as many intellectuals argue that the country has suffered enough from the pan-Arab interests of Saddam Hussein's nationalist regime. "Egypt first" has been the guiding policy in Egypt since Sadat steered the country away from radical politics into the U.S. fold via peace with Israel in 1979. But in Egypt the intellectual community was left behind, as Sadat and his coterie acted entirely on their own

Former Iraqi leader Saddam Hussein as he appeared after U.S. forces captured him in December 2003. (AP/Wide World Photos)

Egypt's president Anwar Sadat was assassinated in 1981 by radical Islamists who opposed his peace with Israel. (TRIP/Art Directors)

Cultural critic and prominent intellectual Edward Said is best known for his writings on Middle Eastern affairs and on the relations between the West and the Arab world. He was a proponent of Palestinian national rights. (Bettmann/Corbis)

in dragging the country into America's and Israel's orbit—one of the reasons why Egypt's intellectuals remain so anti-Western and rejectionist to this day.

The nemesis of thinkers like Ajami and Makiya was Palestinian thinker Edward Said, who died in 2003. Living in New York and writing in eloquent English, Said argued that their pro-American prescriptions for the region were no less humiliating than the totalitarian systems created by the Arab dictatorships themselves and that they offered no solution to the problems of a political-cultural unit defined as Arab. Ironically, Said was never that popular among Arab intellectuals inside the Arab world, despite reams of praise heaped on him when he died. "Edward Said made the people of the colonies become aware of the mechanisms of the mentality of colonialism which could find

their way into their narratives, writings and visions, and he dissipated the illusions that the makers of this discourse hid behind in their actions," Egypt's premier intellectual weekly *Akhbar al-Adab* wrote in a gushing eulogy. But two years earlier, Said was attacked on the pages of *Akhbar al-Adab* for supporting the right of Egyptian novelists to have their work translated into Hebrew by an Israeli publisher.

Amid the bitter standoff between secular-nationalist and Islamist groups, along with the failure of either to remove the existing regimes and the failure of those regimes to challenge the U.S.-Israeli alliance since the 1967 defeat, a certain violence has crept into intellectual de-

(*continues*)

The Arab Human Development Report Stirs Controversy (*continued*)

U.S. president George Bush and British prime minister Tony Blair, the Western leaders who championed the controversial invasion of Iraq in March 2003. (NATO Photos)

bate. Secular liberals were "a bunch of gays and dogs," Islamist judge and lawyer Yehya Refai once said (interview with author, June 1995). Egypt's *al-Shaab* newspaper is a case in point. Since 1985 it was controlled by Adel Hussein, one of a group of Marxist intellectuals who converted to political Islam after the Iranian revolution, seeing it as the paradigm of the future in Arab politics. Hussein, who died in 2001, turned *al-Shaab* into Egypt's most radical broadsheet, but during a mid-1990s Islamist insurgency *al-Shaab* memorably proclaimed in a front-page headline that "tourism is Islamically *haram* (forbidden)"—a virtual call to murder the tourists. "As long as we complain politely, nothing gets done," Hussein once said, when asked about the years of provocative writing. Hussein was a gentle and charming man, which made his politics all the more troubling to the decreasing minority of sober writers and thinkers. In one obituary, secular intellectual Mohammed al-Sayed Said said of Hussein's experiment with *al-Shaab:* "Ideological violence was never the acceptable way of dealing with intellectual issues. Bravery without an idea becomes pure violence and unlimited savagery. I fear that this is what Adel Hussein was sliding into, and I fear that this is what the Arab world in general is sliding towards" (al-Sayed Said, *Akhbar al-Adab,* 24 March 2001). Hussein's descent into Islamist rabble-rousing was symptomatic of a wider malaise in intellectual life.

A Palestinian flag in the window of an electronics shop in Cairo, with the words "Jerusalem is ours." Such expressions of pro-Palestinian support spread after the second Intifada began in 2000. (Norbert Schiller/Focus MidEast)

otherwise treat them as smaller units. The language used to describe the region is telling. Of the ideological terms the Arabs use to describe themselves, the word "Maghreb," referring to the western half of the Arab world, has made it into French and to a lesser extent English usage, but the word "Mashreq" for the Arab East has not. This is a reflection of the nature of imperial power relationships in relation to different areas of the Arab world. But the independence era, when Arab identity came into its own, has molded this language to its own purposes and needs. Paris immigrants, many of whom are now part of a Berber pride movement, turned the designation "Arab" around and called themselves "les Beurs," one of the most strident examples of reappropriating and reformu-

lating an identity imposed by foreigners. "Orientalism" was coined by Palestine intellectual Edward Said living in America as a pejorative term describing Western attitudes toward Arab culture, but over twenty years later Arabs are happily referring to their music as "oriental," often deliberately avoiding the term "Arabic" because it has political overtones. In fact, Said, the author of *Orientalism*, the seminal study of academic attitudes toward Arab-Islamic culture, is little appreciated by Arab intellectuals, and before his death in 2003 he only managed to engage them through articles published in pan-Arab émigré papers, such as *al-Hayat* (published in London and the main daily forum for political commentary from across the region). There are even a few urban Palestinians who remember how, before Zionism changed the cognitive topography of the region, the term "Arab" was ordinarily used by Palestinians to refer to Bedouins in the Negev—some of whom today serve in the Israeli army—and not themselves (interview with Lutfy Mashhour, editor of *al-Senara*, November 1998). (In European diplomatic terms "orientalist," like "Arabist," has meant government officials and associated scholars who are familiar with Arab culture, speak Arabic, and sympathize with Arab nationalism and the Palestinians vis-à-vis Israel, while "Arabist" has become almost a term of abuse in U.S. politics where pro-Israel sentiment is strong.)

To some degree *al-'uruuba* (Arabism) has thrived on the fact that patriotism remains an elusive concept in a region where governments must fight to inculcate loyalty to the nation-state over religious and family loyalty. The Arab historian and sociologist Ibn Khaldoun noted six centuries ago that Arab-Islamic civilization's great advance on tribal fealty was the innovation of loyalty to Islam in the Arab-Islamic city. But since European nationalism arrived in the world in the nineteenth century, loyalty to Islam has not been replaced with much success by loyalty to the modern Arab states, most of which are crude products of colonial meddling. Governments, perhaps because of an acute awareness of this meddling, have tended to rely on clan groups, or some other form of partisanship that views the loyalty of many segments of the population with suspicion. In the extreme case of Saudi Arabia, the state is identified as the embodiment of Islam itself, in the possession of one family that gives its very name to the country and rules via a division of power with clerics. There are many examples of subversion of the official state

structures. Syrian, Palestinian, Lebanese, or Jordanian inhabitants in the Levant may sign on to the idea of a Greater Syria; some Saudis will talk of *al-jazeera al-arabiya* (the Arabian Peninsula) as a code word of disapproval for the Saudi state; Iraqis consider Kuwait an illogical entity, designed and promoted by foreigners to weaken them; and Egyptian Islamist teachers during the 1980s and 1990s would even stop children from singing the national anthem in the morning before classes. Arab states historically have simply been an expression of the extent to which a strong city was able to extend its control. Wider, more inclusive ideologies such as Islamism or Arabism—and many intellectuals argue they are two sides of the same coin—have thrived in this environment.

Historical Background: The Emergence of Postcolonial Arab States

The Middle East changed during the twentieth century more than during any other comparable period in its history. World War I and its immediate aftermath saw the creation of most of the modern, territorially delimited states that make up the Arab world, and that process happened in the shadow of direct European domination throughout the region. It wasn't until World War II and its immediate aftermath that most of these young nations formally threw off the yokes of their colonial masters who, in many cases, had determined the boundaries of the states." To what degree the newly formed Arab states truly gained independence is a debate that rages to this day. Commentators have seen in the Israeli control of Palestinians and the U.S. presence in Iraq a return to the imperial period and collapse of the post–World War II Arab order. But certainly political space was vacated by the foreigners and filled by indigenous political elites, and this process was accompanied by a renewed sense of shared historical experience and cultural affinity.

World War II marked an identity shift in the region, for its inhabitants as much as outsiders. A world "with its core in the former Ottoman territories gives way to a new concept of a Middle East with its heartland in the Arab world," as historian Malcolm Yapp writes (Yapp 1991, 390). It was also the end of a period, dubbed "the liberal age" by historian Albert Hourani (Hourani 1983), when the region's political and intellectual elites had looked to Europe for inspiration. The great sign of these new times was the creation of the Arab League in the Egyptian coastal city of Alexandria in 1945, the result of a half-century of activity by Levantine and Iraqi intellectuals and politicians, the Hashemite rulers of Jordan and Iraq, and the regionwide struggle for independence from the Europeans. As the Europeans went out, pan-Arabism came in. Syria and Lebanon, formerly under a French "mandate" since 1920, were rid of French soldiers in 1946. A year earlier the French gave up in Lebanon but tenaciously held their ground in Algeria, where some 100,000 settlers had made their home, fighting a seven-year war with the Algerians that ended in independence in 1952, at a cost of one million dead among the indigenous population. Iraq, under British mandate since 1920, became independent in 1932. Egypt didn't manage to arrange the exit of Britain from its affairs until 1954, and Britain was only made to relinquish control of the Suez Canal by Egypt's decision to nationalize the crucial waterway in

1956. Britain ended its mandate in Jordan in 1946 and in Palestine in 1947, leaving the Palestinians to fight it out with a strident Jewish colonist movement, sponsored by Britain, despite bouts of discouragement, since 1917, when the Balfour Declaration encouraged immigration of European refugees to the region, thereby increasing the Jewish contingent to almost one third of the Palestinian population in 1947, from less than ten percent in 1917 (Yapp 1991, 117). The creation of the state of Saudi Arabia in the 1920s was largely conditioned by the extent to which Britain attached little importance to the desert wastes where the Bedouin Saudi family carved out a polity in the Arabian Peninsula, the true child of Britain's infamous mid-war promise to the Sherif of Mecca to give Arabia back to the Arabs. The Saudi state formally came into existence in 1932, and it might have incorporated Yemen in 1934 were it not for British and Italian interference. British influence lingered further in the coastal areas of the Peninsula in order to ensure smooth commercial passage in the Red Sea, Arabian Sea, Indian Ocean, and Persian Gulf, a policy that traditionally served to uphold Britain's imperial trade with India and the Far East. Britain didn't formally leave the Gulf until 1971, when the United Arab Emirates came into being. The mandates principally allowed British oil interests to entrench themselves in the region. The U.S.-based Aramco ran Saudi oilfields up to 1990, and the U.S. government helped set up much of the state infrastructure that oil development required in the nascent Saudi state. In North Africa, French dominion was more durable, lasting from 1830 through 1962 in Algeria, from 1881 through 1956 in Tunisia, and from 1912 through 1956 in Morocco (where the Spanish enclaves of Ceuta and Melilla [*Sabta* and *Maleela*] remain a nationalist issue).

The debate over colonial rule has been long and bitter, but suffice it to say that in the Arab world, imperialism took on different forms that have affected the shape of Arab politics and culture today in different ways. Left to their own devices in Algeria, the French were vicious—decimating the population, accentuating differences blurred by Islam between Arabic-speakers and Berber-speakers, and trying to replace the Arabic language with French. The result is that even today cabinet meetings are held in French, yet some Iraqis, Palestinians, and Egyptians pine for the fact that detached British control didn't leave them with any fluency in the colonials' language to show for the experience. British imperialism gave us Kuwait, and in the view of Arab nationalists, American imperialism made sure we still have Kuwait, in the face of Iraqi attempts to undo British conniving. Meanwhile, some Western scholars (e.g., Henry and Springborg 2001) argue that the length and nature of French occupation in Tunisia were just enough to create the modern middle class, which has fueled the country's relative economic success and kept it out of the mesmerizing matrix of pan-Arab reactionism. Out of these experiences in the first fifty years of the twentieth century, a new cultural construct came into existence—a series of countries with a new identity and shared sense of culture. The origins of the modern political ideology known as pan-Arabism are a topic of much controversy and debate. Some intellectuals, such as Lebanese American writer Fouad Ajami, are eager to see an end to what they perceive as a failed project, while others argue that, like the theories of Karl Marx, pan-Arabism was never really given a chance. But it is certain that

the ideology was indisputably new. The concept of the Arabs being the original people of Islam, to whom God made his final and complete revelation—a kind of chosen people, in the fashion of the Jews—had been around since the Arab conquerors first sought to legitimize their rule of a vast empire encompassing the Middle East and North Africa. A series of hadiths (mainly from al-Haythami's al-Zawa'id collection) from the Prophet (which Arab nationalists have often cited and whose authenticity Islamists have questioned) demonstrates a special place for the Arabs, despite the fact that the religion of Islam was eventually to develop as a world religion for all peoples of any ethnic origin: "Godlessness is to be found in non-Arabness. Only a hypocrite could hate the Arabs. If the Arabs are treated with contempt, it is Islam which is being treated with contempt" (Fiqi 1993).

The Arabic term for the conquests is unabashedly ideological. The invasions were *al-futuhaat*, "the openings," which offered the possibility of civilizational advance to a region of tremendous history and energy that had been united by the Arabs. While the Byzantines were occupiers, the Arabs were liberators, and today hundreds of thousands of children all over the region are named after the particular Arab general who "opened up" their slice of the Arab world. There are some intellectuals who denigrate the Arab-Muslim conquests—Tunisian film director Kahina Abbas is named after the Berber princess who tried to fight off the armies of Uqba bin Nafi'—but their voices are marginal. Osama Anwar Okasha, a well-known Egyptian writer of TV soaps, has said: "The Arab civilization interrupted the development of Egypt's Pharaonic/Mediterranean culture, a potentially glorious civilization that could have competed with Renaissance Europe. What the Arabs did was simply preserve Greek texts for the Europeans. It was a copying, not an innovating culture . . . all the Arabs had was poetry and the sword. And they paved the way for the oppressive Ottoman rule that's the main reason for our backwardness today" ("The Sultan of Soap" 2000). But perhaps this issue is better suited for newspaper columns rather than mass-consumption TV serials. Abouda Bahry, one of the few Berber intellectuals left in Tunisia, argues the same, but in bitter tones befitting a people who have been almost entirely assimilated into Tunisia's Arab-Islamic identity. "There's no such thing as Arab culture. It's a mixture of Persian, Greek and North Africa, with some Arabic poetry from Arab tribes in the Arabian Peninsula," he says (interview with author, February 2003). The language used to refer to the region in Arabic is equally ideological in origin. North Africa is the *al-maghrib al-arabi*, often shortened to *al-maghrib* (also the word for Morocco), meaning the Arab West; the Middle East is *al-mashriq*, or Arab East. The Mashreq includes Egypt, the Gulf, and the Levant, while Libya, sparsely populated and in a world of its own to some degree, is more often considered part of the Maghreb. Today, the Arabic phrase *al-aalam al-arabi*, a translation of the phrase "the Arab world," has gained ground in public discourse. For secular intellectuals, the phrase "the Arab world" clearly offers an alternative to the ideologically charged phrase "the Arab nation" (*al-watan al-arabi* or *al-umma al-arabiyya*), and even Amr Moussa, the secretary-general of the Arab League, is given to using the term. Modern scholarship on early Islamic history has come up with scenarios for how the region's Arab identity was formulated, and they go beyond the ideological gloss of conventional Islamic history. A movement of scholars since the 1970s has posited that, rather than see their hegemony slowly fall away if they chose to adopt the Christianity or Judaism practiced by most of the peoples they had conquered, the Arabs set a course for reorienting the Judaic-Christian monotheistic tradition with a new spin. The result, the argument goes, was Islam as we know it today, the product of the interaction between Arab ruling elites and conquered, non-Arab peoples. But it was not recognizable as Islam, in terms of theory of origins, holy book, theology, and schools of law, until at least 200 years after the Arab conquests. (Many Western scholars would concur with Muslim scholars that Islam as it developed offered the peoples of the region one all-encompassing version of the monotheistic tradition, free of foreign [Greek] influence and articulated in one language.) The process of Arabization possibly took a lot longer to make serious inroads among the conquered peoples. Records show that members of conquered communities often became nominal members of Arab tribes and that membership of the new religious community of Islam meant avoidance of paying many taxes levied on Christians, Jews, Zoroastrians, and others. By the thirteenth century, the survival of the Coptic language of the Christians in Egypt was reaching a critical stage vis-à-vis Arabic. By the late twentieth century, standard estimates put the Coptic Christians at 10 percent of a mainly Muslim population, and there were only a reported two families left speaking Coptic, though the language survives in church liturgy.

The Arabic dialects vary widely from one country to another, but the level of mutual intelligibility is more impressive than the divergences. Were it not for classical Arabic's hallowed place in Islam as the language in which God chose to make his final revelation, today's dialects would have diverged even further from each other and from the formal language, in the manner that Spanish, Italian, French, and Romanian diverged from a Latin origin. That is exactly what happened to Maltese Arabic, cut off from the Arab-Islamic mainstream when the islands became culturally oriented toward Christian Europe from the eleventh century onward. What is striking about the linguistic map of the Arab world, though, is the complex extent of overlapping throughout the region. One will find common features between Iraqi Arabic and the Arabic of Palestinian villages in the West Bank and peasants of north and south Egypt, quite removed from urban centers such as Jerusalem and Cairo, which have their own shared linguistic features. Although there is a clear difference in dialect as one moves westward from Iraq and the Gulf to Morocco, there is also a distinct divide between urban Arabic, rural Arabic, and Bedouin Arabic throughout the region, to the extent that a Bedouin from Algeria and a Bedouin from Egypt's Sinai Peninsula might more readily understand each other than they would their settled neighbors, though the modern nation-states are undoubtedly influencing this situation. Today, finally, the self-declared protectors of the language—embodied in an alliance of Arabic language academies in several Arab capitals—have accepted that the next stage of protecting Arab identity requires simplifying the classical language extant today to make it more practical for upcoming generations to quickly learn and use.

By the end of the nineteenth century, as a century of European influence in the region reached its climax with the scramble for Africa, religious thinkers from Egypt

Congestion of people and traffic in central Cairo, Africa's largest city. (TRIP/Art Directors)

and Syria, taking their cue from European criticism, pondered whether Islam itself was the key to explaining why the Europeans had advanced and come to dominate their world. The conclusion of most was that it was the fault of the Turks. Within a few tumultuous decades, which saw the Ottoman Empire crumble and more Arabs fall under direct European control, this line of thought had evolved into calls for a return to an Arab caliphate. By the 1930s, this call became the articulation of an ethnically defined Arab nation. Many of the intellectuals in the Mashreq leading this movement did not consider the Maghreb as part of the project, nor did they even consider Egypt, the most populous of the Arabic-speaking countries, sitting fortuitously in their midst. By the time this anticolonial moment reached its apogee with the Egyptian revo-

Egypt's charismatic Arab nationalist president Gamal Abdel Nasser, who died in 1970. (TRIP/Art Directors)

lution, which was set in motion by a military coup in 1952, the Arab nationalist movement had taken a maximalist course and expanded to include as many as possible—in fact, all those countries that the Arabs had first conquered in the *futuhaat*, where Islam first spread and the Arabic language had taken root. Under Gamal Abdel Nasser, Egypt's charismatic, Peron-like president who ruled from 1954 to his death in 1970, pan-Arabism became a living creed practiced by millions of people. *Al-qawmiyya al-arabiyya*—Arab nationalism—became the new mantra, drummed into schoolchildren and blasted daily on the airwaves. Arab nationalism has found a competitor in political Islam, which had been a force since the early twentieth century and which grew in the aftermath of the crushing Arab defeat to Israel in 1967 (to

the extent that in television quizzes, for the question, "What is the longest journey ever undertaken by a human being?", the answer is the Prophet's ascension, or *mi'raj*, to heaven from Jerusalem). Political writers debate today whether the second Intifada and the invasion and occupation of Iraq have secured the ascendancy of the Islamist trend over secular Arab nationalism. But there's no question that Islamists in the Arab world operate within an Arabist paradigm: the first and the last lands for which they seek a return to religion are those of the original Islamic dispensation, those of the Arabs.

The readiness of countries whose peoples defied the dictionary definition of what an Arab was to submerge their identities into "Arab"—the word that in popular parlance referred to Bedouin tribes—was to some degree rather odd. In 1958 the Egyptian regime acted on its nationalist ideology when it joined a United Arab Republic with Syria, effacing the name of a 5,000-year-old polity from the map. The language of the Egyptians, like the Berbers who formed the main ethnic group in North Africa at the time of the Arab conquests, was part of the Hamitic-Cushitic family of languages, while the Arabic of the Bedouin is part of the Semitic group of languages. They are not unconnected, in the way that Slavic languages are linked to Romance languages, and scholars once upon a time debated whether ancient Egyptian should be classified as a Semitic language. But as Egyptian sociologist Leila Ahmed writes in *A Border Passage*, the key could be found in Nasser's ingenious transformation of a term of derision into a term of cultural pride. Just as Americans of African descent turned the word "black" into "Black," Nasser turned "arab" into "Arab." Europe had humiliated the ancient peoples of the Arabic-speaking Muslim lands. For Europeans, "'Arabs' meant people with whom you made treaties you did not have to honor. . . . It meant people whose lands you could carve up and apportion as you wished. . . . It meant people whose democracies you could obstruct at will" (Ahmed 1999, 267–268). "The European meaning of 'arab' then hollowed out the word, replacing it entirely with itself. Except that now ours is their meaning of the word 'arab' in reverse. Like 'black' and 'Black,' as in 'Black is beautiful.'" Egyptian Christian intellectual Rafiq Habib has even outlined an elaborate theory of Semitic origins for Egypt, a complement to his late 1990s alliance with moderate elements of political Islam through the al-Wasat Party in an attempt to break Egypt's political stalemate.

The pivotal event in the arrival of Arab nationalism was the fighting that ensued between Palestinians and the Zionist movement when the British vacated their Palestine mandate in 1947. The war saw the creation of the State of Israel and the dispersion of up to one million Palestinians into Lebanon, Jordan, Egypt, and, within historical Palestine, the West Bank and Gaza Strip. Pan-Arabism can in many senses be read as a response to the idea of an ethnically pure state for Jews in the midst of the Arab region championed by Zionism. That ideology had consequences beyond the threat to the integrity of Palestinian society: it struck at the very heart of the multireligious nature of many parts of the Arabic-speaking world. Pre-1952 Egypt had been reticently Arabist and sympathetic to the Zionists (who had chapters in Egypt in the 1920s and 1930s) for fear that the Palestinian nationalist movement would provoke anti-Jewish feelings in Egypt and ruin Egypt's complex social fabric. The ruin of that fabric is exactly

what followed from 1948 onward, as the region's Jews gathered in the new State of Israel after the dispersal of the Palestinians. A process, which seems inevitable now, gained momentum, involving Israeli encouragement of Jews to put their Judaism first and get with the Utopian promise by leaving Arab societies to join the Jewish State and independent Arab states pressuring their Jews to get out. Many of those working in entertainment, particularly in Egypt, the cultural motor behind the Arab world, stayed put—the most celebrated such case is singer/actress Leila Murad, who converted to Islam and rejected Israeli enticements to make her the Hebrew Umm Kalthoum. Israeli Jews with origins in Arab countries have begun to delve into these issues and answer honestly what they gained and what they lost. One prominent example is the 1995 novel *Victoria* by Baghdad-born Sami Mikhail: it depicts a Jewish community in Iraq with a sense of alienation from a hostile wider society, which then moves to Israel, where new immigrants encounter more racism and oppression in a state where all Jews are nominally equal but Europeans form the dominant social and political caste. Similarly, Israeli Arab Anton Shammas has been able to produce a Hebrew novel like *Arabesques*, "a supreme instance of the high ground on the Israeli literary scene being taken by a non-Jewish author," as Lebanese human rights lawyer Chibli Mallat has said (Mallat 1996, 58).

Defining Arab Popular Culture: Culture Succeeds Where Politics Fails

Arab nationalism as a political ideology—both as a unification project and mechanism for independence from the West—has been a failure. The only union among the twenty-two nation-states of the Arab League, if we discount the merging of North and South Yemen in 1990, has been an unsuccessful three-year encounter between Egypt and Syria. Even Nasser had his doubts about the 1958 experience and backed off from another go in 1963. The individual states that emerged midcentury have proved remarkably resilient, despite their controversial beginnings. Yet the fact that huge amounts of capital in one of the richest corners of the world are invested outside the region, and that regimes have had to rely on small elites and repressive measures to maintain survival and stability, betrays a continued lack of rhythm: the state system survives but remains dysfunctional. And the system, as the Iraq conflict has shown, has ultimately been unable to stave off a return of the foreigners whom it aimed to replace and repulse forever. Only in recent years have the Arab countries, under Egyptian prodding, set themselves the humble goal of achieving an economic union along the lines of the European Union, with annual Arab summits to help attain that goal. Meanwhile, as the historian of Arab nationalism, Sylvia Haim, writes: "The slogan of Arabism became so powerful and has been so manipulated that it is still virtually impossible for any leader to act without first paying homage to it" (Haim 1976, viii).

On a cultural level, Arab unity has become a remarkably pervasive reality. A cultural lingua franca with its own momentum and divorced from political designs now exists, ranging from *al-muheet ila al-khaleej*, from the Atlantic to the Gulf, according to the Arabic phrase. In television, news media, music, cinema, sports, and so many other aspects of popular culture, Arab identity is a living reality. While political Islam has transplanted Arab nationalism as to-

day's political project of choice, what Adeed Dawisha calls "Arabism" carries on regardless. The examples are endless. One of the pop hits of 2001 was a song called *Arabiyyun Ana*, or "I Am an Arab," by an Armenian-origin Lebanese called Yuri Mrakadi (Muraqqadi). The same year saw an Arabic version of the quiz show *Who Wants to Be a Millionaire?* score huge success all over the Arab world, often offering the spectacle of urbane Lebanese Maronite Christian host George Qerdahi flirt with fully veiled women from the Gulf as they sit in the "hot seat." The dialects are moving closer together. Egyptian has been a street-level lingua franca since the 1960s, but now Lebanese and Gulf dialects are comprehended throughout the region via satellite television, and the once incomprehensible North African argot is becoming more familiar to the Mashreqis. Even within country boundaries, the consolidation process engendered by the modern Arab nation-states has led to linking of peoples and dialects from different environments. The dialect spread by Egypt's massive state media is Cairene, while southern Egyptians have a distinct colloquial language of their own.

A revolution in Arabic-language television has also helped bring the region closer together. Qatar-based satellite channel al-Jazeera has played a key role here, putting in motion fierce TV competition for the huge Arabic-speaking audience of the Middle East and its diasporas in the West. Watched by millions of Arab viewers across the Middle East, Europe, and North America, taboo-breaking al-Jazeera has established itself as a forum for debate on human rights, fundamentalism, religion, and corruption, offending just about every Arab state in the process. In the quest for larger market shares, all of the satellite channels are looking for issues that unite, not divide, and as such their audience is not so much Egyptian, Saudi, or Jordanian as "Arab." Although most Arabs identify first and foremost with their nation-states, the more collective aspect of Arab identity is being indirectly strengthened by this new media. One can observe these shifting identities in the world of entertainment. Singers want to sing in Egyptian and perfect speaking Egyptian, partly because they reach a wider audience, but also because of the prestige of the Egyptian language in the cultural sphere. Yet, for example, pop star Latifa chose her native Tunisian dialect when she appeared on a Lebanese talk show in January 2003—no doubt because both countries see themselves as small, brave outposts of openness and progress in the Arab world today. This multilayering of identities is something that many Western commentators on the region have shown an unwillingness to understand or respect.

As a result, there is a bigger consensus than ever before across the Arabic-speaking world over foreign policy issues like the Palestinian-Israeli conflict and Iraq. Since Palestinians began their uprising, or Intifada, against Israeli occupation in the West Bank and Gaza Strip in September 2000, public opinion has been expressed in every corner of the Arab region, and the Intifada occupies huge space in the popular imagination. Palestine was always a pivotal issue in modern Arab nationalism, but the difference is that, whereas in the past its influence was exercised on a political level from the top, today it is on the popular level, forcing governments to take public stands against Israel. Politicians like to talk about the power of the "Arab street"—a blind hope, which burned strongly in the halcyon days of the 1950s and 1960s, pro-

posing that the masses fired by higher ideals of Arab nationalism will spill forth and make their rulers take stands in emulation of the heroes of early Arabic poetry or the first Muslim conquests. But the truth is that the largely spurious influence of the Arab street has given way to the reality of the Arab living room. Rarely did mass protests change an Arab political elite—most scenes involving the masses were manipulated, such as the hundreds of thousands who poured onto the streets of Cairo to demand that Nasser stay in office when he announced his resignation after defeat at the hands of Israel in 1967. But policymakers are now aware that supranational satellite television, which circumvents the control that governments have over their own media, creates public opinions that the regime might not like. There has been a rush of Arab unity songs, plays, and musicals to accompany the Intifada. One song from 1998, preceding the Intifada by two years, featured major singers from numerous Arab countries crooning in unison about "the Arab dream" (al-hilm al-arabi). State television in many countries refrained from showing the video accompanying the song, because its footage of scenes of Israeli soldiers beating Palestinians were deemed provocative. But they relented in the face of the song's huge popularity and the video's regular airing on the satellite channels.

Palestine has a way of eclipsing other issues in the Arab world, defying the general rule that people feel most strongly about news closer to home. There is no state of Palestine, but there are some six million people in the region, referred to as Palestinians. Over three million live in the territories occupied by Israel in 1967, one million are citizens of the State of Israel, and the others live in various states of national limbo in neighboring Arab countries, while many live and work in Libya and the Gulf. When American secretary of state Colin Powell took part in an MTV youth forum in February 2002, 70 percent of the questions submitted by would-be participants from Egyptian universities concerned Palestine. Not one was on Egyptian domestic affairs, and not one covered the conflict in south Sudan, where at least two million people are estimated to have died in two decades of fighting and four million have been displaced, making it by far the bloodiest conflict in the Arab region over the last fifty years. Sixty percent of people polled in Kuwait, Saudi Arabia, and Lebanon by the U.S.-based Zoghby Institute in 2001 said the Palestinian issue was the most important political issue to them. A Zoghby poll in June 2004 showed an incredible 98 percent of Egyptians had an unfavorable impression of the United States, from 74 percent two years before, and policy towards Palestine and Iraq fueled the disaffection. Slum districts of Cairo are tougher living than Gaza in many ways, but it's Israel's occupation and not their poverty that brings them onto the streets. Yet, wherever they are, Palestinians are denied a range of rights. Palestinian historian Rashid Khalidi has talked of the "shared anxiety" of all Palestinians at frontiers, borders, and checkpoints: "Their identity . . . not only is subject to question by the powers that be; but also is in many contexts suspect almost by definition" (Khalidi 1997, 2). In Lebanon they are confined to squalid refugee camps and denied the right to own property or carry out anything but the most menial jobs. Until 2004, Egypt's nationality laws denied citizenship to children of Egyptian mothers from Palestinian fathers, which in turn denies them the possibility of working in government jobs. Despite Arab-Israeli novelist Emile Habiby's classic enjoinder to Arab intellectuals to "visit us at least once"—to take the Palestinians out of their cultural isolation within Fortress Israel—few ever did. Prominent figures who visited from Egypt, the first Arab country to make peace with Israel, were ostracized, such as playwright Ali Salem in 1994 (who wrote in Arabic *Rihla ila Isra'il*, or *Journey to Israel*) and a diplomat's wife, Sana Hasan, in the 1970s (*Enemy in the Promised Land: An Egyptian Woman's Journey into Israel*). Famed Syrian-Lebanese poet Adonis, who regularly publishes in *al-Hayat*, was expelled from the Arab Writers Union in 1996 for meeting Israeli intellectuals and advocating "normalization" of relations. Debate rages in media throughout the Arab world about the future of the Arabs, the fate of the Arabs, the survival of the Arabs—issues highlighted by "globalization" and new developments in the relationship between Arab countries and Israel throughout the 1990s. Bookstalls on the street corners of Arab capitals are full of titles bemoaning the state of the Arab world and what's to become of it. In general, one can identify a post-1967 "culture of defeat," a psychology of despair and defeatism that has permeated much of the region's cultural output, and politics, since that crushing blow. Japan and Germany faced collapses of such moral and material magnitude after world wars that they succeeded in reinventing themselves and rising again—themes examined by German historian Wolfgang Schivelbusch in his 2003 study *The Culture of Defeat*. But this has not happened in the Arab world, where in any case most of the territories seized are still occupied, conflict remains the region's lot and cultural cohesion is skewed by the jigsaw of political entities. Israel's repression of the Intifada has further inflamed the sense of crisis among intellectuals, as did Israel's invasion of Beirut in 1982 (during which one of the pioneering ideologues of Arab nationalism, Khalil al-Hawi, committed suicide). Oslo fundamentally changed the political and psychological state of the region. Up to then, no Arab country apart from Egypt recognized the State of Israel, and the Arab boycott of all things Israeli remained in place. The file of secret contacts between Arab and Israeli leaders is large and well documented, and the boycott has been circumvented in practice. But with Oslo, the Palestinians themselves were speaking to Israel. Then Jordan made a formal peace with the Jewish State, and Tunisia, Oman, and Qatar opened commercial exchange offices in Israel. The old certitudes of regional politics had gone. In the immediate aftermath of Oslo, Israeli politician Shimon Peres wrote his book *The New Middle East*, which posited a "Middle East market" where Arab countries and Israel would freely interact in a new economic dispensation. Peres even put in an application for Israel to become a member of the Arab League. These developments proved particularly disturbing to the Syrians, whose Golan Heights was still under Israeli occupation, and to the Egyptians, the political and cultural motor of the region. The press and television are engaged in a vigorous debate these days about what Arab identity will mean if and when a solution is found to the Palestinian-Israeli conflict. The Iraqi conflict has increased a sense of foreboding. Iraqi intellectual Kanaan Makiya, author of the infamous portrait of Saddam Hussein's Iraq in *Republic of Fear*, argued in the run-up to

the 2003 war for a new, "non-Arab" Iraq. If Kabyle Berbers gain the upper hand in their struggle against *le pouvoir* (the power, i.e., the authorities) in Algiers, one can imagine similar anti-Arab requests for that state, which was once at the vanguard of Arab radicalism.

But with the end of the Cold War, Arab countries are slowly normalizing their relationships with each other and with the world, and that is making practical cooperation between these countries a more real, attractive possibility than it ever was to ruling elites during the fifty years of revolution and turbulence, when fear of interference from other Arab regimes was a constant factor. The line of Arab League secretary-general Amr Moussa is that "the era of romantic Arab nationalism has passed and now we need to put our minds to the storm of challenges confronting the nation, but we need to avoid self-flagellation and talk of frustration and defeatism" (Moussa 2002). Moussa was under heavy attack in 2003, after the Iraq war, for the League's failure to provide any answers beyond well-publicized shouting matches between leaders in the run-up to the fighting: Gaddafi and the Saudi crown prince, for example, traded accusations over who deserved blame for bringing the Americans into the heart of the Arab region. Ironically, Arabist politics brought nothing but misery to the Palestinians. Hindsight shows that every time the Arabs entered into military confrontation with Israel the Palestinians suffered, losing 78 percent of historical Palestine to Zionist control in 1948 and the other 22 percent in 1967. The fear of Jordan and Egypt is that Israel or their own publics could provoke them into another disastrous military escalation with Israel, which could create a situation where refugees are sent fleeing over their borders (the euphemism "transfer" is a part of Israel's political vocabulary). That's the danger of the Intifada and the new Arab media's stirring of pan-Arab emotions over the Palestinian plight, and that concern underpins the foreign policy of "front line" Arab states. All the countries that at one time sought to export their ideologies by fair means or foul—Egypt, Syria, Algeria, Libya—have moderated their ways. Exceptions remain. The trend across the region at this point in history is toward resolving disputes between Arab states, be it Morocco versus Algeria, Egypt versus Sudan, Syria versus Iraq, Iraq versus Kuwait, or Yemen versus Saudi Arabia, and so on.

This theme of reconciliation can also be seen in the current fad for historical drama. Egyptian director Mohammed Fadel produced the first film about Abdel Nasser in 1996, *Nasser 56*, a black-and-white study of the hundred days leading up to Nasser's nationalization of the Suez Canal in 1956, a move that made him a hero of Arab nationalism throughout the region. Two years later Syrian director Ayman al-Qawadri directed another film, called *Gamal Abdel-Nasser*. Both were shown throughout the region. The biggest success, though, was an Egyptian soap opera about nationalist singer Umm Kalthoum, who dominated Arab music culture from the 1940s up to her death in 1975. The drama was shown as part of the holiday entertainment in the holy month of Ramadan in November–December 1999 on most Arab networks. Though knocking Arab unity is fashionable these days, inside and outside of the region it seems that, despite the upheavals of recent decades, the Arab world is politically moving closer together, not drifting apart, and popular culture,

about the only sphere where the ideology was successful, is aiding the process.

The Globalization Debate: Fear of Foreign Influence and Protecting Arab Cultures

Paranoia over globalization, and what foreigners and their cultures may have in store for the Arabs, is currently rampant in the Arab world. Globalization means different things to different people: some object to the material things of Americana, others fear deeper forms of subjugation to foreigner control. American cultural influences in terms of fast-food restaurants and malls are widespread in the Gulf (Saudi Arabia has allowed McDonald's and Kentucky Fried Chicken to operate in the heart of the holy Muslim city of Mecca). American fast-food names are absent from Syria for political reasons, but neither are they to be found in commerce-savvy Tunisia because the authorities never found the franchise system attractive. Some countries like the UAE and Lebanon have had no qualms about foreign capital investing on their territory; others who dreamed of doing it all themselves have balked. Fear of globalization can mean fear of losing control—over the economy, foreign policy, and public morals. In Egypt all three feature highly in public discourse. Lebanese political commentator Hazem Saghieh critiques this state of terror: "Anyone following events in Egypt, and the opinions of its intellectuals, journalists and politicians, would think that the world woke up one morning, rubbed its eyes, looked at its watch, then said irritably: '7 o'clock. God, I'm late. Time to conspire against Egypt'" (*al-Hayat*, 29 July 2001). Here are some examples of events that Saghieh thought spoke of this paranoia in 2001: the trial of fifty-two suspected homosexuals, a campaign by some intellectuals to prevent writers from translating their novels into Hebrew, a seven-year jail sentence for civil rights activist Saadeddin Ibrahim for "defaming Egypt" through his pro-democracy work, banning of books over sexual content, and panic that Israel had exported to Egypt belts that release deadly chemicals to destroy male procreative abilities. Saadeddin Ibrahim, who has both and Egyptian nationalities, was viciously trashed by Egypt's media. "I hope Saad the American understands well that he no longer has any future on the land of this nation, or in any home or grave in the soil of Egypt. Great Egypt ejects all those who violate its honor and trades in its pride and is biased towards its enemies," newspaper editor Mustafa Bakry wrote (*al-Osboa*, 25 September 2000). In the end, Ibrahim was acquitted of all charges against him. Egyptian investment banker Mansour al-Tarzi explains the current paranoia by reviewing recent history: "We are carrying the burden of our own past and it's a very complicated past, and we're paying the price for it, because the psyche of the Egyptian has been dented by this past. In a sense, one envies those who came into the modern world fresh—carrying nothing but their determination to see their countries grow, prosper and become part of the community. It will take us time to go through it all and see what should be retained, what should be consigned to memory," he said, citing "the obsession with the socialist model, with foreign imperialism, the suspicion of capitalism, the suspicion of money in general, of what the private sector can concoct for the future of the country, of what foreign investors have in mind for Egypt" (interview with author, August 1999). The move to a more individualistic capitalist society implied by Western-led globalization is a challenge to Arab societies throughout the region, all of which to one degree or another uphold communal business ethics (if not socialist, then tribal and familial). The fear of foreign culture and interaction also operates between Arab countries. Faced with economic troubles, Saudi Arabia is less interested than it once was in mass importation of Egyptian labor, and since the late 1990s it has promoted *sa'wada*, or Saudization, of its economy. The wealthy Gulf states have feared since the 1970s that the urban-based, nationalist Arab regimes have an eye on their oil as part of a wider redistribution of Arab wealth. The oil is seen as a curse by many: for secularists it divided the Arabs and let the foreigners in, and for Islamists it corrupted Arab society. Even former Saudi oil minister Sheikh Zaki Yamani once said: "I wish we had found water" ("Post-war Iraq Must Beware the Curse of Easy Riches," Reuters, 25 July 2003). Egyptian newspaper editor Ibrahim Nafie noted during a trip in 2004 to the Gulf that "Countries at the periphery of the Arab world see advantages in political and economic links with countries outside the region, relationships that a country like Egypt at the center would see as the nefarious efforts by Western countries to 'Balkanize' the Arab whole." (*al-Ahram*, 5 March 2004)

Some countries, such as Oman and Syria, are cautiously using tourism to diversify their economies, but they are wary of mass tourism and the clash between foreign and local values. Islamists argue that mass tourism in Egypt contributed to the

Iconography of former Iraqi president Saddam Hussein saw him appear in many personas, including Bedouin chief, military leader, and modern ruler. (TRIP/Art Directors)

war launched against the government of Hosni Mubarak by radical Islamic groups in 1992. The mix of freewheeling foreigners and traditional-minded locals has been difficult in tourist destinations like Luxor, in the center of southern Egypt, where even urban Cairenes can find the values difficult to handle—though the phenomenon of female Western tourists choosing young local men as husbands suggests cross-cultural fertilization is possible in the most unlikely of environments. Iraqis used to joke that Saddam Hussein was nicer to other Arabs than he was to his own people, since he imported Egyptian and Moroccan farmers in the 1970s to set up new communities after massive irrigation projects freed up land.

There has been much resentment at the ethnocentricities of Arab nationalism, in particular Egypt's political and cultural hegemony since the Nasser period. Egypt is heavily present at the point where local cultures merge at a wider level as regional Arab culture, and its dialect has become something of a second lingua franca for Arabs, after the classical language. But many Arabs also have a cringing attitude toward Egypt today. Saghieh wrote that "Egypt was the altar of progress and enlightenment in the Arab world. Now its dominance has become a burden and one of the causes of Arab cultural deterioration" (*al-Hayat*, 29 July 2001). Since the interwar period, Egypt has considered itself the pioneer of progress and democracy in the Arab region, and since the Nasser era it has actively promoted its leadership in cultural, political, and military fields. But the failure of the Nasserist political project and descent into dictatorship, coupled with continued cultural domination and dreams of regional leadership, have prompted much resentment, both among secular liberals, who see Egypt as a huge backward influence on the region, and Arab nationalists, who want Egypt back in the radical camp. Abdul-Kader Husrieh, the son of a well-known Syrian newspaper editor in a brief liberal period in the 1950s, describes Egypt's pioneering role in journalism, for example, as "the worst experience" for Arab countries (interview with author, December 2002). The Baathist officers who took control of Syria in the 1960s borrowed the Egyptian model of heavy state control in all aspects of society, including the media. Western democracy was discredited by the Westerners themselves, through their meddling in Egypt's democratic experiment of the interwar period and allowing Palestine to come under Zionist control, which ultimately brought crushing humiliation upon Arab militaries. Thus, Egypt's switch from the Soviet camp to U.S. alliance and peace with Israel was only a superficial change, in that the apparatus and mentality of the Nasser era remained in place. Now pro-West elites consider Egypt a model best avoided, in the same way that Turkey's secular elite tends to shun the Arab world as a whole as part of a backward past best forgotten.

The latent resentment felt toward Egypt is displayed in every soccer match played with Algeria. When the national teams played in a 2001 World Cup qualifier in the mainly Berber city of Ennaba, the violence shown by the crowd toward the Egyptians betrayed bitterness toward a country that, after independence, sent language teachers to teach the Algerians how to be Arabs again. Egyptian war veterans have even noted that Jews of Yemeni origin who fought against them in the Sinai during the 1967 and 1973 conflicts with Israel were harshest toward Egyptian prisoners, because they remembered the Egyptian army's involvement in Yemen's civil war of the early 1960s. In another example of the Arab world's ethnocentricity, there is almost no awareness in Egypt whatsoever that an Arab—Algerian Mohamed Lakhdar Hamina—actually won the Palme d'Or at Cannes, and Egyptian media, thus Arab media in general, lavish praise and attention on Egyptian director Yousef Chahine as the sole director who has made waves in the outside world. The Islamist military regime that seized power in Khartoum in 1989 clothed Sudan in a strident Arab-Islamic identity that was willfully outside Egyptian control. Even now that the two countries have mended fences after Sudan's support for the Islamic rebel movement in Egypt during the 1990s, Sudanese officials still complain that Egypt doesn't know anything about a country with which it blithely claims a natural geographic and historic unity ("one country, from Alexandria in the north to Juba in the south," as it is said). With literature, in Radwa Ashour's celebrated Grenada Trilogy, Egyptian colloquial Arabic is lurking just below the surface of the dialogue (in classical Arabic) of characters who would in reality have spoken quite different Arabic, in an Iberian Maghrebi culture that merged the Arab with the Berber. As for the Maghreb, newscasts on the Gulf-based satellite channel al-Jazeera often don't include North African cities in nightly weather reports.

The fear of the foreign that is currently gripping Arab countries is entwined with a fascination with the ways of the Westerners. The word "globalization" has had enormous pull on popular consciousness in the Arab world. Neatly translated into Arabic as *al-'awlama*, or "making global," globalization has come to represent all the xenophobic fears of Arab societies at this stage in history. Arab governments are grappling with the problem of how to ensure that the vertical relationships that globalization creates between foreign and local institutions don't rock their inequitable political systems, which are characterized by a divvying up of power among military castes, security forces, business elites, and monolithic ruling parties. But governments also hope that globalization can help pull their economies out of the doldrums and cement stability. High priests of globalization, such as *New York Times* columnist Thomas Friedman, author of *The Lexus and the Olive Tree*, are feted in the region like royalty. (The Saudi royals even chose Friedman and his column to reveal an Arab-Israeli peace initiative in 2002.) Leading Arab intellectual Salama Ahmed Salama wrote in Egypt's leading daily *al-Ahram* that globalization "could be a cover for the interests of the big countries and the developing ones will themselves be forced to accept conditions that don't agree with their own interests" (*al-Ahram*, 25 January 2000). Through globalization, he said, the big countries will "fix the rules of the game" and developing countries will be left to drown in its currents.

Arab states are also fixing the rules of the game, making sure that uninvited elements of the populace don't suddenly get a place at the table through the possibilities thrown open by globalization. Thus they have developed control mechanisms to limit the liberating power of the Internet. Arab countries want the Internet, but they also fear the polluting influences that come with it. Saghieh warned, "The internet is a means not an end. The end should be creating a modern and strong middle class whose knowledge makes it free in relation to the authorities. This requires changes to the social structure, with participation in the political system and an expansion of its reach. What is needed, then, is modernity itself, not modernization. The internet without modernity will just be a passing phase of modernization" (*al-Hayat*, 29 July 2001). Indeed, quoting James Surowiecki, business columnist for *Slate* magazine, Friedman wrote in his book that, with globalization, innovation replaces tradition and nothing matters as much as what will come next (Friedman 2000). So a culture that celebrates reproduction of models perfected in the past is likely to have problems with a globalization posited on that basis.

High versus Low Culture in the Arab World Today

In a region where people have lived alongside each other for thousands of years in radically different geographic locations, it's no surprise that concepts of class play a big role in Arab societies. The major social divide for much of history has been between the urban settled peoples, mainly located on the region's peripheries, and the Bedouin and other desert peoples of the hinterland. Historians of early Islam argue today that this phenomenon conditioned the attitudes of the Arab conquerors when they left the Arabian Peninsula to rule the settled and "civilized" world (the Arabic word for civilization, *al-hadaara*, is connected to the word for sedentary society, *al-hadar*) from its urban centers in Damascus, Baghdad, Jerusalem, and so on, and impelled them to form a new monotheistic religion in the Jewish-Christian tradition with specifically Arab origins rather than simply adopt either Judaism or Christianity as the religion of their newly won empire. Classic tales of the Arab conquests recount the awe of the Bedouin tribesmen at the opulence of the Shah's palaces in the Persian capital of Ctesiphon, near modern Baghdad, when they first entered the defeated city. The modern era saw the same divide, magnified and in reverse, when political elites in Cairo, Jerusalem, Damascus, Beirut, and Baghdad looked on with envy at their Bedouin cousins in the Gulf enjoying independence from the colonial powers after World War I, while their battles against occupation continued.

Throughout the region today, there are large families who enjoy great social prestige, but these urban notables have declined in influence in the Arab nationalist, postcolonial period (Hourani 1983). Morocco has families who trace their origin back to Muslims who were forced to flee Andalusia when Spanish armies ended seven centuries of Arab-Muslim culture in the Iberian Peninsula in 1492 (in contrast to the shame associated with Berber origins). Endless television programs are dedicated to celebrations of Andalusian, Arab-Islamic culture. "Andalucia is not limited to a geographical area, we are all Andalucia," one musician said of North Africa on Morocco's Channel One network (February 2003). Tunisia has a special place in the topography of Arab identity and the spread of Islam, since it has the first mosque in North Africa, established by Uqba bin Nafi' at the Arab caravan city of Kairawan, as well as the famed Zeitouna mosque and religious seminary in Tunis, North Africa's most esteemed center of Islamic learning. The Moroccan and the Jordanian monarchies both trace their origins back to the Prophet Mohammed, and thousands of Muslims in Arab countries bear the title *sherif*, meaning they too have genealogies officially recognized as dating back to the Prophet. In Shi'ite tradition, those who trace their ancestry back to the Prophet's cousin Ali claim the title *sayyid*. In the Gulf, prestige is attached to those bearing surnames of Arab tribal origin, as opposed to other names that suggest nontribal and possibly non-Arab origin; in Egypt, names of Turkish origin can suggest descent from the landed gentry who dominated the country in Mamlouk and Ottoman times.

But since the Arab region saw a huge population explosion in the last decades of the twentieth century, with cities mushrooming with poor districts—a phenomenon seen in all Arab capitals apart from those in the wealthy Gulf states—class divisions between rich and poor have sharpened, and as a consequence issues of "high versus low culture" have become extremely prominent in public space. Whenever figures from poorer backgrounds reach prominence, their cultural background is highlighted by the media. Belly dancing is regarded as a low art form in Arab culture, one step above prostitution, and thus the immense fame and wealth many dancers have attained fascinates the media. The most famous of them, Fifi Abdo, is depicted as something akin to Cairo's version of Nana, Zola's great whore of Paris. A book appeared on Cairo newsstands in 1996 titled *Zaman Fifi Abdou* (*The Era of Fifi Abdou*), which took her success as the cue for a diatribe against the new, rapacious capitalist culture of Egypt and the Arab world. When Abdo bought a flat in the exclusive Nile Towers in Cairo around the same time—an exclusive residence whose opulence exercised huge sway over the public imagination—reports said some Gulf princes had refused to live in the same building as the famed belly dancer. At many of her shows in five-star hotels, professional photographers hawking the events are careful to keep noted politicians and other public figures out of the frame. Belly dancer Dina at one time attracted attention simply for being the daughter of a journalist.

Poor women who make their way into belly dancing are regarded as beyond salvation. But singers from the poor parts of town, who purvey the "low culture" music known as *shaabi*, often try to rehabilitate themselves once they have achieved fame by associating themselves with the pantheon of classical Arab singers of the twentieth century. Ahmed Adawiya became hugely famous in the 1970s as a singer from the slums of Cairo belting out *shaabi* songs that reflected the angst of the times—urban poverty and political uncertainty, as the Arab-Israeli conflict took new twists and turns in the era of Anwar Sadat. Though his star had long faded, Adawiya talked of himself in the late 1990s as the heir to the tradition of performers including Abdel-Halim Hafez, whose perfection of classical singing and clean romantic image made him the epitome of high culture. Similarly, another *shaabi* star called Hakim, who became famous in the 1990s, talked of himself in interviews as a great singer in the style of Hafez.

Some stand out for refusing to be part of these conventions. Another *shaabi* singer, Shaaban Abdel-Rahim, shot to fame in 2001 with a song that stated bluntly, "I Hate Israel." Egypt's intellectual elite had a problem with his success for a number of reasons. The Arab-Israeli conflict has been a central concern of intellectuals since 1948, but in Arab countries on good terms with the United States, those in the mainstream must temper their diatribes. The leftist press in Egypt resented the fact that this barely educated man from a dirt-poor village outside Cairo touched the masses with a message more than they ever did. Furthermore, aware of the limits to his talent, Abdel-Rahim had no pretensions to be another Abdel-Halim Hafez. On one of his first appearances on state television during his early months of fame, he said without shame or fear of ridicule that the shirt he was wearing—a gaudy, flowery affair—was cut from the same material used to cover his mother's sofa. Inasmuch as he recognized that there was something called high culture, he wasn't making any effort to be considered a part of it.

The state in every Arab country, perhaps excepting Lebanon, seeks to control the "agenda" of high culture, be it literature, music, or cinema. As a new artistic development, modern Arabic literature, for example, is generally regarded as suspect by authorities. Good literature often involves a critique of social, political, and cultural realities, and so by definition can be anti-state. There are few cultural programs of substance on Arabic television, though at present some advances are being made on satellite channels (Abu Dhabi TV's *Mubdi'un*, or *Creative People;* Future's *Khalleek Bil-Bayt*, or *Stay at Home*, and *al-Arabiya's Manarat*, or *Lighthouses*). Recently a number of Arab leaders and politicians have even tried to muscle their way onto the literary scene, with short stories by Libyan leader Muammar al-Gaddafi and Egyptian speaker of parliament Fathy Sorour, and novels by Iraqi president Saddam Hussein (before his demise). The works of Gaddafi, incidentally, glorify simple desert living and speak of a disdain for cities—a theme of Arab history since the conquests, which explains much about the political and urban landscape of Libya today. Saddam Hussein cultivated an image of himself as a major patron of the arts, filling Baghdad with sculptures, panoramas, and architecture of a particular totalitarian nature, a kind of fascist chic. Sometimes the artistic community gets its subtle revenge. Sculptor Abdel-Hadi Gazzar was commissioned to produce a work in celebration of the Aswan High Dam that Gamal Abdel Nasser had built during the 1960s. The result was a dehumanized man of sheet metal and wires wearing an amulet, Gazzar's comment on Nasser's Arab socialist revolution (*al-Ahram Weekly*, 1–7 August 2002).

Youth Culture and Its Problems in an Age-Biased Society

Ageism is rife in the Arab world, but not against old people—rather, against the young. Music and cinema are full of older stars who refuse to disappear. The Lebanese singer-actress Sabah is in her late seventies, but due to plastic surgery she now looks a sprightly mid-fifties; in recent years she married Mr. Lebanon, a thirty-something called Omar, then left him when she became suspicious that he was just after her money. Young actors and singers, on the other hand, are a constant cause of carping in the media for the "low" (*haabit*) standards they present. The United Nations Development Programme's first Arab Human Development Report (AHDR) in 2002 specifically singled out the issue of ageism. "Ageism runs counter to the needs of the current era when technol-

ogy and globalization reward innovation, flexibility and dynamism, and it deprives young people in the Arab world of opportunities to participate in and contribute to their societies' development," it said (AHDR 2002, 10). According to the report, 38 percent of the combined population of 280 million comprising the twenty-two member states of the Arab League are under fifteen. American policymakers have noted the consequences this could have for the region's political stability in the near future. But it will have other results too; for one, such a huge segment of the population has massive commercial power, and while today's top young actors are abused by critics, they also command huge fees from directors.

A defining struggle of modern Arab societies is the fight by intellectual elites to maintain their traditional control over those cultural values deemed important by young people. Youth culture in the Arab world never had a radical moment to match the 1960s in the West (as illustrated by the 1996 arrest of heavy metal fans in Egypt on suspicion of "devil-worshipping"). Morocco also prosecuted three heavy metal fans in 2003 for trying to "undermine the faith of a Muslim" by wearing T-shirts with skulls, snakes, etc., and prosecutors accused them of belonging to an international Satanist cult. Commentators in the mainstream media regularly pronounce on the cultural diet of today's youth and the direction that youth should take. "Call on young people to memorize the Quran instead of the Macarena, and let them listen to Quranic analysis instead of the lessons of the devil-worshippers," Egyptian newspaper editor Mustafa Bakry wrote (*al-Osboa*, 1 May 2000). In 2002 there was a state of panic in Egypt's controlling circles

Ayman al-Aathar (left) and Ammar Hassan, clothed in the Palestinian flag, at the finals of the Arab Superstar program in August 2004. Aathar, a Libyan, won despite public sympathy with Hassan because he was Palestinian. (Anwar Amro/AFP/Getty Images)

over the runaway success of a film about a drunken, drug-taking dropout who doesn't aspire to improve his habits, only to have the girl he loves accept him as he is. She does, and the media monitors didn't like it, even suggesting that the director be prevented, somehow, from entering the film (called *al-Limby)* in foreign film festival competitions, lest it "harm Egypt's reputation." In between video clips of "respected" singers, presenters on state television's music shows will trash "low-quality songs" (*al-ughniya al-habta*) and ordinary people on the street to reject the Arabic music/movie industry mantra used to justify lowbrow art, *il-gumhour 'ayz kida* ("that's what the public wants"). In 2001 young Lebanese DJs jazzed up bits of

famous songs by classical singer Umm Kalthoum, a contemporary of Abdel-Halim Hafez, with state-of-the-art disco arrangements. The mixes were a huge success all over the Arab world but provoked strong protest from Arab culture vultures. "There is a trend to take the classics and modernize them, which has some people furious and others excited. But either way this is a deformation of the heritage," wrote Lebanese columnist Ibrahim al-Aris (*al-Hayat*, January 2002). "How can it be right for someone to violate the old melodies and make them contemporary so that their classic form is turned into techno?" Television advertisers will even avoid using classroom scenes in their marketing so that the media authorities do not accuse them of encouraging young people to question the authorities or in some way to "rebel." The official media harbors myriad fears about what would happen to Arab youth without the guiding hand of the state: they might listen to heavy metal music, marry Israeli women, work for Mossad, join radical Islamist groups, forget about Islam, indulge in pornography, or shun Arab identity.

These fears betray an awareness of the distinct sense of alienation that young people in most Arab countries feel toward the state, its ideologies, and its idea of who and what they should be. They also reflect deeply ingrained ideas in Arab culture. In cinema and music, kudos are given to reproducing already perfected forms; to develop them (which, if viewed as positive, is termed *ijtihad*) runs the risk of ruining them. In fact, the word "creativity" is referred to in modern Arabic as *ibdaa'*, but it's a short step from *ibdaa'* to *bid'a*, a pejorative term with origins in Islamic theology that is usually translated as "innovation."

State Attempts to Control Various Aspects of Popular Culture

The control mechanisms in place in Arab societies are strong, encompassing the religious establishment and the state, with its media, police, and official censorship bodies. On political issues, they engender a form of self-censorship—the press in most Arab countries is actually not censored at all, since censors tend to review only foreign literature, cinema, and music. Ruling parties, like state-owned papers, pitch themselves as all things to all people and as the embodiment of the state itself, and they seek to present themselves as at once secular, Islamic, pro-West, and anti-American, according to the political winds. Morocco, Algeria, Tunisia, Libya, Egypt, Syria, and Iraq have all seen this in recent decades, since religious politics took off in the aftermath of the 1967 defeat against Israel. The diversity of political parties is seen as a weak thing. In fact, the term for party politics, *hizbiyya*, has an original reference in Islamic history to a period of political strife in the early days of the caliphate, and regimes today tend to see in *hizbiyya* an undesirable fragmentation of the whole. Moroccan writer Fatima Mernissi has argued that the concept behind the "president of the republic" in the Arab world is quite far from that of the meaning, "presider over the affairs of state," which lies behind the Latin terminology. In Arabic, the terms *ra'is*, president, and *jumhouriya*, republic, derive from *ra's*, head, and *jumhour*, the masses—so the state is embodied in a president whose job is to think for the amorphous, directionless masses. Egyptian civil rights activist Saadeddin Ibrahim has suggested that, in light of the phenomenon of power in Arab republics passing from president to son in the manner of monarchies (the Syrian example in 2000 and expectations of the same in Libya, Egypt, Iraq, and Yemen), Arab politics needs a new word, *jumlukiyya*, or "republicarchy." Political observers consider that the jibe played a role in Egypt's decision in 2000 to jail him over his rights work. Gaddafi famously invented the word *jamahiriya*, a grammatical intensification of the word *jumhouriya*, the normal word for republic, since it makes an abstract noun out of the plural of *jumhour, jamahir*. *Jamahiriya* might best be translated as "state of the masses," though in fact *jumhouriya* means much the same.

States actively engage in culture wars. In 1990, Egypt's culture ministry promoted what it called "one hundred years of enlightenment"—the Egyptian aspect of the process historians term the "Arab renaissance" of the late nineteenth and early twentieth centuries, when liberal arts and politics flourished in a period of "catching up" with the West (which was abruptly brought to an end by the postindependence Arab system). In the choice of singers, writers, poets, and intellectuals promoted in this celebration, one saw the attempts of the state to bolster its self-image as playing a successful game of catch-up with the industrialized and secular West. The canon of greats gave no ground to the Islamist reading of modern Egyptian history, which states that Egypt since the rule of Mohammed Ali in the early nineteenth century has made a fundamental mistake in aping European political systems that do not fit naturally with Arab-Islamic society. State television in Tunisia is way behind its counterparts in Lebanon, Morocco, and Egypt, and as long as the economy continues to be reasonably successful there is no reason for that situation to change. A Tunisian marketing industry expert described Tunisia's television chiefs in this manner: "They are public servants and don't care about what people really want" (interview with author, February 2003). There are no formal pop charts in the Arab world, and music executives say it will be a while before there are, because too many parties in the industry have an interest in keeping the true nature of public tastes and the popularity of the stars obscure, and one can draw a clear analogy here with the political situation, where the parties of state have no desire to be cut down to size in free elections and see their bitter opponents re-

vealed as stronger. Similarly, Egypt's Media Production City—a huge studio complex built in the mid-1990s in the desert outside Cairo—allows a state-guided, airbrushed, and anaesthetized vision of Egypt. Rather than showing the reality of modern Egypt, television and film directors will more often than not head to the Media Production City to shoot scenes in reconstructed alleyways, markets, or poor districts. Promotional campaigns for Egypt's ruling National Democratic Party show the world's cleanest and happiest peasants in the Egyptian countryside.

An exception for some decades was Lebanon, where the state deliberately maintained a low profile as part of a mechanism to hold together the country's complex of confessional communities, some of which had cultural outlooks diametrically opposed to each other (religious/secular, pro-West/pan-Arab). But even Lebanon is today moving in the direction of nations like Syria and Egypt, where the state looms large in an effort to unite the country's different trends under one political and cultural aegis, a process facilitated by the migration abroad of large numbers of the Maronite Christian community, for whose sake the country was carved out of the Levant by colonial power France.

Alternative Cultures and Identities in the Arab World

When the Crusaders arrived in Lebanon in 1099, they were shocked to discover that the Maronite Christians still existed, removed in their mountain recesses from three centuries of Muslim-Arab rule. They came to free the Holy Land from the Muslim Arabs, but the task was not as simple as they imagined. Neither is it today. The Maronites are still one of the largest groups in Lebanon, and the region also includes Berber, Kurdish, Nubian, Jewish, Aramaic, Coptic, and other Christian identities subsumed under the Arab-Islamic whole. Arabic-speaking Maronite Christians of Lebanon, Arabic-speaking Coptic Christians of Egypt, Berber-speaking Muslim Berbers of North Africa, and Kurdish-speaking Muslim Kurds of Iraq and Syria have all had their problems with Arab nationalist ideology, though the Christians of Egypt and Lebanon both maintain Arab identities in public discourse. Arab nationalism has possibly been cruelest to the south Sudanese and the Kurds in Iraq, but both have found the most success in removing themselves from the Arab grip, thanks to foreign intervention in Iraq after the 1991 Gulf War and during the war in 2003 and also to a civil war in Sudan between the Khartoum government and the Sudan People's Liberation Movement (SPLM), which is finally winding down.

Lebanon was essentially created for the Maronites, but now they see it slipping from their control. Even Maronite-run television stations play up to Arab political and cultural unity because that's where the big audiences are to be found—beyond tiny Lebanon, in the wider Arab nation. Lebanon appears for the moment to have reached a consensus that its role is to be, as writer Elias Khoury has said, a window for the Arab world onto the rest of the world. As with the Maronites in Lebanon, Copts have formed the majority of emigrants from Egypt, but their numbers in Egypt have been a dwindling minority since the twelfth and thirteenth centuries, as more and more of the community adopted Arabic and converted to Islam, joining what became the Arabized Muslim majority. Two

families claim today to speak Coptic, the most recent version of the ancient Egyptian language, but they appear to be revivalists speaking the language for ideological reasons, as when the Zionist movement resurrected Hebrew. Angered at being sidelined in Egypt's religiously radicalized society of the last three decades, hardliners among Coptic groups in North America have entertained dreams of a Coptic state in areas of southern Egypt where they are not in a minority, just as the Maronites dreamed of a Marounistan during Lebanon's civil war. Even today's south Sudanese are not the same south Sudanese who took up arms in 1983: since an Islamist regime came to power in Khartoum in 1989, Arabization and even Islamization have made inroads among southerners in the south itself and among southerners who are displaced communities in the north (at least half of Khartoum's six million population is from the south). Rights activists in Khartoum say there is some evidence that the practice of female circumcision is spreading from Muslim communities in the northern cities to neighboring southern non-Muslim communities, as the southerners adopt the customs of the dominant social caste (interview with author, August 2002). Southern intellectuals in Khartoum say that in a federated or independent south Sudan there will be no choice but to use Arabic as an official language, since its use has become so widespread. When outside the Arab world, many minorities speak in a radically different voice. Maronites in North America, in alliance with related Christian groups from Iraq, argue virulently that they are not Arabs. A "Coalition of American Assyrians and Maronites" issued a statement in October 2001, objecting to the identification of Assyrians and Maronites as Arabs, saying,

"Over 2.2 million Assyrians, including Chaldeans and Syriacs (Christian churches with Aramaic cultural origins), and Maronites living in America herewith assert that Assyrians and Maronites are not and have never been Arabs" (Assyrian International News Agency Web site, www.aina.org, 2003). In fact, ethnically and linguistically they are all Semitic and as alike as the Portuguese and Spanish. Within Iraq, Christian intellectuals admit this, but some reject the designation "Arab" or the automatic conflation of "Arab" with "Semitic." Barring the Sumerians, throughout history the people of Iraq's successive empires had their origins in tribes who stormed in from the desert. Perhaps wary of the Arab experience of Zionism, many ordinary Iraqis are reluctant to admit the Sumerians were not Semitic (or Arab). The Christians of the west (Iraq) and east (Syria/Lebanon) spoke variant dialects of the Aramaic language (often referred to as Syriac in the Levant and Assyrian or Ashouri in Iraq). Until the Arab conquests, Aramaic was the dominant Semitic language in urban areas, having overshadowed Hebrew, which disappeared as a vernacular, among others. Jesus Christ was an Aramaic-speaking Jew (as seen in Mel Gibson's *The Passion of the Christ*, 2004, which was seen by Muslim Arabs as a metaphor for Palestinian suffering under Israel and by Lebanese Christians as a metaphor for their suffering under Syria). Today there remain thousands of Aramaic speakers in Iraq, and many were attracted to the secular, Arab nationalist ideology of the Baath Party (founded by a Syrian Christian, Michel Aflaq, who lived his final years in Baghdad). Slogans such as "one Arab nation with an eternal message" and "yes to one nation" had a strong presence in Mosul and the mainly Christian villages in the surrounding countryside during Saddam Hussein's rule. "We have a place in society—not as a sect, but as citizens. We feel we are part of this one body. We have one shared [Iraqi] citizenship and the state has a responsibility to protect everyone," said Archbishop Saliba Isaac, leader of the Syrian Orthodox in Mosul, in January 2003, when there were fears of what the end of Baath rule could mean for the Christian minority (interview with author, January 2003). According to historian Avi Shlaim, Lebanon's Christian leaders told Israel after 1948 that they didn't consider Lebanon to be Arab, but they had to be aware of the sensitivities of the neighborhood they lived in (Shlaim 2000). In 1982 they attempted a peace with Israel, which, given the circumstances of invasion and the Palestinian diaspora, was unsustainable at the time.

Perhaps the most vigorous challenge to Arab identity is being waged by Berbers. This has come in response to strong political and social pressure on Berbers to Arabize, since the old system of Islamic empires in North Africa was superseded by modern nation-states during the twentieth century. These nation-states all chose to adopt a predominantly Arab identity. The Berber response has been to focus on the ethnic aspect of this Arab identity and argue that the Arabic-speakers of North Africa are as ethnically Berber as the Berber speakers (a position incidentally backed up by genetic research published by a group of Spanish and Moroccan biologists in 2000). The main focus of the new Berber-or Amazigh, pride is Morocco—in some ways the soft underbelly of the Arab nation—where Berbers form up to around half of the population, and where the Arabic dialect is more bastardized, with Berber, Spanish, and French elements, than other parts of the Arab world, to the extent that Berber activists argue it should not be considered simply a dialect of Arabic. The first Amazigh World Congress was held in the Canary Islands (also Berber, but under Spanish sovereignty) in 1997. Berber nationalists have even arrived in Egypt's Siwa oasis, the only Berber-speaking area left in Egypt, to promote Berber pride and bolster their Berber dialect in the face of increasing inroads being made by Egyptian colloquial Arabic. Berbers are also using mass media to challenge Arabism. A study by Amar Almasude shows that, since the 1990s the Imazighen (the Berber term for "the Berbers") have used new developments in computer communication, technology, and interactive media to establish themselves both nationally and internationally as a distinct cultural group, and they are fighting to further establish their language in the school curriculum and mass media (Almasude 1999).

But though Moroccan Berbers have faced decades of marginalization and humiliation, the strongest campaigns against them have perhaps occurred in Colonel Gaddafi's Libya, where they form only a small, unthreatening portion of the population. According to Libyan writer Adrar Nfousa, these efforts have included encouraging Berbers to stick to specific areas of the country, so that they don't form communities among Arabic-speakers in Arab cities, and then inserting housing projects full of Arabic-speakers in their midst to deprive the Berber areas of services so that they migrate to the Arab cities and Arabize (policies similar to those adopted by the Baath regime in Iraq toward the Kurds and the Israeli state toward Palestinians, though the preference in the latter case is that they leave the country altogether). Gaddafi is himself known to be the son of a

Berber woman, but there are no reports of him ever speaking the language. In Arab-Islamic culture, it is the father's line that is important—even the Abbasid caliphs often had Persian mothers. "Suppression of the Berber presence, and attempts to cordon it off and deny it, is ongoing and has become institutionalized, reaching its height in the era of Gaddafi. The Berber presence is forbidden and falsified, subsumed under different names in ancient and modern history books and the media," Nfousa wrote in *Sho'un Libiya* in 1999 (Nfousa 1999). "Gaddafi, who is under the illusion that he is the guardian of Arab nationalism and sponsor of Arab unity, propagates the idea that Berbers are ancient Arabs who migrated from Yemen and Palestine in the pre-Islamic era, and that the Amazigh language is an ancient Arabic dialect unsuitable for modern times and an obstacle to progress." These ideas were backed by state-sponsored Arab nationalist writers such as Ali Khosheim, in his books *The Journey of the Word*, *In Search of an Arab Pharaoh*, and *The Berber Arabic Dictionary* (which in turn mirrors modern Turkey's efforts to deny Kurds their identity with theories describing them as "mountain Turks"). The Berbers in Morocco, brought up with similar ideas promoted in schools, have been described by anthropologist David Crawford as "the invisible Imazighen" (Crawford 2002). In Egypt too we find the ministry of tourism issuing a press release promoting desert tourism that states: "Most Siwans are Berbers, descendants of Bedouins that roamed the North African coast from Tunisia to Morocco" (Egyptian Ministry of Tourism Press Release, 23 February 2002).

Arab nationalism has space for Christians, and even for Jews, but little time for those who reject its language. Chibli Mallat has said that perhaps the redeeming factor of Arab nationalism has been the illusion it gave that "Arabic as the vector of identity was more important" than religion. "Where it failed to recognize its limits, Arab nationalism has engendered, sometimes to genocidal extent, new evils. This was the case for Kurds in Iraq and Syria, but also for Armenians and Berbers in Lebanon and North Africa," Mallat says (Mallat 1996, 57). "And yet, Arabic has been a remarkable conveyor of literature produced by minorities, such as that of the Copts in Egypt and the Christians in Lebanon, in a way that has put them in the mainstream." As an ethnic, non-Arabic-speaking bloc, Berbers have been largely outside this process too. The description "Berber" is a designation applied by outsiders that has intrinsically negative connotations. The name probably has its origin in the Latin-derived word "barbarian," after the Romans referred to the rebellious indigenous tribes of North Africa in that manner. The term then found its way into Arabic, so that the word *barbari* means both "Berber" and "barbarian." But the great Tunisian Arab historian Ibn Khaldoun—who stands out in Arab history for his effort to write a history of the Berbers—linked the name to the odd sound of the Berber language to the Arabic ear: they were people distinguished by *barbara*, or "incomprehensible talk."

One of the biggest obstacles to Berber cultural preservation is the belief among many Berber tribes themselves that adopting Arabic, even to the extent of giving up Amazigh, is a good thing from a religious perspective, since it upholds the unity of Islam through its sacred language. The irritation of the Arabizing authorities toward Berber activists is perhaps compounded by an underlying realization that most Arabs in the region are descendants of Berbers who became part of the Arab-Islamic establishment and gave up their language. So, they wonder, why can't the remainder of the "Berbers" just do the same? A similar tension exists in Egypt, where most Egyptian Muslims are descendants of Coptic converts at some stage during the centuries of the Arab-Islamic dispensation. After the U.S. invasion of Iraq, a group called the Egypt Motherland Party appeared, harking back to the "Pharaonism" intellectual movement of the pre-1952 liberal period. "Arabism is manufactured; we are not Arabs," said its leader, Muhsin Lutfy al-Sayed (Dream TV, December 2003). "Iran is completely Muslim but doesn't say it's Arab, Turkey is completely Muslim and doesn't say it's Arab. Speaking Arabic doesn't mean you are Arab. They speak English in the Indian parliament." Interestingly, the process of language switching is also under way in north Sudan, but without the bitterness. Much of south Egypt down to the central Sudan has been ethnically Nubian. Today, different areas on the Nile heading south have their own Nubian dialect, but in the modern era these tribes are losing their dialects as they Arabize in the process of nation-building. Sudanese foreign minister Mustafa Osman Ismail speaks fluent Dongolawi, the Nubian language of the Dongola area in the north that he hails from, yet he is a central figure in an Arabist-Islamist regime for which Islam and Arabic mean unity and progress. Tellingly, Khartoum's National Museum offers a poor commemoration of Nubian civilization compared to the state-of-the-art Nubian Museum in Aswan in southern Egypt, or even to Khartoum's Presidential Palace Museum with its artifacts from the period of British colonial rule. One might say the Nubians—one of three northern tribal groups that monopolize power in Sudan (the two others, the Shayqiyyin and the Ja'liyyin, are considered ethnically Arab)—are an instance of a non-Arab people who have become happy Arabs. Yet, in the manner of these things, many north Sudanese have bitter memories of Syria's initial objection to Sudan's membership in the Arab League when the country became independent in 1956, claiming that it wasn't Arab enough. Arabization is also making inroads in Sudan's neighbor Eritrea, where the dominant Tigrinye language is being challenged by Arabic. Eritrea considered applying to join the League after independence from Ethiopia in 1993. With Muslims and economically powerful Arabic-speaking communities in coastal areas, Somalia is a member of the Arab League, but the wife of its president addressed an Arab League "women's summit" in 2002 in English.

Israel, designed as an exclusivist state with a Jewish majority, fears it will be swamped by Arab culture and go the way of the Maronites in Lebanon. The state of over six million already has a 20 percent Arab minority inside its official borders, and it occupies over three million Arabs in the West Bank and Gaza. Present growth rates mean that by around 2020 Jews will be outnumbered in historical Palestine. Awareness of this issue suddenly leapt to the top of the Israeli-Palestinian political agenda in 2002. Many Israeli and Palestinian parties came to believe that continued settlement activity made the idea of a two-state solution increasingly difficult to implement for the future. Without a system of apartheid or expulsion of Palestinians, Israel will become an Arab state by default. In a sense, Israel promoted Arabization of the region through its success in importing the region's Jewish communities, primarily from Morocco, Yemen, and Iraq, where the polarization caused by the very idea of Israel ruined previously multiethnic and multireligious societies. Palestinian leader Yasser Arafat has often quipped that Israel is an Arab country anyway, since these oriental Jews roughly equal Israel's European Jewry in number, and a few die-hard Jewish intellectuals in Arab countries, such as Morocco's Ibrahim Serfaty, denounce Zionism and maintain an Arab identity (though Arab nationalists in Lebanon prevented Serfaty from attending a Beirut forum in 1998 on the occasion of fifty years since the Palestinian *nakba*).

Nobel laureate V. S. Naipaul has argued that Islam had a "calamitous effect on converted peoples" because it had enslaved other cultures and attempted to wipe them out (*The Guardian*, 4 October 2001). He primarily had in mind non-Arab cultures in the Indian subcontinent. But in fact this process has been at work for centuries within the Arab world. What we are seeing throughout the region is the completion of the Arabization that began with the first Arab conquests. The creation in the region of nation-states along the lines of the European model that has been dominant in world affairs since the late nineteenth century has seen the Middle East's new countries turn to Arabic as the language and culture of modernity and national unity. In the modern era, mass media, popular culture, and the State of Israel have precipitated the completion of this process.

Women, Sex, and Gender in Arab Culture

European photographers Lehnert and Landrock are well known for their early-twentieth-century black-and-white prints

A Tunisian girl some one hundred years ago from the classic set of photographers Lehnert and Landrock. (Library of Congress)

of people and places in the Orient. Their most famous photographs are classic shots of Tunisian women in traditional garb. What's less well known is that the Austrian/German pair persuaded Tunisian girls to throw off their black veils and cloaks for a series of less publicized nude shots. The covered, the naked; the official, the unofficial; that which is fit for public consumption, that which is not—the Lehnert and Landrock prints reflect the duality of attitudes toward women and sexuality in Arab popular culture. When Cairo was full of sex-starved British troops during World War II, prostitutes thrived in special quarters such as Sister Street near the harbor in Alexandria and in the Clot Bey area of Cairo, where they even hung out of balconies to beckon passing men, à la Amster-

dam with its show windows. Today, in keeping with the increased religiosity of the times, prostitutes are more visible in Egypt's movie output than on the streets. Wealthy and Westernized Dubai, on the other hand, is notorious for the public availability of women in bars and clubs.

The "first ladies" of Gulf Arab states—the term applied to the first of up to four wives taken by rulers, according to tribal and Islamic customs—are rarely seen in public life, but recent attempts in Bahrain and Qatar to push political reform have shown them appearing in newspapers and on television. Only in Saudi Arabia does the state oblige them to wear the veil. These systems are deeply entrenched, and the attempts of men in government to change things often come up against male and female forces in society who prefer things to stay as they are. In Kuwait, parliament overturned a decree by Emir Sheikh Jaber al-Ahmed al-Sabah granting women suffrage, and in Bahrain women have failed to win a single seat in elections. There is much domestic opposition to the idea of allowing women to drive in Saudi Arabia. Even in Egypt women win few seats in parliament (Coptic Christians have trouble getting elected too), while Moroccan law now reserves 35 seats for women out of a total 325.

Sex has been the battleground engaging secularist nationalists and Islamists in modern Arab societies. In January 2001, Egypt's culture minister Farouq Hosni, who was up to that point seen as a champion of artistic freedom, announced a war on "pornographic" literature by novelists he said had gone beyond the bounds of public decency. The attack was in fact a clear strategic decision by the government to clamp down on literary freedom in order to keep political Islam at bay. Literature that challenges is seen as a red rag to the Islamist bull. Since the early 1990s the Book Fair, the largest in the Arab world, has regularly seen works by well-known authors, such as Egypt's Nawal al-Saadawi, the Moroccan Mohamed Choucri, and Moroccan anthropologist Fatima Mernissi, ordered for removal by foreign publications censors on the grounds that they go beyond sexual boundaries. The real victim in these book-banning sagas is literature itself. Writers who want to discuss sexual relations risk marginalization at the very least. Even some of Hosni's supporters acknowledged that two of three novels banned by Hosni, in which disillusioned socialists ponder their idealistic youth, had literary merit. In cinema there has been some attempt by the liberal intelligentsia to hit back and return to the freer spirit of 1960s. Critics applauded an art-house film that scored a rare commercial success in late 2001, depicting sexual relations with a directness and gusto rarely seen in Egyptian movies in these conservative times. The film, *Muwatin, Mukhbir wa Harami* (*A Citizen, an Informer, and a Thief*), by auteur director Dawoud Abdel-Sayed, was seen as boldly pushing boundaries, as well as offering a parody of the way the state, through the hapless Hosni, had earlier in the year succumbed to the dominant religious discourse. But it didn't actually involve nudity, which was tried only briefly by mainstream directors and actors in the 1970s (aside from the odd scene in art-house cinema—for example, Khleifi's '*Urs al-Jalil* [*The Wedding in Galilee*]). Of those films, the 1973 *Hamaam al-Malatili* (*The Malatili Bathhouse*), by mainstream director Salah Abu Seif, received the most public exposure—but its actress Shams al-

Baroudi is now veiled and has retired from public life. In another sad coda to this era, actress Nahed Sherif died from cancer caused by a silicon implant operation.

Homosexuality is regarded as a big taboo in public space throughout the Arab countries, but it flourishes as an open secret in different forms behind closed doors, involving famous actors, directors, ministers, and even leaders. After hoping that a flourishing underground gay scene would herald a new era in attitudes, gays in Egypt and Lebanon are leaving for Europe to set up Web sites and campaign with rights groups. Lebanon prides itself on being the Arab world's most open society, but homosexuality is still regarded as perverted and immoral. There are a number of bars and clubs that cater to gays, but they still face the danger of arrest and prosecution for engaging in "unnatural sex." In Egypt, fifty-two men were jailed in 2001 on charges of "regularly practicing debauchery" in an unprecedented campaign against a community that had become too visible in Cairo nightlife and too active on the Internet for the authorities' comfort. There was much public debate in Egypt over the reason for the sudden clampdown, but it's most likely that the state didn't feel society was ready to ditch the age-old attitude of turning a blind eye as long as homosexuals maintained a policy of kiss-and-don't-tell. "Egypt has not and will not be a den for the corruption of manhood, and homosexual groups will not establish themselves here," one prosecutor told the court ("Gay Trial Told Egypt Is No Corrupter of Men," Reuters, 5 September 2001). The campaign, with its lurid press coverage, also conveniently took public attention away from an alarming accumulation of economic troubles. Homosexuality is rarely featured in Arab cinema. Homosexuals appeared in *Hamaam al-Malatili* and Yousry Nasrallah's *Mercedes* (1993), and were alluded to in some of Yousef Chahine's films (e.g., *Iskandariya Leih?*, or *Alexandria, Why?*, 1978).

In general, the inland Arab cities that are surrounded by rural and desert environments are citadels of conservatism, while the coastal cities that are at a remove from these conservative hinterlands are where liberalism has often flourished. Egypt's Mediterranean city of Alexandria, with its pre-Islamic Greek origins, has long been a symbol in the popular Egyptian imagination of openness, freedom, and realization of forbidden dreams. "I wash my clothes, I hang out my worries to dry," sings pop star Mohammed Mounir in his 1989 hit *Oh Alexandria*. Movie director Yousef Chahine has set numerous movies in Alexandria featuring these themes (*Iskandariya Leih?* and *Iskandariya Kaman wa Kaman*, or *Alexandria Again and Again*). But others have seen through the sparkle and found decay. The city is the main player in *The Alexandria Quartet*, Lawrence Durrell's classic depiction of the twisted lives and loves of Alexandria's dwindling foreign communities in the 1940s. And in his 1983 novel *A Banquet for Seaweed*, Syrian writer Haider Haider invents a similar coastal urban center in Algeria, where he mercilessly denudes the city, called Bona, of its airy veneer to reveal the conservative reality behind the Arab seaside city of dreams. "It was a beautiful city, surrounded by sea and woods, but like any Arab city it was desolate, ruled by terror, hunger, middlemen, religion, rancour, ignorance, severity and death. A city that hates strangers," Haider wrote. "Although it was beside the sea and the woods, it seemed sad. Love grows inside it like weeds grow in stone cracks,

threatened with death as soon as it becomes exposed to the sun" (Haider 2000, 11).

The Political Future of the Arab World and Arab Identity

The unwritten, unspoken rule of Arab politics in the fifty-plus years since the postcolonial era began has been that democracy, and a more open society internally at peace with itself, can only really come about when the conflict with Israel, a hangover from that colonial era, is solved in a manner that returns some basic form of justice to the Palestinians. The Oslo peace process, the result of separate, secret negotiating between Yasser Arafat's PLO and Israel, was a jolt to the Arab system, creating pressure for easing the authoritarianism that characterizes all Arab states. Some, like Syria, kept a tight hold; others, like Egypt, loosened up. A debate began on how to ready Arab countries for life with Israel as a partner. But September 11 changed everything. The United States decided that solving the problem of Arab disorder and dysfunction was its priority. Now the Iraqi regime—a major supporter of Palestinian radicalism, at least on the rhetorical front—has been overthrown, and Washington is engaged in a campaign to bring more democratic rule to the region. Although there is now action to try to end the Arab-Israeli conflict, it has clearly taken second place. The consequences of this could be far-reaching. If democracy is discredited in Iraq now, as it was under British imperialism in interwar Egypt, it could mean decades of more of the same for Arab societies. This is the view put forward by most Arab commentators, who sense psychological warfare in pro-Israeli writers in the United States when they talk about the terrible state of the Arab world and argue that Arab regimes should try to end the Arab-Israeli conflict, essentially on Israel's terms. Western observers in general tend to be split, with some focusing on "the Arab-Israeli conflict" camp and others excited by the idea of "democracy now." Those favoring the latter include Israel's supporters and pro-democracy activists who hope that one will inevitably lead to the other (i.e., democracy will lead to accepting Israel on Israel's terms). Those who favor solving the conflict as a necessary condition for democracy believe that, while it is true that minority ruling castes, whether religious or military in persuasion, exploited the Arab-Israeli conflict to shelter themselves and their societies from natural change, the creation of Israel and its corollary, the Palestinian refugee problem, have caused a fundamental state of imbalance in Arab societies, especially in the Mashreq. The creation of Israel and dispossession of Palestinians saw populations shoved around in a region where resources have always been scarce and communities have forever jealously guarded their territory and identity.

Peace processes since 1967 have been underpinned by a basic Israeli desire—for both security and ideological reasons—to avoid returning to the pre-1967 borders and an American commitment to that principle. Such an outcome is likely to mean a peace that leaves Israel with the upper hand in the region, as the dominant force in the Levant. Egypt, seeing itself as the regional leader, is desperate to avoid that outcome. Arab political and intellectual circles question whether the Saudis are as keen as Egypt to check Israeli influence, as long as

it only minimally touches Saudi Arabia itself—"the people of Palestine know better their own valleys," Ibn Saud once famously said (Rasheed 2002, 103), in a comment that has fashioned Arab views of the Saudi commitment to Palestine. Many analysts, both inside and outside the Arab world, think the conflict today is a Palestinian future allied with pan-Arabism or with Israel: Arafat represents the former; Mahmoud Abbas, Ahmed Quria, and whatever other Palestinian prime ministers may come represent the latter. Other observers wonder whether, despite Israel's economic strength, it might be the loser if and when borders open in the region, because of the sheer numbers and cultural vitality of the Arabs. Perhaps for that reason, the Israeli right wants to make sure that if the international community insists on a Palestinian state, it will be one as truncated and troubled as possible, thus discouraging Arabs and Muslims even from visiting it. The Israeli right is well aware of the fact that, in the cramped land of Palestine, it's hardly a forty-minute drive from East Jerusalem to Tel Aviv. Israel, no matter what laws and other stratagems it devises to maintain a Jewish majority, could in practice find itself swamped by Arabs.

The fall of Baghdad to invading foreign forces has left the Arab world confused over the fundamental issue of whether domestic, individual rights must continue to be subordinate to the greater needs of state, religion, identity, and ideology. Many intellectuals are calling for individual rights to come before lofty and rather vague concepts of national rights and principles concerning Palestine, the wider Arab nation, and the community of Islam, and suggest that although globalization clearly undermines old concepts of national sovereignty, the Arab states are in any case weak vis-à-vis a U.S.-backed Israel. Some television channels now carry endless documentaries about the uncovering of brutal tragedies in Iraq under Saddam, but the general tone toward Iraq under occupation is hostile: former Iraqi information minister Mohammed Said al-Sahhaf is remembered not bitterly for false reports of how the war was progressing, but fondly for standing up to foreign arrogance and raising the morale of the Arab nation in one of its darker hours (competing in the nationalist canon with the other modern nadirs of 1948, 1967, and the fall of Beirut in 1982). Few asked questions about the suffering of Iraqis under the Baath regime before it fell. "It is not just bodies that are being dug up at the mass grave near the southern Iraqi town of Mahaweel, nor is Saddam Hussein alone in being conclusively unmasked as a monster. The truth is that Arab media and Arab governments are also being exposed for the crime of having failed to help stop the madman. Who had a greater responsibility than the Arabs to tell 'the truth, the whole truth, and nothing but the truth' about a regime that massacred its own people by the tens of thousands? The dead are therefore not solely victims of Saddam: They are also victims of an Arab world that abandoned its own," as written in a commentary to *The Daily Star* (*The Daily Star*, 16 May 2003). Some writers have asked similar questions about the killings in the Darfur region of west Sudan, though most commentators and governments have closed ranks with Khartoum and asked why Israel's incarceration of Palestinians behind its wall, condemned by the UN's International Court of Justice in The Hague, has not received equal attention. Many familiar figures on Arab television screens are decried as torturers or murderers by someone, somewhere, in the Arab world—for example, Egyptian ex–security chief Fouad Allam, who is the bête noire of the Muslim Brotherhood; Jibreel Rajoub, the security chief of the Palestinian Authority before Oslo collapsed; and any number of veteran politicians in Lebanon. There is much resentment that Washington backs regimes that seem friendly simply based on their relations with Israel or readiness to supply oil at the right price, but which actually are brutal toward their populations. There are a few odd fish: Saudi Arabia is not a typical Arab police state; rather the religious establishment is given free rein on the streets while the police—who number barely 20,000, according to some estimates—take a backseat (though an al-Qa'ida–inspired campaign against the regime in 2003 has forced a rethink). The ruling establishments in these countries may only feel safer broadening the democratic bandwidth once the Israeli-Palestinian conflict has been neutralized to a significant degree. At the same time, they acquire a kind of "negative legitimacy" because of the order they present in the face of chaos like that in Iraq, or because of outside attempts to enforce democratic change while the issue of Israel's occupation remains untouched (for this reason cleric Muqtada al-Sadr's Mehdi Army—by one reading a gang of thugs—won much Arab media sympathy in 2004 for standing up to the U.S. military in Iraq). The classic argument has always been that democracy means the danger of allowing Islamist dictatorships in the door, as with the parliamentary elections that brought the Nazis to power in Weimar Germany. The experience of the Tayep Erdogan's Islamist government in Turkey could help to

Anti-American art showing at the Saddam Arts Center in Baghdad during the 1990s. Former dictator Saddam Hussein was a great patron of a certain kind of art. (Norbert Schiller/Focus MidEast)

moderate Islamic groups in the Arab region and encourage both Arab and Western governments to engage with them.

Postwar Iraq poses unique challenges for two key Arab governments who now see themselves in the firing line. Facing the prospect that they are the ultimate target of Washington's new focus on the region, Egypt and Saudi Arabia have engaged the U.S. administration in the Israeli-Palestinian conflict by playing an active part in supporting the so-called road map, which aims to end the conflict with the creation of a Palestinian state. Some tradeoff with Washington is expected over how much political and economic reform the two countries must engage in. Both regimes want to make sure that whatever change they engage in happens on their terms. Washington's basic measure for reform will

be that extremist anti-American currents in society are cauterized. The quick-fix way for the Egyptians and Saudis to do that is to come up with more security solutions, and those are the very solutions that in the past have provided convenient excuses for postponing real democratic change. The Saudis, constantly fearful of the disintegration of the state (centennial celebrations in 1999 sealed the establishment of an ancestral cult around Ibn Saud), are notoriously slow in instituting change, and President Hosni Mubarak in Egypt has given no indication of how things might develop other than to place his son Gamal at the forefront of efforts to revamp the ruling National Democratic Party. In both countries, many will thirst for more.

The presence of the United States in Iraq, even if its troops are entirely replaced by civilian advisors under a U.S.-allied government, could continue to act as a catalyst for reinvigorating political Islam, much as the Soviet presence in Afghanistan fueled radical politics. For Iraq that could mean a descent into years of destabilization, with law and order extending not much further beyond heavily protected oilfields and government premises, whether they are manned by the foreign forces directly or by the U.S.-allied Iraqi regime. There is also a possibility that Iraq will go the way of Egypt—close ties with the United States could actually hinder democracy and may require the new regime to administer an authoritarian and repressive state, because of the extent of domestic opposition to its reliance on Washington and the "soft" positions on the Israeli-Palestinian conflict required by the regime's backer. Any U.S. administration is likely to have problems turning Iraq into an Israeli-friendly Arab state, since Iraq's Shi'ite establishment is no fan of Zionism, even if the Kurds are open to persuasion. Policymakers in Western capitals and Washington in particular have seemed surprisingly unaware of the fact that both Sunni Arab nationalists and the Shi'ite religious establishment are strongly anti-Israeli and pro-Palestinian. Sympathizers with bin Laden are now feeling sufficiently confident to refer to him reverentially in public as "Sheikh Osama" (al-Jazeera, 10 September 2003), a significant shift brought on by the Iraq war and something that no Arab commentator would have said in the immediate aftermath of September 11. Aljazeera.net even ran a vote in August 2004 asking "Do you support al-Qa'ida's war on the Europeans?" (60 percent answered no, 40 percent said yes).

Any attempt to settle Palestinian refugees in Lebanon or transfer them to other parts of the region (barring Israel, where most of them actually came from) could also stoke the embers of resistance, while the return to their homeland could provoke a civil war situation in Israel (as could a full-scale dismantlement of settlements and Israeli retreat from the West Bank). There is little faith among the Arabs that the United States will deliver a fair deal over Palestine, while at the same time there is more awareness now than there has been since 1967 of the nature of American politics, the influence of Israel, and the deep sympathy that many Americans feel for the Jewish State (whether as pioneering messianic project or place of refuge for the oppressed), so that raising the very question of the U.S. relationship with Israel has come to be seen as "the conversational equivalent of an unclaimed bag on a bus," as American writer Joan Didion has said (Didion 2003). The revelation of U.S. abuse of Iraqi prisoners encouraged the dominant image in the Arab world of the United States as an arrogant neocolonial power whose human rights rhetoric is a cover for geopolitic aims; the abuse appeared to be fed by decades of denigration of Arab culture in Western public discourse to the extent that the Arab intelligentsia wonders why India's cruel caste system, for example, rarely makes the headlines in Western media while all manner of Arab-Islamic rights issues are standard fare. Egypt and Syria went to war against Israel in 1973 because they saw no other way of changing an unacceptable status quo. Field Marshal Abdel-Ghani el-Gamasy, who had tears in his eyes when Sadat caved in to Kissinger's demand that Egyptian forces leave only a token force in Sinai, wrote in his memoirs that Egypt would remain in a state of military confrontation with Israel "until we

Egypt's President Sadat, with his successor Hosni Mubarak on his right and former defense minister Mohammed Abu Ghazala on his left. (TRIP/Art Directors)

regain our full Arab rights"—in reference to the terms of Egypt's peace with Israel in Sinai—and that another Arab-Israeli war would "become inevitable if there is no alternative"—in reference to the wider issue of Palestinian rights (el-Gamasy 1993). Some commentators see the Arab region becoming the launchpad for a counterattack against American neocolonialism: "We could see an occupied Middle East transform itself into the central arena for resistance to the American empire" (Mehio 2004).

In his recent, evocatively titled tract, *The Wandering Arab*, Egyptian political writer Mohammed Hassanein Heikal called for the Arabs to conduct a critical reappraisal of their links with the United States (Heikal 2001) and to resist accepting the demoralizing discourse of Arab failure currently fashionable in the West, and he reiterated the line via the forum of a series of special programs on al-Jazeera in mid-2004. His ideas have been major themes in newspaper columns, political talk shows, and coffee-shop debates. If the road map fails and Iraq fails to recover, many Arab regimes might also begin to wonder whether he isn't on to something.

Bibliography

Print Resources

Ahmed, Leila. *Women and Gender in Islam.* New Haven: Yale University Press, 1992.

———. *A Border Passage: From Cairo to America—A Woman's Journey.* New York: Penguin, 1999.

Ajami, Fouad. *The Dream Palace of the Arabs: A Generation's Odyssey.* New York: Vintage Books, 1998.

Almasude, Amar. "The New Mass Media and the Shaping of Amazigh Identity." In Jon Reyhner, Gina Cantoni, Robert N. St. Clair, and Evangeline Parsons Yazzie, eds., *Revitalizing Indigenous Languages.* Flagstaff: Northern Arizona University, 1999.

Al-Rasheed, Madawi. *A History of Saudi Arabia.* Cambridge: Cambridge University Press, 2002.

al-Sayed Said, Mohammed. Obituary in *Akhbar al-Adab*, 24 March 2001.

Amin, Galal. *Whatever Happened to the Egyptians?* Cairo: American University in Cairo, 2001.

Anonymous. *al-Marouniyya al-Siyasiyya* (Political Maronism). Beirut: Maktabat Ayad, n.d.

Armbrust, Walter, ed. *Mass Mediations: New Approaches to Popular Culture in the Middle East and Beyond.* Berkeley: University of California Press, 2000.

Ashour, Radwa. *Thulathiyat Ghurnata* (The Grenada Trilogy). Cairo: al-Mu'assasa al-Arabiya Li-Dirasat wal-Nashr, 1995.

Benhabib, Seyla. *The Claims of Culture: Equality and Diversity in the Global Era.* Princeton, N.J.: Princeton University Press, 2002.

Benrabah, Mohamed. "Arabisation and Creativity in Algeria." *Journal of Algerian Studies*, nos. 4 and 5.

Bowersock, G. W. *Roman Arabia.* Cambridge, Mass.: Harvard University Press, 1983.

Carey, Roane, *The New Intifada—Resisting Israel's Apartheid.* London: Verso, 2001.

Carey, Roane, Tom Segev, and Jonathan Shainin, eds. *The Other Israel: Voices of Refusal and Dissent.* New York: New Press, 2002.

Chomsky, Noam. *The Fateful Triangle: The United States, Israel and the Palestinians.* London: Pluto Press, 2003.

———. *Rogue States: The Use of Force in World Affairs.* London: Pluto Press, 2003.

Christison, Kathleen. *Perceptions of Palestine: Their Influence on U.S. Middle East Policy.* Los Angeles: University of California Press, 1999.

———. *The Wound of Dispossession: Telling the Palestinian Story.* Santa Fe, N.Mex.: Sunlit Hills Press, 2001.

Cooper, Artemis. *Cairo in the War 1939–1945.* London: Penguin Books, 1989.

Crawford, David. "Morocco's Invisible Imazighen." *Journal of North African Studies* 7, no. 1 (Spring 2002): n.p.

Crone, Patricia, and Michael Cook. *Hagarism: The Making of the Islamic World.* Cambridge: Cambridge University Press, 1977.

Dawisha, Adeed. *Arab Nationalism in the Twentieth Century: From Triumph to Despair.* Princeton, N.J.: Princeton University Press, 2003.

Didion, Joan. "Fixed Opinions, or the Hinge of History." *New York Review of Books*, 16 January 2003.

El-Gamasy, Mohamed. *The October War: Memoirs of Field Marshal El-Gamasy of Egypt.* Cairo: American University Press in Cairo, 1993.

Elgibali, Alaa, ed. *Understanding Arabic: Essays in Contemporary Arabic Linguistics.* Cairo: American University Press in Cairo, 1996.

El-Nawawi, Mohammed, and Adel Iskandar Farag. *Al-Jazeera: How the Free Arab News Network Scooped the World and Changed the Middle East.* Oxford: Westview Press, 2002.

El-Saadawi, Nawal. *The Hidden Face of Eve: Women in the Arab World.* London: Zed Books, 1995.

Fiqi, Mustafa. *Tagdid al-Fikr al-Qawmi* (The Renewal of Nationalist Thought). Cairo: Dar al-Shurouq, 1993.

———. *Al-Arab al-Asl wal-Sura* (Arabs, the Image and the Reality). Cairo: Dar al-Shurouq, 2002.

Fisk, Robert. *Pity the Nation.* New ed. Oxford: Oxford University Press, 2001.

Friedman, Thomas L. *From Beirut to Jerusalem.* New York: Anchor, 1990.

———. *The Lexus and the Olive Tree: Understanding Globalization.* New York: Anchor, 2000.

Gaddafi, Muammar. *Escape to Hell and Other Stories.* London: Blake Publishing, 1999.

"Gay Trial Told Egypt Is No Corrupter of Men." *Reuters*, 5 September 2001.

Gellner, Ernest. *Muslim Society.* Cambridge: Cambridge University Press, 1979.

———. *Plough, Sword and Book: The Structure of Human History.* London: Paladin, 1991.

Gellner, Ernest, and Charles Micaud, eds. *Arabs and Berbers: From Tribe to Nation in North Africa.* Lexington, Mass: D. C. Heath and Co., 1972.

Gordon, Joel. *Revolutionary Melodrama: Popular Film and Civic Identity in Nasser's Egypt.* Chicago: University of Chicago Press, 2002.

Grossman, David. *The Yellow Wind.* New York: Farrar, Straus & Giroux, 1989.

Habib, Rafiq. *Misr al-Qadima* (The Coming Egypt). Cairo: Dar al-Shurouq, 1996.

Habiby, Emile. *The Secret Life of Saeed the Pessoptimist.* 1974 (Arabic ed.) Reprint. London: Zed Books, 1985.

Haider, Haider. *Walima Li A'shaab al-Bahr* (A Feast for the Seaweed). 1983. Reprint. Damascus: Ward Lil-Tabaa'a, 2000.

Haim, Sylvia, ed. *Arab Nationalism: An Anthology.* Berkeley: University of California Press, 1976.

Halliday, Fred. *Nation and Religion in the Middle East.* Boulder, Colo: Lynne Rienner, 2000.

Hamouda, Adel. *Al-Nukta al-Siyasiya: Kayfa Yaskhar al-Misriyyun min Zuama'ihim* (The Political Joke: How Egyptians Laugh at Their Rulers). Cairo: al-Fursan Lil-nashr, 1999.

Hasan, Sana. *Enemy in the Promised Land: An Egyptian Woman's Journey into Israel.* New York: Schocken Books, 1986.

Hass, Amira. *Drinking the Sea at Gaza.* New York: Owl Books, 2000.

Heggy, Tareq. *Naqd al-'Aql al-Arabi* (A Critique of the Arab Mind). Cairo: Dar al-Maaref, 1998.

Heikal, Mohammed Hassanein. *al-Mufawwadaat al-Sirriyya* (The Secret Negotiations). Cairo: Dar al-Shurouq, 1996.

———. *The Wandering Arab.* Cairo: Dar al-Shurouq, 2001.

———. *Azmat al-Arab wa Mustaqbaluhum* (The Crisis of the Arabs and Their Future). Cairo: Dar al-Shurouq, 2002.

Henry, Clement, and Robert Springborg. *Globalization and the Politics of Development in the Middle East.* Cambridge: Cambridge University Press, 2001.

Hirst, David. *The Gun and the Olive Branch: The Roots of Violence in the Middle East.* New ed. London: Faber and Faber, 2003.

"HLA Genes in Arabic-Speaking Moroccans: Close Relatedness to Berbers and Iberians." *Tissue Antigens* 55 (2000): n.p.

Holt, P. M., and M. W. Daly. *A History of the Sudan: From the Coming of Islam to the Present Day.* Harlow, UK: Pearson Education, 2000.

Horne, Alastair. *A Savage War of Peace: Algeria 1954–1962.* 1977. Reprint. New York: Viking, 2002.

Hourani, Albert. *Arabic Thought in the Liberal Age 1798–1939.* Cambridge: Cambridge University Press, 1983.

———. *History of the Arab Peoples.* London: Faber and Faber, 1992.

Ibrahim, Sonallah. *Zaat.* Cairo: Dar al-Mustaqbal al-Arabi, 1992.

———. *Sharaf.* Cairo: Dar al-Helal, 1996.

———. *Warda.* Cairo: Dar al-Mustaqbal al-Arabi, 2000.

Kaplan, Robert D. *The Arabists: The Romance of an American Elite.* New York: The Free Press, 1993.

Kearton, Cherry. *The Shifting Sands of Algeria.* London: Arrowsmith, 1924.

Kepel, Gilles. *Jihad: The Trail of Political Islam.* Cambridge, Mass: Harvard University Press, 2002.

———. *Bad Moon Rising.* London: Saqi Books, 2003.

Khalidi, Rashid. *Palestinian Identity: The Construction of Modern National Consciousness.* New York: Columbia University Press, 1997.

Khoury, Elias. *La Porte du soleil.* Arles: Editions Actes Sud/Le Monde Diplomatique, 2002.

Kienle, Eberhard. *A Grand Delusion: Democracy and Economic Reform in Egypt.* London/New York: I. B. Tauris, 2000.

Kimmerling, Baruch. *The Invention and Decline of Israeliness: State, Society and the Military.* Los Angeles: University of California Press, 2001.

Lane, Edward. *An Account of the Manners and Customs of the Modern Egyptians.* London: John Murray, 1860.

Lavie, Smadar, and Ted Swedenburg, eds. *Displacement, Diaspora, and Geographies of Identity.* Durham, N.C.: Duke University Press, 1996.

Lawrence, T. E. *Seven Pillars of Wisdom.* London: Penguin Books, 2000.

Lewis, Bernard. *What Went Wrong?: The Clash between Islam and Modernity in the Middle East.* London: Phoenix, 2002.

Maalouf, Amin. *On Identity.* London: P. Harvill, 2000.

Makiya, Kanaan. (pseudonym Samir al-Khalil). *Republic of Fear: The Politics of Modern Iraq.* London: Hutchinson, 1989.

———. *Cruelty and Silence.* London: Jonathan Cape, 1993.

Mallat, Chibli. *The Middle East into the Twenty-First Century.* Reading, UK: Ithaca Press, 1996.

Ma'oz, Moshe, and Gabrial Sheffer, eds. *Middle Eastern Minorities and Diasporas.* Brighton: Sussex Academic Press, 2002.

Masalha, Nur. *The Expulsion of the Palestinians: The Concept of "Transfer" in*

Zionist Political Thought, 1882–1948. Beirut: Institute for Palestine Studies, 1992.

Mehio, Saad. Commentary in *al-Khaleej*, 2 May 2004.

Mikhail, Sami. *Victoria.* Trans. Samir Naqqash. Cairo: Dar al-Arabiya for Print, Publishing and Distribution, 1995.

Morris, Benny. *The Birth of the Palestinian Refugee Problem, 1947–1949.* Cambridge: Cambridge University Press, 1989.

Moussa, Amr. Speech at Arab League. 29 October 2002.

Nafie, Ibrahim. Commentary in *al-Ahram*, 5 March 2004.

Nassif, Emad. *Zaman Fifi Abdou* (The Era of Fifa Abdou). Cairo: Dar al-Gumhouriya, 1996.

Nfousa, Adrar. "Al-Amazighiyya Sha'n Libi Asil wa Mughayyab" (Amazighism—An Authentic but Absent Libyan Affair). *Sho'un Libiyah* (December 1999): n.p.

Pappe, Ilan, ed. *The Israel/Palestine Question.* London: Routledge, 1999.

Peres, Shimon. *The New Middle East.* New York: Holt, 1993.

Pipes, Daniel. *The Hidden Hand: Middle East Fears of Conspiracy.* London: Macmillan, 1996.

Qutb, Sayed. *Ma'alim Fil-Tareeq* (Milestones). 1965 Beirut: Dar al-Shurouq, 1979.

Redfield, R. *The Little Community and Peasant Society and Culture.* Chicago: University of Chicago Press, 1973.

Ryan, Nigel, "On the Revolutionary Trail." *al-Ahram Weekly*, Issue No. 597, 1–7 August 2002.

Said, Edward. *Orientalism.* Princeton, N.J.: Princeton University Press, 1979.

———. *The Question of Palestine.* London: Vintage Books, 1979.

Salem, Ali. *Rihla ila Isra'il* (Journey to Israel). Cairo: Akhbar al-Yawm, 1994.

Salibi, Kamal. *The Modern History of Jordan.* London: I. B. Tauris, 1998.

Schivelbusch, Wolfgang. *The Culture of Defeat: On National Trauma, Mourning, and Recovery.* Trans. Jefferson Chase. London: Granta Books, 2003.

Shahak, Israel. *Open Secrets: Israeli Nuclear and Foreign Policy.* Jefferson Chase. London: Pluto Press, 1997.

Shammas, Anton. *Arabesques.* Berkeley: University of California Press, 2001.

Shlaim, Avi. *The Iron Wall: Israel and the Arab World.* London: Penguin Books, 2000.

"The Sultan of Soap." *Cairo Times*, 6–12 January 2000.

Vatikiotis, P. J. *The History of Modern Egypt.* London: Weidenfeld and Nicolson, 1991.

Vidal, Gore. *Dreaming War: Blood for Oil and the Cheney-Bush Junta.* New York: Thunder's Mouth Press/Nation Books, 2002.

———. *Perpetual War for Perpetual Peace.* New York: Thunder's Mouth Press/Nation Books, 2002.

Yapp, M. E. *The Near East since the First World War.* New York: Longman, 1991.

Zayat, Montasser. *Hiwaraat Mamnua* (Forbidden Conversations). Cairo: Dar al-Shurouq, 1995.

Web Sites

www.free-lebanon.com. Site run from Jerusalem by the Christian émigré Lebanese Foundation for Peace.

www.aina.org. Site run by the U.S.-based Assyrian International News Agency.

www.tamazgha.org. A Berber rights site run by the Amazigh Cultural Association in America.

www.libyanet.com. Site called "Libya: Our Home," which is a treasure trove of information on Libyan arts, music, and literature.

www.undp.org/rbas/ahdr/. The official site concerning the United Nations Development Agency's Arab Human Development Reports for 2002 and 2003.

www.freelebanon.org. Site of an anti-Arab Lebanese American lobby group called the U.S. Committee for a Free Lebanon (USCFL).

www.al-bab.com. Site with general political and cultural information on Arabic countries, including Iraq.

www.gaydar.com. A gay Internet dating site, where Egyptian police have used aliases to entrap gay men.

http://www.dubaicityguide.com. A site run by Dubai's Municipality, with in-depth, user-friendly information on the city.

www.marsad.net. Site of London-based Egyptian Islamist dissident Yasser al-Sirry, who runs an "Islamic Research Center."

www.amrkhaled.net. Site of popular Egyptian preacher Amr Khaled.

www.forislam.com. Islamist Web site run by Amr Khaled.

www.islammemo.com. A directory of Islamic Web sites, run by Iraqi Kurdish Islamists.

www.mepc.org. Web site of the Middle East Policy Council, a U.S. nonprofit organization that issues the journal *Middle East Policy*.

www.palestineremembered.com. Site with detailed information on life in Palestine before the 1948 war and refugee crisis, run by a nonprofit group called Palestine Remembered.

www.zawya.com. The prime news site covering the Arab world.

www.avnery-news.co.il. Site of prominent Israeli peacenik and critic of Ariel Sharon, Uri Avnery.

www.meforum.org. Right-wing U.S. think tank, featuring political analyst Daniel Pipes, that works to "define and promote American interests in the Middle East."

www.heritage.org. Site of influential "neo-conservative" think tank, the Heritage Foundation.

www.washingtoninstitute.org. Site of right-wing think tank the Washington Institute for Near East Policy.

www.aei.org. Site of right-wing think tank, the American Enterprise Institute.

www.newamericancentury.org. Site of the Project for the New American Century, another influential "neo-con" think tank.

www.ceip.org/ArabReform. The Arab Reform Bulletin, published by the Carnegie Endowment for International Peace, one of the more liberal think tanks concerning Middle East issues.

www.globalsecurity.org. Site of organization called GlobalSecurity.org concerned with American and global security issues.

www.virtualcountries.com. Site with links to affiliated sites concerning specific Arab countries.

www.ultimatetopsites.com/general/arabtop/index4.html. Site with a page that has a list of the "top 100 Arab sites," which cover entertainment, cultural, religious, and political affairs.

www.oup.co.uk/blsoas. Site of the School of Oriental and African Studies in London's periodical *Bulletin*.

http://arabworld.nitle.org/introduction.php?module_id=5. A Web project by the National Institute for Technology and Liberal Education (NITLE) on "Arab culture and civilization."

www.almash-had.org. Site of mash-had.com, run by Madar, the Palestinian Centre for Israeli Studies.

www.crisisweb.org. Web site of the International Crisis Group, which has much coverage of the Arab world, especially Iraq.

www.cato.org. Site of the Washington-based Cato Institute, which has argued for a U.S. exit from Iraq as quickly as possible.

www.btselem.org. B'Tselem site on human rights issues in occupied territories.

www.fmep.org. Foundation for Middle East Peace (FMEP), a U.S. nonprofit organization concerning the Israeli-Palestinian conflict.

www.mideastweb.org. Pro-peace site run by group of Arab, Jewish, and other intellectuals, in English, Arabic, and Hebrew.

www.csmonitor.com/specials/neocon/spheresInfluence.html. A list of neo-conservative think tanks on the Christian Science Monitor Web site.

www.alhewar.com. Arab American site of the Hewar Center for Arab Culture and Dialogue.

www.aaiusa.org. Site of the Arab American Institute, the main body representing Arab American interests in the United States.

www.hsje.org/homepage.htm. Site of the Historical Society of Jews from Egypt.

2

Television and Radio

Egypt, the Pioneer of the Arab "Media of Mobilization"

Since audio and televisual media became a feature of modern life in the mid-twentieth century, they have been used to further the political and development agendas of Arab governments as well as the rebel, sectarian, and other political movements. The importance of radio was well understood by the officers led by Gamal Abdel Nasser, who instituted a military coup in Egypt in 1952. It would be no exaggeration to say that the model for media as a weapon for state control in the Arab world was established by the Egyptians. Egyptian radio was revolutionary, part of a "media of mobilization" of the masses, and Nasser was in many ways the Arab world's first radio star. Cheap transistor radios spread in the Arab world in the 1950s, just after Nasser came to power. The military coup was announced on the radio by Anwar Sadat, a member of the group of Free Officers, on the very night it took place. Nasser's nationalization of the Suez Canal in 1956 was carried out upon the live radio broadcast of a code word in a speech he gave in Alexandria. After the 1967 Arab defeat to Israel, Nasser also dramatically announced his resignation on radio—with TV cameras, the latest development in media control, filming him reading the speech. Because she had been a favorite of the deposed monarch King Farouk, leading singer Umm Kalthoum was associated in the minds of the masses with the royal Egypt that the military wanted to replace with a new order. But Nasser realized there could no better publicity for the republican cause than for Umm Kalthoum to sing to the nation on state radio. She subsequently developed a close relationship with the regime and with Nasser personally, and to this day she is intimately linked in the minds of people all over the Arab world with Nasserist pan-Arabism.

From that moment on, a host of Egypt's most talented people were drafted into the service of selling the Arab revolution by radio, from poet Salah Jahine, whose nationalist rhyme was put to song, to heartthrob singer Abdel-Halim Hafez, who sang the praises of Nasser's Aswan High Dam and the Arab dream. Abdel-Halim wasn't necessarily the best singer

A Palestinian in the Gaza Strip, called al-Haj Abu Ramadan, listens to news of kamikaze, or suicide, bomb attacks by Islamists in Riyadh, Saudi Arabia, May 2003. (Abid Katib/Getty Images)

of his generation—there were also Karem Mahmoud and Mohammed Kandil—but he had the charisma to carry off songs like *The Charter* (*al-Mithaq*) and *Greetings to Socialism* (*Tahiya Lil-Ishtirakiya*). The majority of people at this time could not read or write, and cassette tape technology—which gave people the freedom to listen to music of their choice—didn't proliferate until the 1970s. As television became more widespread in the 1960s, it was put to exactly the same use. There were two distinct stages: 1956 to 1967, the golden age of Nasser, after his emergence as a Suez War hero up to the defeat of 1967; and 1967 to 1973, when Egypt prepared for war with Israel to try to recover the losses of 1967. Singers from around the region joined together to sing *al-watan al-akbar*, or "The Greater Nation," penned by celebrated

composer Mohammed Abdel-Wahhab, including Egypt's Abdel-Halim Hafez, Nagaat, Shadia, and Fayda Kamel; the Algerian singer Warda; and the Lebanese singer Sabah. Just before the 1973 war, the Israelis might have been able to read the signs from songs broadcast on Egyptian radio, such as Abdel-Halim Hafez's *Keep the Guns at the Ready* ("Keep the guns at the ready/If the world sleeps I'll be awake with my gun, awake day and night with my gun in my hand/Oh revolutionary country our enemy is mighty, so keep the guns at the ready"). Nasser's revolutionary radio wasn't just for Egypt. Egypt set up its Sawt al-Arab, or "Voice of the Arabs" station, as a sort of indigenous Arab version of the BBC's World Service Arabic station, in the service of independence movements throughout the region (the Saudis banned their nationals from listening to its subversive Arab nationalist message, which threatened their controversial rule). Copying Nasser's example, the Palestinian Liberation Organization (PLO) made significant use of radio in its early days. Many senior PLO figures consider that without their propaganda activities, their cause for an independent Palestine may have died. The use of singers on state media in the Nasserist manner continued in Iraq throughout the 1990s, but in a more extreme form. Singers were forced to sing for the regime, though some were more enthusiastic than others. Iraqi singer Dawoud al-Qaysi, famous for his songs in support of Saddam Hussein and the Baath Party, was shot dead in central Baghdad in May 2003. It was al-Qaysi's songs that were played endlessly on state television during the war to bring down the rule of Hussein's Baath Party.

The overkill in the exploitation of the media had its inevitable consequences. The BBC's Arabic Service became extremely popular all over the Arab world because it was regarded as more honest than state-run outfits. Egyptians never really forgave the regime for its false reports of glory in the first days of the Six Day War of 1967, a prelude, as it transpired, to a defeat of large magnitude, not least because of the dreams of unity that preceded it. This event sent the whole Arab world into a state of shock and depression from which it is only just recovering today. When Egypt was ostracized in the Arab world after its 1979 peace treaty with Israel, even more Egyptians tuned in to BBC radio. Until Colonel Gaddafi made up with Egypt in the late 1980s, Libyan radio and television broadcast slanders of Sadat and his successor Mubarak (referred to as Imbarik, meaning "kneeling camel"), which were picked up by all of northern Egypt. During the 1990–1991 Gulf crisis, the BBC and Radio Monte Carlo were widely listened to as the most impartial sources of news available. For televison, those with the means turned to CNN.

The Egyptian state media philosophy today is influenced by a conservative Islamic ethic, which matches the changes in Egyptian society since the discrediting of Arab nationalism in 1967 and also tries to steer a middle way between the religious standards of the Gulf region and the liberal television of Lebanon. There is no soft porn, partial nudity, or obscene language on Egyptian television. Belly dancing, Broadway-style chorus-girl routines, miniskirts and bikinis, movies and soap operas showing alcohol consumption, and love scenes that never climax with acts of sex are all part of the popular cultural scene, but they keep to certain limits on state television. The satellite revolution of the 1990s, led by Saudis, Qataris, and Lebanese, infringed on Egypt and its traditional media hegemony. But Egypt is trying to reclaim its leading role and cultural sovereignty through its vast reserves of talent in actors, singers, dancers, musicians, comedians, journalists, producers, directors, religious scholars, and Quranic reciters. Egypt consciously seeks to present itself as a compromise between openness and propriety, a concept Egypt's state arts censors champion publicly, promoting an Arab cultural ethic that is at once conservative and tolerant.

This was the message that viewers understood in March 2002 during an interview with Egypt's then State Mufti (an official, government-appointed theologian, whose job is to give authoritative religious opinions, or fatwas). The presenter was Mufid Fawzy, a well-known Coptic Christian, who began by explaining to the Mufti, Sheikh Ahmed al-Tayeb, that he was personally "of the Fairouz persuasion" in music, referring to legendary Lebanese singer Fairouz. What was the Mufti? The point of the question was for the Mufti to admit that he listens to music—which more right-wing clerics frown upon—but of a harmless, conservative variety. Sure enough, the Mufti chose this diplomatic middle ground by acknowledging a passion at times in his life, he said, for Umm Kalthoum—a solid, sexless classical choice, as opposed to the liberal, romantic figure of Fairouz. The Mufti was also asked how he had managed to live with a French family in Paris during his younger days, when it's well-known that the French love wine—another no-no in the minds of strict Muslims and political Islamists. The Mufti's response was that he informed the French family that, while he would not partake of the wine, he had no problem being present at the table while they imbibed it. He added that the French family and their guests were always polite and considerate toward his Islamic principles. As a state religious appointee, the Mufti in Egypt sees his role as a guide for Muslims toward an Islamic moral code that allows them to deal with non-Muslims in mutual respect. It's a message designed to undercut the appeal of Islamic radicals of all persuasions, from al-Qa'ida to the austere clerics of Saudi Arabia, where such views would not get an airing on state television.

Arab Satellite TV since the 1990s: The al-Jazeera Revolution

Since the 1990s, Arab television has undergone a revolution led by Gulf and Lebanese satellite television, and the Egyptians have been running to catch up. Saudi businessmen set the ball rolling after the Gulf War in 1991, setting up the London-based MBC (Middle East Broadcasting), with production values and journalistic standards that matched those of the rest of the world. The idea was that MBC would be the CNN of the Middle East. By choosing London as a base for the project, they deliberately moved away from the stifling atmosphere created by government control in Arab countries, though there was a clear subtext of presenting the world to Arabs from an Arab perspective as well as protecting the Saudi regime from the kind of criticism it was subject to after the Gulf War. Next came Orbit, another private satellite channel with close links to the Saudi royal family, which based itself in Rome. Despite a disastrous venture with the BBC Arabic Service, which collapsed in 1995 (after an incident covering Saudi dissidents in London), the channel broke new ground with talk shows that featured leftist and Islamist politicians who rarely if ever appeared on state-run channels inside the Arab world.

In 1996, Qatar's new ruling elite, established after a coup within the royal family, started its own al-Jazeera (meaning "the Arabian Peninsula") satellite channel with the intention of taking the Arab world by storm. With taboo-breaking programs like *al-Ittijaah al-Mu'aakis* (*The Opposite Direction*), which brought together guests from all over the region to talk about domestic, religious, and pan-Arab issues, it was a huge success. Watched by millions of Arab viewers across the Middle East, Europe, and North America, it established itself as a forum for debate on human rights, fundamentalism, religion, and corruption. Presenter Faisal al-Qassem, like many of al-Jazeera's staff, was hired from the BBC's World Service Radio and its Arabic section's failed project with Orbit. His tactic was to let the guests get it all out, and the show often degenerated into shouting matches. The advent of al-Jazeera coincided with the beginning of mass satellite penetration throughout the region, which allowed audiences to see players in their own societies slogging it out on television for the first time, in debates previously confined to the press. Egyptians, for example, could see Islamist preacher Youssef al-Badry face-to-face with Egyptian feminist writer Nawal al-Saadawi in 1997. Libya's Colonel Gaddafi appeared on al-Jazeera with a draft version of the March 2001 Arab summit resolutions, mocking them as not worth the ink they were printed with. "The Arab region needs programs which are strong and I think we've thrown a big rock into stagnant waters," Qassem says of his show (interview with author, June 2004). "I think it has helped to liberate Arabs from the fear of not being able to talk about things. Eight years ago when I began the programme I was looking around left and right for the intelligence people after me. I felt someone was monitoring how I thought; I was frightened to even think about some sensitive political issues." Qassem admits that he does his best to antagonize the two studio guests against one another and incite them to insult each other. "I could do a calm, sober program but I know the viewers wouldn't watch," he says. The program now offers viewers the chance to vote online to answer questions, such as, in early 2004, "Why is it that Arab regimes failed to condemn the pictures of abuse of Iraqi prisoners? Is the torture in Arab prisons not a hundred times worse than Abu Ghraib?" In that case, referring to the U.S. prisoner abuse scandal, 86 percent said yes—Arab torture is worse.

Since its inception, al-Jazeera has offended just about every Arab government. Jordan closed down its offices for four months because a talk show host mentioned collaboration between the late King Hussein and Israel. Opposition politicians said Algeria shut off electricity in parts of the country so people wouldn't see a debate on the country's conflicts. The channel was banned from reporting in Kuwait for a month after an Iraqi insulted the Emir Sheikh Jaber al-Ahmed al-Sabah during a telephone call from Norway on a live program. Egypt's patience ran thin after the Palestinians began the second Intifada against Israeli occupation in September 2000, though al-Jazeera earlier in the year had begun recording some programs at Media Production City, Egypt's glitzy, state-owned studio complex in the desert outside Cairo. Al-Jazeera's talk shows began to air more and more criticism of Egypt after Mubarak took a moderate line at the Arab summit in October 2000 by watering down calls for a mandatory cut-off of all Arab ties with Israel. The debate engendered by al-Jazeera obliged Mubarak himself to appear on Egyptian state television in November 2000. He explained to interviewers that he couldn't afford to take the nation into battle and risk losing everything it had gained politically and economically since making peace with Israel in 1979. After the Intifada began, the channel went so far as to broadcast scenes of children parading in the streets of Bethlehem, carrying a papier-mâché donkey with Mubarak's name daubed on its side. "Some Palestinians have the habit of biting the hand that feeds them," snarled one commentator in the Egyptian press (Ragab, *al-*

Gumhouriya, October 2000). "But because fate has made us the big mother country, the country with weight and leadership qualities, we usually forgive and forget." Not long after that, Egypt deported Faisal al-Qassem's brother Majd, a reasonably well known pop singer, supposedly over visa irregularities, but no one believed that.

Egypt has been particularly vulnerable to attack on al-Jazeera. As the largest Arab country and the self-appointed guardian of Arab nationalism, the average Arab expects Egypt to do a lot to defend the Palestinians, so the Egyptian government finds itself in the position of constantly defending itself before Arab public opinion. The authorities fear that rabble-rousing on al-Jazeera, from callers or studio guests, could contribute to popular pressure to confront Israel. Authorities are also highly suspicious of the channel's motives. The channel was set up by the Qatari royal family, and Qatar is the one country in the region that the channel never criticizes. Qatar's population is so small, and its government so empowered by its huge natural gas discoveries, that it can get away with cutting a maverick, pro-Western role in the region: It can allow the United States to run regional military operations from its soil, and promote normalization with Israel, without any fear of a domestic backlash. The Qataris, like the Kuwaitis, are unpopular in the Arab world, where some intellectuals depict them as selfish peoples in parvenu states that don't make any geographical or political sense and owe their independence to foreign powers. Qatar is happy to allow al-Jazeera to show up the irony in the situation of Egypt—a leading, ancient, historic Arab nation—badgering other states to cut all links with Israel, when Egypt was the first to make peace

with the Jewish State. During a tiff between the two countries in 1997, an Egyptian newspaper editor poured scorn onto Qatar as a country whose population "couldn't fill up a Cairo five-star hotel" (*al-Ahram*, December 1997). In short, al-Jazeera touches on a fundamental fault line in today's Arab world, which runs between the barren desert nations, awash in oil and gas money, and the ancient cultures with long, proud histories, drowning in overpopulation and poverty.

Because of al-Jazeera and the other channels competing with it during the 1990s (MBC, Hizbollah's al-Manar, LBC), the Intifada arguably stoked passions in the Arab world to a more immediate degree than any other event in the long conflict between the State of Israel and the Palestinians since the 1967 war. The Intifada has affected Arab societies from top to bottom and resonated loudly throughout popular culture. In February 2002, well-known actor Farouk Fishawi was asked in a television interview what newspaper headline he would most love to read one day in the future. "Jerusalem, capital of Palestine," he answered gravely and without hesitation. "*Allahu akbar* [God is great]," the interviewer responded. A host of singers churned out material about Jerusalem. In 2001, an all-star cast recorded a patriotic song called *Jerusalem Will Return to Us (al-Quds Hatirga' Lina)*, where singer Mona Abdel-Ghani made a return to the public eye after taking the veil and retiring from music. Egyptian crooner Hani Shaker dedicated his 2001 song, *At the Door of Jerusalem*, to Mohammed al-Durra, the twelve-year-old Palestinian boy whose death in his father's arms was caught on camera: "It was the voice of right/Embodied in a child's cry/In the bosom of death/

A father's sigh in a last look/And a last sound." It is partly because of this very real, direct impact that the satellite channels have had on popular thinking that Arab American academic Hisham Sharabi writes: "In modern Arab history, including during the revolutionary period of the 1960s and 70s, there has been nothing to equal the power of the Arab satellite channels to change the nature of popular consciousness and perhaps in the political attitudes of popular forces in the Arab world" (*al-Hayat*, 18 July 2003). The satellite media with their unifying power across the Arab region, constituting an *Arab* message for the Arab peoples—contrary to past reliance on the BBC World Service or CNN—have crystallized hostility to the American presence in Iraq. The Arab intelligentsia consider that it's not "regime change" in Iraq that will bring democracy to the Arab world, but a just solution to the Israeli-Palestinian conflict, and the satellite channels have helped make this a central tenet of political discourse in the Arab world today.

Al-Jazeera's profile was also high after the September 11 attacks and subsequent to the wars in Afghanistan and Iraq. Its presence in Afghanistan and contacts with Arab Islamists operating there placed it in a unique position to report on the war and broadcast the opinions of al-Qa'ida's leaders. As Saddam Hussein made use of CNN during the 1990–1991 Gulf War crisis, Osama bin Laden has made use of al-Jazeera since September 2001. For a time bin Laden appeared in the manner of a popular hero—Robin Hood cum Che Guevara—standing up to the imperialist West, speaking from his cave while a dapper Bush taped messages from his White House office. Egyptian American Jehane Noujaim

made a fly-on-the-wall documentary about how al-Jazeera covered the Iraq war in 2003 for its estimated 40 million viewers. Like Michael Moore's *Fahrenheit 9/11*, it brings you the graphic images of the dead and maimed that were rarely seen on mainstream Western channels—al-Jazeera's attempt to show that "war has a price," as al-Jazeera producer Samer Khader says in the film. Called *Control Room*, it won a general release in the United States during 2004, despite a government-led public relations campaign against the channel, which Defense Secretary Donald Rumsfeld once dubbed "Osama bin Laden's mouthpiece."

In the face of the stodgy news presentation on state television channels throughout the region, al-Jazeera has also encouraged a new political culture that is more responsive to facts and deals more openly with controversial issues. For Egypt, the traditional media leader, it has prompted an effort to spice up decades of depoliticized programming. After years of drab propaganda, endless soaps, and outdated cabaret acts, new programs with names such as *Breakthrough (Ikhtiraq)*, *In Depth (Fil-'Umq)*, and *Without Censorship (Bidoun Riqaba)* sprang up in the late 1990s in a TV glasnost aimed in part at countering critical views of Egypt that appeared on the Qatari channel. "The private [satellite] channels are not always neutral," *Breakthrough* presenter Amr al-Leithy said (interview with author, Reuters, 5 June 2001). Critics have argued that the apparent loosening of controls on Egypt's state TV simply offers the government a more sophisticated way to sell its policies at a sensitive time, with popular anger running high over Israel's treatment of the Palestinians, the war on radical Islamic groups, and the occupation of Iraq. "Egypt's media

War on Iraq: A Milestone for Arab Television?

The war against Iraq was a milestone for Arab television, though the jury is still out on how lasting the effects will be. The Arab satellite channels featured graphic, fast-paced news on the war that challenged state television stations to keep up. An Arab leader being brought down by an invading foreign force, with accompanying cheers of the populace, is an uncomfortable image for any state-run TV network. The state-run television stations showed the images—only Syrian TV avoided showing the fall of Baghdad—but the stations also provided a barrage of analysis that questioned the motivations behind the scenes of the images. In doing so, they followed the satellite stations. The raising of the American flag on the statue of Saddam Hussein provoked bitter commentary. This is more theatre broadcast by America and its propaganda organs, because the Iraqi people in Basra, Nasiriya and Mosul where they are resisting, are the same as the Iraqi people in Baghdad. Resistance doesn't differ from one place to another. God knows who brought these people who

stood before us today accepting that the American flag be raised on a statue," an Egyptian journalist said on al-Arabiya (9 April, 2003). On al-Jazeera presenters goaded guests and correspondents to suggest that the Americans encouraged looting and breakdown in the civil order to create domestic strife, so that they could run the country with the Iraqi opposition of its choosing. Al-Jazeera's correspondent in Baghdad, Maher Abdullah, provided barbed live commentary as the statue toppled, saying the future of Iraq would now clearly have "an American taste." Al-Jazeera also showed controversial footage of dead British soldiers and gory scenes of dead Iraqis, arguing that they were simply showing viewers the true nature of the war.

After the war was over, al-Jazeera removed its chief executive, Mohammed Jassem al-Ali, who had been in charge of the channel since its inception in 1996 after allegations surfaced that Iraqi intelligence agents had been working inside al-Jazeera to ensure favorable coverage

is basically a media of mobilization and to move to a free media is a very different process," political writer Salah Issa said (interview with author, Reuters, 5 June 2001). The mobilization of the masses involves nine terrestrial channels, dozens of satellite channels, sixteen radio stations, and eight printing houses that publish over fifty newspapers and magazines. Al-Jazeera also regularly interviews Israeli politicians, analysts, and officials to present their viewpoints, and it has been a unifying force in the region. It has brought non-Muslim minority groups into the Arabist-Islamist discourse at the heart of the Arab mainstream, and it has been a factor

in the increasing "pan-Arabization" of Lebanon, introducing Christian political elites and publics to Islamist politics in the "Arab world."

In 2003 a Saudi-backed alternative to al-Jazeera hit Arab TV screens, just in time for the Iraq war. Al-Arabiya—mainly owned by the Saudi-owned MBC—is al-Jazeera minus the Islamist slant and the shouting. Its subtext challenges Qatar's view of the world, which didn't always coalesce with the Saudi view. Saudi companies will not advertise on al-Jazeera because the authorities view it as "anti-Saudi." One Saudi opposition figure was prevented from leaving the country in 2002 after he for Iraq. Al-Ali was granted an interview with Saddam Hussein just before the Iraq war in 2003 (he was later replaced by Waddah Khanfar). With CNN turfed out of Baghdad, it was largely the Arab media's war—a reversal of the situation during the 1991 Gulf War. But on state-run television channels, little has changed for the most part. Most Arab stations still devote a disproportionate amount of airtime to meetings of top officials, protocol items, and religious affairs. Tunisia's state TV network tried to bury news of flooding deaths in the north of the country in January 2003. In Egypt, news about President Hosni Mubarak still dominates coverage, while most of Saudi programming focuses on the royal family and the minutiae of Islam. In one show, aired during the Iraq war in 2003, a caller wanted to know the meaning of flatulence during prayer: He asked, should he continue in his prayers? Had the Devil intervened to soil his faith? The clerics' answer to the distressed caller was, only if a noise was made; in silent flatulence, the clerics said, the Devil had no part and prayer could continue.

U.S. troops, backed by a group of Iraqis, pulling down a statue of Saddam Hussein in central Baghdad during the 2003 war in Iraq—among the many scenes that were shown live on most Arab TV stations. (Christophe Calais/In Visu/Corbis)

criticized Saudi Arabia's position on the Iraqi crisis. Like al-Jazeera, al-Arabiya designs powerful montages of Israeli soldiers putting down the Palestinian Intifada, set to a background of stirring music, but unlike al-Jazeera it does the same to discredit violence from radical Islamist groups like al-Qa'ida who also fight the Saudi regime; it is clear from its overt visual efforts that al-Arabiya has a pro-Saudi agenda. In one such piece, in a reference to a shootout in Mecca between Saudi police and Islamists in June 2003 after which the Saudi authorities said they had found Qurans rigged with explosives, the words "Qurans booby-trapped with bombs" flicked across

the screen. The montage invited viewers to despise the militants fighting the Saudi government. Since the war ended, al-Arabiya has run endless documentaries and discussion shows about mass graves and other human rights abuses in Iraq. Saudi Arabia wasn't happy about America's plans to invade and occupy its neighbor, but its political establishment was at least content to get rid of what they viewed as another Arab nationalist abhorrence in the form of Saddam Hussein. A show presented by Saudi newspaper columnist Hussein Shobokshi was taken off the air in 2003 because of his vocal support of the Saudi liberal reforms. But despite the pro-

Al-Qa'ida leader Osama bin Laden appears on satellite station al-Jazeera shortly before the U.S.-led invasion of Afghanistan in 2001. (Reuters/Corbis)

clivities of al-Arabiya's owners, the fact is that most people working on it are as Arab nationalist in inclination as other satellite and national broadcasters in the region. United States government officials have attacked both channels for their promotion of debate on the occupation of Iraq (airing the views of Saddam Hussein before his arrest and those of Osama bin Laden, either directly or through sympathizers), at the same time as they make available more and more American government officials to give the White House's views on Middle East disputes, a few of them Arabic-speakers. Both channels aim to be the voice of a free Arab world in a largely authoritarian region, or at least that is how their employees view their mission, and even Qatar's Emir Hamad bin Khalifa once said: "I tell my children, if you want to know the issues

of real importance in the Arab world, watch Al Jazeera" (Burns, "Arab TV Gets a New Slant: Newscasts Without Censorship," *New York Times*, 4 July 1999). In the end, the White House appeared to have concluded that al-Arabiya was acceptable and al-Jazeera was beyond the pale: Bush chose to give an interview to al-Arabiya and the administration's own Al-Hurra, set up in February 2004, to address Arab audiences regarding U.S. soldiers' abuse of Iraqi prisoners. After al-Jazeera's reporting on a U.S. military siege of the Iraqi town of Falluja in March and April 2004 the White House said diplomatic relations with Qatar were under strain. Marc Lynch, a political science professor at Williams College, advocates that administration officials should engage in "open debate in credible and independent Arab media" (*Foreign Affairs*,

September–October 2003), an effort that has been ongoing since the September 11 attacks. Both channels make an explicit attempt to solicit Arab American viewers and to educate Middle Eastern audiences with shows about U.S. politics with talkshows, al-Jazeera's *Min Washington* (*From Washington*) and al-Arabiya's *Abra al-Muheet* (*Across the Ocean*).

In general, it's not easy to predict where the satellite revolution is heading. Many of the channels seem to have private, independent initiative, but there are ulterior political motives concerning the promotion of Arab government agendas. As al-Arabiya arrived, Iran began a new channel called al-Aalam, a complement to its Arabic-language religious channel Sahar. There are many rival children's, women's, and entertainment channels, including, to name a few, Zein TV, Heya, the ART network, Dream TV, and al-Mehwar. Few of them are professional in terms of content management and audience retention. For example, Dream TV will air talk shows in the midafternoon, and shows will shift from Dream One to Dream Two for no apparent reason—hardly encouraging to advertisers. Paris-based KTV, run by Algerian businessman Hussein Khalifa, was aimed at the chic youth of Morocco and Tunisia, but he dropped it in favor of music channel ETV. Khalifa hasn't shown political ambitions so far, but they may lurk. The station ANN is the London-based news channel of the pretender to the Syrian throne, Rif'at al-Assad, the dissident brother of Hafez and uncle of Bashar. London-based al-Mustaqilla is run by an opposition Tunisian businessman, but it has changed its tone to feature less criticism and more ads that promote Tunisian tourism, leading Tunisian viewers to conclude he has cut a deal with the authorities. Lebanon's nationalist Christian channel MTV has been closed down by the authorities for alleged sectarian broadcasting, while Christian-run LBC has been more business-savvy in largely pushing a pan-Arabist line. Israel got in on the act with its own Arab satellite channel (in part aimed at its domestic Arab audience, among whom al-Jazeera made great inroads), but it was later cancelled. The British and Americans set up Towards Freedom (Nahwa al-Hurriya) in Iraq after removing the Baath regime in April 2003, but soon dropped it to allow the Iraqi Media Network (later renamed al-Iraqiya) to emerge as Iraq's new "state channel." The U.S. State Department set up its Arabic-language channel Al-Hurra in February 2004, and France is planning an alternative to challenge what it perceives as Anglo-American political and cultural imperialism. Egyptian and Syrian satellite channels even offer a few hours of Hebrew broadcasts in an effort to cultivate the Israeli left wing and perhaps please Washington. One Saudi prince, Mansour bin Nasser bin Abdul-Aziz, has even announced plans for an English station aimed at the West, called ATV (Arab Television), to be based in London. Many of these channels will survive, many of them won't. Commentators hope that those that do survive will offer more political education and less political circus.

Radio is still a big hitter in the region, not least among drivers on the roads, and the audience wars are fast and furious. Washington set up Radio Sawa in 2002, a post–September 11 experiment in "winning Arab hearts and minds," thinly disguised via its twenty-four-hour mix of Arabic and English pop music. Through its news bulletins, it aims to change Arab thinking on issues relating to terrorism. For example, the

Tunisia: Sophisticated Country, Unsophisticated TV

Tunisian television is one of the region's more unappealing state offerings, and it's facing a serious challenge from satellite channels. The state has a monopoly on all television and radio, with two terrestrial television stations (Tunis 7, which doubles as Tunisia's single satellite channel, and Canal 21) and seven radio stations, as well as a plethora of daily, weekly, and monthly newspapers in Arabic and French. According to 2001 government statistics, 28 percent of Tunisia's 10 million population had satellite television, and the advertising industry says at least 50 percent of owners have moved to digital satellites in the Tunis area. Political discussion is strictly off-limits on state TV, including topics of corruption, rights issues, and moderate Islamic movements (whose real strength is hard to gauge because of a long-standing government ban). According to a Tunisian political analyst and journalist: "The government fears that if the door opens to criticizing corruption, it will get wider and wider and they won't be able to control it" (interview with author, February 2003). State television commanded some 80 percent of viewing in 1999, but by 2003 that percentage had dropped to around 50 percent, only rising during the holy month of Ramadan, when state TV aired Tunisian and Arab specially made soap operas to win a captive audience. Opposition figures say the government is upping its entertainment budget at the expense of political and cultural programs as a deliberate ploy to keep Tunisians' minds off serious issues of state.

But even in light entertainment, state television has problems. Statistics show that the Egyptian Satellite Channel (ESC) is consistently the second-most popular channel in Tunisia, while Qatar-based al-Jazeera and Dubai Television are attracting viewers interested in news.

The battle to change state TV is being led by the advertising industry. Tunisian advertisers are confident they can persuade state television to modernize its image and content in the interest of bringing in more advertising revenue. It's a tall order, but also an interesting case of financial interests potentially effecting some sort of political change in the country. "Our big fight now is on TV, which must change and modernize," said Syrine Cherif-Maaref of Label-Ogilvy and head of the Advertising Syndicate (interview with author, February 2003). "It's now at the level of advancement of the 1970s. Television in Morocco, Lebanon, and Egypt is all much more modernized now. All the ad spaces on TV need to be rethought. We have all the information about other TV around the world so we can push them and give concrete examples. So ad people are being given a role in changing TV in general, not just ads per se." The result could simply be a more slickly presented version of the current "TV-lite," though Egyptian terrestrial television offers a good Arab model of how to introduce political discussion shows that allow society to talk about issues of the day without threatening the direction of government policy.

term "martyrdom operation" (*'amaliyya ishtishhadiyya*) is replaced with the Arabic for "suicide attack" (*'amaliyya intihariyya*), and much space is given to the U.S. administration's pronouncements on Middle East peace, Iraq, and its plans for the region. The Arab League has made pronouncements about great plans to spend cash on improving the image of the Arabs in the West and explaining their position on the Arab-Israeli conflict. There has been little action so far, and verbal spats at recent

Arab meetings prior to the Iraq war show that finding a consensus of opinion among the parties is not easy. Radio Sawa has also spurred Egypt into action: the authorities licensed a private radio station run by businessman Adel Adib in mid-2003, called Nile FM. It features state-of-the-art production and DJs imported from London, who pronounce Cairo "the coolest city in the Middle East and Africa." Post-Saddam Iraq has a private radio station called Radio Dijla featuring phone-ins with open talk on everything from electricity to security to politicians. Tunisians have discovered a penchant for radio with the launch of Radio Mosaique in November 2003, a music and news discussion station that has increased the number of radio listeners from 24 to 40 percent of the population (Oxford Business Group 2004).

Hamdy Kandil and Egypt's Attempt to Match Al-Jazeera

The biggest success of Egypt's media opening has been *The Editor* (*Ra'is al-Tahrir*) show, presented by TV veteran Hamdy Kandil, who later moved the show to Dream TV before giving up on Egypt for Dubai Television in 2004. With his large doleful eyes and high moral tone, secular-nationalist journalist Kandil would vent anger every week over issues from Israel to Iraq and voice cynicism toward Washington's intentions for the Middle East. Although no viewing figures were available, the show's combination of current affairs, press reviews, and talk shows became the most talked-about television in Egypt since al-Jazeera's *al-Ittijaah al-Mu'aakis*. Kandil cultivates an image of himself as a figure embodying the "conscience of the Arab na-

tion," an image reinforced by the Palestinian *kaffiya* draped conspicuously on an unoccupied studio chair in front of Kandil's desk in each episode. He is outspokenly anti-American. In one episode directly after September 11, he jeered that the United States, with its technology and intelligence capabilities, could know the color of Iraqi leader Saddam Hussein's underpants at any given time but was still unable to stop the attacks on New York and Washington. "The Americans are boasting that they have the most advanced technology in the world. But the marshals and generals didn't show us the pictures of the innocent people killed in Kandahar or the Red Cross depot they hit," he said on another occasion (Channel Two, October 2001). At the time American officials—never invited on

Egyptian television presenter Hamdy Kandil, known for his nationalist postures. (Norbert Schiller/Focus MidEast)

Kandil's show—staged their own campaign to win Egyptian public opinion. Bush administration figures, including Secretary of State Colin Powell, appeared on a host of programs, initially to counter bin Laden's attempts to court Arab public opinion on al-Jazeera. United States officials were also prominent on Egyptian TV in the run-up to the Iraq campaign in 2003, as again the government sought to appease Washington's anger at what it perceived as media incitement against its war aims.

At the same time, many observers thought that *The Editor* was in essence a government experiment in absorbing the anger of the masses over foreign policy issues the authorities can do little about. "People think there is a plot between me and the government. I'm very upset about this. People are surprised that such a thing is on the screen without the full agreement of the government," Kandil said (interview with author, Reuters, 14 November 2001). "Those who hold the controls would certainly like to have a lighter tone, but our role is always to push and to get nearer to the red lines." Viewers would see jarring edits in the prerecorded show, suggesting ministry officials had their chance to erase some of what they didn't like beforehand. Kandil returned to the Egyptian state media in 1998 after rising to prominence on MBC. He considers that he pushed the boundaries of openness on Egyptian TV and proved that there is a huge market for current affairs coverage. "They [the authorities] were always so sure that people like variety, songs, films, serials. I proved the contrary. And it's not only politics. People are interested in something serious," Kandil said. "I'm happy that I encouraged national television to take freer steps. I'd rather work for national television, I'd prefer that a government kicks me out one day than a businessman—and I'll be kicked out one day, of course."

Satellite TV Popularizes Game Shows

Game shows have taken off in a big way on satellite channels and in turn on state-run terrestrial outfits. The biggest success was a foreign import that captured a worldwide Arab audience: *Who Wants to Be a Millionaire?* There are a host of others, including *al-Fakh* (*The Trap*), *al-Kursi* (*The Chair*), *Waznak Dahab* (*Your Weight in Gold*), and *The Weakest Link.* But it all began with the Arab version of the quiz show *Who Wants to Be a Millionaire?* which was a runaway hit for over two years in the Arab world and catapulted its sex-symbol host George Qerdahi to superstar status. Shown twice a week on MBC, it became the most widely watched show in the region during 2001, surpassing Faisal al-Qassem's *al-Ittijaah al-Mu'aakis* (The Opposite Direction) and Hamdy Kandil's *The Editor.* Qerdahi's version of the catchphrase "Is that your final answer?"—*Jawaab nihaa'i?*—entered into everyday jargon around the region. Media commentators remarked on Qerhadi's overexposure, as he became a favorite with housewives and also appeared on ubiquitous advertisements for various products. In one episode featuring sultry Syrian pop star Assala Nasry, her less attractive husband told Qerdahi dryly, "I hate you. In fact, hatred isn't strong enough a word, but I hate you" (MBC, July 2001). While the audience laughed, Qerdahi just smiled his velvety smile.

The show served to promote cultural unity, with a variety of guests showcasing

A game show called *The Mission* on Hizbollah's al-Manar TV channel, in which contestants from around the region win points toward the goal of being the first to reach Jerusalem, as shown on the map. (Norbert Schiller/Focus MidEast)

the diversity of the Arab world. Viewers were treated to the spectacle of Qerdahi, an urbane Lebanese Christian in a designer suit, appearing with fully veiled contestants from places such as Mecca who are put on the "hot seat" to answer trivia questions in a contest to win up to one million Saudi riyals. The camera would show the eyes of the veiled women, peeking through slits in their black cloaks, while Qerdahi played with their nerves before finally revealing if their answers were right or wrong. Qerdahi's famed poise and composure seemed to betray him when faced with more unresponsive women. Viewers sensed he wanted to flirt, but it's a tall order with only a pair of eyes to play with. "I deal with them, not with reserve, but with bearing. I deal with them with a lot of sensitivity, because you feel that they are very

sensitive," he said (interview with author, Reuters, 10 March 2002). "I'm proper and polite, because I respect the feelings of a fully veiled woman. I respect her circumstances, her environment, her traditions. I respect her convictions." He went on: "I wouldn't be exaggerating if I say that this program brings the whole Arab world together. It brings it together despite all the contradictions of the Arab world. Once in a seminar a woman said to me I had united the Arab world because everyone watches the program. Of course, I was touched. A statistic a few months ago said that 80 percent of Arab viewers watch this program, which is a viewing figure that no program in the world has reached. . . . My identity is Arab. I feel that I belong to all the Arabs. Without exaggeration, this is my feeling, that I belong to all the Arab nationalities."

Saudi TV: Clerics versus Lebanese Women

The fight for the most lucrative television audience in the region is heating up, with clerics, dancing girls, and clean-cut sports shows vying for the hearts and minds of young Saudi men. The popularity of Saudi state-run TV, which gives huge airtime to the religious establishment, is coming up against racy Lebanese entertainment programs and big-time politics on trailblazing pan-Arab stations like al-Jazeera. Forced to rethink its strategy, the state-run network introduced an exclusive sports channel in late 2002 in an attempt to win the huge youth segment of Saudi Arabia's population of over 23 million, and also a raft of political discussion shows.

Media watchers say the network had little choice. The kingdom's interpretation of Islam means women can't be seen or heard singing on television or radio. "Consumers are fed up with Saudi TV," said Karim Younes, general manager of media ad agency Starcom (interview with author, Reuters, 12 April 2003). "There has been a battle between Saudi TV and satellite TV and there is now a major shift."

Saudi TV's market share slipped to around 40 percent in 2002, while London-based MBC—actually owned by a Saudi businessman—led with around 60 percent, overtaking al-Jazeera. All this comes at a time when the desert kingdom grapples with booming population growth, high unemployment, and foreign and domestic pressure to introduce political reforms in the aftermath of the September 11 attacks (the United States has identified fifteen of the nineteen suicide hijackers as Saudi nationals).

Now young Saudi men can ignore state-run TV and take their pick of satellite shows largely aimed at them, which feature Arab women in scanty attire, considered scandalous by Saudi standards. They can even call the station and talk to them. On Sunday night's *Carla-la-la*, seen on Lebanese satellite channel LBC, blonde, Scandinavian-looking presenter Carla Haddad receives calls from around the region requesting the latest Arabpop songs as well as calls complimenting her beauty. At least half the calls come from the kingdom, and some of them have to be cut off for incoherency or com-

---

Despite his confidence, Qerhadi sometimes seemed thrown by Moroccans, whose dialect is notoriously difficult for other Arabs to understand. "We all have a problem understanding each other's dialects when we speak purely in local dialect," Qerdahi said. "Even other North Africans have difficulty understanding a Moroccan if he speaks pure dialect" (interview with author, Reuters, 10 March 2002).

The appearance of the show on Arab television screens in early 2001 coincided with the Intifada, so the show tapped into a rush of pan-Arab popular sentiment throughout the region. Arab Israelis appeared on the program as "Palestinians"

from "Palestine," and some guests even donated their winnings to the Intifada. Once a young Palestinian from Gaza, who spent twenty-four hours getting to the show from Cairo, took home the one-million-riyal prize. It made news headlines because the public around the region felt so sorry for the Palestinians (one Egyptian newspaper ran a cartoon depicting Israeli prime minister Ariel Sharon on a make-believe show called *Who Wants to Kill a Million?*). The MBC network originally brought the contestants to Paris to record the program, but in February 2002 it moved to Cairo's Media Production City, doing a lot for Egypt's ambitions to return to the center stage as a rements that threaten to descend into lewdness. Then on Thursdays, viewers can tune in to LBC's *Ya Lail Ya Ain,* a glitzy quiz show, where three young men face off against three young women amid music, dance, and lots of flirting between the two presenters. This liberal, Lebanese sexual chemistry reacts badly with the strict gender segregation of a purist Islamic state like Saudi Arabia, and the show has provoked an outcry. "This program is based on relations between men and women and in the long run this will affect the nature of relations between men and women outside marriage. It could lead to extra-marital relations," said sociologist Ibrahim al-Juweir, railing against "regulars" with nothing to do but ring in every week (interview with author, Reuters, 12 April 2003). Sixty percent of Saudi advertisers stipulate that their ads should not appear during the show, though that has not stopped the occasional Gulf pop star appearing in some episodes to cavort with the Lebanese women.

Getting it right for the Saudi audience is crucial for Arab satellite stations, because that's where advertisers, Saudi or non-Saudi, want to sell. "For any [Arab] satellite station, Saudi Arabia is the biggest market," Younes said (interview with author, Reuters, 12 April 2003). Satellite penetration in the kingdom is at least 70 percent, way ahead of Egypt, where purchasing power is much lower than in Saudi Arabia. Most Arab satellite channels give their program schedules in Mecca time as well as GMT. Slipping down the ratings table along with Saudi state TV, LBC temporarily shelved the "fluff" shows for Iraq war coverage and a new program dedicated to Saudi soccer. The channel MBC has made a foray into new territory with a women's show called *Kalam Nawa'im* (*Talk among the Gentler Sex*), which boasts the novelty of a Saudi woman as one of its presenters. "It is the second most popular program on MBC after 'Who Wants to be a Millionaire?'" said the presenter, Mona Abu Sulayman. A woman with both career and family, Abu Sulayman doesn't have time for male-oriented fluff on LBC like *Carla-la-la* and *Ya Lail Ya Ain* (interview with author, Reuters, 12 April 2003). "A program should have a duty to the culture it serves. It might serve Lebanese culture, but it doesn't serve Saudi culture," she said.

gional media hub. "Cairo has always been the beating heart of the Arab world and the cultural centre of the Arab world," Qerdahi said. Kandil shares this opinion, though he said Egypt can't hope to dominate the region as it once did in the Nasser period. "The government acknowledges that there is more diversity now. They know well that it's time that we should acknowledge some others who have their production centers, their cultural life, their media. But there is a feeling here in Egypt in general that Egypt will still be there. There is some sense in that because of the cultural life in Egypt, which cannot be compared with any other [Arab] country," he said (interview with author, October 2001). "Here we have the film industry, even if it is going down. In the Arab film archives, 95 percent of films are produced in Egypt. Theatre is flourishing now in Lebanon, but you can't compare it with the Egyptian theatre."

Lebanon's Future Television showed the Arab version of the BBC's hit quiz show *The Weakest Link,* and they managed to find someone to mimic Anne Robinson's (host of the original BBC show) overbearing style with eerie precision. Presenter Rita Khoury appeared with short hair, schoolmarm spectacles, and scathing one-liners—and even a Nazi-style leather jacket. But the show, and her performance, caused considerable outrage in the Arab world, and the show didn't last. The main criticism among men and women was that Khoury behaved like a man and should be more feminine and polite. The setup ran counter to dominant cultural values in many ways (male guests appeared from all over the region, including Saudi Arabia, where women can't vote or drive cars). Pleasantries, not insults, are the form in the Arab world when someone gets it wrong or makes a mistake. Whereas Robinson gained the admiration of British and American audiences who respect her no-nonsense persona, Khoury offended viewers in Arab countries. Sometimes the men pled with the station to edit out some of her remarks to save face back home, though no woman ever complained. When the show first began airing in late 2001, Khoury avoided being seen in public because the insults from passersby were too irritating to handle. "Educated and urbane men who come on the show relish it as a challenge, but the more traditional ones have more difficulty putting up with it. I try to provoke them, not humiliate them, but it's not my problem if they can't answer," Khoury said ("Razor-Tongued Quiz Hostess Outrages Arab Audience," Reuters, 10 June 2002). "No woman contestant has ever got upset. Maybe it's because Arab women are so downtrodden." Khoury moved on to host a "feel-good" afternoon chat show on Future Television.

Reality TV in the Arab World

Reality TV hit the Arab world during 2002 and 2003 but met with limited success. Most of the reality programs were copies of internationally patented shows, such as *Star Academy* and *Big Brother;* one, *'Al-Hawa Sawa (Together on Air)*, was an indigenous product. *Star Academy*, which ran from December to May 2004, was regarded as the most successful in that it drew the least opprobrium from critics, while *Big Brother* was forced off the air after one week when Islamists protested against it in the host country of Bahrain. *Star Academy* was slammed by the Saudi Mufti as "an open call to sin," but the kids were still mobbed whenever they headed into Beirut malls. Now there's a big debate in the Arab media about this form of entertainment. LBC chief Pierre Dhaher has said he thinks it's the future of Arab television in the coming years (LBC, February 2004). "To what extent will the craze of 'reality' reach is still anyone's guess," wrote commentator Omar al-Ghazzi in *al-Hayat* (26 February 2004). "What seems clear, though, is that with all the burdens and troubles of the Middle East, we should add another one, for it seems that reality TV is going to entertain us to death!"

'Al-Hawa Sawa (Together on Air) was a reality TV dating show where male viewers could view the girl participants twenty-four hours a day as they lived in a special Beirut apartment, and contact them via e-mail for a possible meeting in the flat to propose marriage—all of this during the three-month run of the show. But it stirred more than the debate that MBC bargained for when viewers suspected that three of the eight girls from around the Arab world were secretly smoking, thus flouting a ban on cigarettes and alcohol in the luxury flat. The last day saw unexpected drama when one of the contestants, Aicha from Algeria, dropped a bombshell on air by announcing that she refused to get married to her chosen man, Hossam from Egypt. The show

saw another hiccup when Lebanese authorities unexpectedly turned back Hossam at the Beirut airport, refusing to grant him a tourist visa. Viewers chose a Lebanese girl and her Lebanese suitor as the winners, and the couple subsequently departed for a honeymoon in Malaysia (where conservative marriage values are honored in much the same way as in the Arab world).

The Arabic *Big Brother* began in February 2004 but despite a huge media fanfare did not last its three-month stint. MBC got cold feet after complaints that showing unmarried people living together offended Islam. If MBC had chosen to stage the show in more cosmopolitan Dubai or Beirut it's hard to imagine that it would have been forced to shut down in this manner. Considerable efforts had been made to ensure the show acknowledged cultural sensitivities. Unlike the foreign versions of the hit show, the men's and women's sleeping quarters were kept separate, no filming occurred in the bathrooms, and prayer rooms were provided for both religions. Things got off to a risqué start on the first day when the first contestant who entered the house—Saudi national Abdel-Hakim—kissed the female contestants on the cheek in greeting. As the show proceeded, it proved to be compelling viewing. For example, Amal from Egypt talked frankly with the other girls about her messy divorce, and three of the girls caused a crisis in the house with their public joking about the ungainly and uncharismatic male contestant Abdullah, a Saudi Somali. This disrespectful joking led to an Arab League–style crisis meeting around the kitchen table among all twelve contestants: "We should leave this committee meeting as one, with one voice, and anyone who has anything else they want to say must say it now!" Abdullah said, thumping the table in defiant nationalist tones.

Dream TV, Egypt's Experiment with Private TV

The most recent development in Egyptian television has been the rise of private satellite station Dream TV. Dream is mainly owned by Ahmed Bahgat, one of a small clique of businessmen who are close to the authorities, and the government's Egyptian Radio and Television Union (ERTU), which owns a 10 percent stake in the company. Between programs it regularly runs comic skits that lampoon al-Jazeera, as part of an effort to promote Dream as the Egyptian patriot's satellite station of choice. But the channel has made major waves in Egyptian politics by showing interviews with senior political figures that have included harsh questions about the unrepresentative political system that still prevails. It has also shown the latest pop videos before most other channels, making it popular throughout the Arab region. In 2002 it ran into problems with the government over a program featuring its main presenter Hala Sarhan, who made her mark as a talk show host on the Arab cable network ART in the 1990s. She was attacked in Gulf and Egyptian newspapers in October 2002 as the "porno presenter," based on an edition that discussed the problems of young people who can't afford to get married in Egypt's conservative culture, during which studio guests started talking about masturbation. The ministry of information issued a vague threat that it might stop the channel from broadcasting from Egyptian studios. Sarhan's defense was indicative of the way

Egyptian talk show hostess Hala Sarhan, who helped establish private Egypt satellite station Dream TV. She left for music channel Rotana not long after appearing on a show that discussed sexual issues, including masturbation, which annoyed the government. (Reuters/Corbis)

the channel presents itself. "This is not about one particular programme, it's bigger than that," she told the opposition *al-Arabi* newspaper (27 October 2002). "It's that there are several vested interests which have come together to explode this issue and destroy a successful Egyptian channel which has made its mark everywhere. It's about other channels, businessmen and even states. It's no puzzle. These people's interests are in there being no free successful Egyptian channel open to everyone which has pulled the rug from under the feet of some rival channels, a channel that has returned confidence in Egyptian media, Egyptian dialect, Egyptian art and

Egyptian intellectual and artistic life." Cast in this light, Dream is part of Egypt's strike back at the Lebanese and Gulf media revolutions. Dream also provoked controversy with the space it gave to Mohammed Hassanein Heikal, the right-hand man of Gamal Abdel Nasser and former editor of *al-Ahram*, whose opinions are accorded enormous respect in the Arab world. Heikal appeared in three irregular hour-long slots during 2002, termed *The Professor (al-Ustaz)*, in which he simply sat before a camera at a desk and gave his analysis of the state of Egypt and the Arabs vis-à-vis the Iraqi crisis and the Israeli-Palestinian conflict (he did the same with a wider audience on al-Jazeera in August/ September 2004). His line is that Egypt is frightened to challenge the Americans by mobilizing Arab countries against Washington's pro-Israeli policies. The programs irked the Egyptian authorities, as did Dream's airing of a Heikal lecture at the American University in Cairo in which he openly attacked the idea of Mubarak's son Gamal becoming the next president. Many Egyptians consider that Gamal is being groomed for the presidency.

Dream is based in Media Production City, a massive studio complex outside Cairo that rents space to satellite channels, including al-Jazeera. The studios also offer facilities for Egyptian TV and film directors to churn out drama for the Arab world. Media Production City was the brainchild of Information Minister Safwat al-Sherif, and the majority of its stockholders are state-owned companies. By law all radio and television in Egypt are state-owned and run by the Radio and Television Union. Dream and another private Egyptian channel, al-Mehwar, have been allowed to operate because the Media Production City is classed

Egypt's Media Production City was built in the mid-1990s to help maintain Egypt's central role in Arab media and entertainment. (Sandro Vannini/Corbis)

as a "media-free zone." There are other Egyptian-run satellite channels, including the music station Melody and the religious channels Iqra (Recite!) and al-Majd (The Glory), all of which are run from abroad. The increase in regional tension, with the Intifada, the September 11 attacks, and the crisis in Iraq, has hardened the government's resolve to hold on to the terrestrial media. For the moment, there is little prospect for independent terrestrial television channels in Egypt.

Ramadan TV—An Annual Carnival of Arab Television

The Muslim holy month of Ramadan has become a television bonanza, along the lines of the intense television coverage that surrounds the Western Christmas, but to an even greater degree. Commentators have seen in it a debasing of the religious meaning of the month, when Muslims fast from dawn to dusk, and a sign of how increasingly consumerist Arab societies have become. The Egyptians excel with a massive nightly output of specially made soap operas, cabarets, quiz shows, religious programs, and celebrity interview shows, the planning of which takes up much of the previous year. As soon as it's all over and critics in the press and on television have debated to death the merits and demerits of a particular year's offering, state television begins work on the next Ramadan package. For Egypt it's big money, since the programs are sold to the Arab satellite channels and beamed around the region. When the mosque muezzin announces sundown, millions of Arabs begin hours of binge eating in front of the television. It's a boom time for advertisers. An estimated 80 percent of the Egyptian population tunes in

Arab Soap Accused of Antisemitism

The Egyptian private satellite channel, Dream TV, was at the center of much controversy in late 2002. It showed a drama that dealt with Israel and the early Zionist movement, promoting the idea that the Protocols of the Elders of Zion—an infamous tract in the history of European antisemitism—was authentic. The U.S. administration and Israel both condemned Egypt over airing the show in the holy month of Ramadan, though Egyptian state TV was one of some twenty Arabic stations to buy it from Dream TV. The drama, called *Faris Bila Gawad* (*A Knight without a Horse*), featured actor Mohammed Sobhy playing the son of a Turkish noblewoman and an Egyptian peasant in British-occupied Egypt in the late nineteenth century. Sobhy undertakes guerrilla operations against the British, but then occupies himself with finding out the secret of the Protocols, a book that a group of secretive, aging Jews are imploring the British to remove from Egypt. The underlying premise of the drama was that the Arabs weren't aware of Zionist plans for Palestine to effectively stop them, but that they would have if they had read the book.

In the face of the bad publicity, Arab media throughout the region engaged in a debate over the show and whether it was antisemitic or not. In Egypt, nationalists furiously defended it in the face of foreign interference, while a small number of writers, including Mubarak's political advisor Osama al-Baz, said the show had been a big mistake, helping Israel's lobby groups in Washington once again present the Arabs as antisemitic. "It is possible to expose the fallacies and dangers of Israeli policy through rational argument and there is no excuse for borrowing from an alien, inhuman and outmoded anti-Semitic lore," al-Baz said, urging Arabs in their conflict with Zionism not to employ a racist polemic of antisemitism that has little to do with the Arab world and everything to do with Europe ("Contaminated Goods," *al-Ahram Weekly*, 2-8 January 2003). In one piquant observation, human rights activist Yousry Mustafa wrote that by airing the show on state television, Arab governments were once again playing to the gallery of public opinion in order to divert the minds of the masses away from issues like failed economic policy and domestic repression. "The Arab regimes have tried hard to feed the demagoguery [surrounding the drama], to make use of it and benefit from it, because it helps create illusory battles in times of crisis—so that we don't think about the unemployment, backwardness, fear or the frustration that has afflicted us," he wrote in the Egyptian weekly *al-Qahira* (26 November 2003).

The serial was clearly crafted to back up the Arab view of today's Israeli-Palestinian conflict.

prior to and after breaking the fast, and the cost of advertising in this period as well as the number of advertisements rises dramatically. Ramadan 1999 alone netted 23 percent of the $153.2 million in annual television expenditure in Egypt. In keeping with the back-to-our-roots tone of the month, soap operas dramatizing famous events in Islamic history are aired late at night, and Western movies are off the air for the entire month. The intelligentsia are routinely disgusted with what they consider fluff designed to keep minds off of pressing issues of politics and economy. "Egypt as we see it on television has become a happier and brighter place that takes away our worries and makes us forget the sadness, but in the end TV remains

وقام بتأليف الأغاني و الأشعار :   الصورة :   المنتج :

محمــد بغــدادى   عصــام فريد   محمـــد عمـــارة

شـركة دريــم للإعــلام

A poster advertizing controversial TV drama *Faris Bila Gawad (A Knight without a Horse)*, in which actor Mohammed Sobhy is a master of disguise who hopes to foil Zionist plans for Palestine. (Norbert Schiller/Focus MidEast)

Each episode ended with the coda, "he who resists occupation is not a terrorist," in reference to the Intifada. Yet the drama concluded with a clumsy attempt to appease the critics and get the Egyptian government off the hook: Dream TV appeared to have concocted a new ending for the show that contradicted everything that had gone before it. The final scene showed Sobhy planning to bomb a meeting of Zionists in Egypt, but when he sees a woman with her child among them he changes his mind. The message up to then had been that resistance can involve choices that some might deem terrorist. Suddenly the message seemed to be that peaceful resistance was best after all. The controversy was repeated in 2004 when Hizbollah's al-Manar TV aired a Syrian-made drama about Zionism, called *al-Shataat* (*The Diaspora*). Again, it was attacked by Washington as "anti-semitic."

a mask which distorts reality and lets us stick our heads in the sand so that we don't see the bitter truth," said Islamist intellectual Fahmy Howeidy (*al-Wafd*, 16 November 2001). Regarding 2002's Ramadan offering, presenter Hamdy Kandil said, "It's impossible to see everything Egyptian TV makes but this year it's a festival, with adverts three or four minutes in every show and talk shows where interviewers ask historic questions like 'what's the most funny situation you've ever found yourself in?'" (Dream TV, December 2002).

As well as providing a chance for actors to make names for themselves, the Ramadan soaps offer the state and its major directors and writers a chance to debate social and political issues with the certainty

Iraqi Television Battles the Arab Satellite Stations

Iraqi state TV after the fall of the Baathist regime was surprisingly bad. The country had more than a hundred newspapers and more than a hundred political parties, but the state television network known as the Iraqi Media Network (IMN), which was set up by the coalition authorities, did not reflect this at all. A U.S. State Department poll in October 2003 established that of the one-third of the Iraqi population that had access to satellite dishes, only 12 percent got their news from IMN, and the pan-Arab channels al-Jazeera and al-Arabiya were gaining ground. The Arab channels regularly hosted Iraqi commentators, intellectuals, and religious figures, who were largely absent from the state broadcaster when it was controlled by the occupying forces. At the same time, the satellite channels were attacked by the Iraqi authorities as "anti-Iraqi," because they aired so many views antagonistic to the American presence. During Ramadan 2003, when Arab television usually puts on a light entertainment extravaganza for the captive evening audiences, the offering was pretty poor—a mixture of old Egyptian films, year-old talk shows, and a nightly soap opera from Japan. In fact, it was not much different from television during the era of Baath dictatorship.

In November 2003 a shake-up saw a new director take over, broadcaster Shameem Rassam, and the station's name changed to al-Iraqiya ("the Iraqi channel," echoing al-Arabiya, "the Arab channel"). Rassam left Iraq in 1990 for the United States, where she worked in Arab media. She was on the U.S. State Department committee that worked on ways to recreate Iraq's media when Washington had removed Saddam Hussein's regime. "Al-Jazeera is a news channel and I don't want to compare IMN to al-Jazeera. We want to cover that of course and we're trying to establish more talk shows," she said (interview with author,

---

that their message will reach the masses. Ramadan in December 2000 saw an Egyptian drama tackle the sensitive issue of marriage between Coptic Christians and Muslims, spearheading a Ramadan theme of national unity. Recent years have seen a number of violent incidents between the two communities in rural areas. A state of paranoia subsequently gripped the political elite over American attempts to uphold Christian rights (the history of French involvement in Lebanon to protect the Maronites looms large throughout the region). In the series *Awaan al-Ward* (*The Blooming of Roses*), the grandchild of the marital union between a Coptic woman and Muslim man is kidnapped and the parents and their families agonize over whether it was an act motivated by religious zeal and whether this is a sign that the two communities are better off staying apart. Radical nationalist papers violently objected to the series as "meaningless licentiousness" (these same papers relentlessly hounded famed Egyptian American civil rights activist Saadeddin Ibrahim in the 1990s over his championing of Copts as a minority who are denied full rights as citizens). Following early reactions to the soap, state television censors cut lines from some episodes later in the month. For example, told by one character that "at least in America they protect the Copts," the kidnapped child's Coptic grandmother retorted angrily that "in America they only protect their own interests" (*al-Wafd*, 13 December 2000).

November 2003). "We're still young and we're still on the road, but I think we've established the first steps. We plan to have more bureaus in Iraq and bureaus around the region so that we are the voice of Iraq abroad. We are training people now. We want young Iraqis, but they were under control of that system for thirty years, so it's rehabilitation of the mind." Too much so, many Iraqis would say. The term "resistance," referring to insurgents fighting the occupying troops, is regularly used by the pan-Arab satellite channels and most Iraqis, but the IMN channel, which later changed its name to al-Iraqiya (the Iraqi Channel), avoided using the term, preferring "rebellion" instead. "Who says it's resistance? That's what al-Jazeera says. But we are Iraqis—let's use our own terminology," Rassam said. Her aim is for the channel to emerge as a semi-autonomous state body, such as the BBC in Britain. "All Arab countries have a state-run media. Iraqis are used to that but we thought to do something new. If we are semi-state, then we can get funding from the

people and the community. That experience is new for the Arab world. The time is right to attempt such a thing," she said.

But those who wanted to reinvent the channel were racing against the clock. A private network called al-Sharqiya (the Eastern Channel) was set up in June 2004, and is owned by Saad Bazzaz, an ex-Baathist dissident who brought Iraq the popular, independent daily *Azzaman.* Washington-based Arab station Al-Hurra launched Al-Hurra Iraq to target Iraqis. The authorities in the new Iraq have said they intend to license as many channels as possible. Their thinking is that the best way to combat the pan-Arab channels is to make them just one option in a sea of television choices. However, they have also resorted to threats. Al-Arabiya was banned in November 2003 after it aired a taped message from Saddam Hussein, just weeks before his arrest, and al-Jazeera was banned for a month in August 2004 for airing tapes from groups kidnapping and killing foreign hostages.

Ramadan 2002 was the occasion for a marked opening up in Syrian state television and a challenge to Egypt's Ramadan dominance. Syria made twelve soaps compared to Egypt's seventeen. In general, cheaper Syrian soaps are being bought up by state operators in many Arab states, and there is a current fad for Latin American soaps, which are dubbed into Arabic in Lebanon. There is also a trend toward collaboration between directors and actors from different countries. As yet, the American style of comic soap hasn't been too successful in Arab culture: a version of *Friends*, called *Shebab Online (Youth Online)*, is carried on MBC. It features a mix of Egyptian and Lebanese actors, similar plot lines, and one-liners, but it hasn't

caught on. Syria's record number of soaps and satirical shows in 2002 tackled social and political issues with a new gusto. Most talked about by Syrians was *Spotlight (Buq'at Daww)*, a comedy series produced, directed, and acted by a group of young actors criticizing corruption, the role of intelligence services in clamping down on freedoms, and, as the show put it, "how the sons of the officials and those close to the government are behaving." This sort of television was unheard of in Syria before Bashar al-Assad became president in 2000. Observers reckon the authorities felt it was time to allow some margin of criticism, or a release valve, as economic and political pressures in society increase. One episode of *Spotlight* featured a detained citizen who kept asking the authorities what the charges were against him. The officer investigating him finally revealed that "opposition" was suspected to be in his genes, since his great-grandfather was a known dissident, so a DNA check might be in order. Another episode discussed the widespread presence of intelligence informers in Syrian society. According to director al-Laith Hajjo, a number of senior officials were annoyed by the series and some episodes were heavily edited before airing. "I heard that some people were not pleased because of a certain character or accent we used in the series," he told the Syrian paper *al-Domari* (9 December 2002). In another satirical show called *Mirror* (*Miraya*), one memorable sketch had Arab leaders arguing over whose national dish should be printed on a unified Arab currency, while each suggestion was essentially a variation on the same thing.

Ramadan 2001 showed what happens when state television doesn't pay enough attention to the material it puts out during the holy month. The soap *The Family of Hagg Metwalli* (*'Aylit al-Hagg Metwalli*) became the subject of heated debate around the Arab world because of its almost comic-nostalgic depiction of a patriarchal Cairo clothes merchant who marries an Islamically sanctioned four wives. But it wasn't intended as a comedy of manners. The show incensed not only civil rights and women's activists but also most ordinary newspaper columnists, who were angered that a practice that most Arab societies are, at least at an official level, trying to discourage was presented as a sort of rosy ideal. The English-language *al-Ahram Weekly* in Egypt fumed: "State-controlled television is exactly that: 'state-controlled.'

It is designed to indoctrinate the masses. It is by default an instrument of propaganda. Call it popular culture as much as you like, call it popular art if you must, but please remember that all discourse is political. And the idea that Metwalli is promoted as an ideal by the official discourse is simply shocking" (Elbendary, "Pride and Prejudice," 27 December 2001). In a nice example of the confusion of messages that crowd popular culture in the region, the *Metwalli* series was interspersed with commercial breaks in which Egypt's National Council for Women promoted the notion of gender equality between girls and boys. The cast appeared on a stream of talk shows about the drama, but seesawed between arguing that the idea was to show polygamy in a bad light and arguing that polygamy solves the problem of large numbers of unmarried women in Egyptian society. Egypt's religious authorities have often said polygamy is an answer to the problem of aging, unmarried women who can't find someone to marry in a society that looks down on late-marrying females. It appeared that the authorities had intervened to assuage public concern when, in the last episode, Metwalli told his son that his multiple marriages had perhaps been a mistake after all—but the touch of remorse was entirely out of kilter with the rest of the show. Either way, the character of Metwalli has entered popular parlance around the region as the epitome of a middle-aged man living a pampered life of pleasure as his twilight years beckon—or as the Egyptians say, *mabsout 'al-akhir*, "as happy as Larry."

Ramadan has also spawned television events that have acquired a hallowed place in the televisual firmament of the Arabs: a song-and-dance show called *Fawazeer* (*Riddles*) and Egypt's version of *Candid*

Actress Sherihan made the *Fawazeer*
(Riddles) show famous during the month of
Ramadan, which is the prime holiday season
for television entertainment. (Norbert Schiller/
Focus MidEast)

Camera, al-Kamira al-Khafiya. The
Fawazeer show has a famous or upcoming
actress act out scene after scene with a
dance troupe as her cabaret foil, and the
whole is meant to give a clue to the "rid-
dle" that viewers try to solve by the end of
the month. The breathtaking (if somewhat
cheesy) energy of *Fawazeer* has brought
fame and fortune to those who pull it off,
most notably Sherihan and Nelly, both of
whom were asked to perform the show for
several years running. Other actresses
who followed were unkindly compared to
them in physique and movement, and they
didn't last more than one season. In November–December 2001, Egypt's main
channels ditched the show altogether.

Candid Camera, meanwhile, continues after comedy actor Ibrahim Nasr in 1998 began dressing up for routines as an aging
Egyptian dame called Zakiya Zakariya,
who reveals her true identity as the mis-
chievous Nasr at the end of each set-piece.
Nasr has branded his memorable Zakiya
Zakariya character on popular concious-
ness with catchphrases of made-up Arabic
words that he uses in his tussles with unsuspecting members of the public. Zakiya
Zakariya dolls uttering the terms *bikh* and
tatatata—roughly translated as "stuff you"
or "poo to you"—are sold in shops, a Zakiya Zakariya film came out in early 2002,
and the team produced a successful play in
Cairo's 2001 summer season, in which, as
the title proclaimed, *Zakiya Zakariya
Challenges Sharon* (*Zakiya Zakariya
Tatahaddaa Sharon*). The idea of the play
was that if Arab leaders couldn't stop Israeli prime minister Ariel Sharon from per-
secuting Palestinians, perhaps Egypt's
most formidable old bat could do the job.
Political analyst Mohammed al-Sayed Said
said that although the play did not rise to
the level of high art, it nevertheless reflected the level of disgust at Sharon's policies. "Sophisticated intellectuals think this
is vulgar art, but it reflects the public
mood," he said (interview with author,
Reuters, 7 September 2001). The show is
losing touch, though. Having done Zakiya
Zakariya to death, Nasr moved on to
Ghobashy Noqrashy, a show featuring an
overweight boy of the same name in tasteless clothes who, for example, persuades
restaurant guests to hide in the kitchens,
clean the floors, and knead dough in order
to trick visiting tax inspectors about the
number of people he employs. The key to
the humor in these shows is a general perception in Arab countries that, with the on-

slaught of capitalist consumer culture, manners have plummeted and values have gone out the window, and it's not too far-fetched to imagine a restaurateur, for example, abusing people in this way.

A to Z:
Key People and Terms

ARAB RADIO AND TELEVISION NETWORK (ART)

Network of entertainment, culture, and religion channels owned by Saudi businessman Saleh Kamel, who throughout the 1990s acquired a significant percentage of

Saleh Kamel, the Saudi owner of the major entertainment network ART (Arab Radio and Television), speaking in Lebanon in September 2003 at a football event. (Ramzi Haidar/AFP/ Getty Images)

the total Arabic films ever produced, most of them Egyptian. Egyptian financial house EFG-Hermes began its own project to buy up Egyptian film rights in 2000. The activities of both groups have raised fears of the Arab cinematic heritage falling into the hands of private money. The network usually scoops up the main Arab soap opera productions, with special rights to screen them first or at advantagous times of day. The channel also focuses on sports coverage and bringing foreign films to Arab audiences. Most of its output is pay-per-view channels, though it has set up Iqra as a free-to-air religious channel on Egypt's Nilesat satellite.

AL-ARABIYA

New satellite channel set up before the Iraq war as a rival to al-Jazeera. Mainly owned by the Saudi-owned satellite channel MBC (whose owner, Walid al-Ibrahim, is a brother-in-law of King Fahd), it usually censors all negative references to Saudi Arabia in statements from Osama bin Laden. But it rapidly established itself as the worthy rival of al-Jazeera during the Iraq war in 2003 and regularly trumped al-Jazeera with its contacts with Iraqi insurgents fighting the American occupation there. Iraqi authorities temporarily banned the station in November after it aired the latest of audiotapes it had obtained from Saddam Hussein. Iraq's new state television consciously aped the channel with its choice of the name al-Iraqiya ("the Iraqi Channel" versus al-Arabiya's "the Arab Channel") and used the same stylistic features in its graphic format as the distinctive imagery used by al-Arabiya. Its main shows include *Min al-Iraq* (*From Iraq*), presented by Elie Nacouzi (formerly of Lebanon's MTV); *Nuqtat Nizam* (*Point of Order*), presented by Hassan Muawwad (formerly of the BBC World Service Arabic radio); and *Bil-Arabi* (*In Arabic*), presented by Giselle Khoury.

BAYWATCH

An Arabic version of the show about sexy Californian lifeguards, called *Action in Hurghada*, an Egyptian resort on the Red Sea. Despite objections from the Muslim Brotherhood to Miss Egypt beauty pageants, its makers hope it will win an Arab audience because of its promotion of Egyptian tourism, via coral reefs and women in swimsuits (though in fact most women in Egypt swim with their clothes on). With a script that mixes Arabic and English, it plans distribution in some Asian countries and the United States. The plots revolve around a team of lifeguards of Arabic and other nationalities who perform sea rescues, crack crimes, and capture villains.

BBC WORLD SERVICE ARABIC

Radio station that has traditionally attracted listeners since the 1960s in times of crisis because of its perceived lack of bias in comparison to the media in other countries. The national media in many countries often slam it as anti-Arab, since it is owned by the British government. The station is commonly referred to throughout the region as *izaa'at london*, or Radio London, a term that implies status as the "official" mouthpiece of Britain, dismaying the station's administrators. Despite that, the station has at times been accorded mythical levels of trust from ordinary listeners. In the 1990s its influence waned somewhat, due to strong competition from Radio

Monte Carlo, budget problems, and reorganization within the wider structure of the BBC—as well as the emergence of groundbreaking, televisual Arab media.

DUBAI MEDIA CITY

Set up in 2001 as a media and information technology center. It has drawn in major Arab channels MBC and al-Arabiya, CNN, and the major international news agencies Reuters, AP, and AFP. It is part of the Dubai Technology, E-commerce, and Media Free Zone Authority, which also includes Dubai Internet City and Dubai Ideas Oasis. It offers 100 percent foreign ownership and tax exemptions for both companies and individuals, plus guarantees of an atmosphere in which media people can work more or less freely. The authorities in Qatar have been miffed at Dubai's success in attracting foreign money in this way, though Dubai has had a head start, working on establishing itself as a major finance and business center since the 1970s.

EGYPTIAN RADIO AND TELEVISION UNION (ERTU)

The Egyptian Radio and Television Union (ERTU) has sole rights to own radio and terrestrial television, guaranteed by Egypt's constitution. In the 1990s, the opposition Wafd Party attempted to set up an independent Egyptian radio station based in Cyprus, but their attempts were thwarted when the government interceded with the Greek Cypriot authorities. The ERTU is probably the biggest producer of drama in the Arab world. Slowly it is being rolled back, with Egypt allowing private radio station Nile FM in summer 2003, in an apparent attempt to undermine the U.S.

government's Radio Sawa, run by the State Department.

FAWZY, MUFID

Veteran Egyptian state television presenter, famed for his small stature, goblinlike appearance, and camera shots showing the back of Fawzy's head as he interviews people. This produced one memorable cartoon in the Egyptian opposition *al-Arabi* newspaper, following Fawzy's interview with President Hosni Mubarak on the eve of parliamentary elections in November 1995. It showed the back of an interviewer's head, but in front of Fawzy was the back of another head. The figure meant to represent Fawzy shouted, "Open!" The implication was that Fawzy had carried out an obsequious interview with the president. Fawzy is derisively referred to on the Egyptian street as "Mustafid Fawry"(meaning ""immediately benefiting"), implying he curries favor with officials for personal gain. He currently presents the popular state TV show *Hadith al-Madina* (*Talk of the City*). A Coptic Christian, he is known for his anti-Islamist political views.

FUTURE TELEVISION (AL-MUSTAQBAL)

Lebanese satellite channel officially licensed in 1996, aiming to represent Sunni Muslims. Owned by Lebanese prime minister Rafik al-Hariri, this Lebanese station maintains the right connections and rarely gets into trouble with the authorities. Along with LBC it has pioneered the introduction of Western styles of liberal programming, with good-looking presenters, fashion shows, and music shows. Since 1999, it is now rivalled by NTV, which is owned by Tahsin Khayyat, a prominent Sunni Muslim businessman opposed to Hariri's policies. NTV has been subject to a number of threats of closure and legal action, ostensibly over alleged dealings with Israelis, but observers suspect the rivalry with Hariri is the real source of trouble.

Al-Hurra, the Washington-based Arabic satellite channel funded and administered by the U.S. State Department, was created to counter what the U.S. administration saw as anti-American reporting on al-Jazeera and al-Arabiya. Its main political discussion show is hosted by Lebanese presenter Ziyad Njeim, who formerly appeared on now-banned Lebanese channel MTV. The channel, which aggressively focuses on political reform and human rights in Arab countries, has provoked public condemnation from Saudi clerics. U.S. president George W. Bush accepted an interview on the channel in May 2004 to address Arab public opinion concerning the scandal over American troops abusing Iraqi prisoners. (President Bush also granted an interview to al-Arabiya, which was seen as marginally less subversive than al-Jazeera.)

'AL-HAWA (*ON THE AIR*)

This was one of a wave of political shows in the late 1990s on Arab satellite channels that first brought serious political debate from the press to the TV screen. It is presented by Emad Adib, editor of the Egyptian financial daily *al-Alam al-Youm*, and it airs on the Saudi-owned Orbit channel. Adib also set up the Egyptian financial daily paper *al-Alam al-Youm* in an attempt to create a culture of business reporting in Arabic journalism. Adib has been superseded by the popularity of shows and presenters on free-to-air channels like al-

Jazeera and al-Arabiya, but he is still regarded as a pioneer of the Arabic broadcasting revolution of the last decade.

AL-ISLAH (REFORM)

A satellite channel run by the Saudi opposition group Movement for Islamic Reform in Arabia, based in London, which was launched after the suicide bomb attacks in Riyadh in May 2003. The group's head, Saad al-Fagih, said the channel would be more dangerous to the Saudi royals than Osama bin Laden. The location of the channel's studios has been kept secret, and callers from within the kingdom are promised that their voices will be disguised to encourage them to speak openly against the Saudi government. But the channel has only managed to broadcast intermittently, suggesting that Saudi financial interests have made their influence felt in order to muzzle the dissident project.

JAHINE, SALAH (1930–1986)

A giant of the nationalist Egyptian intelligentsia. He was primarily a cartoonist and poet famous for writing the lyrics to nationalist songs used by the state in the 1950s and 1960s. Like many in the intellectual elite of the time, he truly believed in the dream of building a new society promoted by President Gamal Abdel Nasser. Consequently, Jahine was one of the many who were devastated when it all came crashing down in 1967, and many people say he never fully recovered from the shock. He seemed to find a new zest for life in the early 1980s when French singer Dalida returned to Egypt, where she grew up. Jahine penned a series of haunting, bittersweet pop songs for her, which spoke poignantly of love for the nation. These songs, such as *Hilwa Ya Balady* (*So Sweet My Country*), are still hugely popular in the Arab world. But Jahine committed suicide in 1986, and Dalida, who also had a depressive streak, did the same a year later in 1987. Jahine's songs and images colored popular culture throughout the Nasser years; indeed, in many ways they have come to define the period.

JORDANIAN MEDIA CITY COMPANY

A large production and uplink center in Amman established as a private free zone in 2001 by Saudi Sheikh Saleh Kamel's Dallah Media Production Company. Its main tenant and client so far is Kamel's own Arab Radio and Television (ART) network. ART offers Jordanian TV access to the international soccer matches covered by ART. Egypt's and Dubai's "media cities" have outdone the Jordanian version so far.

KANDIL, HAMDY (B. 1936)

Kandil rose to prominence in Egypt in 2000 when his program, *The Editor*, led a new wave of political programming on Egyptian state television, inspired by the revolution on the satellite channels. His show came into its own after the Palestinian uprising broke out in September 2000, when he presented himself as the "conscience of the Arab nation," railing against moral injustice and neoimperialism in classic Nasserist fashion. He moved to the Egyptian satellite network Dream TV, where he had more freedom to speak his mind, but because the station operates from Egypt's state-owned Media Production City, there were still parameters within which he had to work. In 2004 he moved to Dubai Television as part of an effort to increase viewership for the network, which was declining in popularity.

KHALLEEK BIL-BAYT (STAY AT HOME)

A culture and literary program on Lebanon's Future satellite channel, in which the presenter, poet Zahi Wahby, engages in an in-depth discussion with a well-known literary figure. The word *bayt* means "a verse or line of poetry," as well as "home." It is one of the few cultural discussion shows on Arab screens. In a bid to maintain its success and sustain further seasons, it has moved into entertainment territory, hosting famous actors and actresses. Similar shows on Arab television include Abu Dhabi's *Mubdi'un* (*Creative People*) and *al-Arabiya*'s *Manarat* (*Lighthouses*), presented by Tunisian Kawthar Bishrawy. Bishrawy left al-Jazeera in 2002 on bad terms, claiming the channel's Qatari bosses didn't take cultural television seriously.

LAHHAM, DOREID

Much-loved Syrian comic actor and director who now chairs a talk show on the MBC satellite channel. He rose to prominence in the 1960s as part of a TV and film comic duo, paired with Syrian Nihad al-Qalie. They were a couple in the style of Laurel and Hardy. Like Algerian comic Rouiched, he makes much use of comic set pieces, a style heavily promoted in Egyptian cinema and drama. Following the Arab defeat in the war of 1967, Lahham moved into theater with Mohammed al-Maghout, a political playwright. The plays of Doreid Lahham became the only outlet for marginal political criticism and relief throughout the 1970s and 1980s in Syria.

LBC

Lebanese satellite channel officially licensed in 1996, with the aim of representing the interests of Maronite Christians (though owned by Essam Fares, a Greek Orthodox businessman). It has led the way in bringing Western entertainment programming to the Arab world, copying the formats for pop and youth culture shows in Europe and North America. Much of it, ironically, is aimed at ultraconservative Saudi Arabia, the viewing public targeted by Arab advertisers. LBC has consciously led Lebanon's attempt to bring the West to the Arab world, but the channel has become synonymous with scantily clad women whose faces are surgically altered. In fact, a joke among men in the region is that LBC stands for *libnaniyaat bidoun culottes*—"Lebanese women without trousers."

AL-MANAR

Lebanese channel set up by the Shi'ite Hizbollah group in the early 1990s. It was officially licensed in 1996, despite the fact that the state had already authorized four other channels to represent Lebanon's main sects, including the Shi'ites. NBN is the Lebanese channel intended to represent the Shi'ites, owned by parliament speaker Nabih Berri. Al-Manar's continuing existence was testament to the growing prestige in Lebanon of Hizbollah because of its role in fighting Israel's occupation of the south. Its future is in the balance, as Washington pressures Lebanon and Syria over Hizbollah. It is one of the independent satellite channels that have changed the face of Arab media, including al-Jazeera, MBC, and LBC, by breaking the stranglehold of state television operators.

Reporter Farah Noureddin of Lebanese satellite station al-Manar, which is run by Hizbollah. (Kontos Yannis/Corbis Sygma)

MANSOUR, AHMED (B. N. A.)

One of al-Jazeera's leading presenters, with a background as a political journalist from Egypt and Islamist sympathies and connections to the Muslim Brotherhood. His interviews with major political figures and former government ministers, prime ministers, and presidents usually serve to back up the Islamist argument that the era of secular Arab nationalism failed for the Arabs. The show, called *Shahid ala-Asr* (*Eyewitness of the Era*), usually lasts over several episodes and involves Mansour asking tough questions about the morality of the interviewees' actions. His other show is *Bila Hudoud* (*Without Limits*) and usually involves an hour-long interview with one person, with whom Mansour is sympathetic, concerning a current issue.

MEDIA PRODUCTION CITY

Huge Egyptian studio complex at Sixth of October City outside Cairo—a "media-free zone" available to local Egyptian and Arabic film productions and shows. Al-Jazeera shot some shows there in 2000, and Egypt scored a major success when the top game show *Who Wants to Win a Million?* moved there from Paris in February 2002. Its chairman, Abdel-Rahman Hafez, also doubled for a while as chairman of the ERTU, making him second only to Information Minister Safwat al-Sherif (in the post from 1981 to 2004 and still a powerful regime figure) in Egypt's hierarchy of media moguls. Egypt jealously guards its control of media: the complex and its tax breaks for Arabic stations "doesn't mean privatization of the Egyptian media or infringement of existing terrestrial broadcasting," Sherif said

("Taboo-breaking Arab Broadcaster to Set Up in Egypt," Reuters, 17 April 2000).

MTV

Lebanese music and entertainment channel officially licensed in 1996 under the ownership and management of the Greek Orthodox Murr family (hence the "M" in "MTV"), intended to represent the interests of that group in Lebanese society. The station was closed down in 2002 after pushing the envelope on Syria's presence in Lebanon—the station made itself a forum for Christian nationalists opposed to any Arab or Muslim interference in the country. The closure provoked an outcry in a country widely considered a bastion of the free press in the Arab world. The specter of religious violence is still strong in Lebanon after the 1975–1990 civil war, and most stations are linked via ownership, editorial stance, or both to specific sects or sectarian political groups. MTV also faced charges of stirring sectarian strife over its coverage of a Muslim office worker's killing of Christian colleagues, which officials had warned the media not to depict as sectarian violence.

POLITICAL SATIRE

There is little political satire on Arabic television, though of late it has begun. Lebanese television has a few comedy sketch shows that poke fun at government ministers, and the satellite channel MBC is trying to break into the territory with its program *CBM*. Egypt is trying with a *Spitting Image*–style, puppet-based show called *Illi Fat Sat*; Syria is trying with *Mirror* (*Miraya*) and *Spotlight* (*Buq'at Daww*); and Iraq's new independent al-Sharqiya has comedy shows that also skirt

the dire situation in the country. Much fodder was found in the figure of former Iraqi information minister Mohammed Said al-Sahhaf, known for his colorful abuse in classical Arabic and denials of the obvious when Iraq was at war in March and April 2003. An impersonation of him is the key hook to the MBC show.

AL-QASSEM, FAISAL

The presenter of al-Jazeera's *The Opposite Direction* (*al-Ittijaah al-Mu'aakis*) and object of frequent attacks in the media in many Arab countries. Qassem is a Syrian Druze who made his name in the early 1990s on the BBC World Service Arabic radio station. His brother, Majd, is a well-known singer who suffered for al-Jazeera's spats with Arab governments. He was turned back at the Cairo airport by Egyptian authorities when relations were particularly tense in 2000. On *The Opposite Direction*, Qassem leads stormy discussions between two representatives of opposing schools of thought, but he is well known for doing his best to stir up arguments. The program has touched on the big, sensitive issues in nearly every Arab country and been the cause of political standoffs between Qatar and numerous Arab states since al-Jazeera began transmission in 1996. It was a novelty when the program first appeared for viewers to see taboo issues brought out of the closet in a rambunctious way, because the show often descends into shouting, insults, and walkouts.

QERDAHI, GEORGE

Heartthrob Lebanese presenter of the Arab version of the global hit show *Who Wants to Win a Million?* (in Arabic, *Man Sa-*

yarbah al-Milyoun? lit., *Who Will Win the Million?*). Qerdahi's background was in political journalism with Radio Monte Carlo in the 1980s and then with London-based MBC in the 1990s. In 2001, MBC asked him to take the plum job of hosting the Arabic version of the globally popular game show. He has become a household name throughout the region and has lent his presence to the promotion of products, including mobile phone networks and men's fashion. As a Maronite Christian, he is also known for his pan-Arab politics.

SUPERSTAR

The Arabic version of the British talent show *Pop Idol* and *American Idol* in the United States (with even the same theme song), which airs on Future Television, featuring a panel of experts from Lebanon, Kuwait, and Egypt. The show debuted in October 2002 to great fanfare. Crowds attacked the Beirut studios in September 2003 when the Lebanese contestant who was the local favorite failed to win. The format has been a big success, although music commentators have noticed that the first winner, Diana Karazone from Jordan, hasn't really risen above the level of one of the hundreds of second-tier pop singers in the Arab world, and that the show focuses more on looks than on vocal talent. Although Palestinian singer Ammar Hassan was the toast of the 2004 contest, Libyan Ayman al-Aathar was the final winner.

Bibliography

Print Resources

Armbrust, Walter, ed. *Mass Mediations: New Approaches to Popular Culture in the Middle East and Beyond.* Berkeley: University of California Press, 2000.

Burns, John. "Arab TV Gets a New Slant: Newscasts without Censorship." *New York Times,* 4 July 1999.

"Contaminated Goods." *al-Ahram Weekly,* 2–8 January 2003.

Eickelman, Dale, and Jon W. Anderson, eds. *New Media in the Muslim World: The Emerging Public Sphere.* Bloomington: Indiana University Press, 2003.

Elbendary, Amina. "Pride and Prejudice." *al-Ahram Weekly,* 27 December 2001–2 January 2002, Issue No. 566.

El-Nawawi, Mohammed, and Adel Iskandar Farag. *Al-Jazeera: How the Free Arab News Network Scooped the World and Changed the Middle East.* Oxford: Westview Press, 2002.

Heil, Alan L., Jr. *Voice of America: A History.* New York: Columbia University Press, 2003.

Mostyn, Trevor. *Censorship in Islamic Societies.* London, Saqi Books: 2002.

Oxford Business Group. "Tunisia Report." 17 March 2004.

Ragab, Samir. *al-Gumhouriya,* October 2000.

"Razor-Tongued Quiz Hostess Outrages Arab Audience." Reuters, 10 June 2002.

Said, Edward. *Covering Islam: How the Media and the Experts Determine How We See the Rest of the World.* New York: Vintage Books, 1997.

"Taboo-breaking Arab Broadcaster to Set Up in Egypt." *Reuters,* 17 April 2000.

Wood, James. *History of International Broadcasting.* Vol. 1. London: Peter Peregrinus, 1992.

Web Sites

www.tbsjournal.com. Site of the Adham Centre for Television Journalism of the American University in Cairo.

www.aljazeera.net. Al-Jazeera's site in Arabic.

www.english.aljazeera.net. Al-Jazeera's site in English.

www.alarabiya.net. Site of the rival to al-Jazeera, al-Arabiya.

www.amin.org/jourmag. Site of the Arab Media Internet Network, with links to and information on Arabic broadcast and print outlets inside and outside the Arab world.

www.voanews.com/arabic. Voice of America's Arabic-language Web site.

http://news.bbc.co.uk/hi/arabic/news. The Arabic-language Web site of the BBC World Service.

www.mbc1.tv/home.asp. The Web site of MBC Television.

www.art-tv.net. The Web site of ART (the Arab Radio and Television Network).

3

The Press

How the Arab Press Grapples with Censorship

There is not a single Arab country that enjoys a free press, and yet the Arab world probably has a more thriving print media than any other region in the world. The reasons for this are many. In Egypt the state owns, funds, and produces a massive output of newspapers and magazines. This output is based on the idea that since the state aims to be all things to all people, it should also provide every kind of publication imaginable—pro-government, opposition, Islamist, youth, Arab nationalist, and so on. Egypt's flagship daily *al-Ahram* aims to be all of these things rolled into one. Lebanon once had a rabid free press—a function of a central state made deliberately weak in order to accommodate the country's delicate confessional balance—and was the center of all kinds of political publishing for groups based in other countries in the region, a function of the lack of freedoms elsewhere. Algeria's complex society, which has been Arabizing by degrees since its independence in 1962, has seen a growth in publications, particularly those in Arabic (though many that appeared after liberalization in 1988 have been closed down for Islamist leanings, leaving French-language publications to comprise the majority of some thirty dailies).

In general, the written word in the Arabic language has power and influence over Arabs, perhaps beyond that of other cultural groups around the world. There are several reasons for this situation: The formal Arabic language has a hallowed status as the language of Islam; large numbers of people have been coming into literacy since the mid-twentieth century (Lebanon has the highest rate, with 85 percent literacy; Egypt and Morocco have around 50 percent; and Mauritania has a regional low of 40 percent); and literacy and the written word are central factors in the story of early Islam and the life of the Prophet (tradition depicts him as illiterate, yet he was the one through whom God chose to reveal his final message to humankind).

Censorship is prevalent throughout the Arab world. Some of it is laid down by the state in opaque, vaguely worded statutes, but most of the

A Cairo street vendor displays a range of newspapers on the street. (Bettmann/Corbis)

censorship is self-imposed, done in fear of the state's heavy hand. Each country has its own sensitive story. The state-owned papers, independent papers, opposition papers, and Arabic and non-Arabic press based abroad all must adhere to each country's codes if they want their publications to sell without hindrance from the authorities. In most countries, the taboo subjects include the integrity of the ruler and his family, dissident groups fundamentally opposed to the existing system (in the 1960s these dissidents were leftists; since then they've become Islamists); and anything sexual or religious that could lead to street demonstrations. To take one example: Moroccan editor Ali al-Murabet was sentenced to four years in prison in May 2003 for "insulting the king" and "undermining the monarchy" in articles and cartoons published in two satirical weeklies. They included an interview with a vocal opponent of the Moroccan monarchy, a comic photomontage lampooning government officials, and an article on the Royal Court's finances. Amendments to Morocco's press law in 2003 drew criticism from human rights organizations for retaining prison sentences of up to five years for journalists and publishers found guilty of undermining the monarchy, Islam, or Morocco's claim to the disputed western Sahara territory. "Control of the media in the Arab world differs from one country to the next," says Jihad Khazen, former editor of *al-Hayat* (Khazen 1999). "The Arab media are anything but monolithic. There is no state committee that meets in secret and assigns parts of the control to this prince or that sheikh." For journalists, it's a game of daring an official mindset that rules by instilling fear of its ability to strike at any time. Many decide that cohabiting with and being co-opted by the authorities is the better part of valor. Arabic literature is full of tales of writers, journalists, and other intellectuals torn between living comfortably by selling out to the regime and living on the edge for the sake of "the truth."

Book publishing itself is considered to be in a state of crisis, with a decline in the total number of publications produced in the region annually. A best-seller in Egypt sells only 10,000 copies, even though the country's population is around 70 million. The Arabic novel didn't mature as a literary genre until the 1950s, mainly due to Egypt's Naguib Mahfouz, the only Arab to win the Nobel Prize for literature. Today, the publishing market is increasingly driven by the religious establishment, with books sponsored by Islamic foundations, Islamic publishing houses, religious governments, and so on. Continuing tension between religious lobbies in the region and secular intellectual and political elites has further narrowed the opportunities for literary creativity. The annual Cairo International Book Fair, the largest publishing forum in the Arab world, saw up to eighty publishers fail to display their books in January 2002, because Egyptian customs and censorship authorities objected to works dealing with taboo religious, sexual, and political subjects. The Arabs in the region do read, and avidly. But what they read is for the most part an extraordinarily diverse and thriving array of newspapers and magazines. In these publications, an easier form of Arabic is presented to the reader, rather than the heavier, classical language of novels, religious works, and school textbooks.

The Egyptian Press Today

Egypt's immense national press is an enigma. Though it considers itself the leader of press freedom in the Arab world, it is a model of how to maintain state control and allow freedom within certain strictly patrolled boundaries. Though the press was conceived in the 1950s as part of Egypt's "media of mobilization," and remains essentially that, it has become harder to handle for the authorities. The president or prime minister will every so often call a private meeting with editors of state, opposition, and independent papers to ask the press to tone down some of their attacks on corruption, or to emphasize positive developments at a time of national depression over economic woes, or to be more understanding of the limits of foreign policy in the Arab-Israeli conflict. And in a culture where the political and the moral spheres are subject to rigid controls, there is a big market for sensationalism.

The state has no less than eleven bodies that publish newspapers and magazines, including eight publishing houses and three government ministries. The leading publishing house, al-Ahram, prints about a dozen daily, weekly, and monthly papers and magazines, intended to appeal to the entire spectrum of Egypt's complex society—a women's weekly, a children's magazine, a sports weekly, a weekly magazine aimed at the Arab world, English and French weeklies for the foreign communities in Egypt, and a daily that tries to house all of the intellectual trends in the country. The flagship paper, *al-Ahram*, is the oldest daily paper in the Arab world. It was founded by two Lebanese brothers in 1875 and later nationalized after 1952. It is now viewed by the president as "his" paper, the state's most prestigious mouthpiece. The paper has come under severe criticism in recent years for being a shadow of its former self, no longer the beacon of freedom and democratic progress it once was, certainly in the pre-1952 period, while some would argue it remained a model into the 1970s. Since the early 1990s, the paper has played a central role in the government's propaganda campaign against (1) radical Islamist groups who had taken up arms against the state; (2) the moderate Islamist trend of the Muslim Brotherhood and political parties allied with it; and, most recently, (3) human rights groups and civil society. On occasions such as the president's birthday, businessmen will fill page after page with advertisements of congratulation, and co-opted cartoonists will get their chance to decorate entire pages with drawings whose message is that Mubarak is the honest guardian of national unity.

The Arab-Israeli conflict has always taken up the lion's share of analytical space in the Egyptian press, in part because of the enormity and importance of the issue for Arab countries and also, to some indefinable degree, as a means of avoiding pressing issues of political and economic reform that present the government and entrenched elites with difficult choices. In the immediate aftermath of the 1993 Oslo accords between the Israelis and Palestinians, it seemed that this historic breach was heading toward closure, and, as a consequence, talk of political and economic reform spread through the press in some countries as regimes began to prepare for life without the conflict. But the rise of the Israeli right, as well as subsequent world economic crises and their effects on the region, set the process in reverse, and "the national security argument"—that open so-

ciety exposes the country to Israeli Mossad mischief and Palestinian meddling, and that domestic Islamists and nationalists can't be trusted—gained ground again. How serious the government ever was about reform during the 1990s is open to question. Some writers have argued that after Mubarak secured an almost immediate write-off of $25 billion of external debt, in return for taking part in the 1990–1991 Gulf War, the regime has been disingenuous about the political and economic reform it claims as its ultimate goal.

Since the late 1970s, when Sadat created a form of multiparty democracy as the complement to his controversial peace with Israel, the opposition and independent press have given the state-owned papers a run for their money,. The main opposition parties each have their own paper —the liberal Wafd Party has a daily, *al-Wafd* (*The Delegation*); the Islamist-leaning Liberal Party has a daily, *al-Ahrar* (*The Free*); the Nasserist Party has a weekly, *al-Arabi* (*The Arab*); and the leftist Tagammu Party has a weekly, *al-Ahali* (*The Community*). The ruling National Democratic Party issues a weekly paper called *Mayo* (*May*) and a religious weekly called *al-Liwa al-Islami* (*The Islamic Banner*). The Muslim Brotherhood, by far Egypt's biggest opposition force (but—partly for that reason—banned since 1954), found its main press outlet in the Islamist-leaning Labor Party and its biweekly *al-Shaab* (*The People*). But both the party and its paper were suspended in 2000 after leading a campaign against allegedly blasphemous novels, a campaign that caused a riot in Cairo. *Al-Shaab* had been one of Egypt's most colorful papers, constantly provoking fights with the authorities over corruption, secularism, and the government's pro-West poli-

Kahil and His Beleaguered Dove of Peace

One of the best practitioners of the art of the political cartoon was Mahmoud Kahil, who was sixty-six when he passed away in 2003. Kahil's savage caricatures were usually seen in the Saudi-owned daily *Asharq al-Awsat* and its sister publications *al-Majalla* and the *Arab News,* but he reached the wider world in his regular contributions to the journal *Middle East International.* Kahil was a "cartoonist's cartoonist" in his classical style of drawing, which he used to lampoon Arabic leaders. Kahil left for London when the civil war broke out in his native Lebanon in 1975, and from there his reputation spread. In a sign of how accurate his work was, he rarely used captions in his work. One of his cartoons in 2002, after a donor conference in Paris to help the Lebanese economy, depicted Lebanese prime minister Rafik al-Hariri as a surgeon with an upturned Eiffel Tower syringe, injecting a pick-me-up into a sick, human embodiment of Lebanon.

Kahil cast himself as a supporter of the downtrodden everywhere. One of his classic cartoons shows a beleaguered-looking "Mr. World," a figure with a moustache representing the Arab world. He was a scathing critic of Israeli prime minister Ariel Sharon, whom he often depicted with a mouth dripping with Palestinian blood. Kahil was also known for his "peace dove" cartoons, which he used to comment on the depleted hopes for ending the Israeli-Palestinian conflict and building a better future. This dove appeared in every pose imaginable, beaten-up, browbeaten, or packing its bags. In one cartoon, former U.S. president Bill Clinton was shown at a fast-food restaurant handing out flaming doves. These images lived in the Arab mind for a full two decades and also did much to color the way foreigners thought about the region.

cies. Since 1985 it was controlled by former Marxist intellectual Adel Hussein and his Brotherhood-allied nephew Magdy Hussein. Adel Hussein, who died in 2001, was admired by many across the Arab world for refusing to tone down his ideology and rhetoric. He tried to turn the Labor Party into a real political party, and its paper into a real newspaper, in an era when regimes want to reduce modern governance to what a colloquial Egyptian term refers to as "décor." He was one of a group of Marxist intellectuals who converted to political Islam after the Iranian revolution, seeing it as a paradigm of the future in Arab politics, and he turned *al-Shaab* into Egypt's most radical broadsheet. Many think he went too far, with, for example, headlines that

blatantly goaded radical Islamists to murder foreign tourists. Secular intellectuals saw in the Husseins and *al-Shaab* a sign of the intellectual violence gripping the Arab world, as governments refused to share power, and opposition movements proved incapable of overthrowing them.

Sensationalism, questionable ethics, and paranoia are rampant elsewhere. The government has made some efforts to control this type of journalism, demonizing it as the "yellow press," though many state-owned papers and magazines also engage in sensational journalism. A common theme in the more rabid opposition and independent papers is that Israel and its intelligence agency Mossad are out to corrupt Egyptian youth. Some examples cited are alleged imports from Israel of belts with radioactive buckles sold in Cairo, "factories of death" that churn out shampoo to make Egyptian hair fall out, Nescafé that brings on AIDS, creams that gnarl the skin, chewing gum that makes women horny, and the music of a transsexual Israeli singer whose Arabic-Hebrew pop songs were a big hit in 1995–1996 until the government banned her tapes. The underlying themes of the way Israel is covered are that Egypt is a more moral, religious, peace-loving, ancient, and authentic polity and culture. Israel, on the other hand, is dissolute, parvenu, and warmongering. Egypt is real; Israel is plastic. In one typical reference, the tabloid weekly *al-Khamis* revealed in shocked tones that homosexuality is rife in Israel. "Gays and lesbians are everywhere. More than 10,000 Israelis of both sexes have revealed this deviancy at a festival held in Tel Aviv. Israel revealed its filthy social face during this odious festival. Male youths were keen to exchange kisses, engage in obscene acts and take commemorative pictures of this," it said (*al-Khamis*, 23 November 2000). "There is a statistic that shows that homosexuality in Israel represents 25 percent of the population of the Jewish state!!" The press howled as if somone had pulled a fast one on them when they discovered that Israeli singer Dana International had made a promotional trip to Cairo in 1995, posing by the Nile on horse-drawn carriages and flirting in coffee shops with the punters. "They had written about me before and that's why we went in very quietly," said the singer, who went on to win the Eurovision Song Contest in 1998 (interview with author, *Cairo Times*, 15 May 1997). She was the subject of a subsequent best-seller by an opposition journalist, peddled on Cairo street corners, which described her as a "Jewish prostitute" manufactured in Tel Aviv, like those shampoos, "to unleash her moans and shameless words from the city of a thousand minarets" (al-Ghaity 1996).

Crime coverage is fairly lurid and highly moralistic. The weekly *Akhbar al-Hawadith* (*Crime News*) regularly takes murderers back to the scenes of their crimes, where they relate the dastardly deeds in detail or report last words of remorse before they're hanged. Being a state-owned publication with a direct line to the attorney general's office, the paper plays a big role in trashing the reputation of rights activists, alleged Israeli spies, homosexuals, affluent youth who listen to heavy metal music (and who have been arrested on suspicion of "devil-worshipping" in a number of cases since 1996), and other people facing trial in controversial cases where a political point is being made by the state. Sensationalism has also benefited from computer graphics software, which provides extra glitter to controversial stories. *Al-Arabi* caused a minor diplomatic incident in 2001 when it announced Israeli foreign minister Shimon Peres, who was on an official visit to Cairo, by photomontaging his head onto a photograph of Adolf Hitler: Israel as Nazi state is a favorite theme in the nationalist papers. Months later, the same paper offered a front-page photomontage of Ariel Sharon as a baby in George Bush's arms, directing a large spout of urine onto the face of the supposed leader of the free world. On occasion some publishers try to push the envelope with nudity. During the two weeks of the Cairo International Film Festival, the authorities allow printing of the schedules in garish, sensationalist newspapers, flagging films containing sex scenes alongside

A protester holds a cartoon portrait of U.S. president George Bush in a protest in Cairo against the 2003 war in Iraq as it raged in late March. (AP Photo/Denis Doyle)

hot pics and headlines such as "black women are crazy for violent sex and prefer it oral" and "Hollywood stars challenge the world with their breasts," to quote two examples. Some Lebanese papers that are ostensibly about crime news are trying the same approach. One, called *al-Adala* (*Justice*), features seminaked women on the cover and headlines such as "Ahmed makes love to his daughter in Tripoli?!" and "Khadija lures Shahida so that her husband Tewfiq can rape her!" (December 2002).

At present, Egypt's press is arguably more under the state's sway than at any time in the last decade. Most of the opposition papers have either been co-opted to tone down their rhetoric against the state, or they have been marginalized and closed down. *Al-Wafd*, the leading opposition paper, offers only token opposition to the

government in economic and foreign policy, and *al-Shaab* is now only on the Web (www.alshaab.com). Government concern about the plethora of privately owned publications is largely misplaced in that few have circulation figures of note and fewer still are concerned with politics—most are tabloids writing about belly dancers and actresses. The Journalists Syndicate is strictly under government control, led by *al-Ahram*'s editor Ibrahim Nafie. It's the one professional organization that Mubarak has made clear he will never allow to fall under the control of an opposition faction. The state-owned press dominates membership, shutting out many opposition journalists who then miss out on the considerable social and financial benefits of officially registered journalists, presenting young journalists with another dilemma—

whether to fight with the impoverished op-position and independent press or to sell out for an easy life in the state's mammoth media empire. As a consequence, there has been a huge outflow of journalistic talent to London and the Gulf.

Despite all the problems of the press—censorship, obtaining information, finding hard news in Egypt's notoriously slow po-litical and economic climate, obtaining a li-cense from the government—people still want to read newspapers and people still want to own them. They offer publishers and their editors prestige in society be-cause of the hallowed status of the written word. The press also offers opportunities to make money through attracting advertis-ing, to attack one's business or political op-ponents, to take money for writing puff pieces, or to threaten others if they don't pay protection money. There is hardly any developed press covering local news, an in-dication of the shrunken nature of civil so-ciety in Egypt's highly centralized, authori-tarian system.

The Prominent Role of the Emigré and Foreign-Language Press

Arabic papers based outside the Arab world and foreign-language papers within the Arab world have more freedom to dis-cuss domestic and global issues than local Arabic-language papers throughout the re-gion. In both cases, the reason given is that their readership is very small, restricted to elite groups of society, and therefore poses little threat to stability. Often the degree to which they have censorship problems with the authorities reflects the degree to which their reports of domestic issues present information to the outside world. Other

times they simply provide cheeky com-ments or analyses that go too far. Mo-rocco, Algeria, and Tunisia, where for a significant sector of society French is still a native language alongside Arabic, have a series of French-language dailies that op-erate to all intents and purposes according to the same rules as the Arabic-language press.

The London-based *al-Hayat* and *Asharq al-Awsat* (*The Middle East*) are the two main Arabic-language publications based abroad and aimed at the Arab world as a whole, as well as Arabic-speaking communi-ties around the world. London is also home to the Palestinian émigré *al-Quds al-Arabi* (*Arab Jerusalem*). Within the region, the main foreign-language publications are Le-banon's *Daily Star*; the *Gulf News*, based in Dubai; the Saudi-based *Arab News*; Egypt's *Cairo Times* (which suspended publication in 2004), *al-Ahram Weekly*, *al-Ahram Hebdo*, and *Middle East Times*; Jordan's *Jordan Times*; Sudan's *Khartoum Monitor*; and Morocco's respected mainstream daily *L'Economiste*. These are the ones that stand out and are taken seriously, but there are others, such as the notoriously outmoded *Egyptian Gazette*, whose look and style have changed little since it began in 1880. The al-Ahram publications, though state-owned, are given a considerably wider berth than the publishing house's Arabic papers; they also distill the best of the immense ana-lytical output of the Arabic press for repro-duction in translation. The same goes for the *Arab News*, owned by the Asharq al-Awsat group. The others are to some degree or another "opposition" papers, lobbying for political and economic changes toward a more liberal environment. Some publica-tions within the region can be added to the two London-based publications (and their

A Syrian reads the pan-Arab daily *al-Hayat* in May 2004. The daily is based in London and sold on newsstands in many Western capitals. (Louai Beshara/AFP/Getty Images)

sister magazines, *al-Wasat* and *al-Majalla*), and together they are considered to be the main intellectual forums of the Arab world: from Egypt, *al-Kutub: Wughaat Nazar* (*Books: Viewpoints*), *al-Hilal* (*The Crescent Moon*), *Adab wa Naqd* (*Literature and Criticism*), *Sotour* (*Lines*), and *Akhbar al-Adab* (*Literature News*); the Palestinian *al-Karmal* (*Carmel*); the Lebanese *al-Zawaya* (*Angles*) and *Adab* (*Literature*); Jordan's *Amman;* and the Kuwaiti *al-Arabi* (*The Arab*) and *Alam al-Fikr* (*The World of Thought*). Iraqi poet Samuel Chamoun is involved in an English-language periodical focused on Arabic literature called *Banipal*, which has been published in London three times a year since 1998.

Al-Hayat and *Asharq al-Awsat* have established themselves as credible pan-Arab dailies that cover the entire region's political, economic, and cultural news, as well

as analyze and intellectualize it. Seeking to address the whole region, the British prime minister has used both papers for the simultaneous publication of "letters" to the Arab world on major issues such as Western policy toward Iraq and the Palestinian-Israeli conflict. Both managed to attain this position of respect because of and/or despite—opinions vary—Saudi ownership. A Saudi family from Jeddah that has a history in publishing launched *Asharq al-Awsat* in London in 1978. Now its chairman is the Saudi royal prince, Ahmed bin Salman bin Abdel-Aziz. Initially a Beirut paper set up in 1946, *al-Hayat* was relaunched in 1988, after a twelve-year hiatus due to the Lebanese civil war, under the private ownership of another Saudi royal, Khaled bin Sultan bin Abdel-Aziz, who was the leader of Saudi forces during the 1991 Gulf War. Both dailies formed the early stages of a "Saudization" of pan-Arab me-

Iraqi Media: Pre- and Post-Saddam

Iraq's media before the war was dominated by the Baath regime and the family of Saddam Hussein. His son Uday owned the main daily newspaper, *Babel,* as well as a TV channel for young people called "Shebab" (Youth). Only a few privileged Iraqis had access to satellite channels. Virtually all papers were state-owned, 100 percent beholden to the regime, and carried no dissent whatsoever. In the weeks leading up to the 2003 war, the personification of Saddam as Iraq and Iraq as Saddam was complete, and the final fusion of the two was achieved through the media. In a televised speech to the nation in January on the anniversary of the beginning of the 1991 Gulf War, Saddam called the Americans preparing to invade Baghdad the "new Mongols," invoking the forces of Hulagu Khan in 1258. But this time, Saddam vowed, it would be different. Unlike the bloodbath that Baghdadis suffered then (involving the death of the Abbasid caliph and his two sons), the new invaders would be routed on the city walls by a united and steadfast leadership, army, and people. "The army of Hulagu has now come at this time to clash with Baghdad after it was born again. Tell them in a clear voice: Stop your evil against the mother of civilization, the cradle and birthplace of the prophets and the messengers," he said (Shebab, 17 January 2003). "Baghdad, its people and leadership, is determined to force the Mongols of our age to commit suicide on its walls. We have planned to defeat the aggressors." The regime always cast itself in a melodramatic historical light, making use of figures from Mesopotamia's long past. Saddam was variously Sargon, Nebuchadnasr, Hammurabi—even some of the prophets—rolled into one. Everyone was expected to suffer and sacrifice as much as Saddam, whose words of wisdom were quoted endlessly on television, murals, signposts, and stelae (like the other modern Arab hero-villains who sought a place in the firmament, Gamal Abdel Nasser and Muammar al-Gaddafi).

Now it's a different world. Iraqis can watch the Arab satellite channels—pulling them into the Arab community—as well as the new state TV channel al-Iraqiya, set up by the Coalition Provisional Authority (CPA) after the 2003 Iraq war. Scores of papers covering politics, economics, sports, gossip, Arab entertainment, and news scandals have also sprung up, taking Iraq back to where it was before the Baath came to power in 1968. In the first year after the Baath fell, the largest-circulation daily to emerge was *Azzaman* (*The Times*), run by urbane and secular former dissident Saad al-Bazzaz. A journalist from Mosul, al-Bazzaz started the paper in London in 1997 as an outlet for opponents of the regime. The moment the regime fell, he was ready to move into Baghdad with up-to-date print and publishing facilities. The new press did a roaring trade in Baghdad, a city of four

dia in the 1990s, which extended to satellite and cable television too. Though there is no direct government involvement in either paper, both have to tread carefully when dealing with Saudi news. If they don't, then Saudi companies will boycott them, and that would be disastrous. As Jihad al-Khazen, a former editor of *al-Hayat,* says (Khazen 1999), "Without the Saudi market, neither newspaper, nor any of the large Arab television networks, would survive. We need the pan-Arab and local advertisements from that market. Hence, the indirect—some would say unhealthy—influence of the state over the media" (http://muse.jhu.edu/).

A mural of Saddam Hussein depicts him as the Babylonian ruler Nebuchadnezzar. (Françoise de Mulder/Corbis)

million, with print runs of 50,000 for the major dailies. From five political dailies and twelve weeklies in the Baath era, the press expanded to include over 100 newspapers and magazines, including a satirical tabloid called *Habizbooz* (run by a journalist who used to work on Uday's *Babel*). However, most of these publications were little more than poorly printed outlets for political parties, highlighting the speeches and visits of their leaders—similar to the press under the Baath regime. Already the press is reflecting the new divide in Iraqi society, post–Saddam Hussein: those with the new, U.S.-led order and those against it. The CPA issued regulations in summer 2003 warning papers against "incitement to violence" after one paper accused American troops of rape and another published a list of Iraqis "collaborating" with the CPA. Shi'ite cleric Muqtada al-Sadr's *al-Hawza* paper was banned in March 2004, leading to weeks of disturbances between his supporters and U.S. troops. The sovereign Iraqi authorities reopened it several months later.

Ordinary journalists are not so charitable. They say the Saudis and other Gulf monarchies have bought the Arabic media—its papers, journalists, and writers—in an effort to stave off mounting criticism of the status quo. Gulf papers like the UAE's *al-Ittihad* (*The Federation*) are full of columns by senior writers from Egypt and other poor Arabic countries, lured by money to write "pro-Gulf" opinions (depicted in Egyptian writer Bahaa Taher's novel, *Love in Exile*). The phenomenon started after the 1991 Gulf War, when the Gulf regimes suddenly found themselves subject to huge criticism in the Arab world over their alliances with the United States, alliances that many in the urban Arab countries believed were at the root of the problem that led to the war in the first place. At the same time, the Gulf monarchies came under intense scrutiny in the West for lacking democracy and women's rights. It was at this point that Saudi Arabia moved to place a stranglehold on the Arabic media, gaining control of the major pan-Arab papers and being the first to get into satellite television.

Lebanese Press: A Haven for Arabic Publishing

Considering its size, Lebanon has a huge media. Lebanon, along with Egypt, has been at the forefront of progress in the field since the latter half of the nineteenth century. While Cairo was the locus of most major publications at that time, their founders and major journalists were usually Lebanese or Syrian. Today Lebanon, with a population of around 3.5 million (including Palestinian refugees), has at least thirteen dailies, including eleven Arabic, one English, and one French, and over a thousand other weekly and monthly magazines and papers, covering topics including sports, business, luxury living, and (a Lebanese preoccupation) beauty tips for women. The main dailies are *al-Nahaar* (*The Day*), whose editorials are often anti-Syrian and "Lebanon first," and *al-Safir* (*The Ambassador*), which styles itself as "an Arabic political daily" and tends to be more concerned with the Arab-Israeli dispute and the wider Arab world. Beirut has also been the base for Syrian and Iraqi publications.

At present, Lebanon's print, radio, and television media are going through some changes because of the shifting undercurrents of the Arab-Israeli conflict. With Israel ending its occupation in south Lebanon in 2000, Lebanon appears to be more aligned with Syria than ever. Efforts by Christians to protest this situation have failed, confirming the ascendancy of Shi'ite Muslims and Muslims in general, and leading to the emergence of stricter limits on press freedom. The clearest example of this was the rough treatment meted out by security forces in August 2001 to Christian students protesting against Syrian influence in Lebanon's political life. The students demonstrated after the arrest of other anti-Syrian activists, who were, according to government officials, suspected of working for Israel. The incident was a double shock for proponents of civic freedoms, first because Lebanon is not used to this sort of heavy-handedness from the authorities, and second, because many had expected expansion, not a shrinking, of liberal space after the Israelis pulled out of the country. The media was intimidated by the new atmosphere—where security-force informers and phone taps are now widespread—to underreport the events. The business monthly *Executive* published a whole issue of blank white pages in protest and afterward wrote that an assault on civil rights could have repercussions for the economy if the country's reputation abroad suffered. "President Lahoud is an army man who the Syrians understand, we now realize that's why they wanted him. This country is becoming more like Syria, after Hafez al-Assad and the Israelis have gone. The Syrian mentality is now within us, via Lahoud and his control of the security and the army," one Lebanese magazine editor said (interview with author, January 2002). Since it reported in December 2001 an alleged attempt on Lahoud's life, *Asharq al-Awsat* has had to submit its daily publication for advance approval to state security force offices. Other papers have faced legal action for "disrupting relations with a sister country," but rights activists joke that since the Syrian army and intelligence are still in Lebanon, relations can't have been disrupted very much by any press article.

The Entertainment Press— A Burgeoning Market

News in the region is often synonymous with scandal, and there's a huge press that trades in it. The entertainment press is the main arena for promoting actors and singers (and trashing the competition). The press operates in a crowded market and is desperate to generate publicity in order to claim high sales and bring in more advertising revenue. "Respectable" and "scandalous" are important categories in the Arab world. The stars strive to be seen as more moral, religious, and Arab nationalist than the rest, while still aiming for sex-symbol status within those boundaries. Conversely, being depicted in the media as disdainful of religion, soft on Israel, and rude about other Arab nationalities could be a public relations disaster. Top belly dancer Fifi Abdo had to rebut press claims that she had accepted huge sums to perform in Israel on numerous occasions in the mid-1990s, when "normalization" was a major issue in Egypt after the 1993 Oslo Accords. The entertainment press is the prime arena for this schizophrenic game.

Currently, a major issue in the movie press regards "sex scenes"—what are referred to as *ighraa'* in Arabic ("seduc-tion"). This seduction involves provocation of the viewer's sexual appetite by acts of kissing, simulated foreplay between an actress and an actor, and depiction of an actress in underwear or a bikini. The ambiguity of the phrase allows actresses to appear in print saying, "I don't mind doing *ighraa'* scenes," or others to say, "I would never do *ighraa'* scenes," or, as one magazine wrote in a headline, "my husband doesn't mind me doing *ighraa'* scenes" (*Shashati*, 14 March 2002). None of this actually signifies nudity as a Western moviegoer would understand it. Journalists will produce these headlines in formal Arabic, regardless of whether the interviewed star actually made the statements, because *ighraa'* is an issue that sells in the entertainment press, and the dichotomy between classical and colloquial Arabic is easily abused. Upcoming and established stars alike will pay money to get their pictures on the front cover of major publications, though only smaller names pay for features about themselves inside glossy magazines.

In 1997, the Lebanese singer Najwa Karam was hit badly on the morals front when a Gulf newspaper reported that the Christian starlet had started calling her dog after the Prophet Mohammed. The story caused such a scandal that she was subsequently turned back at Cairo airport by angry security officials. Her next album was marketed in Egypt with large posters showing her in a headscarf and dark glasses, in the manner of affluent and pious Muslim women, with a signature reading, "to my dear public, my very spirit." Similarly, the Tunisian singer Zikra was reported by the Gulf press in 2002 to have compared her move from Tunisia to the Gulf to the Prophet's *hijra*, or migration, from Mecca to Medina. That provoked reports that a Gulf religious figure had issued a fatwa, or religious edict, denouncing her as an unbeliever, which she subsequently denied in a series of interviews in various entertainment publications. Zikra was murdered in Cairo by her jealous husband in November 2003. A number of singers have fallen afoul of Egypt's state television and the Musicians Union because of press reports alleging they had slandered the standard of Egyptian orchestra players. The Lebanese conductor Selim Sehab, Lebanese singer Magda Roumi, Tunisian singer Latifa, Iraqi heartthrob Kazem al-Saher, and Zikra were all briefly "blacklisted" from appearing on television and/or performing in Egypt because of such slights. Another theme in the entertainment press is catty remarks among the stars. Interviewers never stop needling them to say something nasty about their rivals. Lebanese pop star Nawal al-Zoghby has taken legal action against her Lebanese rival Diana Haddad and Haddad's producer husband over stories in newspapers saying they had questioned Zoghby's vocal ability. Zikra and the Syrian singer Assala also appeared in press wars, which saw them attack the standards of pop stars who do not match their own considerable vocal talents. Lebanese singer Ragheb Alama was once obliged to deny reports that he had called Sudanese women "ugly." "An Arab artist could never utter such words. I have respect and appreciation for all the Arab peoples," he said (*Asharq al-Awsat*, 10 March 2004), after a Sudanese women's group in Cairo threatened legal action.

The most glittering of the glitter press, whose names say it all, include Egypt's *Akhbar al-Nugoum* (*News of the Stars*) and *Sayidaty* (*My Ladies*), and Lebanon's *al-Maw'id* (*The Appointment*) and *Kalam al-Nas* (*People's Talk*). There is a host of women's, lifestyle, and fashion magazines as well, most of them Lebanese, including *al-Shabaka* (*The Network*), *Noura*, *al-Basha* (*The Pacha*), *Party*, *Snob*, and *Hawaa* (*Eve*) from Egypt, and the Kuwaiti magazines *al-Yaqaza* (*The Awakening*) and *al-Nahda* (*The Renaissance*). Advertisers will say, though, that the most sophisticated market in the Arab region is Saudi Arabia, which has a wealthy, large, and diverse population that requires advertisers to think in terms of regions. To take daily newspapers as an example, *Okaz* sells in the west, *al-Riyadh* sells in the central region, *al-Yawm* sells in the east, and *Asharq al-Awsat* sells all over the country. Niche markets are also valuable to advertisers: *Alam al-Sayyarat* (*The World of Cars*), *Zahrat al-Khaleej* (*Flower of the Gulf*), *Laha* (*For Her*), and *Kolenas* (*Everyone*) (among the lifestyle magazines), and the men's magazine *al-Rajul* (*Men*). This kind of branding and building up loyal readers is still in its primitive stages in other Arab countries.

The Repressed Press: Nuisance Publications That Annoy the Authorities

Egypt's *al-Shaab* is the most well known of a genre of gadfly publications that made a profession of irritating Arab regimes and dancing around their restrictions. These have included *al-Maw'ed* (*The Appointment*) in Algeria, *al-Mawkif* (*The Stance*) in Tunisia, Syria's satirical political weekly *al-Domari* (*The Lamplighter*), Egypt's *al-Destour* (*The Constitution*) (which lasted for two years in the mid-1990s), and Egypt's state-owned *Rose al-Yousef*. At least fifty-eight journalists have been killed in Algeria, either by security forces or opposition groups, since violence erupted there in 1992. "What is published or not published reflects the balance of power between the clans," said Henry and Springborg regarding the military and the constellation of interests around it (Henry and Springborg 2001).

Tunisian journalists have a particularly bad time of it. The government and ruling RCD Party own a small number of major newspapers, including the main French-language daily *La Presse;* the privately owned *as-Sabah* (*The Morning*) and *al-Shurouq* (*The Sunrise*), the main Arabic dailies, rarely challenge the government on serious policy issues. The newspapers of opposition parties that are allied to the government have run into the ground for lack of readership, leaving only two opposition papers that put up serious opposition to the government in business—the opposition Renewal Movement's monthly *al-Tariq al-Jadid* (*The New Way*) and the Progressive Socialist Rally's weekly *al-Mawkif.* Since the beginning of 2001, *al-Mawkif* has appeared irregularly because of pressure exerted by the state, including withholding advertising from government ministries and public sector companies, after it published articles highlighting corruption and criticizing the government's policies on democracy and the media. "Today you can't produce a weekly paper that is concerned with news because the government will make it too difficult," said Rachid Khashana, a leading political writer involved with the paper (interview with author, February 2003). No paper opposed constitutional changes in 2002 that allow the president to stand for unlimited terms in office—a referendum for a fourth five-year term was due in 2004. Tunisia even issued an effective press ban on pictures of U.S. Democratic presidential candidate John Kerry when he first emerged as a credible contender to Bush (Tunisian Human Rights League report, 30 April 2004).

As a result there are two styles of journalism in Tunisia: anodyne daily news reports of government actions, which differ little from newspaper to newspaper, and tabloid-style crime, entertainment, and gossip news. "The Tunisian main papers are seven versions of *Pravda*—they all are the same. Tunisia, North Korea and Libya are the only countries that still have a Stalinist media," said one writer, who would only speak off record. "There is a cordon around the Tunisian reader." The only exceptions are economic news, which appears in the weekly *L'Economiste Maghrebien* and the Paris-based *Jeune Afrique*, and occasional issues of the London-based *al-Quds al-Arabi* that make it into the country. The major pan-Arab daily *al-Hayat*, also based in London, has been prevented from distribution in Tunisia for over two years, and France's *Le Monde* and *Liberation* have also been blocked from distribution for running articles critical of the government. Licensing regulations are restrictive, and the government's system for deciding where to place daily advertising from state bodies results in pressures on content. The government buys printing paper from abroad and sells it to the Tunisian press at a discount, forming another control mechanism that can be used to exert pressure when necessary. The authorities can also interfere with the postal service to remove subscription issues of papers carrying articles they object to.

Since 1998, the Tunisian president has been on the New York–based Committee for the Protection of Journalists' (CPJ) list

Adel Hamouda: Egypt's Tabloid King

The king of the tabloid press in the Arab world is Adel Hamouda. From 1992 to 1998, he transformed the Egyptian magazine *Rose al-Yousef*—considered a pioneer of Egyptian journalism since its founding in the 1920s—from another staid, state-owned weekly into the stronghold of a virulent new form of journalism that mixed sexual innuendo and politics. A maverick liberal and anti-Islamist, Hamouda did things that no state editor had done before—suggesting that the peace process was a waste of time, treating the United States as an enemy, and demanding a total overhaul of pro-Western government economic policies. He not only championed secularism but also openly attacked the religious establishment as hypocritical, backward, and corrupt. All this was done in a provocative and titillating style, using Photoshop technology. He spent hours perfecting every issue's front cover, ridiculing politicians, clerics, and stars. With its new, *Private Eye*–like presentation, what was formerly a drab publication with some 8,000 sales per week suddenly registered sales of 150,000 copies per issue.

The facts were usually subordinate to the conspiracy theory in Hamouda's style of journalism. He had no compunction about accusing the American ambassador in Cairo of prior knowledge of the 1995 attempt on the life of President Mubarak in Ethiopia. He always claimed he had "proof," but no one ever saw it. The tabloid mindset believed it was just the kind of thing the Americans would probably do, since they were seen as not liking Egypt's ability to outsize Israel in regional political influence. In Hamouda's thinking, the end—forcing the state to give up its nefarious alliance with America—justified the means. In 1997 *Rose al-Yousef* led a campaign to stop *al-Ahram* from printing the syndicated cartoons of Israeli American cartoonist Ranan Lurie. It also ruined a plan to produce an Arabic edition of Lurie's weekly *Cartoon News* with the unproven claim that Lurie had fought Algerians in Algeria and Egyptians in Egypt and thus hated the Arabs in general. But for Hamouda, as for most of the opposition press in Egypt, this was an example of the state "normalizing" relations with Israel by stealth—something the political intelligentsia has been sensitive to since President Sadat single-handedly dragged Egypt out of the Arab-Israeli conflict with his maverick peace with Israel in 1979.

The Hamouda revolution saw a raft of newspapers adopt the same style in the mid-1990s, most notably the weekly *al-Destour,* which had similar leftist-nationalist leanings. But it all came crashing down in 1998 when the government revoked *al-Destour's* print license and a decree summarily removed Hamouda from

of the "10 worst enemies of the press," and in 1997, the Tunisian Newspaper Association was expelled from the World Association of Newspapers over its alleged failure to support a more open press. In recent years there has been a string of infamous incidents, documented by international press watchdogs and the U.S. State Department in its annual human rights reports.

Most took place during a period of bad relations with France in 2000–2001, when a number of journalists and rights activists complained of harassment over critical opinions expressed in the local and foreign media. In one incident, journalist Fethia el-Beji was fired from her position at *as-Sabah* for articles about the books of Taoufik Ben Brik, a prominent dissident

In 1997, Egyptian daily *al-Ahram* cancelled plans to publish the work of U.S. Israeli cartoonist Ranan Lurie after protests by Egyptian journalists. (Hank Morgan/Time Life Pictures/Getty Images)

"*Roza*," as it's affectionately referred to in Egypt, and reassigned him to a columnist's position on another state-owned publication, *al-Ahram.* Their crime was to publish a story that pushed the envelope: alleged threats from extremist Is-

lamist group al-Gama'a al-Islamiya to murder prominent Coptic Christian businessmen. The story ran afoul of Mubarak's fear of fomenting sectarian strife in Egypt and giving pro-Israeli lobbyists in the United States ammunition against Egypt in order to influence U.S. government policy. Why did the state tolerate *Rose al-Yousef* under Hamouda's stewardship for so long? Most likely because of Hamouda's implacable opposition to political Islam. Radical groups began an open insurgency against Mubarak's regime in 1992. The government thought it was a price worth paying if the only genuinely popular weekly magazine opposed the insurgency, so they gritted their teeth while the editor assaulted government corruption, attacked government-allied religious leaders, and soured relations with the United States and Israel. But when Hamouda was finally removed and the magazine came under the control of a former presidential spokesman, an important forum for Egyptian secularism was lost. Hamouda is one of the few public figures who brazenly trashes the religious establishment. "Religion simply supports the authorities. *Al-Azhar* [government-backed religious establishment and magazine] told us war in 1967 and peace in 1979. Okay, the Quran is the word of God, but as soon as it's interpreted, it becomes the word of its interpreter," he said (interview with author, *Cairo Times,* 2 October 1997).

now in France. Ben Brik's brother, rights campaigner Jalel Zoghlami, failed to win official approval for a new paper, to be called *Qaws al-Karama* (*Arch of Dignity*). And opposition journalist Sihem Bensedrine resorted to the Internet to publish her newspaper *Kalima* (*Word*), where it joins Egypt's *al-Shaab* in the cyberworld of marginalized Arab media.

The government says it is promoting press freedom as much as possible. In April 2001, the parliament passed a series of amendments to the Press Code, eliminating an ambiguously worded article prohibiting "defaming public order," removing prison penalties for violating advertising regulations and other restrictions, and decreasing the time period for government

Tunisian journalist Taoufik Ben Brik (center) and Reporters Without Borders secretary general Robert Menard (right) in Paris after Ben Brik ended a hunger strike to protest alleged Tunisian government harassment. (AP Photo/François Mori)

suspension of newspapers. In interviews with *as-Sabah* and *al-Shurouq* in May 2001, Ben Ali said: "I will say to you once more loud and clear: Do write on any subject you choose. . . . There are no taboos except what is prohibited by law and press ethics" (Committee for the Protection of Journalists, Tunisia report 2001, www.cpj. org). The authorities say they must defend public figures against bad and sensationalist reporting in Tunisia's still-undeveloped media culture, as well as prevent the temptations of media outlets to go beyond rules of public morality. "The state has created an atmosphere for freedom but not for talking about people's private life," said Mohamed Ben Ezzeddine, head of the state

news agency Tunisian Afrique Presse (interview with author, February 2003). "The aim of the tabloid papers is commercial, not principles—there is no editorial line; they are only after their own interests. I fear that we'll see nudity in papers. We have always been very open but I fear for our morals." Critics say this is just an excuse for covering up the corruption at the center of Tunisia's mini economic miracle of the last decade.

In Syria, government control has been far more obvious, so recent improvements have also been more conspicuous. Two independent papers have made waves since 2000, a satirical weekly called *al-Domari* and an economics weekly called *al-*

Iqtisadiya (*The Economist*). Amid the initial euphoria about press reforms, some hundred requests were submitted to the information ministry for licenses to set up new papers in 2001. But a year later, the country had only about fifteen new publications, most of them concerned with sports, lifestyle, entertainment, and classified advertising. When it first appeared, *al-Domari* was a revelation for ordinary Syrians, who for the first time in years were exposed to ridicule of the bureaucracy, empty government promises, corruption, and even specific ministers. It has made way for the state television's venture into more open programming. Though it is still a far cry from the satirical political publications Syria knew in its liberal age in the 1960s, before the Baath Party took over—such as the famed *al-Mudhik al-Mubki* (roughly translated as "something to make you laugh and cry")—the paper has broken important boundaries in free expression. "We face many official obstacles. But what we have done is break the barrier of fear," said its editor, cartoonist Ali Farzat (interview with author, December 2002).

Farzat's wordless cartoons dominate *al-Domari*. In one, a man sits wearing a medal around his neck, but a thought bubble shows that he wishes it was a roasted chicken. In another, a cartoon cop weeps as he watches a television soap opera. The sad joke is what he ignores just behind him: a bloodied prisoner in chains, implying police brutality. The paper runs headlines not found in the government press, such as these from a recent analysis of Syria's economy: "ministers and the parliament only do paperwork" and "people with degrees cannot find jobs." One exposé criticized a politician's ties to a plan to raze a neighborhood for a new hotel complex, and another detailed bribe-taking among police officers. It was apparently Bashar al-Assad himself who encouraged Farzat to issue the paper, which began life as a satirical pamphlet in left-leaning intellectual circles. Farzat was awarded a major accolade in December 2002, when the Dutch Prince Claus Awards Committee chose him as one of their nine winners of the year for "exceptional achievements in the field of culture and development," a list that included Israeli journalist Amira Hass and Senegalese singer Youssou N'Dour. "Farzat utilises all that he has to hand and takes it as far as possible to create a space for social comment and debate. His pointed caricatures, published in the domestic and foreign press, inspire his readers to reach sincere interpretations of their daily lives and to consider politics, economics and society from new angles," the committee said.

Farzat said that difficulties faced by the paper have worsened. "Our paper is going through difficult stages and our aim now is just to survive. Some people don't like this paper so they place obstacles in our path, both practical and psychological. This paper has no outside or internal funding except its sales. This is enough to show how popular the paper is," he said, adding that the government has obliged the paper to use its official state distributor, limiting its reach, and has prevented state companies from advertising in the weekly. At the same time, Syria's state Arab Advertising Institution (IAA) takes 27 percent of the cost of any advertising, while the distributors take 35 percent of the paper's annual revenue. "This is not a commercial project as much as it is a democratic project to increase the space for constructive criticism," Farzat said. "We are like someone in the bathroom who finds the water is hot one minute and cold the next. We are forced to talk in symbolic terms. Some months we can't talk about certain ministers and some social issues, but we must expect such things." The success of the independent press has shocked the authorities. Despite a print run of 50,000 copies, the official state-owned daily *al-Thawra* is said by informed insiders to sell as little as 4,500 copies a day—in a population of 18 million—and the Beirut-based *al-Kifah al-Arabi* (*The Arab Struggle*) sells more. Farzat said he was printing 100,000 copies himself until the state took over and reduced his print run to 50,000.

Jordan: A Model Press?

The press situation in Jordan, like Saudi Arabia's, is a possible model for other Arab presses, though there are still problems. Jordan has two main Arabic daily newspapers, *al-Rai* (*The Opinion*) and *ad-Dustour* (*The Constitution*), both originally private ventures that are now partly state-owned. The English-language daily *Jordan Times* went through a popularity boom when King Abdullah first came to the throne in 1999, because as a speaker of fluent English he would read it from cover to cover to know what was going on in the country. All dailies speak on behalf of the government or agree with it on major issues. Jordan, like other U.S.-allied Arabic states such as Egypt and Saudi Arabia, has had a difficult time balancing ties to Washington and peace with Israel with popular anger that supports the Palestinians since the second Intifada began in 2000. The invasion in Iraq complicated things further, and the media, like the government, is very

much on the defensive in public debate in the Arab world. For example, the Arab media around the region said the United States would use Jordan to launch part of its attack on Iraq, prompting Jordanian editorial writers and columnists to spring to the government's defense in regional Arabic press wars. The government regards editors in chief as high-ranking state officials, and a number of the editors have indeed held high official offices, such as minister of information. There have been a few failed attempts at independence, such as *al-Arab al-Yawm* (*The Arabs Today*) in 1998 (until the government bought into it), and the English-language *The Arab Daily*, which folded after a few months under financial pressure and mismanagement.

Media laws are prohibitive, with liberal use of prison sentences for crimes of publication, and in general a "press culture" has not developed that allows the industry self-regulation and responsible journalism. "Professionalism is lacking and the government wants more control. If it had been a professional press with ethical standards and commitment to factual reporting, the government would have a less easy time in maintaining control of the media. The political culture is not conducive, but the press is not assertive," said one editor (interview with author, July 2002). The outbreak of the Palestinian uprising put a strain on all aspects of political and economic life in the country. It's always been that way in Jordan to some degree. As the saying goes, Jordan's political culture may not be Sweden's, but then its neighbors are not Norway and Denmark. And when there is death in the West Bank, condolences are paid in Amman. "The whole atmosphere has got tense and this reflects on all aspects of public life, including the press. But moderation is a characteristic of Jordan's political culture. There are not the same deteriorations as in Egypt and Syria, for example. The overall character of public life is moderation and there is no excessive use of methods to restrict freedoms," the editor said.

In 1998, a press and publications law granted the government wide discretionary powers to issue fines, withdraw licenses, and order shutdowns, as well as banning reports on criminal cases or crimes without the consent of the public prosecutor. The law also criminalized, with vague language, media coverage that disparages the royal family or any individual, the armed forces, religion, heads of friendly states, or the national currency. Amendments in 1999 set fines at $700 to $1,400 and also set fees of $700,000 to obtain a license for a daily newspaper and $70,000 to obtain a license for most other publications. In one case, Toujan Faisal, the only woman ever elected to Jordan's parliament, was sentenced to eighteen months in prison in May 2002 for a range of crimes of speech in the press, on the Internet, and at public demonstrations, which in the judge's ruling amounted to incitement to civil disorder and harming Jordan's image abroad. The crimes included telling a pro-Iraq solidarity conference in Baghdad that Jordan's policy toward Iraq "fluctuates like the stock market" between supporting an American attack and supporting Baghdad, and using the Internet to accuse the prime minister of corruption. Journalists and academics have complained of being forced out of their jobs because of their political views, whether pro-Islamist or anti-Israeli. According to a 2001 report by the Euro-Mediterranean Human Rights network on press freedom in Jordan, "until the [1998] law is repealed, Euro-

pean Union officials should closely monitor developments in Jordan." The U.S. State Department report on Jordan for 2001 noted that "during the year, the government broadened its authority to prosecute journalists and close publications" (March 2002). But that's not bad compared to the rest of the Arab press.

Cartoonists—Bearers of a Noble Tradition in the Arab Press

Cartoons in the Arab world are politicized, and because illiteracy and censorship of the written word are still widespread in the region, cartoonists are accorded great importance in Arab popular culture. As with many journalists, cartoonists have paid for their work with their lives. Palestinian cartoonist Naji al-Ali was murdered in London in 1987 (theories on the perpetrators vary from the PLO to Israel to the Saudis). To this day he is marginalized in Egypt's educational curriculum because of his bitter cartoon attacks on former president Anwar Sadat and his peace treaty with Israel. The Egyptian government has periodically raised the issue of withdrawing Mohammed Hakim's Egyptian nationality on the grounds that he is really Sudanese as a means of pressuring him over his work in the leftist weekly *al-Ahali*. And Essam Hanafi of the Islamist *al-Shaab* was in and out of prison for his contributions to the paper's attacks on government ministers until the paper was banned in 2000.

The daily papers all have cartoonists who draw a wide public. *Al-Hayat*'s Gomala has adopted the figure of the cartoonist Kahil, a moustached man with a globe for a head, who is meant to represent the Arab world or "Johnny Arab" and his many regional worries. The figure appears in national press cartoons throughout the region. Palestinian cartoonist Naji al-Ali made famous the small refugee boy called Handaleh, who showed how the little guy in Palestine was always the victim of big politics. Amr Okasha of Egypt's opposition *al-Wafd* newspaper has made an impression on public consciousness with his constant ridicule of Egypt's parliamentary democracy, including touches such as a limelight-hogging female TV presenter, who asks a citizen a question holding a huge microphone in one hand but stuffing the other hand in the clueless citizen's mouth to stop him from saying something for himself. Here the message and the accompanying caption are as important as the image presented (despite the cartoonist's limited ability as a caricaturist). Many cartoonists forgo sophistication for simplicity: uneducated people are unfamiliar with things like perspective and shading, leading to some bizarre misunderstandings. Egypt's popular Mustafa Hussein once experimented with the idea of characters who have shadows: "I had to stop. People thought they had wet themselves" (Negus, "The Character Assassin," *Cairo Times*, 29 May 1997). Many of the biggest names have only limited outlets and elite audiences, such as Egypt's Golo and Mohieddin al-Labbad, Iraq's Mu'ayyid Ne'ma, and Syria's Yousef Abdalki. Cartoonists who appear in the daily papers generally honor the taboo against caricaturing their leaders, which helps keep them to some degree immune to the unpopularity of their government's policies. Other well-known cartoonists around the region include George Bahgoury, Gomaa Farahat, and Ahmed Hegazy in Egypt; al-Arabi al-Sabban in Morocco; al-Zawawy in Libya; and Algeria's

Qasi Said and Ali Dilem (the latter recently had trouble with the government over cartoons implying corruption among the military).

Mustafa Hussein is probably Egypt's most famous contemporary cartoonist. Since 1974 he has worked with partner Ahmed Ragab, who comes up with the jokes, on the state-owned daily *al-Akhbar* and its weekly version *Akhbar al-Youm* (*The News of Today*). Since the death of the multitalented Salah Jahine in 1986, he has inherited a mantle as Egypt's most senior cartoonist. For the most part the Hussein-Ragab duo target Egyptian society, its corruption, and its poverty. Their main characters are not sympathetic. "To be honest, a few of them are real bastards," Hussein once admitted (*Cairo Times*, 29 May 1997). Perhaps their most famous is Abdel-Routine, the archetypal government employee, incapable of getting anything done unless it comes with three stamps and four signatures. Another favorite is Ali al-Komanda, a snazzily dressed government spokesman who specializes in saying nothing in as many fancy words as possible, including the made-up words *dikhooma* and *dikheima* ("this-here" and "that-there"). Kuheita is the pair's dirt-poor good-for-nothing, happy in his poverty and with his head in the clouds, who is often invited over for drinks and a cigar by another Hussein-Ragab classic, Aziz al-Elite, the self-obsessed snob utterly unaware of the people's suffering. Hussein's only vaguely sympathetic characters are to be found in his "civil servants' café," where state secretaries and desk jotter-blotters, half-naked and starved on paltry government salaries, sit all day doing nothing but debating such trivialities as whether *Lahma* (meat) is a football player, a minister, or what.

A to Z: Key People and Publications

AB'AAD
Lebanese intellectual quarterly.

ABWAAB
London-based literary and intellectual periodical published by Dar al-Saqi, a London- and Beirut-based publishing house.

AL-ADAB
Lebanese literary monthly, which tries to introduce Arabic readers to new literary styles and trends abroad.

ADAB WA NAQD
Cultural weekly published by Egypt's leftist Tagammu Party.

AL-AHALI
Weekly paper published by Egypt's opposition Tagammu Party. www.alahali.com

AL-AHRAM
Egypt's state-owned flagship daily. www.ahram.org.eg

AL-AHRAM HEBDO
French-language weekly produced by Egypt's al-Ahram publishing house. www.ahram.org.eg/hebdo

AL-AHRAM WEEKLY
English-language weekly produced by Egypt's al-Ahram publishing house. www.ahram.org.eg/weekly

AL-AHRAR
The daily mouthpiece of Egypt's opposition Liberal Party.

AKHBAR AL-ADAB
Cultural weekly issued by Egypt's state-owned Akhbar al-Youm publishing house. www.akhbarelyom.org.eg/adab

AKHBAR AL-HAWADETH (CRIME NEWS)
Popular blood-and-guts weekly produced by Egypt's *Akhbar al-Youm*. www.akhbarelyom.org.eg/hawadeth

AL-ALI, NAJI
Palestinian cartoonist murdered in London in 1987, most likely for his cartoon depictions of the plight of Palestinians.

ARAB NEWS
Leading English-language publication in Saudi Arabia striving for wider regional market share among English-language papers. www.arabnews.com

ARABESQUE
Bimonthly journal on Middle East dance and culture. www.arabesquejournal.com

AL-ARABI
Weekly mouthpiece of the opposition Nasserist Party in Egypt and a sensational-

ist regime-baiter, regarded by the government as "irresponsible" opposition.

AL-ARABI
Kuwaiti cultural monthly.

ASHARQ AL-AWSAT
London-based, Saudi-owned, pan-Arabic daily. www.asharqalawsat.com

ASSABAH
Tunisia's main Arabic-language daily.

AZZAMAN
Iraq's main independent daily, run by businessman Saad al-Bazzaz www.azzaman.com

BABEL (BABYLON)
The main Iraqi daily, owned by Uday Saddam Hussein, son of the Iraqi president, before the regime was brought down in 2003.

AL-BAHITHAAT (THE WOMEN RESEARCHERS)
Lebanon-based publication with a focus on women writers, which aims to transcend gender divides in Arab culture.

AL-BAHRAIN AL-THAQAFIYYA
Bahraini arts and culture journal.

BIDOUN
New York–based cultural quarterly about the Middle East and its diaspora artists in various fields in the West. www.bidoun.com

CAIRO TIMES
Leading independent Egyptian English-language weekly, established circa 1997, and pushing a liberal pro-democracy line. www.cairotimes.com

DAILY STAR
English-language daily in Lebanon. www.dailystar.com.lb

AL-DESTOUR
Popular Egyptian opposition weekly, whose sensationalist nationalist tone led to its closure in 1998.

AL-DOMARI
Syrian political-satirical weekly started by cartoonist Ali Farzat in 2001. Named after the man who would light the way with a lantern in the dark streets of premodern Syria.

AD-DUSTOUR
One of the main Jordanian dailies. www.addustour.com

L'ECONOMISTE
Moroccan paper that began as a business weekly in 1991. It has been a daily since 1998 and now covers political and economic news. www.leconomiste.com

EXECUTIVE

Lebanese monthly business magazine in English.

GULF NEWS

Main English-language daily in the UAE. www.gulf-news.com

HABIBI

A journal of Middle East dance and arts. www.habibimagazine.com

HANDALEH

A Palestinian refugee child created by famed Palestinian political cartoonist Naji al-Ali. The name means "bitter gourd," an allusion to the bitterness of the refugee experience. Ali, assassinated in London in 1987, was considered to be a supporter of the Popular Front for the Liberation of Palestine (PFLP), and his Handaleh image became a kind of cult symbol of the Palestinian Left.

AL-HAYAT

The foremost pan-Arab daily, which also has an English-language Web site. It is now London-based and Saudi-owned, but it began life in Beirut in 1946. Its reporters now work in alliance with satellite channel LBC. www.daralhayat.com

HEIKAL, MOHAMMED HASSANEIN

As Egypt's most famous living journalist, Heikal was Nasser's right-hand man. Though he is still today Nasser's main apologist, Heikal is accorded enormous respect around the region as a political writer of distinction. He is regarded as having pioneered investigative reporting in the Arab world as editor of *al-Ahram* in the 1960s.

AL-HILAL

Monthly intellectual magazine produced by Egypt's state-owned al-Hilal publishing house.

HUSSEIN, MUSTAFA

Egypt's best-known cartoonist, the daily scribbler in the *al-Akhbar* newspaper.

AL-IJTIHAD

Intellectual quarterly based in Beirut, edited by Islamic studies academic Ridwan al-Sayyid.

ISSA, SALAH

One of Egypt's most humorous but sober political columnists, whose column titled *Mushaaghabaat* (*Hooliganisms*) appears in various papers. He is editor of the cultural weekly *al-Qahira* (*Cairo*).

JERUSALEM REPORT

Israeli publication concerned with Jewish, Israeli, and Middle East affairs. www.jrep.com

JORDAN TIMES

Jordanian English-language daily. www.jordantimes.com

AL-KARMAL

Palestinian cultural quarterly, produced in Ramallah under direction of its chief editor, Palestinian poet Mahmoud Darwish.

KHARTOUM MONITOR

Sudanese daily set up in 2000 by south Sudanese in Khartoum, aimed mainly at the city's large south Sudanese community and expatriates.

AL-KHAZEN, JIHAD

Lebanese former editor of *al-Hayat*, where he now has a prominent column.

AL-KUTUB: WUJHAT NAZAR

Egypt's premier monthly review of books.

AL-LIWA AL-ISLAMI

Islamic weekly issued by Egypt's ruling National Democratic Party.

AL-MAJALLA (*THE MAGAZINE*)

A Saudi weekly magazine aimed at the whole Arab world, published in London by the Asharq al-Awsat group.

MASHAREF

Palestinian literary periodical based in the Israeli city of Haifa. Set up by late writer Emile Habibi and currently edited by Siham Dawoud, it is one of the few intellectual forums where Israeli and Arab culture come together.

THE MIDDLE EAST

London-based monthly on Middle East affairs.

MIDDLE EAST INTERNATIONAL

Fortnightly journal on Middle East affairs. www.meionline.com

MIDDLE EAST TIMES

Cairo-based English-language weekly. www.metimes.com

MU'ALLIM, IBRAHIM

Head of the Arab Publishers Union, based in Cairo.

NAFIE, IBRAHIM

Head of the Egyptian publishing house al-Ahram and editor of its main paper, the daily *al-Ahram*.

AL-NAHAR

Lebanon's main Arabic daily. www. annahar.com.lb

OKAZ

One of the main Saudi dailies. It is named after a famous pre-Islamic custom of regular poetry reading and debating among tribes living in western Arabia—an early form of political forum. www.okaz.com.sa

AL-OSBOA (*THE WEEK*)

Independent Egyptian weekly run by

Nasserist firebrand Mustafa Bakry, a favorite talking head on Arab satellite channels, along with Abdel-Bari Atwan, the Palestinian editor of *al-Quds al-Arabi*.

QANTARA

French intellectual and literary quarterly published in Paris by the Arab World Institute.

AL-QUDS AL-ARABI

Palestinian émigré daily produced in London. www.alquds.co.uk

RAGAB, SAMIR

Editor of Egypt's semi-official daily *al-Gomhouriya*, Ragab, with his daily column, is one of Egypt's most infamous columnists. He has a unique, flowery style that Mubarak once said was one of his personal favorites, and he is seen as a regime stalwart.

AL-RAI

One of Jordan's main dailies. www.alrai.com

AL-RIYADH

The main daily in Saudi Arabia, run by businessmen with close ties to the monarchy. www.alriyadh.com.sa

ROSE AL-YOUSEF

Egyptian magazine founded in 1925 by an entertainer named Fatima al-Yousef, who then went on to become the Arab world's pioneer in opposition journalism. It was nationalized with the rest of Egypt's press by Nasser, then became a leftist center of criticism of Sadat in the 1970s, before reinvention once again as a sensationalist political tabloid in the 1990s.

AL-SAFIR

One of Lebanon's leading Arabic dailies. www.alsafir.com

SALAMA, SALAMA AHMED

One of the most respected of the numerous daily columnists, or op-ed writers, in Egypt, appearing in *al-Ahram*.

SAWT AL-UMMA (*VOICE OF THE NATION*)

Egyptian weekly paper run by Adel Hamouda, Egypt's tabloid king who transformed the fortunes of *Rose al-Yousef* magazine in the 1990s.

AL-SHAAB

The paper of Egypt's opposition Labor Party, suspended by the government in 2000 after it was accused of inciting a riot over an allegedly blasphemous novel. Now it publishes exclusively online, where it has to be careful—Egypt prosecutes for Internet crime. www.alshaab.com

SOTOUR

Cultural monthly published in Cairo.

AL-TARIK

Intellectual Lebanese bimonthly journal, edited by Mohammad Dakroub. www.afric-asia.com/themiddleeast/index.php

LE TEMPS

Tunisia's main French-language daily.

TISHREEN

The main Arabic daily in Syria, state-owned.

AL-WAFD

Egypt's main opposition paper, the daily *al-Wafd*, is the mouthpiece of the Wafd Party, named after the delegation of nationalist leaders who petitioned Britain for independence after the First World War. www.alwafd.org

AL-WASAT (*THE CENTER*)

The respected weekly political magazine of *al-Hayat*.

AL-WATAN (*THE NATION*)

Saudi paper based in Jeddah, which is leading calls for political reform in the kingdom and envisions Saudi Arabia as leading the Arab world into a new era of sobriety and modernization. Texts and cartoons argued for a more relaxed, enlightened, and inclusive form of Islam than that championed by the Wahhabi religious establishment. Well-known political analyst Jamal Khashoggi was sacked by the government in May 2003 after two months editing the paper, when he pushed the limits of criticism in the kingdom. www.alwatan.com.sa

AL-ZAHF AL-AKHDAR

Main Libyan paper whose name, "the green march," refers to Gaddafi's "green" revolution.

AL-ZAWAYA

A new cultural bimonthly issued in Beirut.

Bibliography

Print Resources

"The Character Assassin." *Cairo Times*, 29 May 1997.

al-Ghaity, Mohammed. *A Scandal Called Saida Sultana.* Cairo: Dar al-Gumhouriya, 1996.

Henry, Clement M., and Robert Springborg. *Globalization and the Politics of Development in the Middle East.* Cambridge: Cambridge University Press, 2001.

Al-Karikatir wa Huqouq al-Insan (Cartoons and Human Rights). Cairo: AOHR/ UNESCO/Egyptian Cartoonists Association/ Dar al-Mustaqbal al-Arabi, 1990.

Khazen, Jihad. "Censorship and State Control of the Press in the Arab World." *Harvard International Journal of Press Politics* 4.3 (1999): 87–92.

Mostyn, Trevor. *Censorship in Islamic Societies.* London: Saqi Books, 2002.

Negus, Steve. "The Character Assassin." *Cairo Times*, 29 May 1997.

Tunisian Human Rights League Report, 30 April 2004.

Web Sites

mahjoob.com/index.php. Site of Palestinian cartoonist Emad Hajjaj.

www.al-bab.com/media/freedom.htm. Al-bab's special section on media freedom in the Arab world.

www.state.gov/g/drl/rls/hrrpt/2003/nea. U.S. State Department's annual human rights report on countries in the region, including press freedoms.

www.pmwatch.org/awi/. Site of Algeria Watch International.

www.cpj.org. Site of a watchdog group, the Committee for the Protection of Journalists.

www.marweb.net. Site with news from North African countries.

www.mees.com/dotcom/newspapers/index.html. *The Middle East Economic Survey*'s press directory.

http://meionline.com. Web site of the journal *Middle East International*, a fortnightly journal.

www.merip.org. Site of the U.S.-based Middle East Research and Information Project.

www.indexonline.org. Web site of the journal *Index on Censorship*.

www.rsf.fr. Site of media watchdog Journalists Without Borders.

www.cafsco.nl. Netherlands-based organization working to promote independent press in the developing world.

www.meed.com. Site of the *Middle East Economic Digest* (MEED), a business weekly.

www.haaretzdaily.com. The English-language Web site of Israel's main daily paper.

www.iraqiwriter.com. List of Web sites of Iraqi newspapers and Iraqi organizations, run by a group of Iraqi writers and artists, who also run the Web site.

4

The Cinema Industry

The Emergence of Arab Cinema in the Early Twentieth Century

Cinema has a hallowed place in Arab culture, in both a physical and metaphysical sense. The huge billboards that dominate the urban landscape in a city like Cairo are a reflection of the space cinema occupies in the cultural psyche of the Arab world. But cinema is also part of the idea of a golden era of Arab culture that is, in turn, inextricably bound up with the aggressive march of Arab nationalism in the mid-twentieth century. Today's cinema is unfavorably compared to the works of that era, and along with color film is seen as the emergence of a crass commercial cinema. The media today also propounds the idea that the black-and-white era was somehow more moral, though in fact it was more sexually liberal than today's cinema. Observers have pointed out that, in the past, the industry was peopled by elite sectors of society that have since been weakened by the national-socialist policies of Arab regimes like that of Abdel Nasser. As Palestinian director Michel Khleifi told the arts show *al-Mubdi'un* (*Creative People*): "When the cosmopolitan communities left Egypt under the Nasserist experience Egyptian cinema became weak. Whereas before it was one of the best in the world" (Abu Dhabi TV, June 2002).

Film as a medium was invented in the West, and Arab cinema has often been criticized as evidence of Westernization. Cinema was one target of armed Algerian-Islamist groups in the 1990s. One of the last films made in Algeria, Merzak Allouache's *Bab el-Oued* (named after an old poor district of Algiers), which dealt with the issue of Westernization, was shot under difficult conditions in Algiers in 1994. Yet, as with many other facets of the industrial West imported into the region, the cinematic form was repackaged and made relevant to the cultural realities and requirements of the Arab setting. Public cinema screenings have been forbidden in Saudi Arabia for over two decades, and a taboo exists on portraying the Prophet or the first four so-called righteously guided caliphs (actor Yousef Wahbi's ill-fated plan to portray the Prophet Mo-

A series of billboard posters for foreign and Arabic films in Luxor, Egypt. (TRIP/Art Directors)

hammed on screen in 1930 partly explains his muted presence in today's cultural canon of cinema "greats"). At the same time, commentators with a secular nationalist outlook often present the existence and health of the cinema as a benchmark of the region's success or modernization, as a sign of keeping up with the pace of the West and maintaining a sense of cultural self-respect in the globalized world.

Egypt was the country that was best placed to produce its own version of the West's cinema, partly because its relationship with the British colonial masters was less restrictive to indigenous culture than the relations of other countries in the region with French authorities. Short, silent, and full-length films were made in Egypt, Tunisia, and Syria in the 1920s, but Egyptian entrepreneurs worked hard to see that an independent national industry developed in Egypt. It was partly Egypt's head start that led to the distribution of Egyptian films and awareness of Egyptian dialect all over the region. Indigenous industries elsewhere were later to make use of Egyptian technical and directing expertise. They adopted genres of melodramatic movies and musicals (with their origin in nineteenth-century shadow plays) that Egyptian cinema made popular, and even used Egyptian dialect, as happened in many Lebanese films up until the civil war broke out in 1975. Viola Shafik notes in her study of Arab cinema that although Algeria had more cinema houses than Egypt in 1933, not a single film was made by a native Algerian director before independence in 1962 (Shafik 1998). In the 1940s France set up various studios in North Africa to counter Egypt's indigenous and Arab-nationalizing cinema. In fact, a debate rages today over whether North African cinema has truly removed its colonial shackles, since much of its production is French-funded and/or directed by French-educated directors, and the themes dealt with seem to reflect European perspectives on indigenous culture. The public, meanwhile, often votes with its feet and heads for the Egyptian films.

From the 1970s to the mid-1990s, the Egyptian-led Arab cinema was in decline. Without the drive of the nationalist period, the region's unreformed economic and political systems militated against thriving cinema industries. Ironically, nationalization of the film studios killed creativity. Lebanon's fifteen-year civil war and Iraq's woes since it entered war with Iran in 1980 squashed their industries. Egyptian cinema found a new niche in the 1980s with the so-called contract films, made with little expense at the behest of wealthy Saudi entrepreneurs, featuring formulaic, bawdy humor for video distribution to Gulf Arab audiences. But the general trend over the period was a drop in production while television culture took off, driven by video ownership in the 1980s and the satellite boom in the 1990s. In the late 1980s, Egypt was still making sixty films a year, but by the mid-1990s production had dropped to only around twenty or twenty-five a year. By contrast, Iran, with a population size similar to that of Egypt, produces up to sixty films a year and has over three hundred cinema houses. Still, Egyptian cinema has witnessed a revival, via "low-culture" blockbuster comedies that have made huge stars of some young actors. These films are formulaic and heavily panned by critics, but they have nevertheless tapped into a desire among the burgeoning younger generation for new faces and films that deal with the realities of today's youth. These films bring in huge audiences and profits,

but the number of productions annually is still low, and it sunk lower after the Iraq war dealt a further blow to the economy. The industry also remains shackled by a corrupt star system dominated by a small clique of actors and directors, which acts to stifle talent and limit the types of films produced. Age is no limit to stars' longevity—their age is simply kept a closely guarded secret, masked by toupees and plastic surgery, unlike in the West where actors' ages are exposed in the press. The main tendency in Egyptian cinema is to deliver what one critic called "tawdry treatment of desire," the result of which is that film perpetuates the very social malaise its makers often claim to remedy (El-Bishlawi "Matrimony of Extremes," *al-Ahram Weekly*, 3–9 May 2001).

Globalization is also making inroads in the cinema. The topics dealt with are diversifying and reflect the region's increased and deeper contact with life beyond the Arab world, or at least show the region struggling with the challenges of globalization. There has been a wave of films about political figures, sexual issues, and America. In 1998's *An Upper Egyptian at the American University* (Sa'idi fil-Gami'a al-Amrikiya), comic star Mohammed Heneidy learns that the Westernized elites haven't lost their nationalist spirit. In 2001's *Days of Sadat* (Ayyam al-Sadat), the first-ever treatment of the Egyptian leader who became the first Arab to make peace with Israel encourages the viewer to see Sadat as a wise visionary. Most local industries have broken free of their reliance on Egyptian cinema. In fact, some of the region's alternative identities have managed to show through as well: in the last decade, Berber-language films have been released in France, such as Algerian Belkacem Hajjaj's

1995 film *Machaho*, and in 1993, Iraqi Kurd Ibrahim Salman directed *A Silent Traveller*. Saudi female director Haifaa Mansour managed to write and direct three short films (2003's *The Only Way Out* received a special mention at the 2004 Rotterdam Film Festival) that deal with Saudi Arabia's domestic problems, despite the lack of a cinema industry in that country. But apart from a few exceptions, such as the films of Tunisian director Ferid Boughedir, Arab cinema is yet to develop a language that speaks at once to an indigenous public and a global audience, in the way that Iranian cinema has managed in recent years. Arab cinema survives, then, but in a different form from its heyday: in general, smaller and with less Egyptian dominance, but with clearly defined national industries in the movie-producing countries of the region.

Arab Cinematic Language since the Swinging Sixties

Despite globalization, there remains a basic difference of emphasis in the elements that are important in Western and Arabic films. When celebrated American actor John Malkovich headed the judging committee at the 1998 Cairo International Film Festival he publicly criticized Arabic films, with particularly harsh words for one Syrian film ("The Accidental Patron: I Owe It All to Cairo," *New York Times*, 9 January 2000). Although by the technical standards of most Western films, Abdel-Latif Abdel-Hamid's 1998 *Nasim al-Ruh* (*Breeze of the Soul*) was an inferior adventure in celluloid, in terms of content it was a charming film, very much rooted in the concerns of Arab culture, personal relationships, and music. "It had a real human spirit," said

Syrian actress Raghda (interview with author, *Cairo Times*, 28 April 1999).

Those films that speak a global language often get mixed reactions at home. A 1998 movie by young Lebanese director Ziad Doueiri, *West Beirut* (*Bayrout al-Gharbiya*), became the first Arabic-language film to have a general release in North America. But it didn't get a general release in Cairo and fared poorly when shown in Beirut. The film focuses on two teenagers growing up in Beirut during the civil war, and the acting and colloquial language are convincing in a way rarely achieved by mainstream Arab cinema. It manages to be politically subversive in showing the teenagers' disregard for the ways that political and religious realities supposedly circumscribe the lives of all those caught in the conflict. The Egyptian viewers who got a chance to see the film at the 1998 Cairo International Film Festival gasped, giggled, and were obviously enchanted. According to Egypt's film censor at the time, Ali Abu Shadi: "People can like many things, but they will still walk out of a film like that and say confidently that it shouldn't be shown in public. It's a form of schizophrenia, but it's a natural, inherited instinct in this culture. It touches on a very fundamental problem we have in this culture" (interview with author, *Cairo Times*, 22 July 1999). Censorship has had a minor effect in Lebanon, where things are generally looser than in Egypt: security police forced forty minutes of cuts in Randa Shahal Sabbagh's *Civilisées* because of representations of militia fighters engaging in mindless violence during the civil war. In neighboring Syria, director Mohammed Ali Atassi got away with portraying veteran dissident Riyadh al-Turk after his release in 2001 with *Ibn al-Aam* (*The Cousin*), but

Riyadh was soon reincarcerated over demands for political reform.

Censors are as much prisoners of public taste as they are arbiters of what the public ought and ought not see. Tunisia's relative liberalism is a "political decision," as Abu Shadi puts it, and the corollary is that there's absolutely no margin for politics. "In Egypt it's the opposite. There's quite a lot of freedom to discuss political issues, but sex is always a problem. The law forbids nudity and lovemaking in a big way," Abu Shadi said (interview with author, *Cairo Times*, 22 July 1999). Egypt's stricter moral code in cinema is part of the state's attempt to appease religious conservatism, recognized as a powerful force in society. "This trend [political Islam] is there, and we can't deny its existence, so we have to appease this part of our public," Abu Shadi said. He hopes that Egypt will ultimately return to the liberal standards of the 1960s. Until then, in his view, Arabs and the rest of the world collectively had the right balance between modesty and freedom in cinema. An Islamist critique would label the period before the 1960s as a postcolonial aberration in the Arab world, but for Abu Shadi and other members of the secular-nationalist intelligentsia it was a veritable time of renaissance, led by Egypt. "It was a time of freedom in the arts, but at the same time, there was no nakedness, for example. We were moving in the same direction as the rest of the world then," he said. But this renaissance was ruined in the Arab world by the discrediting of secular Arab nationalism and in the West by the sexual revolution—both major events of the 1960s. And if the arts in the Arab world need some loosening up today, in the West they need to reacquire a sense of limits, Abu Shadi argues. "We will never go too far, as they

have done in the West," he said. "Here maybe we can get back to where we were in the 1960s, but even that's being ambitious" (interview with author, *Cairo Times*, 22 July 1999).

Egyptian director Inas al-Degheidy has turned this whole debate on its head. After a run of films seen as defending women's rights, she cast two serious actors in her 1996 film *Istakoza* (*Lobster*), a Benny Hill–style, bawdy comedy, filled with cleavage shots and featuring the lead actor, Ahmed Zaki, exploding with desire for the actress Raghda. The movie came off as an attempt to titillate male audiences, but from a supposedly feminist director. Those involved heartily defend it. "I love that film and I'm really proud of it," says Raghda (interview with author, *Cairo Times*, 28 April 1999). "It doesn't work the mind. Partly it shocked people because it was me and Ahmed Zaki, two actors who critics expected something heavy from. But the public liked it." According to Degheidy, "I was saying that manliness is not located in the male organ but in other things, like love and affection. That was the idea. A relationship between a man and woman isn't just sex" (*Cairo Times*, 9 December 1999). Neither audiences nor critics saw it that way, and Degheidy has come to be seen as just another commercial director using sex to bring the masses to the cinema houses. "Maybe people didn't get it," she says of *Istakoza*'s message. Degheidy might perhaps be considered the Arab world's only truly libertarian director, a woman guided by anger at society for imposing an inhibiting moral code and who would happily break all the taboos if she thought she could get away with it. "What is daring in my films is that they are different from others. I don't recognise the word '*ayb* [shame] in art.

Islam on Film

The history of early Islam is fairly rollicking stuff, but it has received far less attention in the English-language world than Christianity or Judaism. The first feature-length film of the story of the Prophet's mission to spread the message of Islam was Mustapha al-Akkad's *al-Risala* (*The Message*) in 1976, shot in Arabic and in English. Mainstream Sunni Islam prevents depiction in any form of the main figures of early Islam in order to discourage their idolization, which would run counter to the monotheistic spirit of the religion (depictions of Ali, the Prophet's cousin and central figure of Shi'ite Islam, are common among Shi'ites). So Akkad had to tell the story while keeping central characters like Mohammed, his wife Khadija, his cousin Ali, and the first caliph Abu Bakr, as well as other, more minor figures. The viewer hears the voices of Mohammed and Ali, accompanied by their shadows, and views scenes from their perspectives, but they are kept out of the frame. Akkad's other technique was to boost the role of Hamza, the Prophet's uncle and one of the first converts, casting Anthony Quinn for the part.

In 2002, British Disney animator Richard Roth tackled the same subject again, but as an animated feature. No stranger to the biblical epic, Roth previously directed *Joseph in Egypt* (1992), *Abraham and Isaac* (1992), *Moses* (1993), and *Joseph's Reunion* (1995). But with *Mohamed, the Last of the Prophets,* Roth faced the additional obstacle of having to keep Hamza off screen because of a ruling by Egypt's al-Azhar. But the production came at a time when Islam as a radical and violent force was the prevailing image in the West, after the September 11 attacks. The film acts as a corrective, emphasizing the element of social justice in the message of peace that Mohammed brought to the Arabian Peninsula. The ruling elite of Mecca are portrayed as a rapacious capitalist class who promote pagan cults and are cruel to women and the poor, beat their slaves, fleece pilgrims, and drink heavily. Battles are presented as self-defense and not proselytizing acts. The film, however, failed to make waves, possibly because it was done in the cartoon format, though its makers likely hoped they could follow Disney's string of successes throughout the 1990s.

Unfortunately, people are judging art as *'ayb, haram* [morally wrong], *halal* [morally right], God said this, God didn't say that. I have faith, but cinema has nothing to do with religion. Religion is one thing, art is another. The artist should be able to realize everything that he imagines. . . . There are many things I'd like to be able to do," she says; with society as it is, she can't (*Cairo Times*, 28 April 1999).

Censors are under constant pressure from society at large. In 1995 Egyptian actress Yousra was taken to court over a scene in *Tuyour al-Zalam* (*Birds of Darkness*) because her bare legs offended an Islamist fundamentalist sheikh, Yousef al-Badri. Two years later, Egyptian actress Maali Zayed received a prison sentence because a bedroom scene in the film *Abu Dahab* (1996) disgusted a member of the public who saw it with his little boy. In Morocco, attempts begun in the early 1990s by director Abdel-Qader Laqtaa to portray sexual relationships have come up against problems. There was a ruckus over Laqtaa's 1991 film *Love in Casablanca* (*al-Hubb fi al-Dar al-Bayda*) because an actress was shown in a nightgown; over

A billboard poster in Cairo for a film starring popular Egyptian actress Yousra. (TRIP/Art Directors)

Mohamed Lotfi's 1995's *Rhesus* (known in Arabic as *Dam al-Akhir*, or Blood of the Other) because of French kissing; and Laqtaa's 1995 film *al-Bab al-Masdoud* (*The Closed Door*) was banned because of a scene in which a couple make love. The extent of kissing and cuddling in Egyptian films is seen as highly risqué in Morocco. Islamists in Morocco forced Yousef Chahine's 1995 *al-Muhagir* (*The Emigrant*) to be pulled from screens because it depicted a Muslim prophet; the film was for a while banned in Egypt for the same reason.

Politics has also imposed cruel realities on the Arab cinema. The establishment of the State of Israel and subsequent exodus of Jewish communities in the Arab world to the new state—which climaxed in Egypt after the 1956 Suez War—ruined the career of Leila Murad because she was born a Jew. A conversion to Islam after marriage to ac-

tor Anwar Wagdy didn't help. Wagdy subsequently left her for actress Leila Fawzy. After Suez, Murad retired at the age of thirty-eight. She died penniless and ignored in Cairo in 1996, despite the fact that her films and their immortal songs of grace, innocence, and hope are still regularly shown on TV as classics of Arab cinema. She reportedly turned down numerous offers to quit the Arab world for Israel and become a Jewish Umm Kalthoum, presumably in Hebrew. Similarly, Soad Hosni, the most beautiful and diverse of the "Golden Age" actresses, committed suicide in 2001 in London at age fifty-eight, a forgotten, drunken recluse. She appeared to have thrown herself from her apartment balcony, but the Egyptian media suspected something more sinister, since Hosni, like other actresses, had been caught up in the heady world of intelligence agencies in the 1960s and many officials from that era hold high positions of power today. Comedian Ismail Yassin died a pauper in 1972, pursued by tax authorities and banned on television. Shadi Abdel-Salam died in 1986 without managing to shoot a follow-up to his 1969 masterpiece *The Mummy* (*al-Mumyaa'*), because producers who had no desire to see serious and intellectual cinema develop and thrive denied him funding. As cinema moved out of its Golden Age, a few directors, such as Kamal al-Shaykh, tried to fight the prevailing penchant for plots descending into farce and slapstick, a constant stream of dialogue, and song-and-dance routines. Farce has become so much the norm in Egyptian cinema that no one knows anymore if art is reflecting life or life is reflecting art. Few stars of the Golden Age have survived with their careers intact. The only director still producing films is Chahine, though his later attempts to critique fundamentist Islam have been seen as lavish flops: *al-Masir* (*Destiny*), 1997, and *al-Akhar* (*The Other*), 1999. His autobiographical trilogy—*Iskandariya Leih?* (*Alexandria Why?*), 1979; *Hadouta Misriya* (*An Egyptian Tale*), 1982; *Iskandariya Kaman wa Kaman* (*Alexandria Again and Again*), 1989—was pilloried for being self-indulgent. His acclaimed 1991 twenty-minute documentary, *al-Qahira Munawwara bi-Ahliha* (*Cairo Lit Up by Its People*), was banned by censors after Chahine refused to excise scenes of Cairo poverty and religious zeal.

In another sign of the times, the movie world has seen the phenomenon of female actresses retiring from the industry and taking the veil, in "repentance" for their sinful days looking pretty on camera. The wave began in the late 1970s, when the Islamist trend was growing in many Arab countries, with Syrian actress Shams al-Baroudy, star of the famous 1973 risqué film *Hammam al-Malatily* (*The Malatily Bathhouse*). Then followed Golden Age actress Shadia in the mid-1980s, and a host of others in her wake: dancer Sahar Hamdy; singers Mona Abdel-Ghani and Hanan; actresses Shahira, Hoda Ramzy, Suhair al-Bably, and Abeer al-Sharqawy; Syrian actresses Hanaa Tharwat and Nisreen; and another Golden Age actress, Zubayda Tharwat. Since 2000, a few more Egyptian actresses have taken the veil for periods of time—young actresses Mona Lisa, Ghada Adel, Abeer Sabry, Myrna al-Mohandis, and Wafa Amer and the older actress Sabreen —and this recent wave has coincided with the mass emotion stirred by the Palestinian uprising against Israeli occupation. Some took the veil and then disposed of it in well-publicized returns to the limelight, including actresses Sawsan Badr and Farida Seif al-Nasr. Singer Yasmeen Khayam, daughter of the famous Egyptian preacher Sheikh al-Hosary, cast off her veil in the 1980s only to put it on again. Some men have "repented" too, such as the Egyptian, "B"-rated soap actor Mahmoud al-Gindy, who now does television interviews in the white robes of a pilgrim to Mecca.

Omar Sharif, the only Arab actor who moved from the Golden Age to global stardom, is an odd case. He is back in Egypt now, but rarely acts. When he misspoke while receiving a special award at the 1999 Cairo International Film Festival, unintentionally saying he was "artificial" as opposed to "touched" (*mufta'al* instead of *munfa'il*), it was taken in some press quarters as proof that he was no longer an authentic Egyptian since life with the foreigners had ruined his Arabic. Since his role opposite American Jew Barbra Streisand in

Funny Girl, his opinions on the Arab-Israeli conflict have been regarded as suspect back in Egypt. He was in trouble in the media again in 2004 after he joked to *Time* magazine that he was working on ensuring that his Muslim granddaughter grew up "not to have any religion" at all while he had given his oldest grandson "the biggest bar mitzvah ever" (*Time*, 8 December 2003), provoking a scathing attack in Egypt's main daily *al-Ahram*, though he was feted on al-Jazeera later in the year. Overall, 2004 was a good year for Sharif: he won best actor in France's prestigious César Awards for his role as a Muslim shopkeeper in 2003's *Monsieur Ibrahim*, directed by François Dupeyron, where he befriends and becomes a spiritual father to a young Jewish boy who frequents prostitutes, and starred in the Hollywood epic *Hidalgo* (directed by Joe Johnston, 2004). No one emulated his Hollywood success and few even tried to follow in his footsteps (Lebanon's Madeleine Tobar made an attempt in the 1980s before settling for fame in Egyptian soaps today). Sharif appears more than a little sad to have given up Egyptian cinema for glamour in the West, which by his own admission left him empty and unfulfilled. It's a line that plays well. When he first made his permanent return to Egypt, Sharif appeared on television commercials for stylish home floor tiles, in which he tells Yousra, regarded as Egypt's most classy female actress today, with dramatic poise and intensity: "I've missed Egypt so much."

In subsequent interviews Sharif (born Michael Shalhoub) seemed genuinely relieved to have come to a realization that he belonged back in Egypt, where he has done four films since 1984. Now he's become famous for giving bad-tempered interviews.

Legendary actor Omar Sharif on a French television show in September 2003. (Eric Fougère/VIP Images/Corbis)

One example from 1996, in the Egyptian magazine *Alive*, seemed to be an extended spat between interviewer and interviewee over the media's expectations of how a star should act. They were, he told them, lousy interviewers with lousy questions based on lousy perceptions on how the stars live (he also flouted convention by declaring prostitution was an honorable profession, that he had no problem with homosexuality, and that he may have slept with more than one thousand women). Sharif was either cleverly turning the media experience on its head or providing an example of a rather bitter, bad-tempered star in his twilight years. He says he made some forty or so bad films simply because he had gambled away his money on bridge (*Cairo Times*, 5

March 1998). He heavily indulged his other passion, women, but ruined a happy marriage to Egyptian actress Faten Hamama (for whom he became a Muslim) for the sake of Hollywood. Sharif turned down an offer from Chahine—the two fell out in the 1950s—to play the last Andalusian caliph in his 1997 film *Destiny.* "The script was very bad," he says with his disarming honesty. "I've done many horrible films with bad scripts, but I hate to do a bad film with a good director" (*Cairo Times,* 5 March 1998).

The "Golden Age" before the 1970s

Most critics agree that Egyptian cinema's high point was Shadi Abdel-Salam's 1969 movie *The Mummy*—Arab cinema's contribution to the world's movie classics and the only serious attempt in cinema to critique modern Egypt's direction and identity. "The film presents a complex set of symbols about the problems of modern Egypt, its relationship with its Pharaonic past, its perspective on the West, and its Arab identity," critic Mustafa Darwish writes in his portrait of Egyptian cinema, *Dream Makers on the Nile* (Darwish 1998, 42). *The Mummy* is set during the time of foreign archaeological discoveries in Thebes in 1881. Two sons of a recently deceased clan leader are shocked to learn that for generations their family has been living by robbing tombs. One son is murdered by the family for fear that he will give away the tombs' whereabouts to foreign archaeologists. The other—filled with wonder at the incomprehensible ancient language of his ancestors left on the walls of temples—decides to succeed where his brother failed out of respect for the past.

He is determined to count the forgotten and ignored years (as invoked by the film's alternate title, *The Night of Counting the Years*), finding meaning in the monuments of Pharaonic Egypt. As long as the natives fail to ascribe value to their own past and endeavor to preserve it, the foreigners will continue to disdain them. But doing so means overcoming Arab and Islamic political and intellectual barriers to examining this past. As Shafik writes, "History may be used as a weapon in the fight for political or cultural positions. The resulting historicism serves to strengthen the chipped identity, particularly when a society is subjected to rapid changes" (Shafik 1998, 164).

The three decades preceding *The Mummy* had seen the development of a remarkable cinema that fed the dreams of the entire Arab world. Its women stars included Soad Hosni (dubbed "the Cinderella of the Egyptian Screen"), Faten Hamama (famed for her image of a passive moral girl who bore injustice rather than struggle against it), Laila Murad (whose films are adored to this day for their innocent exuberance), Tahiya Carioca (noted for her belly dancing and femme fatale mystique), Hind Rustum (the only true sex symbol of Arab cinema), the great singing diva Umm Kalthoum (who made six films between 1936 and 1947), and a host of others. Its male stars included Rushdie Abaza (Egyptian Italian ladies' man), Omar Sharif (a star in the Arab world for a decade before his 1963 breakthrough in the West with *Lawrence of Arabia*), Anwar Wagdy (dashing Syrian actor and director, married for a time to Laila Murad), comic Ismail Yassin, Elvis-style singer-actor Abdel-Halim Hafez (the first young male sex symbol of Arab pop culture), singer-composer Mohammed Abdel-Wahhab (strait-laced precursor of Abdel-Halim), Lebanese singer and oud player Farid al-Atrash, Ahmed Mazhar (who played the lead role in Chahine's epic *Saladin*), and others. Most of them were products of Egypt's multicultural melting pot in the first half of the twentieth century.

That period churned out some hundred films a year. Many of these films linger in today's popular cultural memory, and many are still shown regularly on terrestrial and satellite channels all over the region—a canon that every Arab comes to know. Some landmarks and favorites are *Widad*, a musical feature film starring Umm Kalthoum that heralded the beginning of the Golden Age; 1939's *Determination* (*al-Azima*), Egypt's first venture into realist cinema, depicting Cairo's poorer social classes; Salah Abu Seif's *A Beginning and an End* (*Bidaya wa Nihaya*), an adaptation of the Naguib Mahfouz novel starring Omar Sharif; 1965's *The Sin* (*al-Haram*), directed by Henri Barakat and starring Faten Hamama; 1958's *Cairo Station* (*Bab al-Hadid*), Chahine's first classic; *My Father Is Up the Tree* (*Abi Fawq al-Shagara*, 1969), a massive box-office success that has never been shown on Egyptian television because of its numerous scenes of kissing between Abdel-Halim and Nadia Lutfi; and 1971's *Watch Out for Zuzu* (*Khalli Baalak min Zuzu*), where a respectable girl by day, Soad Hosni, hides her secret dancing at night. Some of these early films are artistic gems. An example is the 1941 film *Dananir*, with Umm Kalthoum starring as a girl with a beautiful voice in the harem of Abbasid caliph Haroun al-Rashid. It is a singing-dancing-acting extravaganza that reconstructs the historical dance of court maidens in the Abbasid era. But most of the early films are romantic tearjerkers or social commentaries that implied that various aspects of traditional culture required reforms to suit the modern state.

Outside Egyptian cinema, one film that has shone is a 1976 Algerian film by Merzak Allouache, *Omar Gatlato al-Rujla* (*Omar, Killed by Manliness*). According to Shafik, "in the last twenty years no film has described the ordinary relation of Arabs to music better than *Omar Gatlato*" (Shafik 1998, 101). Omar is a typically impoverished young Algerian with no job prospects and fewer prospects for knowing women. Through contemporary Algerian pop music and Indian musical films, the film shows that he is able to feel the love and happiness denied by ordinary life. His friends give him a tape recording of a girl talking about everyday things, and he resolves to find the girl whose voice he listens to. But he faces ridicule from his safe world of male chums if he goes through with his plan. Algerian Mohamed Lakhdar Hamina's *Chronicle of the Years of Embers* (*Waqaa'i Sanawaat al-Jamr*, 1974) depicts Algerian pre- and postindependence through the eyes of an idealized, heroic, suffering peasant. It is the only Arab film to win the Palme d'Or at Cannes. Algerian cinema saw major success with a series of films starring comic actor Ahmed Rouiched, starting with *Hassan Terro* in 1967. These films used satire to begin a new cinematic trend questioning the plethora of films that dealt with and glorified the independence struggle with France. Women had no central role in these nationalist Algerian films, though Chahine made *Jamila Bouharid* in 1958, which idolized the Arab woman's role in nationalist struggle through its tale of a famous Algerian independence fighter of the same name.

Tunisian Noury Bouzeid's *Man of Ashes* (*Rih al-Sadd*, 1986) depicts two young men, who were abused as children by a carpenter, trying to find their way in life. One, Farfat, is thrown out of the house by his father who thinks he's a homosexual. The other, Hashimi, is forced by his parents into an arranged marriage. Some friends mock Farfat's masculinity when they go to a brothel, so he storms out, finds the carpenter, and murders him. The story is an allegory for a broken younger generation trying to recover from the abuse of the generation that took control of Tunisia after independence. Syrian director Samir Zikra's *The Half-Meter Incident* (*Hadithat al-Nisf Mitr*, 1981) offers a subtle, subversive message. The film depicts an apolitical and sexually frustrated white-collar worker, living with his family, who meets a woman at the university. Life opens up before him, and he becomes a self-aware, self-confident womanizer who abandons his girlfriend after he gets her pregnant. The 1967 war is on the horizon, and his employers, who have noticed how he has changed, give him a job organizing civil defense. But the Arabs' disastrous defeat doesn't hurt him at all. Instead, he obtains a promotion because of his opportunistic commitment to the useless war. The defeat of 1967 simply reinforces all the negative phenomena in society that in part led to defeat in the first place.

The New, Egyptian-Led Commercial Cinema

Egyptian cinema has seen a revival since the late 1990s, partly as a natural development from the satellite channel revolution and the money pouring into music videos, but also due to limited government encouragement and a burgeoning youth population looking for new faces and films. It all began in 1997 with *Ismailiya Rayih Gayy* (*Ismailiya Back and Forth*), a crudely made comedy produced on a tiny budget, which defied all expectations to become Egypt's biggest-grossing film up to that time. Comic actor Mohammed Heneidy, who appeared in a supporting role with pop singer Mohammed Fouad, was propelled to sudden stardom. Thus producers realized that one young actor with huge popularity could be the way to revive box-office fortunes. The next year Heneidy starred in the made-to-order *An Upper Egyptian at the American University*, which broke previous records as the highest-grossing film, raking in the equivalent of eight million dollars. His next film, *Hamam in Amsterdam* (1999), in which he pursues the dream of emigration to Europe, was another huge hit. "Some people hadn't been to the cinema for thirty years before these films," said Medhat al-Adl, who produced both of them (interview with author, November 1999). A rash of other comedies did well on the back of the "Heneidy phenomenon," as private-sector firms opened new cinema complexes and the government lowered taxes on ticket prices. Ahmed al-Saqqa now commands huge fees for any film because his good looks have made him the heartthrob of teenaged girls. A number of films starring other new comic stars have done reasonably well, such as Ahmed Adam's *I Didn't Intend to Become a Filipino Maid* (*Wala Fi Niyya Ab'aa Filibiniyya*, 1998) and *Cinema Action Hero* (*Shagi' al-Sima*, 2000) and Alaa Walieddin's *Saladin the Headmaster* (*al-Nazir Salaheddin*, 2000) and *Abboud 'al-Hudoud* (*Abboud on the*

Border, 1998). The film *al-Limby* by Wael Hassan, with a goofy comic lead role played by Mohammed Saad, repeated the experience of *Ismailiya Rayih Gayy* by coming from nowhere in summer 2002 to become the biggest box-office hit yet in Arab cinema.

Heneidy was the most unlikely of big-screen stars. He's small, bald, and baby-faced, but people would burst into fits of laughter when they saw him on the street at the height of his fame. He has tapped into a desire for a return to old-fashioned values of decency, filial piety, and nationalism uncorrupted by Westernization, an attempt to re-create the black-and-white world of Arab cinema's Golden Age. His summer 2000 effort, *Bilya and His Big Head*, in which he befriends homeless street kids, bombed—mainly because its appeal was to children only. Critics and senior actors have warned that the wave of "fast-food films" won't support a long-term revival as long as the acting and story lines are lightweight. Heneidy's poorly received *Saheb Sahbo* (*His Friend's Friend*) from 2002 backed up this argument. Whether Mohammed Saad can sustain his success or fall like Heneidy did remains to be seen. With the number of films made per year still low, many fear that American films will flood the new cinema houses. The nervousness over what globalization could do to the indigenous industry erupted in a furor in 2000, over news that a private-sector company had gone on a two-month spending spree, buying up a third of all Egyptian films ever made. Most of them were black-and-white films from the "Golden Era" and were in a deteriorated state. The company that bought them, a specially created offshoot of the financial house EFG-Hermes, said it was doing the nation a favor. But critics said that it was dangerous for so much of the national heritage to be in the hands of a single, non-state-owned enterprise.

Prior to the new comedy films, Arab cinema was dominated by Egyptian actor Adel Imam and, to a lesser extent, Egyptian actress Nadia al-Gindy. Imam was the highest-paid actor in the Arab world, and Gindy was dubbed *nigmat al-gamaheer*, or "star of the masses." Such monikers are usually products of a star's marketing team rather than of an adulating press or adoring public, but they stick nevertheless. Egyptian singer Hany Shaker, newspapers have reported, has nagged television presenters and concert promoters to refer to him as *amir al-ughniya al-arabiyya*—"prince of the Arab song"—and the term has gained currency, though more in Egypt, where there is interest in promoting Egyptian singers in the Arab world. Both Imam and Gindy played supposedly attractive thirty-somethings well into the 1990s, when they were in fact sixty-somethings, but they pulled it off with a degree of success. But the current huge jump in popular interest in cinema, fueled by a new generation of stars, suggests that the public is ready for new acts.

Imam dominated cinema in the 1990s with a series of political comedies attacking the Islamist extremist groups that had launched open warfare against the state. The films, penned by leftist screenwriter Wahid Hamed, formed part of a successful government propaganda campaign against the radicals and attempts to demonize them. In return for that, the filmmakers managed to direct a fair amount of criticism at the state itself for corrupt, undemocratic practices, with implications about why radical Islam had gained so much

Nadia al-Gindy and Adel Imam, two of the celebrated icons of Egyptian cinema, at an awards ceremony in 2004. (Amro Maraghi/AFP/Getty Images)

sway in Egyptian society. The most celebrated of these films is *al-Irhabi* (*The Terrorist*), where Imam is an Islamist on the run who is taken in by an unsuspecting family who lead the kind of liberal, middle-class lifestyle that his ideology has taught him to despise. But in the process of living among them and experiencing their humanity, Imam's character comes to question his radical beliefs. This simplistic approach gave way to the more revealing 1992 *al-Irhab wal-Kebab* (*Terrorism and Kebabs*), where Imam is a hapless Egyptian caught in a Kafkaesque bureaucratic nightmare in a well-known government building in Cairo known as the Mugamma. After a group of disgruntled citizens express anger at the restrictive government, police decide that Imam is leading a band of terrorists who have come to storm the building.

The movie suggests that Egypt's modern state is a failure and that mass disaffection in society allowed terrorism to grow. Imam deserves some credit for challenging the public with his brief sendup of popular religious preacher Sheikh Metwalli Sharawi in the 1999 film *Mahrous, the Minister's Boy* (*al-Wad Mahrous Bitaa al-Wazir*). The leftist intelligentsia think Sharawi, who died in 1998, was one step away from the terrorists and blame state television for making him so popular.

Gindy, on the other hand, is famed for emotional roller-coaster performances, where she overcomes all odds through the will-to-power that only a woman can muster to triumph over some form of social, economic, or political evil. Her roles generally fall into three categories: wronged woman, power-hungry woman,

Tunisian Director Nouri Bourzid on Egyptian Commercial Cinema

In a rare interview in *al-Hayat* (27 December 2002), director Nouri Bourzid said, "The drama we have now is responsible for our backwardness and it's from Egypt. But it's only Egyptian drama that can get it out of this. If one day the Egyptians realize that the view of the public has to be changed and the door opened to directors who have courage to say things—people like [art-house film directors] Merzaq Allouache, Lakhdar Hamina, Mohamed Malas, Michel Khleifi, Burhan Elwiya and others—then we will have entered a period of respecting the public. You can't give me a film like *al-Sukariya* [a commercial adaptation of the eponymous novel by Naguib Mahfouz, starring Egyptian actress Nadia al-Gindy] and erase the important characters like the Muslim Brother, the communist and the homosexual. It was because of these characters that I wanted to do a version of this contemporary novel, but it's been done.

"Egyptian cinema lost a chance when people like Dawoud Abdel-Sayed, Mohammed Khan, Atef al-Tayeb and Khairy Beshara came along. They are brave writers, not necessarily about politics, but about the individual. But those who control the market—and we don't know their intentions—held them back. They have talent, knowledge and the idea of renewing society, but they have been encouraged to make progress. The Egyptian state must take a stance and set up a fund to support films that want to get out of the commercial strait-jacket. This would be in defence of Egypt's heritage and the Arab public that likes well-made films. There are shortcomings and the private sector is dominant. But the problem goes far beyond cinema. It's an issue of culture, Arab societies and educating generations. The day will come when creative work is considered heresy and that's what's frightening. What I build in two hours they spend years destroying in Egyptian soap operas. Change is necessary."

and crusading woman. Critics love to hate her and she's often accused of vulgarity, of cheapening women, and of being too fond of portraying sex as a weapon. Most of her films are seen as another episode in the continuing adventures of her own ego. One opposition paper memorably dubbed 1995's *The Woman Who Shook the Throne of Egypt* (*Imra'a Hazzat Arsh Misr*)—which was allegedly about a paramour of King Farouk's—as *The Woman Who Twisted History* (*al-Arabi*, July 1995). In other adventures she has battled Mossad agents, giving her a certain cult following in Israel. She is the grande dame of Egyptian cinema, the Arab Joan Collins.

In 1999's *al-Imberatora* (*The Drug Baroness*), Gindy appears in the guise of a maid, luscious Zenouba, working in the home of a police officer who is rising in the ranks. When their love affair is uncovered by his mother, the policeman shuns the maid, and our heroine is turfed out ignominiously. It's one of those soul-destroying moments when love turns to hate. So Gindy embarks on an epic voyage of revenge by building herself up as a drug "baroness" in poor districts of Cairo, taking the name Madame Zizi and wearing ever more outlandish costumes. She becomes a big shot in the state, cutting deals with Israelis to smuggle Lebanese heroin into Egypt (a common theme in the Egyptian press). When Gindy's brother and husband are killed by cops, she has her ex-lover's wife machine-gunned to death. At that point the police officer telephones her to say, with laughable lightness considering the circumstances, "Let's stop this war between us and come to an understanding." So the final scene is set for a romantic resolution—but she's poisoned his drink and he's secretly placed a bug under the table. He dies in her arms, and the scene freezes on the face of our heroine in the anguished realization that life in prison with neither family nor lover awaits her. It's because of films like this that Egypt's film industry went from being known as Hollywood on the Nile in the 1960s to being known as Bollywood on the Nile today.

Today's Art-House and North African Cinema

What appeals to Arab audiences today or leaves them cold is an issue that's taxing the local movie industry. Yousef Chahine's glossy 2004 *Destiny* (*al-Masir*) bombed at the box office, while *Ismailiya Rayih Gayy*, one of the most inexpensive films in Egyptian cinema history, was the industry's biggest financial success. Serious directors and actors took fright. "When they saw a film like *Ismailiya Rayih Gayy* breaking all the records they had to go back and rethink everything," Raghda said (interview with author, *Cairo Times*, 28 April 1999). "It wasn't a film, it was a bunch of kids doing what they want, as if the director had left the camera running and gone home." Art films such as the late Radwan al-Kashef's lavish *Araq al-Balah* (*Date Wine*) from 1998 tend to be well received abroad and do well on the international film festival circuit, but they are shunned in Egypt. Dawoud Abdel-Sayed's *Ard al-Khof* (*Land of Fear*, 1999) was nominated in the Best

Foreign Film category of the 2001 Academy Awards, but it had only limited success at home. Mohammed Khan scored a major coup for independent cinema with his 2004 *Klephty* (*Thief*), the Arab world's first major film made using digital camera technology, but Khan preferred to sell it to Arab TV channels rather than fight with distributors over a general release. Osama Fawzy's 1999 film *Gannat al-Shayateen* (*Devils' Paradise*) was well received by critics, and Mahmoud Hemeida won the best supporting actor award at the 1999 Alexandria International Film Festival in Egypt for his role as a drunkard's dead corpse, suggesting there is a danger of tokenism being mistaken for art in an industry still struggling to regain a sense of itself after three decades of decline.

A billboard in Cairo for Egyptian director Yousef Chahine's 1997 film *al-Masir* (*Destiny*). (Attar Maher/Corbis Sygma)

Ferid Boughedir is known only for two works of an as-yet-uncompleted trilogy, and two other films that preceded them, but he is probably one of the best directors in the Arab world and one who has made truly world-class cinema. Egyptian directors Shadi Abdel-Salam and Yousef Chahine once did the same, but Abdel-Salam died in 1986 and Chahine's oeuvre of the nineties has been disappointing. Boughedir's 1989 *Halfaouine* (named after a district of Tunis) depicts a young boy who spies on women from a rooftop and public baths, his only access to a supposedly secluded world of Arab women. Boughedir's glossy and colorful palette adds to the sense of watching an orientalist painting come to life. The film and its 1986 sequel, *Seif fi Halq al-Wadi* (*Summer in La Goulette*), both scored commercial successes in Tunisia. The films were made with French money, as are many films in formerly French-occupied North Africa, and many in the Arab East consider that the French money comes with expectations from directors of a certain take on Arab culture, one that fits the Western view of the East. "There's not one film that France doesn't have a hand in. Their native cinema has French money and half-French actors and directors. At least in Egypt it's an indigenous product," actress Raghda said (interview with author, *Cairo Times*, 28 April 1999). Many Lebanese directors have experienced this influence, with one foot in the Francophone world and the other mired in the Arab Mashreq scene. French funder FondSud notoriously won't give money to a film that has a significant amount of English dialogue, and they have problems with treatments that present liberated, independent women. Numerous directors have related experiences that illus-

Tunisian film director Ferid Boughedir at the Berlin Film Festival in 1996. (Ronald Siemoneit/Corbis Sygma)

trate this, including Ghassan Salhab (who directed *Terra Incognita*). Elie Khalifeh (director of *Taxi Service* and *Merci Natex*) had to drop plans for a film called *Bint Sur* (*A Girl from Tyre*), in which a free-spirited young woman has a love affair in Israeli-occupied south Lebanon with an Irish peacekeeper; the film traverses sectarian problems in Northern Ireland and sectarian problems in the Middle East.

In Boughedir's view, Tunisia has followed a progressive censorship policy on sexual and women's issues that has encouraged directors to make challenging cinema and allowed the public to develop a taste for the highbrow (interview with author, *Cairo Times*, 9 December 1999). "It's the nicest censorship in the Arab world and this is the key to success," Boughedir said, though he acknowledges that liberal cinema has been used by the Tunisian regime as a way of diverting the minds of the masses from political issues, with censorship as harsh as it is anywhere else. Yet Tunisian audiences don't seem to see the Western cliché in their cinema that some Egyptian directors and critics claim to see in French co-productions. Boughedir sees *Halfaouine* as working on different levels, only one of which is Western. "*Halfaouine* shows the move from childhood to adolescence. It starts off local, as something that only people of that neighborhood [where it's shot] would understand. Then it addresses the Arab audience and then it becomes something with something to say to people even in Japan," he said (interview with author, *Cairo Times*, 9 December 1999).

Boughedir does for Tunisia what novelist Ahlam Mostaghanemi does for Algeria in her Arabic novel *Dhakirat al-Jasad* (*Memory in the Flesh*), the first postindependence novel in Arabic by an Algerian woman, which accomplishes what Palestinian American writer Edward Said said Palestinians must do in the arts: narrate indigenous experience and make it comprehensible for the rest of the world as part of a liberating process of asserting cultural identity. "We need to create a new cinema which is deeply located in identity. We need to show how our people love, how our people cry, how our people dream. But we have to make it relevant," Boughedir said (interview with author, *Cairo Times*, 9 December 1999). Doueiri's *West Beirut* achieved this, creating a new cinematic language through which Lebanese see themselves (see, for example, Danielle Arbid's *Ma'arik Hubb* [*In the Battlefields*], another depiction of life in Beirut during the Lebanese civil war, which aired at Cannes in 2004). "In *West Beirut* Ziyad Doueiri comments on the political, social and historical reality in Lebanon. It gives us information on how Beirut lived in the time of the war, how people spoke, how kids lived the war and how it affected their dreams. At the same time it's entertaining," Boughedir said (interview with author, *Cairo Times*, 9 December 1999). Some young Egyptian directors are trying too. Atef Hetata, son of Egyptian feminist and novelist Nawal al-Saadawi, won the top prize at the Thessaloniki Film Festival in 1999 with his film *Closed Doors* (*Abwaab Mughlaqa*), but the film didn't last long in Cairo cinema houses when it was released in 2001. Another notable example is the late Kashef's *Date Wine* (*Araq al-Balah*), with its lavish colors and tale of cruel realities in an oasis of the Western Desert, which was critically acclaimed in Egypt and abroad but failed to bring in audiences. The film is often cited as an example of an Egyptian falling into the trap that North African directors have fallen into, that of relying on European money but losing cultural legitimacy as well as popular appeal. According to popular entertainment Web site Elaph.com, "these films try to package the Arab reality in a folkloric form that is behind the rest of civilization, like something out of the 1,000 Nights" (14 February 2004).

In his satire *Summer in La Goulette*, Boughedir subtly challenged Arab and Israeli conventions regarding Jews who left Arab countries for the Jewish State in the years after its creation in 1948. La Goulette is a coastal district of Tunis, where foreign communities, including Jews, lived in the colonial era. The film's message, that the Jews who lived in Arab countries (in

Scene during the shoot of one of Yousef Chahine's later films, *al-Youm al-Saadis* (*The Sixth Day*), which starred the late Egyptian-born French singer Dalida. (Tony Frank/Corbis Sygma)

Tunisia, Egypt, Morocco, Yemen, Iraq, Syria) were cut from the same cultural cloth as the rest of the Arabs, annoyed Israelis and was misunderstood by Arabs as a call to normalization of relations between Arab states and Israel. "I lived among the Jewish minority, and they were Arab. Their culture is Arab, their food, their music," Boughedir said (interview with author, *Cairo Times*, 9 December 1999). "I hate to forge reality. Art can't be based on denial of reality or propaganda." The film celebrates the tolerance and diversity that once characterized Arab countries. It starred Italian actress Claudia Cardinale, who was born and raised in Tunisia.

In this effort, Boughedir mirrored Chahine's casting of Egyptian-born French Italian singer Dalida in his 1986 film *The Sixth Day* (*al-Youm al-Saadis*).

Most of Chahine's films have been French co-productions, often with Francophone leanings. His *Adieu Bonaparte* (1985) even celebrated France's cultural role in Egypt's modern history, suggesting that Napoleon's 1898 invasion of Egypt should not be seen as entirely negative. Boughedir argues that France is doing the world a service by standing up to Hollywood's domination of international cinema and funding co-productions with countries of the developing world. But he says he's optimistic that Egyptian cinema will reclaim its place as the leader of an Arab cinema that goes beyond identifying itself with the rest of the world too. "The strength of Egyptian culture means cinema will never die," he said (interview with author, *Cairo Times*, 9 December 1999).

A-to-Z: Key People and Terms

ABAZA, RUSHDIE (1927–1982)

Son of an Italian mother and an Egyptian father, Abaza was one of the biggest actors in Egyptian cinema from the 1950s to the 1970s. Large and handsome, he was its leading ladies' man, though he often played villainous rakes too. He died at only 55 in 1982. His prime decade was the 1960s, when he began a series of thirteen memorable films starring opposite Soad Hosni. Unlike many other actors of this era, he stepped straight into cinema without any background in theater.

ABDEL-SALAM, SHADI (1930–1986)

An Egyptian director, idolized by critics and other intellectuals concerned with modern Egypt for his 1969 classic *The Mummy* (*al-Mumyaa'*; also known as *The Night of Counting the Years*). He followed it up with the equally outstanding 1970 *Complaints of the Eloquent Peasant* (*Shakawi al-Fellah al-Fasih*). But he died in 1986 without ever having made a third film from his script for *Tragedy of the Big House*, about Egypt's iconoclastic Pharaoh Akhnaten. Rumor has it that the Egyptian government has acquired rights to the script and is looking for a director. Abdel-Salam's classics mixed love for ancient Egypt (in an era when that was not politically correct) with an eye for detail, plus technical skills he learned as a set and costume designer in American and Italian films.

ABDEL-SAYED, DAWOUD (B. N.A.)

One of Egypt's realist directors who emerged in the 1980s, Abdel-Sayed has managed to mix art-house indulgence with commercialism, producing a number of notable films. They include the comic satire *al-Kitkat* (*Kitkat Square*, 1991) set in the poor Cairo district of Imbaba, based on the novel *Malik al-Hazin* (*The Heron*) by Egyptian writer Ibrahim Aslan. He also directed the critically acclaimed *Ard al-Ahlam* (*Land of Dreams*) in 1994, the last film with Golden Age actress Faten Hamama; the 1999 *Land of Fear* (*Ard al-Khof*), which was Oscar-nominated for Best Foreign Film; and 2001's *Muwatin wa Mukhbir wa Harami* (*A Citizen, an Informer and a Thief*), which critics praised despite controversy over its "sex scenes."

ABU SEIF, SALAH (1915–1996)

Probably Egypt's most successful director of social realist films, usually focused on Cairo's poor districts. Many of them are part of today's canon of best-remembered films of the Golden Age, including *The Tough Guy* (*al-Fitiwwa*, 1957), *A Woman's Youth* (*Shabab Imra'a*, 1956), and *A Beginning and an End* (*Bidaya wa Nihaya*, 1960).

AKKAD, MUSTAPHA (B. 1935)

A Syrian director based in the United States, famous for his English-language film *Lion of the Desert* (also, *Omar Mukhtar: Lion of the Desert*, 1980), the story of Libyan anticolonial resistance fighter Omar al-Mukhtar. The epic film, starring Anthony Quinn as the Libyan outwitting Italian military leader General Rodolfo Graziani, played by Oliver Reed, is shown on Egyptian television whenever Libya's Colonel Gaddafi visits Cairo. Akkad also directed a famed film from 1976 about the life of the Prophet, *al-Risala* (*The Message*). Through his successful crossover to Western cinema, Akkad has acquired cult status in Arab countries, but his output has been slim due to funding problems.

ALLOUACHE, MERZAK (B. 1944)

An Algerian director now based in France, who gained notoriety for his popular 1976 film, *Omar, Killed by Manliness* (*Omar Gatlato al-Rujla*). He later received critical acclaim abroad with his 1994 *Bab al-Oued*, named after a district of Algiers where Islamist groups became strong after Algeria experimented with political liberalization in 1988. Allouache turned the film into a novel of the same name.

BAGHDADI, MAROUN (1940–1993)

Lebanese director whose documentaries were noticed by Egyptian Lebanese director Yousef Chahine, leading to his first film, *Beirut, Oh Beirut*, about Lebanese politics after the 1967 defeat, and made in 1975, the year Lebanon's civil war erupted. His 1982 film *Small Wars* (*Huroub Saghira*) was about the beginning of that war, shot and shown in Beirut when the war was entering its most dramatic phase. His 1991 *Beyrouth Hors la Vie* took the Special Jury Prize at Cannes. He died in Beirut in 1993.

BESHARA, KHAIRY (B. 1947)

One of today's key Egyptian directors, who has carefully mixed commercial cinema with more experimental work. His 1986 *The Necklace and the Bracelet* (*al-Tawq wal-Aswira*), shot among the peasants of southern Egypt, established his reputation.

Subsequently he made *Kaburya* (*Crabs*, 1991), *Ice Cream in Glim* (1992, starring pop star Amr Diab), and *Abracadabra America* (*Amrika Shikabika*, 1993, starring pop star Mohammed Fouad), establishing his reputation. His 1995 *Traffic Lights* (*Ishaarat Murour*) was a move back to experimental realist cinema.

BOUGHEDIR, FERID (B. 1944)

Acclaimed Tunisian director known mainly for his film *Halfaouine* (also known as *Rooftop Bird*, or *Asfour al-Sath*, 1989), where a young boy spies on near-naked women in Turkish baths. The film is part of a trilogy, the third of which is due for release soon. He resides in France where he teaches, but his Francophone ties are regarded with suspicion by the nationalistic and commercial cinema industry in Cairo.

BOUZID, NOURI (B. 1945)

One of Tunisia's best directors, whose works include *Golden Horseshoes* (*Safaa'ih min al-Dhahab*, 1989), with scenes of sexual intercourse and police torture that were censored, and also the politically sharp *Man of Ashes* (*Rih al-Sadd*, 1986). Bouzid once described Arab cinema after the 1967 debacle against Israel as "post-defeat cinema"—a statement of the immense impact that war has had on Arab intellectual and cultural life.

CAIRO INTERNATIONAL FILM FESTIVAL

The biggest film festival in the Arab world, begun in 1976. Since 1998 the festival has strived to repair a bad reputation for appalling organization, obscure films from Eastern bloc countries, and last-minute schedule changes, along with sometimes overstating the sex content of films in publicity to attract viewers. The festival offers Cairenes two weeks a year of uncensored foreign movies—without subtitles—and that fact has been the event's main attraction since its inception. When Egyptian actor Hussein Fahmy took over as festival director in 1998, he made strenuous efforts to bring in well-known actors and directors from abroad, such as John Malkovich, Alain Delon, Sophia Loren, Peter O'Toole, and Omar Sharif.

CHAHINE, YOUSEF (B. 1926)

Probably the best-known Arab director abroad due to screenings of his films at international festivals, particularly Cannes, which presented him with a lifetime

Egyptian film director Yousef Chahine. (Neema Frederic/Corbis Sygma)

Chahine Attacks America in September 11 Short

Arabs had their input in a French-produced omnibus of eleven short films called *11'09'01': September 11,* released in 2002. Eleven directors from around the world each contributed a submission that was 11 minutes, 9 seconds, and one frame long, intended as a personal response to the September 11 attacks. Egyptian Yousef Chahine, the Arab director who is most well known internationally, chose to direct an anti-American message in his contribution. It tells the story of a filmmaker who cannot handle the news conference for his latest project because of the news reports of the attacks, and who then enters into a dialogue with the ghosts of an American marine killed in the Beirut attack of 1982 and a Palestinian suicide bomber during the second Intifada. He continues the theme of years of growing Arab resentment toward the United States in his 2004 film, called *Anger* (*al-Ghadab*), in which he explains how his own young, idealistic love affair with America gave way to disillusion in later life. Other contributions to the omnibus included Israeli director Amos Gitai, who hears news of the attacks while filming the aftermath of a Palestinian attack in Israel; Iranian director Samira Makhmalbaf, portraying Afghan refugee children who don't know what a skyscraper is and are preoccupied with news of an accident at a local well; and British director Ken Loach, who focuses on how the U.S.-backed coup against Chile's socialist leader Salvador Allende brought to power the dictator Augusto Pinochet. Other contributing directors included Mira Nair of India, Danis Tanovic of Bosnia, Claude Lelouch of France, Sean Penn of the United States, Shohei Imamura of Japan, Alejandro Gonzalez Inarritu of Mexico, and Idrissa Ouedraogo of Burkina Faso.

achievement award in 1997 to mark the festival's fiftieth anniversary. The only Arab director of his era to study in America, his work has spanned pro-Nasser historical drama, social realism, autobiography, lightweight musicals, and anti-Islamist flops, along with some of the most critically acclaimed films made in the Arab world. He is treated today as a grandee of Egyptian cinema, and his invitation to actors to appear in his films is seen as their gateway to fame. His 2001 film, the lighthearted *Silence, We're Filming* (*Sukout, Hansawwir*), starred Tunisian pop star Latifa. His protegés have included Yousry Nasrallah, whose art-house output has so far included *Mercedes* (1993) (with a rare depiction of homosexuality), the film documentary *On Boys, Girls and the Veil* (1995), and 2000's *The City* (*al-Madina*).

AL-DEGHEIDY, INAS (B. N.A.)

An Egyptian female director, who has stirred up scandals with a series of films that seemed designed to provoke controversy regarding sex and politics. Her last movie, *The Diary of a Teenage Girl* (*Muzakkaraat Muraahiqa*, 2002), provoked a court case from a housewife, who said that the film, with its depiction of a teenager transgressing sexual taboos, had defamed Egyptian womanhood when one character said that most Egyptian girls get pregnant through engaging in premarital sex. Censors made her change the name of the one before that from *Nakedness* (*al-Uri*) to *Night Talk* (*Kalam al-Lail*, 1999).

ELWI, LAILA (B. N.A.)

A luscious Egyptian actress, known for her sex appeal. She has been fighting a weight problem for the last ten years, à la Oprah Winfrey, with her weight sometimes up and sometimes down, but her size has made her popular with Egyptian and other Arab audiences, whose traditional preference is for big women. Despite her weight issues, she has enjoyed a run of popular and well-regarded films, including *Silence, Please!* (*Sama, Hoss*, 1990) and *Oh Milk Pudding* (*Ya Mehallabiya Ya*, 1991), both directed by Sherif Arafa.

AL-GINDY, NADIA (B. 1940)

One of Egypt's most prolific actresses, who has been acting in commercial cinema since the 1960s. Her distinctive looks and wily "femme" roles have made her one of the most famous Egyptian actresses of the last thirty years. She first became known after her role as a femme fatale drug dealer in a 1970s TV soap opera, *The Whirlpool* (*al-Dawwama*). She was briefly married to Emad Hamdy, one of the big stars of the Golden Age, whose most famous works include Ezzeddin Zulficar's *I Am Leaving* (*Inni Rahila*, 1955) and the religious epic *Rab'a al-Adawiya* (1963). Hamdy had a long marriage to the actress Shadia, with whom he starred in many films produced by a production house they set up together.

EL-HAGAR, KHALED (B. 1963)

Young Egyptian director who began his career with Chahine's Misr International film company in Egypt. He has reached a mass audience in the West making English-language films from his base in England, including 2000's Anglo-French production *A Room to Rent*, starring Paris-based Moroccan actor Said Taghmaoui (and also starring well-known Anglo-Saxon actors Juli-

THE CINEMA INDUSTRY 135

ette Lewis, Rupert Graves, and Anna Massey). The film was badly received by some mainstream critics in the West, though its style and concerns were typical fare for Arab cinema; it offers an amusing take on life in London seen through Arab eyes. His first full-length movie was 1993's Arab film *Small Dreams* (*Ahlam Saghira*), which was well received on the international film festival circuit. He subsequently studied at London's National Film and Television School, and his films preceding *A Room to Rent* included *A Gulf between Us* (*Hagiz Baynana*, 1994), a forty-minute film that looked at how the 1991 Gulf War ruined a relationship between an Arab and a Jewish girl in London. His debut in mainstream Egyptian cinema was 2003's *Hobb al-Banat* (*The Love of Girls*).

HAMAMA, FATEN (B. 1931)

One of the most famous actresses in Egypt who appeared in a huge number of tear-jerkers from the 1950s to 1970s, including *Call of the Curlew* (*Du'aa al-Karawan*, 1959), as well as mature, well-acted roles in films such as *I Want a Solution* (*Uridu Hallan*, 1975). She acquired a reputation for playing characters who embodied the modern Arab ideal of the attractive and liberal, yet obedient and moral, daughter. Her marriage to Omar Sharif in his younger days before Hollywood, when he was an Arab acting star, also helped establish her legendary status. The marriage collapsed after he found fame in the West. She revived her career in the late 1990s with lead roles in a number of Egyptian soap operas, where directors went to extraordinary lengths to iron out her wrinkles and present her as audiences remembered her in the 1960s, using a soft-focus lens around

her head that gave the impression of a halo.

HAMINA, MOHAMED LAKHDAR (B. 1934)

A major Algerian director, whose well-known works include *The Wind of the Aures* (*Rih al-Awraas*, 1966), *Chronicle of the Years of Embers* (*Waqaa'i Sanawaat al-Jamr*, 1974), and 1967's *Hassan Terro*, the comedy of a cowardly resistance fighter starring comic Ahmed Rouiched (the latter started a series of popular Algerian films featuring Rouiched). His *Chronicle* won the Cannes Palme d'Or in 1975, making Hamina the only Arab director to achieve the prize.

HOSNY, SOAD (1943–2001)

The most revered actress of the Golden Age, who died in tragic circumstances in London in 2001. For a decade Hosny had kept away from the lights, but her death, probably by suicide, shocked the Arab world. She looked tired, overweight, and washed-out in her last film, 1991's *The Shepherd and the Women* (*al-Raa'i wal-Nisaa*), directed by Maher Awad, and the industry seemed too quick to forget her, which explains the sense of guilt that now permeates media discussion of her. She was one of the great actresses whose demise seemed to parallel the demise of the nationalist cinematic dream since 1967. "It was a long suicide," as arts critic Ibrahim Aris said (*al-Wasat*, 2 August 2004).

IMAM, ADEL (B. N.A.)

An Egyptian comic actor who became the most famous cinema star in the region in

Cinema poster from the 2004 film *Klephty*. (Photo courtesy of Rola Mahmoud)

the 1980s and 1990s. He first shot to fame through his manic improvisations in the 1971 play *School for Hooligans* (*Madrasat al-Mushaaghibeen*). He has been undercut somewhat by the emergence of a new generation of comic actors, including Mohammed Heneidy and the current youth heartthrob Ahmed al-Saqqa, who both hit the big time in the 1998 box-office smash *An Upper Egyptian at the American University*, directed by Said Hamed.

major political figures in the Arab world. The film was a critical and commercial success, partly because of lead actor Ahmed Zaki's uncanny portrayal of the deceased leader, and also because the film did a fair job of leaving the audience to make up its own mind on his controversial policies. His 2004 film *Klephty* (*Thief*) was seen as a major comeback for independent cinema d'auteur in Egypt, and the beginning of digital filmmaking technology in the Arab world.

KHAN, MOHAMMED (B. 1943)

An Egyptian director who made 2001's *Days of Sadat* (*Ayyam al-Sadat*), one of a series of films in recent years focusing on

KHLEIFI, MICHEL (B. 1950)

A Palestinian director known for the documentary *Fertile Memory* (*al-Zakira al-Khisba*, 1980), the semidocumentary *Song* of the Stones (*Nashid al-Hajar*, 1990), and the 1989 film *Wedding at Galilee* (*Urs al-Jalil*), which looks at how patriarchal society weakens Palestinians' ability to challenge Israeli oppression. It won the Cannes Critics Award in 1987. Most Palestinian directors, whether Israeli citizens or residents of the occupied territories, have worked on documentaries rather than fictional movies.

MURAD, LAILA (1918–1995)

A Jewish-born Egyptian singer-actress who was the number-one star of the late 1930s and early 1940s, featured in films by Jewish director Togo Mizrahi. But with the creation of Israel in 1948, her days as an Arab cinema star were numbered. She retired in 1956, when Britain, France, and Israel went to war with Egypt in 1956 over the Suez Canal. She had a number of high-profile marriages, including one to comedy director Fatin Abdel-Wahhab and another to Syrian film star Anwar Wagdy. Wagdy was responsible for some of Laila Murad's best films, including the 1951 *Ghazal al-Banat* (*Girls' Flirtation*), which he directed. Murad died in penury in Cairo in 1996, a sad statement on the fate of Egypt's once-evanescent cinema industry, which fed the dreams of the entire Arab world.

RUSTUM, HIND (B. 1933)

A sultry Golden Age actress who was regarded as the only Marilyn Monroe–style sex symbol of Egyptian cinema. She starred in 1957's *Give My Heart Back* (*Rudd Qalbi*), directed by Ezzeddin Zulficar; Chahine's 1958 *Cairo Station* (*Bab al-Hadid*); Hassan al-Imam's 1965 film *The Nun* (*al-Rahiba*); and Hossameddin Mus-

tafa's 1972 *A Word of Honor* (*Kalimat Sharaf*), plus the popular Chahine-directed comedy from 1957, *You Are My Love* (*Inta Habibi*). Half Turkish, she was one of a group of actresses known for their exotic foreign looks, including half-Hungarian Mariam Fakhreddin, half-Polish Nadia Lutfy, and Turkish Shadia. Rustum withdrew from the spotlight in the 1970s.

SABBAGH, RANDA CHAHAL (B. N.A.)

Sabbagh was the winner of the Silver Lion director's award at the 2003 Venice Film Festival for *The Kite*. It subsequently became the director's first film released to the general public in her native Lebanon, where she has a history of trouble with the censors. The film is set in the Golan Heights and tells a love story about two members of the Druze community who are betrothed, a girl who lives in a Lebanese village and a boy who lives in the Israeli-occupied area and serves as an Israeli soldier. Sabbagh's previous work includes 1998's *Civilisées* (*A Civilized People*), dealing with Lebanon's civil war, from which Lebanese security censors cut forty-seven of the total ninety minutes due to bad language. Sabbagh has said this showed Lebanon was not yet ready to discuss the war.

SALEH, TAWFIK (B. 1927)

In a career spanning over forty years, Saleh has made only seven films, but most have been quality works that challenged prevailing trends. His *Mister Bulti* (*al-Sayyid Bulti*, 1966) and *The Rebels* (*al-Mutamarridun*, 1967) both ran up against censorship problems for their cynical view of justice and socialism in Nasser's

Egypt. Forced out by the public and private sectors, he then headed to Syria. His 1972 film *The Duped* (*al-Makhdu'un*), financed with Syrian money and based on a novel by celebrated Palestinian writer Ghassan Kanafani, is a statement par excellence of Palestinian suffering in the diaspora at the hands of Arab regimes. Like many Arabs in the 1970s, he believed that Saddam Hussein's Iraq was going to lead the Arabs into the First World and achieve what Nasser failed to do. Thus his 1980 *The Long Days* (*al-Ayyam al-Tawila*), about Hussein's revolutionary younger days.

SHARIF, OMAR (B. 1931)

The Arab world's most famous actor, who scored success in Egyptian cinema in its Golden Age before going on to global success in Hollywood, a feat not emulated since by any other Arab actor. He is currently settled back in Egypt, acting as a kind of cultural ambassador for the country but not making movies—unless he gets a good script, as he often says. He was born Michael Dmitri Shalhoub to an Alexandrian family of Lebanese descent, and he represents a cosmopolitan Egyptian culture that disappeared after the revolution, though his cosmopolitan ways have often conflicted with the Islamist nationalism of the Egyptian public. He shot back into the international limelight with 2003's *Monsieur Ibrahim et les Fleurs du Koran* (*Monsieur Ibrahim*), directed by François Dupeyron. It garnered him the best actor prize in France's prestigious César Awards of 2004 for his role as a Muslim shopkeeper who befriends a Jewish boy.

AL-SHERIF, NOUR (B. 1946)

One of Egypt's best and most well-known male actors. He has been around since the 1970s in famed film roles, but arguably he achieved more renown in the Arab world with the 2001 soap opera *Hajj Metwalli*, the story of an Egyptian self-made businessman happily married to four women.

SULEIMAN, ELIA (B. 1960)

A Palestinian director whose 2002 *Divine Intervention* (*Yadun Ilahiya*) is a satire about a Palestinian couple in the occupied territories trying to manage their love affair amid the reality of checkpoints and urban warfare during the second Intifada. The film received the Special Jury Prize and the International Critics Award at the 2002 Cannes Film Festival. He is from Nazareth, whose residents are typically described as Israeli Arabs, though he was identified as purely Palestinian in the Cannes coverage. His previous full-length film, *Chronicle of a Disappearance* (1997), also attempted to present the realities of the Palestinian situation.

AL-TAYEB, ATEF (1947–1995)

Al-Tayeb's films debuted in the 1980s, and he is regarded as one of the best of Egypt's new wave of directors. His *The Bus Driver* (*Sawwaaq Utubis*, 1982) shows the corruption of values wrought in society by the 1970s economic-liberalization policies of the Egyptian regime. *The Innocent* (*al-Baree'*) from 1986 depicted political injustice and had problems with the censors specifically due to a scene where ordinary citizens rebel against injustice. Showing injustice may be one thing, but suggesting that your audience rebel against it is another.

TLATLI, MOUFIDA (B. 1947)

A Tunisian woman director who made the acclaimed 1994 film *Silence of the Palaces* (*Samt al-Qusour*), portraying a servant girl kept as a virtual slave in the palace of Tunisian aristocrats on the eve of Tunisia's independence from France. A young nationalist teacher befriends her and opens her mind, but after independence he comes to see her as too "low" to marry and wants her to abort their child, thus showing that social liberation and national liberation don't necessarily go hand in hand. Her 2000 follow-up film, *The Season of Men* (*La Saison des Hommes*), was well received in Europe.

TURK, HANAN (B. N.A.)

Turk is currently the young darling of Egyptian cinema. Her big break came when Chahine cast her in his lavish biblical epic *The Emigrant* (*al-Muhagir*) in 1994. But Turk had to reconstruct her career after she was briefly imprisoned in 1996 with another actress, in what police claimed was a vice ring. She was never formally charged and always maintained her innocence, but even when she returned to movies over a year later in *Ismailiya Rayih Gayy* (produced by singer Mohammed Fouad in 1997), audiences tutted in reproach when she appeared on the screen. Now she is a major box-office draw in the new wave of youth films that *Ismailiya* spawned. Her main competitor is Mona Zaki, another member of the new brat pack in Egyptian cinema, who rose to fame as Heneidy's love interest in *An Upper Egyptian at the American University in Cairo* and later secured a contract as an ethereal woman wafting through white curtains in Lux soap commercials.

YOUSRA (B. 1955)

Yousra is today's premier actress in Egypt and the one seen as the most classy. After years of appearing in nondescript comedies as a wafer-thin actress, she emerged in the 1990s as the leading lady opposite Adel Imam in most of his blockbusters, and her reputation grew. She now looks better than she did ten or twenty years ago, but critics have mauled her for a recent foray into pop music with a song (*Everybody Needs to Love*) and an image (looking compassionate with children) that seemed intended to present her as some kind of Arab Princess Diana, Queen of Hearts.

ZAKI, AHMED (B. 1949)

One of Egyptian cinema's major actors, with a long list of impressive roles to his name. They include controversial historical dramas of past presidents. He played the role of Gamal Abdel Nasser in 1995's *Nasser 56* and portrayed Anwar Sadat in 2001's *Days of Sadat*.

Bibliography

Print Resources

"The Accidental Patron: I Owe It All to Cairo." *New York Times*, 9 January 2000.

Al-Aris, Ibrahim. *Rihla fil-Sinima al-Arabiya* (A Trip through Arab Cinema). Beirut: N.P., 1979.

Al-Hadari, Ahmed. *Tarikh al-Sinima fi Masr* (The History of Cinema in Egypt). Cairo: N.p., 1989.

Armbrust, Walter. *Mass Culture and Modernism in Egypt*. Cambridge, UK: Cambridge University Press, 1996.

Darwish, Mustafa. *Dream Makers on the Nile: A Portrait of Egyptian Cinema*. Cairo: Zeitouna/American University in Cairo Press, 1998.

El-Bishlawi, Khairiya. "Matrimony of Extremes." *al-Ahram Weekly*, 3–9 May 2001, Issue No. 532.

Farid, Samir. *Directors and Directions in Egyptian Cinema*. Cairo: General Authority for Culture Palaces, 2000.

Gordon, Joel. *Revolutionary Melodrama: Popular Film and Civic Identity in Nasser's Egypt*. Chicago: University of Chicago Press, 2002.

Said, Edward. *Orientalism*. Princeton, N.J.: Princeton University Press, 1979.

Shafik, Viola. *Arab Cinema: History and Cultural Identity*. Cairo: American University in Cairo Press, 1998.

Shohat, Ella. *Israeli Cinema*. Austin: University of Texas Press, 1989.

Wassef, Magda, ed. *Egypte 100 Ans de Cinema*. Paris: N.p., 1995.

Web Sites

www.arab-celebs.com. Site that provides the alleged dates of birth of some Arab actors, singers, and TV presenters.

www.legend-sabah.com/legend-sabah/. Official Web site of Lebanese phenomenon Sabah.

www.dreamsofanation.org/films.html. Site with a comprehensive listing of films by Palestinian directors.

5

Music and Arabpop

Overview: From a Classical Tradition to Arabpop

Like modern cinema, Arabic music also had its Golden Age. The greats of Arab cinema were often singers, and the two forms of entertainment fed each other. The guardians of high culture consider that when cinema began to deteriorate in quality and quantity after the 1960s, music began a steady descent from high art into the realms of popular culture. The conventional opinion is that the Golden Age of music ended with the discrediting of Arab nationalism after 1967 and also the passing in that same decade of Umm Kalthoum and Abdel-Halim Hafez, symbols of high culture. In their place came the sounds of low culture, and by the late 1980s the pop industry had come to totally dominate the Arab soundscape with a new, infectious genre aping Western pop. It was still rough at the edges then, but today the music industry has entirely caught up with the West by merging state-of-the-art production with Arabic musical forms to create a successful indigenous sound that, like India's pop industry, competes with Western pop, at least in the minds of the Arab public (though Arabic pop music has yet to make the splash that Punjabi "Bangra" music, for example, has made in Europe). When in 2001 Lebanese producers began taking famous sections of music from Umm Kalthoum songs and singers did pop versions of Mohammed Abdel-Wahhab favorites—despite the outrage in some quarters of the press—it was a sure sign that what has sometimes been called "Arabpop" had come of age. Yet Arabpop is still depicted by the elites of high culture as the product of a decadent society that has lost its sense of worth. "When political and economic stability is restored in our societies and our conditions flourish, the original song will come back because it represents ourselves and our heritage in a true manner," classical Syrian singer Sabah Fakhri said in the Emirates daily *al-Bayan* (March 2002). "A serious dialogue should be conducted between the generations in order to be able to maintain our heritage. These days we are living the age of the deterioration of the Arabic song, but this doesn't mean there is nothing good. . . . Music is the language of the universe which God created before human beings. The splendid music makes me live a state of Sufism on the stage, so I dance and shake deep from inside."

One notable feature of Arabpop is that it is almost entirely apolitical. It is a mainstream genre designed to score maximum success by offending no essential constituencies—except classical purists, who don't matter anyway from a commercial viewpoint. The music veers away from the standard love song format only to promote Islam as a religion of peace or to back the Palestinians or occasionally slam the United States over its regional policies, but it steadfastly avoids domestic political and social issues. Some Western-style rap groups have emerged in recent years—Egyptian group MTM won a "rap" genre award at the first Arabian Music Awards in Dubai in 2004—but their major hit *Ummi Musafra* (*My Mother's Away*) was about nothing darker than a teenager who holds a dance party when his mother goes on holiday. Algeria has come closest to producing a mass dissident music, through the *rai* genre that developed from the 1960s to the 1980s, before reaching a foreign audience through France-based *rai* singers. The success of Maghrebi sounds in the West has caused the Mashreq to sit up and pay attention. Arabpop in the East is using more and more of the rhythms used by *rai*, and *rai* singers are teaming up with Arabpop stars for hit duets (the Moroccan-turned-Egyptian singer Samira Said sang with Algerian Cheb Mami in 2002, and Amal Hegazy of Lebanon followed with Cheb Faudel). By contrast, Khaled's success with his first big European hit, *Didi*, was originally met with indifference in the Arab East, where his Algerian dialect was hard to follow and the style of singing was alien. Another fad of the moment is reworking classic songs

as pop hits, such as Lebanese singer Dania's 2002 hit *al-Hilwa Di* (*This Gorgeous Woman*), a version of an Abdel-Wahhab classic (originally, in another era and time, about oppressed workers), whose chic video had the voluptuous Dania bouncing around the streets of Cuba. Though based in Cairo and Beirut, this mainstream pop industry is a mélange of local sounds accessible to all Arabs. At the same time, each country and region has its own music traditions, some of which have had limited success as pop genres in their own right (such as Algerian *rai*, Moroccan *shaabi*, Egyptian *shaabi*, and Gulf pop).

Most Arab countries also have their own classical Arabic music traditions and modern classical singers—Tunisia has Lutfi Boushnaq, Iraq has Nazem al-Ghazali, Morocco has Abdel-Wahhab Doukali, and Iraq has Afifa Iskander (who in 2004 reemerged in public in Baghdad after years of seclusion, *al-Hayat* of 9 August 2004 reported). North Africa has Andalusian music, the classical sound of the Arab-Islamic culture in the Iberian peninsula, which lasted from the eighth to the fifteenth centuries A.D. *Al-Andalus*, as Andalusia is called in Arabic, lives on today, from restaurant and nightclub names, to a reference point for intellectual discussion of the Palestinian-Israeli conflict, to the name of an Arabic satellite channel. In fact, the districts of Riyadh attacked by suspected al-Qa'ida suicide bombers in May 2002 were named after the Arab cities of Andalusia—Ghurnata (Grenada), Qurtuba (Cordoba), and Ishbiliya (Seville). Oriental and Occidental cultures crossed paths in Muslim Spain, resulting in three styles of Andalusian music: the flamenco of southern Spain; classical Arabic-Andalusian tradition, which is cultivated today in Algeria, Tunisia, and Morocco; and

Israel and Arabic Music

Music is as entangled in the great debates over Zionism and Arab identity as anything else in the Arab world. According to a study by Egyptian musicologist Farag al-Antari, the twentieth century witnessed "the Zionist plunder of Arabic music," as the title of his 1997 work explains (*al-Satu al-Sahyouni 'ala al-Musiqa al-Arabiya*). In 1932, when Zionism still had a certain respectability at least in Egypt, an Arabic music conference was held in Cairo with government backing. Its organizers were mainly European Jewish musicologists who had settled in Palestine, and the result was an enormous compilation of musical samples from North Africa and the Levant that ended up in the library of the Hebrew University in Jerusalem. Further Israeli studies of Bedouin music in the Sinai, while it was under Israeli occupation between 1967 and 1973, concluded that this music was not connected to the wider traditions of Arabic music. Al-Antari argues that these attempts undermined a unifying element of pan-Arabism. He also notes claims by some Israelis that the harp is of Jewish rather than Pharaonic origin and that the music of Jewish Egyptian composer Dawoud Hosni belongs to a Jewish rather than an Arabic tradition.

These debates give a sense of the immense identity battles raging in the region: Can we talk of "Arabic music"? Should we more correctly talk of smaller traditions of Jewish, Coptic, Egyptian, and Bedouin music? Who are the custodians and where are the citadels of the regional musical heritage—Egyptians in Cairo or Israelis in Jerusalem? Despite this, some Arabpop singers have ventured into Israel to perform for the Palestinians, including Medhat Saleh, Hani Shakir, Samira Said, and Hakim. Few public figures other than government officials in countries with diplomatic relations with Israel would risk the opprobrium of their peers for making such trips. The "anti-normalization" argument says that to reach the Palestinians in the occupied territories or Israel one has to deal with the State of Israel. Israeli Arab writer Emile Habiby once famously beseeched Arab intellectuals to "visit us at least once." But few ever have. At the same time, Arabic sounds are periodically popular in Israel—witness Ofra Haza (of Yemeni origin), Zava Ben (who sang Umm Kalthoum songs), and most recently Dana International, a transsexual of Yemeni origin, whose lyrics cleverly mix Arabic, Hebrew, Yiddish, and English. She won the Eurovision Song Contest in 1998.

Palestinian singer Ammar Hassan got to the finals of the "Arab Superstar" program on a wave of sympathy for Palestinians. (Anwar Amro/AFP/Getty Images)

Jewish-Andalusian music, found in Sephardi Jewish communities throughout the Arab world, which they carried to Israel. The classical Andalusian music that is cherished in Morocco today—especially by families who fled Spanish persecution after the Muslim regime was overthrown—is sung in classical Arabic or the lost Arabic dialect of Grenada. The sound also survives in the popular Tunisian genre of classical Arabic music known as *ma'louf*. Arabpop is of course informed by classical Arabic music. Arabic music has around seventy *maqamat*, or scales, which use tonal intervals smaller than the halftones used in Western music. Unlike in Western music, in Arabic music the melody of a particular scale is central, not the meter or rhythm. Each *maqam* is meant to induce a different mood in the listener. For example, the *rast* is connected with a feeling of power, health, and strength; the *bayaati* is for joy, vitality, and femininity; *hejaz* is for the size and eternity of the desert; and *saba* is for sadness and pain. Even the most hip pop ditty today will still be rooted in this Arabic tradition.

The Golden Age: 1952–1977

The period from the 1940s through the 1960s was a time of revolutionary change throughout the Arab world, when there was much hope and optimism, and when classical Arabic music enjoyed a renaissance. There has been considerable debate over who were the true greats of this period (singers, writers, and players). In *The Seven Greats of Modern Arabic Music*, Victor Sahab selects Sayed Darwish, Mohamed al-Qasabgi, Zakariya Ahmed, Mohammed Abdel-Wahhab, Umm Kalthoum,

Riyadh al-Sonbati, and Asmahan (Sami 1998). The most celebrated singer of the era was Umm Kalthoum, or *al-Sitt* ("the Lady"), as she was affectionately known, or least she has come to leave the biggest impression on subsequent generations. It was against the background of struggle for independence and search for identity in the Arab world that her career developed, and for Arabs her appearance at this particular time in history seemed almost providential. When in 1923 she moved to Cairo from her northern Egyptian village of Tammay al-Zuhayra, the Arab world was in the midst of a great colonial division. Egypt was independent only in name. Part of Palestine had been promised to the Zionist movement. Only in the empty desert of the Arabian Peninsula, where Ibn Saud and his family were plotting their future state, could one speak of anything approaching independence. The rise of Arab nationalism was mirrored by the career of this prodigal child-singer who took the high culture of Arabic poetry to the masses via her singing.

Umm Kalthoum publicly associated herself with the Arab nationalist regime of Gamal Abdel Nasser after it came to power in Egypt in 1952, and the two got on famously well. She had everything to offer in the way of cultural symbolism that Nasser's pan-Arab state could want. In *The Voice of Egypt*, biographer Virginia Danielson recounts that it was Nasser himself who, in the first days of the military coup of July 1952, reversed a decision to take her off state radio because she used to sing for deposed King Farouk. Nasser saw that to reinforce his regime's legitimacy and fire up the masses for his development plans, he could do no better than to have Umm Kalthoum on his side. For her part, she genuinely believed in him. After the disastrous defeat of the 1967 Arab-Israeli war, Umm Kalthoum came out fighting, and embarked on four years of concerts for Arab audiences around the world to raise money for Nasser's effort to rebuild Egypt's military.

Lebanese conductor Selim Sehab has provided a summary of her musical talents (lecture given by Sehab in Cairo, November 1994). At the beginning of her career, she had already perfected the pronunciation of Quranic Arabic; her vocal range extended from baritone to soprano; she sang from her larynx and not her diaphragm; and her voice was strong enough to break glass, so that microphones had to be kept at a half-meter distance from her mouth. Sehab considers that in global terms she was the greatest singer of the twentieth century. She also attracted around her the best players, lyricists, and songwriters in the Arab world, putting her at the pinnacle of Arab high culture. Her monthly performances were broadcast on radio throughout the Arab world for thirty years until her death in 1973. Throughout her career she perfected what is known in Arabic as *tarab*—a state of rapture induced by music, singing, and verse. She attracted a constellation of stars around her, including songwriters Mohammed Abdel-Wahhab, Baligh Hamdy, Mohammed al-Qasabgi, and Riyadh al-Sonbati and poets Bairam al-Tunsi, Ahmed Rami, and Ahmed Shawki. She also contributed to pushing sexual conventions through songs where she spoke directly to her lover about her feelings, such as *Inta Umri*. Even today the convention in pop songs is for men to refer to women from the masculine point of view, for otherwise such public acknowledgment of premarital affection would be scandalous for a woman in traditional society.

A 1968 image of Umm Kalthoum in Cairo, taken after she decided to donate the proceeds of her concerts to Egypt's war effort to regain the Sinai Peninsula from Israel. (Bettmann/Corbis)

Umm Kalthoum is currently back in vogue, partly because it's around a hundred years since her year of birth (variously set at 1898, 1904, and 1908) and partly because she fills a need in the collective Arab consciousness at present. In Egypt, a major soap opera about her life was a huge hit all over the Arab world in 1999, and an Egyptian film director, Mohammed Fadel, has made a major film biography of her life, *Kawkab al-Sharq* (*Star of the Orient*). The Arab World Institute in Paris has for years held an annual Umm Kalthoum week of musical performances. The rush of interest in the 1990s came at a time of unease about the future among political elites. Since the end of the Cold War, and when Palestinians and Israelis entered into the Oslo peace process in 1993—then fell out of it when talks collapsed in 2000—the old certitudes

Image of Arab nationalist singer Umm Kalthoum, taken early in her career, on the cover of a magazine. (Patrick Godeau/Focus MidEast)

Umm Kalthoum shown at the height of her fame on a coffee shop wall. (Patrick Godeau/Focus MidEast)

of regional politics were no more. The press and television are engaged in a vigorous debate these days about what Arab identity will mean if an end is found to the Palestinian-Israeli conflict and Iraq becomes allied with the United States in the manner of some of the Gulf monarchies. Bookstalls on the street corners of Arab capitals are full of titles bemoaning the state of the Arab world and what will become of it. The Arabs are searching for heroes and Umm Kalthoum fits the bill.

The other great star of the postindependence era, before Arabpop gripped the region, was Abdel-Halim Hafez, the first sex-symbol singer (in the Elvis Presley mold). The media made much of the twentieth and twenty-fifth anniversaries of his death in 1997 and 2002, with reams of newsprint

about the Egyptian who replaced the rather staid and proper Mohammed Abdel-Wahhab as the role model for youth. Even Umm Kalthoum was disturbed by Abdel-Halim's success. "Boy, you're a crooner, not a real singer," she once snapped at him in front of the press (Danielson 1997). Afflicted with bilharzia as a child, due to playing in the Nile, Abdel-Halim died at age forty-eight in 1977. His illness denied him foods, drink, and marriage, providing him with a persona in accordance with the dominant culture of repressed sexual desire, which he embodied in his songs. He remains a role model for men and women today, as a handsome male with manners and a soft heart—an Egyptian cultural ideal adopted by the rest of the Arab world. Recent films have consciously tried to create the aura of Abdel-

Halim around certain pop stars. One vehicle, for singer Mustafa Qamar, even re-created scenes from classic movies where Abdel-Halim sang certain songs, but it didn't go over with the public (2000's *al-Hobb al-Awwal*, or *First Love*).

However, the memory of singers today does not necessarily reflect how they were thought of at the time. Mohammed Abdel-Wahhab and Abdel-Halim Hafez are revered in today's official public discourse in Egypt, though they were both discredited in the latter stages of their careers. Cultural anthropologists argue that musicians were subject to posthumous hagiography to make them part of a modernized national identity. The state media in Egypt chooses to forget that Abdel-Wahhab was once ridiculed for his effete European ways. First rising to prominence in an earlier era, Abdel-Wahhab was outgunned by the association of Abdel-Halim with the nationalist regime that overthrew the monarchy in 1952. But Abdel-Halim's star faded after the 1967 defeat discredited Nasser's regime, and nascent Arabpop and foreign music eventually came to replace Abdel-Halim in the affections of the masses. In fact, the generation that lived during the Nasserist era came to be known as the "defeat generation." Its spirit died with Abdel-Halim, and the reverence his memory enjoys today is a measure of how depressed Arabs feel about the state of the current political order.

The Birth of Arabpop since the 1970s

The Arabs are mad about music. As Egyptian music producer Tarek al-Kashef said, "Everyone is crazy about music, they never stop talking about it. You hear it everywhere, it's probably even coming out of the taps" (interview with author, *Cairo Times*, 6 March 1997). Today's music industry is an extremely sophisticated, multimillion-dollar operation, but twenty years ago it had only just begun. That beginning was the rise of Ahmed Adawiya, the Arab world's first modern pop star. His politically subversive tapes, sold in the backstreets of Cairo and sung in the lowest form of colloquial Arabic, dominated popular culture through the 1970s—a time when the greats of the Golden Age of music were passing away. He rode the wave of a new musical genre called *shaabi* music, or music "of the people"—traditional songs of lament transformed into a raw urban scream in the slums of Egypt's expanding cities.

Music moguls today idolize Adawiya's memory. His first album in 1972 sold a million copies, and he went on to sell five million tapes over five years in Arab countries, making him the first pop star to successfully exploit the spread of cassettes and cassette players around the region. With his last tape in 1982, Adawiya sold 250,000 units in one week. This was at a time when there wasn't an industry as such, just backstreet recordings, pirated tapes, and authorities concerned about a new underground culture developing in the slums. Although the music had a traditional Arabic orchestra sound, it differed in that it was packaged into a five-minute format in the Western pop fashion. And then there were the words. In contrast to the dramatic love songs and politically correct sounds of the Umm Kalthoum era, here was a very ordinary young man, with a passion to move mountains, singing about the maddening trivialities of modern Egypt—for example, in his most famous song, *Zahma* (*Overcrowding*), he sings of a woman called

Arabpop Still Waiting to Break into the West

The September 11, 2001, attacks delayed the launch of Arab pop music on the Western stage. Encouraged by the worldwide success of English rock star Sting's 1999 collaboration with Algeria's Cheb Mami on *Desert Rose*, major record labels were busy placing themselves in the Middle East to take advantage of what they thought would be "the next big thing" in the West. But the attacks in the United States changed all that, as "Arab" was no longer "in," and in 2002 Sony Music closed down its Cairo operation. Sony had been the only one of the five major worldwide record labels to have a fully owned subsidiary in the Arab region. "There was general interest in Middle East artists, and the majors had initiated plans to set up a direct presence in the Middle East, but September 11 changed that," said Ahmad Marei, who was managing director of Sony's ill-fated Egyptian division (interview with author, September 2002). The distinctive Arabic sound, characterized by quarter notes and belly dance–inspired beats, remains marginalized outside the Middle East. "International music accounts for 30 percent of sales in the Arab world, while Arabic music from the region accounts for only 0.3 percent of sales in the rest of the world," says Shuckri Bundakji of the IFPI (interview with author, May 2004).

Global fame (*al-'aalamiya,* as it is termed) is the current obsession of many of the top artists in the Arab world. Inspired by the success of Colombian Lebanese singer Shakira, who is hugely popular in the Arab world, singers like Lebanon's Nawal al-Zoghby and Morocco's Samira Said have shifted their image and sound in an attempt to follow in her footsteps. The Algerian *rai* singers like Cheb Mami and Cheb Khaled have had a fair amount of success in the West, especially among North African immigrant communities in France. There have been other exceptions to the rule, such as the

Popular Algerian French singer Cheb Mami in 2001 after his success in the *Desert Rose* duet with British singer Sting. (Eric Robert/ Corbis Sygma)

southern Egyptian Musiciens du Nil, who were packaged as gypsies and made waves as "world music." In 2002, one time British sex symbol Jane Birkin visited Beirut to publicize the album *Arabesque,* featuring Serge Gains-bourg songs reworked in an Arabic style. But for the most part mainstream Arab music doesn't interest the West and vice versa.

Ahmad Marei is skeptical about any of the Arabpop stars making it without a major label behind them. At the same time, major labels have too many problems with the internal workings of the Arabpop market for them to gain a regional foothold. Sony should know, being forced to close down its Egyptian division in 2002. "There are no statistics, no retail audits, no charts. You don't know how many [copies of] an album sold. You're dealing in a complete vacuum and it's difficult to get market share data," Marei said (interview with author, September 2002). Local artists are used to agreeing to huge flat fees instead of royalty deals with local labels, meaning they have little interest in carefully plotting album promotion with their companies.

Even the big stars rely more on hype than on concrete sales to justify their status and huge fees for appearances at weddings and special parties for the elites in various Arab capitals. Just as governments don't want free elections to establish the real strengths of different political groups (lest the low popularity of government parties be exposed), the music industry has no interest in showing the real strengths of its stars. "The media presence of any artist doesn't reflect their sales," Marei said (interview with author, September 2002). Cassette tapes sell more than CDs throughout the region, limiting the profits of record labels, and pirating is rife. Compact discs comprise around 5 percent of the market in Egypt, up to 40 percent in Lebanon, and 30 percent in Dubai. But local retail outlets will make pirated copies of compilation CDs and tapes to order. For example, there are now over forty hit compilations of an illegal series that is similar to the "Now" series in Britain. The only major Western retail outlet in the region is Virgin, with stores in Beirut and Dubai. Although Egypt accounts for around two-thirds of sales of the biggest Arab artists, Egyptian unit prices are much less in dollar terms. In the current climate of global market slowdown, the most successful albums will sell 1.5 million units in Arab countries, 1 million of them in Egypt. Western music accounts for only around 10 percent of sales in Egypt, Marei said (interview with author, September 2002).

Umm Hassan, crying babies, and traffic jams. These were anthems for changing and confusing times in the Arab world after the death of Gamal Abdel Nasser. He also starred in a few films, including an experiment in the horror genre by director Mohammed Shebl, his 1981 *Anyab* (*Fangs*).

Adawiya's success was met with a horrendous snobbery. For the leftist intellectual elite he was a symbol of everything wrong with the times: the pro-American policies of Nasser's successor Anwar Sadat, Sadat's peace with Israel, his apparent ditching of the Palestinians, and his loosening of the socialist command economy, which lasted in nationalist states like Libya, Algeria, Iraq, and Syria through the 1990s. To these intellectuals, under Nasser there was Umm Kalthoum, but with Sadat the Arab world was left to the insidious silliness of Adawiya songs. Leftist political commentator Salah Issa wrote that Adawiya's natural audience consisted of people who peddled bad foodstuffs, built shoddy apartment blocks, and made a fortune dealing drugs—all features of 1970s Egypt. For most of the decade Egypt's information ministry kept Adawiya off national television. For the state, the glorious road to development meant inculcating the masses with knowledge and culture according to an official canon, but then the masses decided for themselves what they liked by buying Adawiya tapes. The authorities didn't like that. As Walter Armbrust writes in his book, *Mass Culture and Modernism in Egypt*, "It is Adawiya's frank appeal to the masses—without any of the rhetoric of 'raising their cultural standards'—that sets him apart from singers backed by the cultural establishment in print and on television" (Armbrust 1996, 184).

The irony is that Adawiya himself was blissfully unaware of the power of his music. It was the work of producer Atef Montasser and lyricist Hassan Abu Itman, who both understood the appeal to the common man of a backstreet kid with a strong voice like Adawiya's. They took that voice and mixed it with themes that touched on everyday life. In *Zahma*, Umm Hassan was a metaphor for the uncertainties in Egypt in the early 1970s, after Nasser's death, and the wailing baby was Sadat craving the demagogic appeal of Nasser. "It sounded uncultured and unintellectual, but he really sang from the heart—so if he had understood the words he might have sung them differently," Kashef said (interview with author, *Cairo Times*, 26 June 1997). "I was simply very happy and thank God for what I was blessed with," Adawiya said (interview with author, *Cairo Times*, 26 June 1997). By the late 1990s Adawiya had turned to religion, putting out religious tapes under his own record label that featured star preachers and Quranic reciters. Any chance of a comeback for Adawiya himself, though, painfully ended in 1998 when a cuckolded Kuwaiti husband inflicted serious damage on the singer. Rumors surfaced that the Kuwaiti husband performed surgery on the singer under the influence of drugs, thus leading to a botched procedure. When Adawiya subsequently appeared on television, he was weak and could hardly stand up, and on the streets a phrase was coined, "*Ahmed Adawiya baad il-amaliya*" (Ahmed Adawiya after the operation).

The nascent industry that went on to take the Arab world by storm has desperately strived to emulate Adawiya's phenomenal success. It wasn't until the late 1980s that a coterie of experimenting producers succeeded, led by Libyan singer/producer Hamid al-Sha'iri. The song was called *Law Leki* (*If Not for You*), sung by Libyan Ali Hemeida and featuring a format that dominated Arabic pop for the next ten years: Libyan clapping, finger cymbals, and a drum machine with a beat that mimicked the hip swings of belly dancing, which every Arab learns as a child. *Law Leki* sold some 60,000 tapes and established a new, insidiously catchy sound, dubbed at the time as *jeel*, or "generation music." Though no one in the *jeel* era approached the success of Adawiya, with few stars selling more than 300,000 copies of each album, this was the time when "Arabpop" took off. Hundreds of singers flooded the airwaves with songs, which, though derivative and similar-sounding, attested to the fact that the Arab world had successfully developed its own peculiar music industry (as opposed to doing copies of Western hits, such as Egyptian singer Simone's version in Arabic of the Pointer Sisters' *Frankie*). Sha'iri is widely regarded as the genius who, after the Adawiya phenomenon, almost single-handedly invented Arabpop. In a traditionalist culture like the Arab world, which places special value on its musical heritage, that's not easy. "Before him we didn't have anyone with the guts to do something like he did," said young Lebanese composer Hani Siblini (interview with author, January 2002). "And it was because he's not Egyptian—he brought something different to Egypt. I don't think anyone can invent now as such; we're living in a mixing era, a mixing of cultures." Sha'iri is still going strong. He had his own huge hit with Egyptian singer Hisham Abbas in 1997, *Aini* (lit., "my eye," meaning "my love"); he produced the "Arab dream" (*al-hilm al-arabi*) song, where a host of pop stars sing about Arab unity; and he has produced the hits of Lebanese pop star Nawal al-Zoghby.

The late 1990s saw a second wind for

Lebanese singer Nancy Ajram at the Jerash Festival in Jordan in July 2004. (Ali Jarekji/ Reuters/Corbis)

Egyptian singer Ruby during an interview in 2004 after her music videos, which are considered risqué, annoyed some Egyptian politicians and media commentators. (Aladin Abdel Naby/Reuters/Corbis)

Arabpop. With the advent of Arabic satellite stations, pop video culture has taken off and new sounds have developed that are much closer to Western pop but still distinctively Middle Eastern. Most of the stars of the moment are reinventions. There are two eras of video culture, pre-satellite and post-satellite. The Syrian Asala was once a dumpy-looking singer of long poems by poet Nizar Qabbani. Now she's shaped for the video era, with good looks and well-crafted pop tunes for private Arabic music channels, which, as of this writing, now number at least thirteen. The same goes for all the other major stars, with some of them provoking huge controversy. In Lebanese singer Nancy Ajram's first video clip, 2002's *Akhaasmak Aah* (*I*

Would Fall Out with You), she belly dances her way through a men's coffee shop in a tight-fitting dress, leading to protests when she performed in Bahrain and calls in numerous Arab parliaments for a ban on broadcasting the video. Egyptian singer Ruby provoked a similar outcry with her 2004 song *Leih Byidaari Kida* (*Why Does He Hide Like That?*). In his critique of a video by Lebanese pop star Nawal al-Zoghby, Egyptian academic Ashraf Galal noted that there is "the absence of Arab identity and positive values and a clear approval of Western values, and there is no presence for the Arab environment, and there is a complete cancellation of higher meanings and values" (*al-Hayat*, 20 April 2004). There's a sort of separation of functions that's emerged in the industry now. Beirut used to be the center of Arabic music until the 1975–1990 civil war ruined the industry there. Cairo become a production center as Arabpop developed as a genre in the 1990s, while Gulf-owned satellite television channels aired the music videos that ultimately made the singers megastars. Some Lebanese stars are producing their albums in Beirut again, but those with big ambitions go to Cairo to market their work. Cairo is still seen as the capital of Arabpop, but few of the biggest stars are actually Egyptian, an irritant to Egypt's cultural establishment. Lebanese singers will come to Cairo to appear on Egypt's terrestrial channels, while Egyptian stars and other Arabs will head to Beirut to appear on Lebanese satellite shows. The biggest sellers have been Egypt's Amr Diab and Lebanon's Ragheb Alameh.

The industry is a huge moneymaker for lyricists, composers, musicians, agents, sound engineers, and others. The small state of Lebanon is a big motor for the industry. Lebanon currently has music sales of around $30 million a year, with a population of around 4 million, compared to $80 million in Egypt with a population of 70 million, $80 million in Saudi Arabia with over 23 million, and $50 million in the United Arab Emirates with nearly 4 million. Considering Lebanon's size, that's impressive. Some fifty Lebanese singers are known in the Arab world, with around half of them recording their songs in Egypt with Egyptian composers. Pirating is rife. Samir Tabet, a Lebanese lawyer fighting music piracy, said at least five million dollars is lost a year in unpaid rights to record companies in Lebanon, including domestic pirating, imports, and unlicensed performing of material. Tapes are pirated even more,

comprising about 70 percent of the total CD sales in Lebanon (Lebanon has the biggest CD market in the region). "We raise cases and wait for the state to do something. But the state has other priorities, such as economic problems," Tabet said (interview with author, January 2002). "The effect is that small producers fear to enter the business, not only because of piracy, but because big companies monopolize even if they make losses." But despite the piracy, the streets are still alive to the sound of new singers. A record contract can get a major star $700,000, no matter how many units are sold. "We need an infrastructure of legislation and the concept of supporting artists," says Shuckri Bundakji, Middle East representative of the International Federation of Phonographic Industries (IFPI) (interview with author, May 2004). "One of the big problems in the Arab world is there's no taxes, like in the GCC. Most of the support in France and Italy, for example, comes from tax money in order to help their art and their culture." The maverick musicians mixing classical Arabic songs with techno beats are mainly Lebanese. They have been accused of tampering with the sacred canon of Arabic singing giants of the twentieth century. After watching a program on Future Television that aired a rejigged version of the classic *Inta Umri* (*You Are My Life*), culture commentator Ibrahim al-Aris wrote in *al-Hayat*, "Is it right for a modern person to take phrases from the music introduction to one of the songs of Umm Kalthoum and turn it into a dance rhythm which moves the young people of today in nightclubs? . . . There is a trend to take the classics and modernize them, which has some people furious and others excited, but which is in general a deformation of our heritage" (*al-Hayat*, January 2002). Siblini disagrees: "It's a very big thing to say I'm ruining tradition. People are too humble to do something like that," he said (interview with author, January 2002). "Many people are now buying Umm Kalthoum and original mixes by Baligh Hamdy [the composer of *Inta Umri*]. I'd be happier if someone could compose like Baligh Hamdy, but no one today could even create something like those four bars of music [the classic intro to *Inta Umri*]. In the Arab world we're used to getting techniques from the West and then arranging Arabic songs with it. So the West has helped us in music since it made us discover in the Arab world that our music, our treasure, can't really be modernized—we didn't touch Umm Kalthoum's voice. New generations will see that we had genius in our world." He adds: "We are witnessing a new generation of composers and they are doing very well."

Establishing some sort of order in the industry will be a challenge. The IFPI organized its first Arabian Music Awards in May 2004 in Dubai, an event that threatened to lay bare the true popularity of the big pop stars. Most categories were split between the four main music regions of the Arab world—North Africa, Egypt, the Levant and Iraq, and the Gulf—in what organizers said was an attempt to keep everyone happy. The winners were chosen by Arabic music listeners around the world via the Internet and phone text messages over a period of a month, with international auditing firm Ernst & Young hired to ensure no vote-rigging. But hardly any Arab stars who were not asked to perform bothered to come and the few who did walked out when their rivals got awards that they felt should have been theirs. Plugged as the Arabic Grammies, the ceremony began over two hours late and the live broadcast on Lebanese Future TV had to be cut eight minutes into the airing because microphones didn't work and trophies could not be found on stage. Without explanation, the ceremony ended without the awarding of the most prestigious prizes—overall best male and female performer.

Egyptian *Shaabi* Music Today

Shaabi music didn't die in Egypt with the end of Ahmed Adawiya's career. Egypt has a whole host of *shaabi* stars, and the genre is even aped by non-Egyptians, such as the Lebanese Fadi Badr. The most popular mainstream *shaabi* singer over the last decade has been the Egyptian singer Hakim, with a *shaabi*-meets-Arabpop sound that diehards say isn't really *shaabi* at all. With Hakim, *shaabi* is repackaged for respectable public consumption and airplay on the satellite channels. The son of a village mayor in central Egypt, Hakim hails from a family of social standing who tried to prevent him from entering the low-class world of music. With Hakim, *shaabi* music is cleverly exploited to craft an image of an authentic Egyptian, who, despite life's myriad irritations in an overcrowded country of 70 million people, still manages to smile through it all—though in fact *shaabi* music was originally characterized by its dramatization of life's problems and histrionic complaining, as in Adawiya's classic moan *Zahma* ("How overcrowded the world is / You lose your loved ones in the chaos / Crowded so there's no more mercy / Like a saint's festival without a saint"). Whereas the state shunned Adawiya, it has welcomed Hakim with open arms, and that likely goes some way to explaining the flip from raw *shaabi* songs of complaint to polished, *shaabi*-esque ditties of hope. Hakim's smile is central to the sell. Most of his album covers and publicity photos feature his infectious grin. "We try to get people to smile. We don't want heavy tunes and sad words. The words can touch the listener who is sad, but it'll make him smile," Hakim said (interview with author, *The Middle East Magazine*, November 2000). "There's no one who hasn't been treated unfairly in life. No matter how content people are, they feel that somehow they have been wronged at some point. No one is happy with his lot in life when it comes to money, but everyone is convinced they deserve more."

Shaabi music, Hakim-style, sells. Hakim's producer, Hani Sabet, claims that Hakim's recent albums have sold a million units apiece, with piracy covering a fifth of that figure. His 2000 album *Aho!* (*Hey, People*) benefited heavily from the advance publicity of a starring role in TV ads for an Egyptian mobile phone card, Alo! And he's extremely popular at Algerian weddings. Hakim said his popularity lies in the fact that the vast majority of people in Arab countries today come from limited-income backgrounds. "Ninety percent of people in the Arab world are simple folks. Most of the Arabs who've gone abroad and become Americanized and European are originally *shaabi*. You'll find it's the same in all the fancy districts of Cairo—everyone originally comes from the poor districts, so they have nostalgia for this kind of music," he said. "When they sit in my concerts they loosen their ties and live. I make them forget that they are fancy folks now with a car waiting for them outside. They go back to their roots" (interview with author, *The Middle East Magazine*, November 2000).

But Hakim has acknowledged a debt to Adawiya. "He is a legend; there will never be anyone like him again," he said on Rotana TV (14 April 2004), before offering a rendition of his own favorite Adawiya song, *Telephone*.

The original form of *shaabi* has made a comeback, though, with the sudden stardom of Shaaban Abdel-Rahim. This Egyptian singer became the toast of the nation when his song, *I Hate Israel* came out following realtime television coverage of Israel's attempts to crush the Palestinian uprising against occupation that began in September 2000. The song was so popular that it even provoked a media spat over who wrote the lyrics. Poet Awad Badawi claimed the refrain was picked up by Abdel-Rahim's friends at a musical soiree and next thing he knew it had become something akin to the national anthem. "Abdel-Rahim is a working-class, illiterate singer, so how could he sing about politics and Israel? It was my idea, he would never have thought about a subject like that," Badawi said (interview with author, Reuters, 8 May 2001). Even the official arts censor, who has the power to censor lyrics deemed politically or religiously offensive, tried to claim credit. "Originally it was 'I don't like Israel' but I made a recommendation that they choose another word equal to the state of people's feelings," Madkour Thabet said (interview with author, Reuters, 8 May 2001). Abdel-Rahim's follow-up song had him claiming he would give up smoking and become a new man in the new year, but he ventured into populist politics again with his 2004 song *Ya Am Arabi* (*Hey, Arabs*), whose video clip had cartoon images of Israeli prime minister Ariel Sharon sending the September 11 planes to attack New York

Egypt's Dissident Duo

Singer Sheikh Issa Imam and poet Ahmed Fouad Nigm are the best known of Egypt's small repertoire of dissident singers. Probably the most important political songsters of the post-Nasser era in the Arab world, this duo sang of the disgust ordinary people felt for the ruling order after the 1967 defeat, and they did so in the most barbed and sarcastic colloquial language. Nigm wrote the poetry and the blind Sheikh Imam sang and played the oud. Their fame took off after the 1968 song *Oh how Nice, Our Soldiers Have Returned from the Frontline* (*Ya ma ahla, rij'it zubbatna min khatt il-nar*), a parody of the 1967 farce that reportedly angered Nasser. The duo's skit on Gulf regimes surviving on their oil wealth in alliance with Sadat, "Welcome Nixon, Watergate hero, the sultans of beans and oil wealth highly valued you," inspired massive student protests in Cairo in 1977. Class divides and a spectacular poverty gap that emerged throughout the 1970s fired much of their work. Nigm once wrote: "They wear the latest fashions, we live seven in a room/They eat pigeon and chicken, we eat beans that make us ill/They travel in airplanes, we die in minibuses." The pair later separated amid personal disputes, and Imam died in 1995.

Nigm is something of an unofficial national institution in Egypt today, a living leftist legend. His three-part autobiography, titled *al-Fagoumy* (a made-up word meaning something like "the morally depraved attacker"), stands out as one of the most honest, crude, and subversive pieces of writing that hasn't been banned by censors. He eschews the false bravado and tales of glorious political struggle from the cradle that litter the autobiographical genre in Arabic political writing and he uses expressive colloquial language. Even Arab League secretary-general Amr Moussa once said he was a fan. From works by Anwar Sadat and his wife to those of newspaper editors close to the president, self-hagiography is an art form that is alive and well in Egypt. Nigm's insane brilliance won him many female admirers—he's on his fifth wife, despite admitting to violence against his first, singer Azza Balbaa. Yet despite this fame, he is ignored by the state and lives in an unattractive low-income housing estate in the desert outside Cairo. Nigm has been attacked by some in the opposition press as the latest in a line of leftists to be co-opted by the state, though he still lives his celebrated life of poverty while leftist poets like Abdel-Rahman al-Abnoudy are treated in hospitals abroad at the government's expense. Naguib Sawiris, chairman of the Egyptian mobile phone company Orascom and a symbol of the new capitalist order, held an evening in honor of Nigm's seventieth birthday in June 1999. "Sawiris wanted to do something for someone he admired and used to listen to as a student in the 1970s, while the state doesn't want to celebrate him at all," said political commentator Salah Issa (interview with author, *Cairo Times,* 8 July 1999).

and U.S. president George W. Bush carving up the Arab world like a cake, as the British and French did after World War I. Some voices in Arabic music have spoken out against this. "The public is hungry for real art," composer Helmy Bakr said (news conference in Dubai, 15 May 2004).

"Songs are about more than just insulting Sharon or Bush . . . or wiggling your behind."

With Abdel-Rahim in particular, though, there is a specific cultural cringe felt by Arab intellectuals and other purveyors of high culture. His success rattled Egypt's left-leaning intelligentsia. They always wanted to bond with the masses over a defining nationalist issue like Palestine, but because the state is formally allied with America and at peace with Israel, they can't. Then suddenly, in the first weeks of the Intifada, an amazing window of opportunity opened up. The Left tried to take advantage of it by organizing demonstrations, but the state always puts limits on that sort of expression. Then in one fell swoop this tasteless, cultureless, bad singer from a dirt-poor village outside Cairo managed to make that magic connect with the masses with a statement of immediate simplicity: "I hate Israel" (*Ana Bakrah Isra'il*). The literary weekly *Akhbar al-Adab* received angry protests after one article compared Abdel-Rahim to Sheikh Imam, the blind singer who sang the anti-regime verse of leftist poet Ahmed Fouad Nigm after Nasser's defeat and in Sadat's time. The Imam-Nigm duo have high cultural caché for leftists throughout the Arab world. But *Akhbar al-Adab* realized that Abdel-Rahim's popularity was a sign that the elites were, once again, out of touch with the people. "There is another culture that we don't know anything about, and that is the culture of the lower classes, which encompasses millions of Egyptians. It is a culture marginalized by resentment and arrogance from the cultural elite," it wrote (April 2001).

Like Adawiya in his heyday, Abdel-Rahim symbolizes everything the government and its massive state media does not want Egypt to be. He is a good example of a class of Egyptian that public discourse on cultural values deems as requiring reconstruction. But Abdel-Rahim himself was disarmingly happy with who he was. He didn't aspire to be a great singer and he didn't hide his impoverished background.

He told one TV presenter that the shirt he was wearing—a gaudy, flowery affair—was cut from the same material used to cover his mother's sofa. He didn't pay lip service to the official canon by playing up Abdel-Halim as a role model. Inasmuch as he recognized that there was something called high culture, he simply didn't consider himself to be part of it. "Abdel-Rahim is illiterate and has no culture, so of course we can't show him on television. It's not real art. Why don't people listen to Hany Shakir?" TV presenter Amr Leithy said, referring to Abdel-Halim clone Hany Shakir (interview with author, May 2001). Leftists have noted with satisfaction that Abdel-Rahim's Arab nationalism is hollow, as they always suspected—he briefly sang a reworded version of the *I Hate Israel* ditty in advertisements for a new McDonald's sandwich called the McFalafel (a contract he soon lost after a complaint from the American Jewish Committee), and he is now taking huge fees to appear in slapstick films that milk his popular appeal while it lasts.

Algeria *Rai*, the Maghreb's Answer to Mashreqi Arabpop

The Algerian music known as *rai*—meaning "opinion" or "view" in Arabic—became a big industry in its own right in the 1980s, broke into the Western music market in the 1990s, and in recent years has begun to influence the pop sounds of the eastern half of the Arab world. In Algeria, *rai* was the first music whose lyrics addressed the feelings of everyday people—on personal as well as political matters—and this was a leap ahead from traditional religious lyrics. The initial reaction to the music in the Arab world was similar to the reaction of conservatives in Algeria itself when modern *rai* developed from the 1960s through the 1990s: distaste. Several *rai* singers, including Cheb Hosni and producer Rachid Baba Ahmed, were assassinated by Islamist radicals in the 1990s, and after that those who still remained left for Paris. It's easy to see today why traditional-minded religious constituencies are disturbed by this alluring mix of Arabic classical music and Western rock music. Many of these singers have voices as powerful as muezzins during the call to prayer, and many of their vocal showpieces in *rai* songs appear to imitate the call of the muezzin—such as Cheb Mami's input in English rock singer Sting's *Desert Rose* hit from 1999. *Rai* involves a process of deconstruction of Arab-Islamic music culture, taking certain aspects and reformulating them in a Western rock-pop context. It's a form of world music, but it is practiced by the indigenous culture itself. Peter Gabriel's World Music project offered two versions of Pakistani singer Fath Ali Khan, his synthesized modern version and the original sound. One sounds exotic, erotic, and atmospheric, appealing to the Western ear, and the other sounds traditional, appealing to devotees of that form of traditional Pakistani music. With *rai*, the Algerians themselves—with French help—present a repackaged modern sound.

The music originated as a product of the rural migration to cities in West Algeria in the 1930s. In this new environment, a number of popular religious forms of music and singing emerged, such as the poetry known as *malhoun* and the singing of the *maddaha*, a woman who would sing Sufi songs in praise of the Prophet (known as *madh*, or praise) at ceremonies such as weddings and circumcisions. After independence in 1962, local groups of musicians began to replace reed flutes with brass (trumpets and saxophones), and then with electric guitar and the wah-wah pedal. Brothers Rachid and Fethi Baba Ahmed introduced a complete synthesizer and drum-machine sound into *rai* in 1982, when the reed flute made a comeback in the form of a keyboard. A key component in this process was the use of the accordion and other instruments in the Oran area to develop the *malhoun*, and musicologists say that Oran and *rai* were originally quite distinct forms, though today the term *rai* has become a catchall phrase covering the lot. As in Egypt, the flood of cheap cassette recorders opened fresh avenues for the spread of novel forms of popular music that spoke to a new generation of disenfranchised and disenchanted youth in a failed modern state.

Rai took off when Cheb Khaled collaborated with the Baba brothers in the mid-1980s. Having taught himself guitar, bass, harmonica, and accordion, Khaled was a player at clubs, parties, and weddings. Then he met Rachid Baba Ahmed, the Hamid al-Sha'iri of *rai*, who revolutionized the form with Western electric instruments and studio techniques. Khaled was the right voice at the right time. The addition of drum machines, synthesizers, and guitars took the music to a new generation, even though much of it continued to be censored by the Algerian government, which considered the style subversive. After leaving for France in 1986, Khaled's first big commercial success was the 1992 album *Khaled*, featuring the Arabic funk-rock hit song *Didi*. This was the big international break for *rai*, and producers Cairo and Beirut wondered how to advance the Arabpop sound of the Mashreq. Arabpop was a carefully constructed Frankenstein monster from the studios of

The "king of *rai*," Cheb Khaled, performing in Cairo in 1993 at the height of his fame after the success of *Didi*. (Thomas Hartwell/Corbis)

Cairo, which largely hijacked the potential for Egypt's *shaabi* to develop as Algeria's *rai* had. The album *Khaled* had tracks mixed by American producer Don Was, and Steve Hillage directed proceedings on 2000's *Kenza* (*Treasure*), by which time Khaled was using Egyptian musicians for his backing orchestra.

Marginal Music and Instruments Still Extant in the Arab World

Every region of the Arab world has its own distinctive musical forms and instruments. Rhythms, instruments, and vocal styles mark the cultures of the Gulf (which has developed a commercial pop style of its own), Lebanon, Sudan, Nubia, and the Berber regions of North Africa. Algeria's

foremost Berber singer, Matoub Lounes (Ma'toub al-Wannas), was murdered in an attack by masked gunmen, presumed to be Islamists, at a roadblock in June 1998. Lounes had been at the forefront of the Berber cultural movement for two decades, and ironically his assassination took place a week before an Algerian law making Arabic the only official language of government, business, and education went into effect. Berbers blamed his death on the government that he had spent years bitterly lampooning in his protest songs. Born in 1956 in the midst of Algeria's war of liberation, Lounes was a product of the Francophone secular educational system that was on its way out, but which Berbers of the Kabyle area have clung to as a lifeline amidst the state's Arabization plans. After a stint in France, he began public performances in 1980, the year Berbers first clashed with the state via demonstrations and strikes, known as the Berber Spring. Lounes arrived just at the right time to capture the spirit of resistance and make it his own. He played the part to the full, often performing in army fatigues as a statement that the Kabyle Berbers were at war with Algeria's Arabist state. Infamy turned to farce when he survived being shot five times by a policeman during the riots of 1988, which led to the legalization of political parties, a critical event in modern Arab politics. Then, in September 1994, he was held for two weeks by the rebel Armed Islamic Group (GIA). Kabyle singer and political rival Ferhat Mehenni accused Lounes of staging the entire incident to the advantage of the Rally for Culture and Democracy (RDC), a Berber-oriented opposition party that was associated with Lounes. Two years later he accused another singer, Ait Menguellat, of making a deal with the GIA to keep them off Menguellat's back.

Lounes didn't just attack Arabism, he attacked Islam too. His famous parody of the Algerian national anthem stated: "No use waiting for hope nor shall we abdicate / Never they'll let Kabyles govern, bright and learned may they be / Fondling injustice, their own hands have rotted like evil / They soiled our origins / They dyed the face of Algeria with Islam and Arabic / Along with deceit and lies." If the authorities thought *rai* was subversive, Lounes's Berber-language songs were something else entirely. In *The Solidarity Fund (Sunduq al-Tadamun)*, he pilloried a fund created by Algeria's first postindependence president, Ahmed Ben Bella, filled from jewelry that women would donate to the new state, which saw itself as a postcolonial developing world power in the non-aligned move-

ment. Most presume the money was pocketed by the regime. The policeman who shot him was ridiculed as the "gendarme of shame" in a subsequent song. Despite all this he was never arrested by the authorities, though less popular singers often were hauled in. But he was the fifth singer in four years to die. *Rai* singer Cheb Hosni died in the same incident that Lounes survived in 1994. The *rai* singer, producer, and composer Rachid Baba Ahmed was gunned down in 1995. Singer Lila Amar and her husband were killed the same year, and twenty-eight-year-old *rai* singer Cheb Aziz was killed in 1996. They are among around seventy artists, including journalists, writers, poets, and theater directors, who have been killed since the Islamic insurgency erupted in 1992. Leaders of the Islamic Salvation Front (FIS), the Islamist party banned in 1992 because it was on the point of winning general elections, often attacked Algeria's artistic community in public statements as a source of moral depravation.

Al-Malouma bint al-Midah is the only renowned singer from the West African Arab country of Mauritania, but she has acquired quite a reputation in the Arab world. She met with fierce resistance when she first began performing her songs of love and sensuality, including threats against her life and attacks on her instruments. But fans stood behind her, forming the al-Malouma club, and through appearances at the Carthage Song Festival in Tunisia and on the Arabic satellite channels, she has become known outside Mauritania, which is a forgotten corner of the Arab world. Like *rai* singers, she sings in colloquial Arabic and mixes traditional instruments with modern. At the moment she's on a drive to "take the Mauritanian song to the whole Arab nation" (*al-Hayat*, May 2002). "Mauri-

Iraqi Music Scene Sees Hopes for Post-Saddam Revival

Despite being tainted by association with the old regime, Iraqi pop stars have tried to make a comeback, but as in politics the exiles are hogging the limelight. Iraq once had dozens of young pop singers, but during the 1990s they had to sing the praises of Saddam Hussein, forcing many to flee abroad and others to give up altogether. Dawoud al-Qaisi, head of the Musicians' Union, was so close to the ruling elite that he was gunned down in May, prompting many others to go into hiding while Washington was setting up its civilian administration and the Governing Council was dominated by dissidents abroad. "They are frightened since most of them were forced to sing for the previous government," said video producer Bari Jabbar (interview with author, Reuters, 10 December 2003). "Ordinary people had been repressed so they didn't want any reminder [of the past]. But they were naive since we were all in one way or another part of the system." Singing under Saddam brought problems, usually because of Saddam's vindictive son, Uday, who ran the youth and entertainment channel Shebab. "Me and another singer, Haitham Yousef, were really popular with the girls, so Uday stopped us appearing on television. Then last year they produced a list of singers who had not sung for Saddam yet [on TV], so I had to do it—twice," said Nizar al-Khaled (interview with author, Reuters, 10 December 2003). Yousef fled the country after Uday had a group of girls beat him up at a concert, Khaled said, and former workers at Shebab recall similar incidents, including one in which Uday urinated on a singer because he didn't like his looks. Those like Khaled who stayed and suffered the system's madness say things have hardly improved. They avoid public performances because of the security situation, face threats from religious extremists, and suffer from an open season on copyright theft. "I wouldn't put out an album now because it wouldn't be worth the effort," Khaled said (interview with author, Reuters, 10 December 2003). Despite that, "people are thirsty for Iraqi songs, Iraqi films, Iraqi dramas; just to hear something in the Iraqi dialect."

But Iraqi studios say they are doing a roaring trade and proclaim the rebirth of Iraqi pop. "Production now is stronger and we've got loads of orders. It's a revival," said Jawdat Mutashar, an owner of Studio Hikmat (interview with author, Reuters, 10 December 2003). "We even have Syrian and Jordanian singers coming here to record, partly because it's cheaper. When the situation in Baghdad stabilises things

---

tanian society remains closed to Arab countries in terms of media, perhaps because the country lies in the northwest of the Arab Maghreb. Its people are still holding on to their Bedouin ways, and still give great value to the Bedouin Arab life." Her first album released in the West, 1998's *Desert of Eden*, had a haunting, captivating sound that mixed the African sounds of West Africa with the Arabic-Berber sounds of North Africa. Featuring a group of Senegalese and Mauritanian musicians, it was recorded at Youssou N'Dour's studios in Dakar and featured Malouma playing the ardine, a traditional instrument played by women. But released for the benefit of the world music market, the album has taken her music to foreigners more than to the Arab world. Africa-meets-the-Arabs can also be heard in the music of Sudanese, Ethiopian, and north Kenyan singers. The tunes of Gulf pop music are mostly of

will really take off." One of the artists recording at the studio is Salah al-Bahr. The chic thirty-three-year-old has a deal with a Saudi recording company that will also shoot video clips for his songs in Dubai. In the lucrative world of Arabpop, that means Bahr has made it. "I don't do politics because people are sick of it, but I do sing about the new Iraq and freedom," Bahr said (interview with author, Reuters, 10 December 2003). Bahr regularly sang for Saddam, when he made annual trips to the country from France, where he lived with his wife. "We had no choice so I think we can be forgiven. Most people understand this," he said (interview with author, Reuters, 10 December 2003). The industry has a lot of catching up to do: stars from other Arabic countries now dominate Iraqi popular culture. The current biggest sellers, according to music shops, are Egyptians Amr Diab and Sherine and Syrian diva Asala. "I hope we can catch up with the rest of the Arabs," said poet and lyricist Adel Muhsin, who writes for most of the Iraqi singers returning to the music business (interview with author, Reuters, 10 December 2003). "But the public will most appreciate the singers who stayed in the country and suffered with them." The most famous of the exile singers is Kazem al-Saher, who from a base in Cairo became one of the biggest pop stars in the Arab world during the

Iraqi pop star Kazem al-Saher, one of the Arab world's top pop stars, singing at Lebanon's Beiteddine Festival. (Mohamed Azakir/Reuters/Corbis)

1990s while singing about Iraq's suffering under sanctions. The new Iraq has also proved to be a marketable commodity abroad. Saher featured on English diva Sarah Brightman's album *Harem,* and another exile singer, Ilham al-Madfai, had an international release on the major music label EMI, titled *Baghdad.*

Yemeni origin, with an array of rhythms from different tribes around the peninsula, but there are also heavy Indian and Iranian influences.

The distinctive instruments of Middle Eastern and North African music include a variety of drums such as the *tabla* or *darbuka*, a reed flute called the *mizmar*, violins and a variation known as the *kamanja*, the *rabab*, the oud, and a distinctive, tinny-sounding, zither-like instrument called the *qanoun*, whose strings are strummed and plucked by a sitting player. The oud is the direct ancestor, in both form and name, of the European lute. There are different varieties—the North African oud, sometimes called the *mondo* or *mondola*, has eleven strings arranged in five double courses with a single bass string. The instrument is well designed for heterophonic, modal music. It is built to promote single-string rather than chordal playing, and the fretless neck allows for practically infinite gradations of intonation. The oud is typical of Arabic music in general, both classical and modern popular music. Rhythm has an important place in Middle Eastern and North African music. As in the Qwali music of North India, clapping is also a feature, and there are many kinds of drums. Arabic and Arabic-Berber rhythm-based music draws listeners into its infectious grooves and melodies, much like Qwali music. The *darbuka* is usually made from clay, is goblet-shaped, and has a fish-skin head. It can be played between the legs, on the thigh, or on the shoulder. Egypt, where the drum is called the *tabla*, is a big producer of modern aluminum varieties that can be tuned, but musicians complain they lack the sound quality of clay. Players of the *tabla* are seen as purveyors of low culture. Mubarak once memorably fumed against Islamist radicals fighting his regime by saying that they were all "sons of *tabla* players and belly dancers."

Algerian *rai* music also has the *gellal*, a drum made from a piece of piping with a skin affixed at one end around the natural bulge of the pipe joint. It has a snare fixed inside this head. Modern *rai* has moved on to include instruments such as the drum kit and other standard Western instruments, which tend to trim down the rhythmic complexities of the traditional version. The *tarr* is a small, round frame drum with jingling disks set into the frame, just like a tambourine. Right-hand strokes on the head and disks combine with complicated twists and shakes of the left hand to produce a wide variety of rhythmic patterns. The *ta'rija* is a small, hourglass-shaped vase drum, held in the hand rather than under the arm, with two small snares under the single head. North Africa also has a tra-ditional Berber instrument called the *bendir*, a frame drum made from wood and covered with animal hide. A frame drum is basically any drum in which the shell is less deep than the head is wide, and like many Maghreb percussion instruments it can be played one-handed. Metal castanets called *krabeb*, or *kakabou*, are also essential as building blocks of rhythm. Sufi practitioners of the music known as *gnawa* make heavy use of them.

A-to-Z: Key People and Terms

AJRAM, NANCY (B. N.A.)

Lebanese pop singer who shot to sudden stardom in 2002 with the song *Akhasmak Aah* (*I Would Fall Out with You*). Her coquettish movements in the song's music video caused a furor in Arab countries but made her an instant sex symbol. Riots ensued in Bahrain when angry Shi'ites protested at her concert in 2003. The entertainment media covers her profusely, with much discussion about her background, appearance, plastic surgery, and love life. Unusual for Lebanese female pop stars, she is a Muslim.

ALILECHE, MOHAMED (B. 1959)

Kabyle Berber singer whose music is less political than that of Matoub Lounes. In 1990, he left Algeria for California, where he has since made CD recordings and become a noted world music singer. His 2000 album *Tragedy* (*Tawaghit*) is a tribute to Lounes, highlighting the Berber sound of the Kabyle region, and featuring Alileche's vocals and playing of the *mondo*—a guitar-like instrument commonly used in Algeria, but allowing an extra two quarter notes to give it a distinctive Kabyle flavor. He signs in the Kabyle Berber dialect called Tamazight, which was finally given formal recognition in Algeria in 2002. Berber music features bagpipes, Celtic-style oboes, and pentatonic scales reminiscent of Chinese music. Berber music was first modernized in the 1970s by Ammuri Mbarak, appealing to urbanized Berbers who seldom returned to their villages in the Atlas mountains of Morocco. The electrified Berber bands had names like Usman ("lightning") and Izenzarn ("thunder"), playing modified traditional tunes on western instruments. They argued that since city dwellers will listen only to European-style pop music, the best way to preserve Berber music in a modern urban context was to repackage it in Western form.

ASALA (B. N.A.)

Syrian singer who started off singing the verse of famed poet Nizar Qabbani in the early 1990s, then gained attention for a number of shorter pop songs, such as *Ma Bahibbish Hadd Illa Anta* (*I Love No One but You*). But in the late 1990s she transformed her look and sound, becoming one of the best-selling female artists in the Arab world, with hits including *Ya Magnoun* (*Crazy Guy*) and *Yamin Allah* (*Swear to God*). She was supported by her business-man-husband, Ayman al-Dahabi.

ATLAS, NATACHA (B. 1964)

Daughter of a Moroccan Jewish father and Greek Alexandrian mother, Atlas grew up in Belgium and became known on the London dance scene in the 1990s, with her combining of Eastern and Western influences and world music with pop and rock. She has three albums: 1995's *Diaspora*, 1997's *Halim*, and 2001's *Ayeshteni* (*You Made Me Live*), and she appeared at Jean-Michel Jarre's Pyramids Party in Egypt at the millennium and also on his subsequent album. Like the Paris-based Tunisian singer Amina al-Nabi, who once won the Eurovision Song Contest for France, her music remains a niche interest among Westernized audiences in the Arab world.

AL-ATRASH, FARID (1907–1974)

Son of a princely Druze familiy in Mount Lebanon, which spearheaded resistance to French occupation in the Levant after World War I. He rose to fame in Egypt in the 1940s with his singing sister Asmahan and went on to make thirty much-loved films that are seen as classics for their song-and-dance routines. He stayed unmarried after his sister's tragic death in 1944, but he was a ladies' man who lived the high life in Cairo. His classic songs include *al-Rabee'* (*Spring*), *Awwal Hamsa* (*First Whisper*), *Lahn al-Khuloud* (*Eternal Melody*), *Tuta* (*Raspberry*), and *Raqsat al-Gamaal* (*The Dance of the Camels*). When he died in Beirut in 1974, he had not fulfilled his dream of composing a song for Umm Kalthoum. He was buried in Cairo by his sister.

BAALBEK

Lebanese song festival held in the ancient pre-Islamic town of Baalbek in the Beqaa Valley. Famed for the appearances there of Lebanese diva Fairouz, it has become eclipsed by other festivals in recent years.

Fairouz: Living Legend

A few singers have successfully crossed the divide from the classic era to today. The best example is Lebanese diva Fairouz, a huge star of the 1950s and 1960s who still makes albums and is seen as a living legend. She came to prominence as a Christian (Greek Orthodox), whose renditions of the rural folk music of Mount Lebanon (through the music of the Rahbani brothers) appeared to make her a symbol of Lebanese particularism. But with her songs about Jerusalem, rejection of commercialism, and studied refusal to speak to the media, Fairouz went on to establish a reputation as the symbol of a dignified Arab nationalism. Since 2000, with the Arab world highly attuned to the Palestinian issue, Fairouz's series of concerts has touched a deep chord in the soul of many. Her first musical efforts (written by the Rahbani brothers, one of whom she married) modernized the traditional sounds of Lebanon and took them to a mass audience, but since the late 1970s she has mixed classical Arabic sounds with jazz (written by her son Ziad Rahbani) and offered it to a mass audience. No Arab singer has managed to merge the traditional and modern as Fairouz has. Neither has she been averse to the need to sell an image. When she first entered the public eye, her large nose gave her an almost eerie look, but she later appeared as a stunning beauty with a perfect nose, standing almost motionless in long flowing

Lebanese singer Fairouz, one of the icons of modern Arabic music, performing in a Beirut church in April 2004. (Haitham Mussawi/ AFP/Getty Images)

dresses as she performed with her ethereal voice. Her image has gone a long way toward establishing her mythical status in Arab culture, placing her on a par with the late classical diva Umm Kalthoum. A saying in the Arabic world goes, "Play Fairouz in the morning and Umm Kalthoum at night." Today Fairouz sticks to Arabic jazz sounds that don't stretch her voice as much as the romantic ballads that made her famous. Her last album was *Wala Kaif* (*Not in the Mood*), released in 2002.

Lebanon also hosts the Beiteddine Festival in July and August, which in 2002 featured cabaret singer-actress Ute Lemper, the musical *Cats*, and singers Youssou N'Dour, Cheb Khaled, Hakim, José Carreras, and Fairouz and Ziad Rahbani. It was begun in 1985 by the Jumblatt family, Lebanon's leading Druze family, and held at the seventeenth-century Beiteddine Palace in the

Chouf mountains near Beirut. Other major music festivals include Jerash, held in the Roman ruins at Jerash in Jordan, and the Fez jazz and folk music festival.

DALIDA (1933–1987)

Egyptian singer of Italian origin who became famous in France in the 1970s, not least for her relationship with French leader François Mitterand, and returned to Egypt in the 1980s. She made a series of Egyptian pop songs with writer Salah Jahine that are well-remembered in the Arab world to this day. They've recently been remastered as disco tracks, giving her the cult status in the Arab world that she also has in France, but based on a completely different oeuvre. She committed suicide in 1987 after a string of failed love affairs. Born in the Cairo suburb of Shubra before it became an overpopulated poor district, she was miscast as a Bedouin woman in Chahine's *The Sixth Day* (1986).

DARWISH, SAYED (1891–1923)
In the 1920s, when jazz musicians in the United States and Europe began breaking down traditional song structures, Egyptian Sayed Darwish and other Arab songwriters were transferring tunes from simple improvisation to clear melody. Though Darwish died in 1923 at 32, in his short life he had been the first to put greater importance on the role of the composer rather than the singer—a key development in modern Arabic music. He was an early pioneer of the Arabic operetta, a form later utilized by Lebanese singer Fairouz.

DIAB, AMR (B. 1961)
Egypt's biggest male pop star and probably the most successful of all the Arabpop singers. Like most others of the genre, he began his career in the late 1980s. Roles in a few films maintained his heartthrob status until the advent of music video technology in the late 1990s, of which he was one of the primary beneficiaries. His recent hits have included 1998's *Allamouni* (*They Taught Me*) and 2001's *Wala 'ala Baal* (*She Doesn't Care*). He is also one of the most well known Arab singers in the West.

ELISSA (B. N.A.)
Lebanese pop singer who has risen to prominence since her first album in 1999, *Baddy Doub* (*I Want to Melt*), and a subsequent duet with Lebanese pop star Ragheb Alameh. Her biggest hits since 2001 have been *Aishalak* (*I'm Living for You*), whose video was the work of French director Fabrice Begotti, and *Agmal Ihsas* (*The Most Beautiful Feeling*), and she also featured in a duet with Irish singer Chris de Burgh, *Lebanese Nights*. Her video clips have been controversial for what is regarded as her risqué appearance, which prompted criticism by some members of the Egyptian parliament. The entertainment media has also been preoccupied with allegations that she has had plastic surgery.

FADELA, CHABA (B. N.A.)
An Algerian Jewess, Chaba Fadela was one of the first stars of the modern *rai* era in Algeria with her 1979 hit *Ana Mayihlali al-Nom* (*I Don't Like to Sleep*). She left for Paris in 1988 with her husband Cheb Sahraoui, where they made their debut album *Ns'el Fik* (*You Are Mine*), the title track of which became a *rai* anthem that announced the genre's arrival as legitimate fare for modern pop music.

FAIROUZ (B. 1935)
Legendary Lebanese singer, now in her twilight years but still making music and maintaining her image. She began singing rustic Lebanese songs and romantic ballads, then moved into Arabic jazz in the 1970s after the death of her composer-husband, Assi,

and assumption of her son Ziad as her chief songwriter. But in the minds of the masses in the Arab world, she has come to represent the high values of Arab nationalism long after the politicians had failed to live up to them.

FAUDEL (B. 1978)

Currently the rising star of *rai* music in France, his first album, *Baida* (*White*), was a big success, mixing traditional *rai* with hip-hop, rap, rock, and flamenco. In 1998, he took part in the Un, Deux, Trois Soleils Concert in Paris with Cheb Khaled and Rachid Taha, which led to an album with a hit song of the same name, *Abdel-Qadir*, on which all three Algerian stars sing. In 2001 he had a hit with Lebanese singer Amal Hejazi, part of a wave of duets between Mashreq and Maghreb stars.

FOUR CATS

Lebanese all-female group with four members, whose song *Ashar, Hdaach, Itnaach* (*Ten, Eleven, Twelve*) resembled the Spice Girls' *Do You Wanna Be My Lover?* The band members change frequently—one has her own show now; another is trying to make it as an actress in Egypt—but they always raise eyebrows around the region. Other hits have included 2002's *Tal Intizari* (*I've Waited So Long*) and *Ya Nasini* (*You, Who Have Forgotten Me*), a remake of a song by Georgette Sayegh, a Lebanese pop singer of the 1970s. Most of their songs are written by Elias al-Rahbani, a Svengali-like character who started the band.

GNAWA

Music traced back to slaves deported to North Africa in the sixteenth century from what was then known as the Guinea Empire (today's Senegal, Guinea, and Mali). The music is a powerful mix of Arabic song and African rhythm and is used by Sufi groups in their trance-inducing rites. Other Moroccan song-dance forms include *al-guedra* (of the Tuareg Berbers), the *ahouash* (which in Berber means "dance") of Berber women in the High Atlas mountains, *ahaidous* singing of the Middle Atlas, the *tissint* from south of the city of Agadir, and *taskiouine*, also of the High Atlas.

HADDAD, DIANA (B. 1976)

Lebanese pop singer from the Shi'ite south who is known as "the voice of the mountains." She has become one of the biggest female hits in today's Arabpop and is regarded as having one of the best voices. With an eye on the lucrative Gulf market and an Emirati producer-husband behind her, she's recently taken to singing Gulf-style pop. The Gulf market has proved a lucrative complement to Cairo-Beirut Arabpop. The main female singer from the Gulf is UAE-based Ahlam, from Bahrain.

HAFEZ, ABDEL-HALIM (1929–1977)

Egyptian heartthrob singer, known as "the dark nightingale" (*al-andalib al-asmar*), who was the forerunner to today's pop stars. He dominated Arabic song via his film roles throughout the 1950s and 1960s, starring opposite all the leading women of the day. His sympathetic, innocent, and very Egyptian look made him a model of the perfect lover still cherished by women to this day.

AL-HAGGAR, ALI (B. 1954)

Seen as Egypt's best male singer, Haggar has resisted the temptation to make big-time pop songs, unlike other singers of his genre such as Hani Shakir. As a child, he was a prodigy in singing, from a poor family south of Cairo with a musical history. He gained overnight success in 1977 with *'Ala Add Ma Habbina* (*As Much as We Loved*), but he is most remembered for his album *Tigeesh Na'eesh?* (*Let's Start Living?*).

HAKIM (B. 1962)

Egyptian singer of *shaabi* music, a kind of folk-rock Arabic rap. Possessed of enormous charisma, Hakim manages to inject his personality into songs in a way that has made him a marketable commodity all over the Arab world, not just in Egypt, where his music is located. He is the son of a village mayor in Maghagha in the southern Egyptian district of Minya—a social status that makes his rise to fame as a singer unusual. He was discovered by the mastermind behind Arabpop, Hamid al-Sha'iri. He had a huge hit in 2003 with Spanish singer Olga, *Ah, Ya Albi* (*Oh, My Love*).

JAJOUKA

World music from a village in Morocco that became popular on the American college and alternative music circuits in the mid-1990s, played by a troupe known as the Master Musicians of Jajouka. Seen as purveyors of magical and otherworldly music when they were "discovered" in the 1950s by British painter Brion Gysin, in 1982 they became a worldwide phenomenon (in the manner of the Bulgarian trio Mystère des Voix Bulgares, who became internationally known after English singer Kate Bush used them on her 1989 album *The Sensual World*). They were first made famous in the West in 1971 by Brian Jones of the Rolling Stones, and they took off as a major commercial concern after the concept of "world music" was conjured up by London record labels in 1987.

KHALED (B. 1960)

Since the first *rai* festival was held in Oran in 1985, Khaled has been known as "the king of *rai*." Since the album *Khaled* featuring the song *Didi* in 1992, he has been the most successful Arab artist to cross over into the Western mainstream, making the entire *rai* format fashionable in Europe. *Aicha* (1996), from the album *Sahra*, was a big hit all over Europe. And in 1999 he headlined the Un, Deux, Trois Soleils Concert in Paris with Rachid Taha and Faudel; it was the biggest Algerian show ever staged in France. He made a song with Amr Diab, bringing together one of the biggest stars in the Arab world with the biggest Arab star to achieve international success. He has also sung duets with an Israeli singer, though he has resisted offers to visit Israel.

KHALIFEH, MARCEL (B. 1950)

Lebanese "dissident" singer, along the lines of Sheikh Imam and Ahmed Fouad Nigm, who was taken to court in 1999 for alleged blasphemy. His 1995 song *Ana Yousef, Ana Abi* (*I Am Yousef, I Am My Father*) was set to the words of a poem by Palestinian poet Mahmoud Darwish, which included a direct quote from the Quran. Khalifeh sings the words to oud playing. At a court acquittal in December 1999, he agreed that in future performances he would stop playing the instrument at the point when he utters the Quranic verse, because adding musicality to the Quran is what offends some Muslims. Although Khalifeh is a Maronite Christian, he is famed for his Marxist, pro-Palestinian beliefs. During the civil war, tapes of Khalifeh's music were confiscated by controlling Christian militias.

LATIFA (B. N.A.)

Tunisian pop singer from the 1980s who has become one of the most successful female singers from her Cairo base. She had the lead role in director Yousef Chahine's 2001 film *Silence, We're Filming*. She was one of the first Arabpop singers to delve into her own local culture as material with her 1999 song *Inchallah*, which was based on a traditional Tunisian rhyme. She starred in a musical at Lebanon's Beiteddine Festival in August 2004, *Hukm al-Ru'yaan* (*Rule of the Shepherds*) by Mansour Rahbani, which critics attacked as a superficial critique of Arab politics.

MAMI, CHEB (B. 1966)

Algerian singer born and raised in the southwestern Algerian village of Saida. He moved to Paris at nineteen, changed his name from Khelifati Mohamed to Cheb Mami, and went on to become the biggest *rai* star after Khaled. His first internationally distributed album was 1989's *The Prince of Rai*. The music's popularity among Algerian immigrant communities in France showed the potential to reach European audiences too. He collaborated with British rock star Sting on his mainstream hit *Desert Rose*, the first duet between a Western singer and an Arabic singer. He sang a duet, *Youm Wara Youm* (*Day after Day*) with Moroccan Egyptian

pop star Samira Said, mixing *rai* with Arabpop.

MOUNIR, MOHAMMED (B. 1958)

Egyptian Nubian star who has been very successful recently. His album of 2000, *Fi 'Ishq al-Banat* (*In the Love of Girls*), was one of his most popular sellers. Veering away from the vacuous pop sounds he dallied with in recent years, Mounir's sound here was heavy and oriental and boasted high production standards—much like the France-based Algerian stars who have had quite an influence on Arabic pop over the last three or four years. It was light-years away from the rough Nubian sounds he started with in 1980 and for which he first became famous with the 1982 album *Shababik* (*Windows*). In 2002 he made an album of Sufi devotional music about the Prophet, called *Earth, Peace* (*al-Ard, al-Salam*), inspired by his recent pilgrimage to Mecca. His move away from his Nubian roots has left Nubian singer Ali Hassan Kuban as the carrier of the authentic Nubian sound.

OUAZZA, NOUJOUM (B. N.A.)

Leading figure in the development of Morocco's own mainstream pop, or *shaabi*, music in the 1970s and 1980s. Ouazza was singer and guitarist in the band *Lem Chaheb* and then the band *Dissident*, whose jazzy Arabic sound influenced mainstream Egyptian star Mohammed Mounir.

RAHBANI, ZIAD (B. 1956)

The son of Fairouz and her chief songwriter for the last two decades. Rahbani has produced a number of albums of his own, in the leftist-dissident style best summed up by his song *Ana Moush Kafir* (*I'm Not an Infidel*), featuring the famed lyric "I'm not an infidel, it's hunger that's the infidel" (*ana moush kafir, il-joa' illi kafir*). The song implies that a society that makes people indigent and deprives them of their rights has no right to spout the religious piety and principles that are the preserve of the rich—a subversive theme in popular culture, famously echoed by actress Nabila Ebeid in the 1990 film *al-Raqisa wal-Siyasi* (*The Dancer and the Politician*): "Morals are something the rich invented to cheat the poor."

AL-ROUMY, MAJIDA (B. 1956)

Lebanese singer famed for her nationalist songs sung in classical Arabic. She first gained prominence with a leading role in Chahine's 1973 film *al-Ard* (*The Land*), and became well-known throughout the region after the Lebanese civil war ended in 1990. Her 1995 song *Qana*, named after the village in south Lebanon where civilians were killed in an Israeli air raid, further bolstered her popularity around the Arab world. It was her father, Abdel-Halim al-Roumy, who discovered Fairouz. Both Fairouz and Roumy are partly of Palestinian origin.

SABAH (B. 1927)

A famous Golden Age Lebanese singer-actress, now in her seventies but still in the public eye with her distinctive, orange-colored hair and a flashy-looking husband in his forties. The expectations of gossip columnists played out when news broke in early 2002 that she had finally had enough of her philandering husband, Fadi Lubnan, and she demanded a divorce. She is much admired. Most of the Golden Age actors are deceased, in dire circumstances, depressed, secluded, penniless, or ignored. Sabah, whose films from the 1950s still show on television channels, insists on appearing as if she was forty years younger, occasionally singing, and taking a younger man as a husband. She was once infamously married to Rushdie Abaza for one day before they divorced.

AL-SAHER, KAZEM (B. 1961)

Iraqi singer who has managed to mix classical sounds, mainly Iraqi in style, with today's pop to become one of the biggest singers in the region. His fame spread after he appeared on Egyptian TV screens in 1995 and subsequently made a number of albums in Cairo, at a time when sympathy for ordinary Iraqis languishing under United Nations sanctions was growing in the Arab world. Saher came at the right time to ride the wave of sympathy and at the same time bring the romantic tradition of Abdel-Halim Hafez back into fashion. He revived classical musical sequences that died with Mohammed Abdel-Wahhab as well as bringing to the rest of the Arab world uniquely Iraqi musical structures, some of which date back to the Abbasid caliphate over a thousand years ago in Baghdad, which had become lost in the cacophony of modern Arabpop. His first regionwide success was *Salamtak Imn al-Ah* (*Keep Safe from the Pain*). Recently his pop hits have borrowed heavily from the rhythms of the modern Algerian *rai* stars in France.

AL-SHA'IRI, HAMID (B. N.A.)

A Libyan singer-songwriter-producer who is acknowledged to be the mastermind behind the growth of Arabpop music since the 1980s. He writes for many of today's biggest names, and occasionally puts out a song on his own or with another singer, such as the 1997 hit with Hisham Abbas, *Ainy* (*My Love*). Many of today's stars have sought him out for his production skills and ability to think up catchy hooks for songs.

SLIMANI, ABDEL-ALI (B. N.A.)

One of the few *rai* singers to end up in London as opposed to Paris. In Algeria he learned guitar and performed as a drummer at soccer matches, and then headed to Paris in 1982. In London he worked as a club DJ before signing on as a vocalist and percussionist with bassist Jah Wobble's Anglo-Arabic unit Invaders of the Heart. In 1996, Wobble co-produced Slimani's solo debut *Mraya* (*Mirror*), which mixes traditional *rai* with in-vogue Western music.

TAHA, RACHID (B. 1958)

One of the best-known Algerian singers of the moment, who sang with Khaled and Faudel on the hit song *Abdel-Qadir* in 1998. After emigrating to France with his family, he worked as a DJ before forming a group called Carte de Séjour, which tried to create an Arabic rock music that went beyond the modern *rai* sound still being perfected in Algeria before Mami and Khaled unleashed it in France in the late 1980s. When he went solo in 1990, he moved into dance music. Steve Hillage produced his first album in 1995 (*Rachid Taha*), but he scored a major hit in France and Arab countries with his 1998 album *Diwan*, with the hit song *Ya Rayeh*, a haunting, oud-based tune about the regrets of emigrants to France. The 2000 album *Made in Me-*

dina (referring to the holy city of Islam) was recorded in Paris, London, Marrakech, and New Orleans.

UMM KALTHOUM (CA. 1904–1975)

Egyptian child-prodigy singer who became a legend of classical Arabic music in the modern age and a symbol of the hopes and dreams of Arab nationalism, both during her lifetime and after her death. A peasant's daughter, she was taught by her father, a Quranic reciter, who was astonished at the strength of her voice and her ability to memorize text. A museum in her honor, featuring music, artifacts, and information about her life, opened in Cairo in 2001. At her death, up to four million people took to the streets of Cairo in her funeral procession. During the 1960s she became the confidante of kings and presidents, first among them Egypt's president Nasser.

WARDA (B. 1939)

One of the longest-lasting and most famous singers, known as Warda al-Jaza'iriyya (Warda the Algerian) after her Algerian background, though her mother was Lebanese. She scored two huge hits in the mid-1990s with *Harramt Ahibbak* (*I Stopped Myself from Loving You*) and *Garrab Nar il-Ghira* (*Try the Fire of Jealousy*), Gloria Gaynor–style stompers guaranteed to fill the dance floor. She was married in the 1970s to Egyptian composer Baligh Hamdy, who wrote some of Umm Kalthoum's most famous songs. Warda originally came to prominence as a classical singer in the same vein, and starred in a number of films. A throwback to the era of Umm Kalthoum, Warda worked with most of the same great composers, including

Riyadh al-Sonbati, Baligh Hamdy, Mohammed Abdel-Wahhab, Sayed Mekkawy, Mohammed al-Mougy, Farid al-Atrash, Hilmy Bakr, and many others. She's admired for her staying power and ability to stay contemporary.

WARDI, MOHAMMED (B. 1932)

Popular Sudanese singer with leftist leanings, who left Sudan for Cairo after the 1989 military coup of Omar Hassan al-Bashir brought in an Islamist regime. He returned to Khartoum in 2002. A Nubian from the far north, Wardi's early schooling was in Egypt. His first hit was in 1960, just four years after independence for Sudan, so he has come to represent the entirety of Sudanese experience, hope, and failure over the last fifty years. Known as the "golden throat," he has a unique ability to enter into emotional zones for Sudanese that others don't reach.

ZIKRA (1961–2003)

Tunisian singer regarded as having one of the best female voices in the Arab world, who has scored a number of pop hits in recent years. She found herself in trouble with religious figures in the Gulf after press reports quoted her as comparing her career to that of the Prophet Mohammed, but she met an untimely death in November 2003 when her Egyptian husband murdered her in a drunken fit, shocking the Arab world.

AL-ZOGHBY, NAWAL (B. 1971)

The most successful of all the female pop stars has been Nawal al-Zoghby. Since 1998 she has had a string of cleverly composed pop songs, including *Mandam Alayk* (*I Don't Regret You*) and *Layaly* (*Nights*). Her 2002 hit *Illi Tamannayto* (*What I Desired*) was clearly influenced by Venezuelan singer Shakira's hit songs, and al-Zoghby's new look appeared to be modelled on the Lebanese-origin Shakira too. Critics, turned off by her brusque personality in media interviews, are constantly predicting her demise.

Bibliography

Print Resources

Abdel-Fattah, Wahid. *al-Ustura* (The Legend). Cairo: N.p., 2002.

Al-Attar, Soliman. *al-Muwashahat al-Andalusiya* (The Andalusian Muwashah). Cairo: General Organization for Cultural Palaces, 2003.

Armbrust, Walter. *Mass Culture and Modernism in Egypt*. Cambridge: Cambridge University Press, 1996.

Asmar, Sami. "Remembering Farid al-Atrash: A Contender in the Age of Giants." *Al Jadid Magazine* 4, no. 22 (Winter 1998).

Danielson, Virginia. *The Voice of Egypt: Umm Kulthum, Arabic Song, and Egyptian Society in the Twentieth Century*. Chicago: University of Chicago Press, 1997.

El-Antari, Farag *The Zionist Plunder of Arabic Music (al-Satu al-Sahyouni 'ala al-Musiqa al-Arabiya)*. 2nd ed. Cairo: Dar Al-Kalima Publishers, 2001.

Nelson, Kristina. *The Art of Reciting the Qur'an*. Austin: University of Texas Press, 1985.

Web Sites

www.al-bab.com. Site with much useful information about music around the Arab region.

www.naima-project.org. Project to document the life of Egyptian singer Na'ima al-Misriyya (1911–1937) and the early phonographic era in Egypt.

www.israeliscent.com. A site called "Israeli Scent: Ethnic Moroccan Music from Israel," with information about Moroccan and Iraqi Jewish music in Israel.

www.dafina.net. A Moroccan Jewish Web site with information on Moroccan Jewish music.

www.arab.de. Site run by Arab Germany Consulting with a mine of music information.

www.gatewayofafrica.com. The Web site of the *North Africa Journal and Maghreb Weekly Monitor*, with music information.

www.amazighonline.com. Site run by Amazighonline, a Berber culture group.

www.beiteddine.org. The official Web site of the Beiteddine Festival in Lebanon.

www.turath.org. The U.S.-based Web site of turath.org, which is dedicated to traditional Arabic music.

www.jerashfestival.com.jo. The official Web site of the Jerash Festival for Culture and Art.

www.azawan.com. Site of azawan.com, which is dedicated to Amazigh/Berber music.

www.mazika.com. Egyptian site in English and Arabic called the Arab Music Network, focused on Arabpop stars and music.

www.6arab.com. An Arabpop site called the Arab Music Revolution, with songs by classical singers too.

www.oghnia.com. Chic Arabpop site that includes video clips and offers downloads.

www.7alim.com. A cyber-shrine dedicated to Abdel-Halim Hafez, with information and downloads.

www.amrdiab.net. Site of the Amr Diab Fan Network.

www.Aramusic.com. An online shop for ordering Arabic music.

www.fairouz.com. Site of fairouz.com, dedicated to the Lebanese diva Fairouz.

www.ziad-rahbani.com. A site dedicated to Fairouz's son Ziad, run by fans.

www.maqam.com. Site that defines itself as a "promoter and seller of Arabic and Middle Eastern music and artists," with information on Arabic musical forms including belly-dance music.

www.farid-el-atrache.com. Site dedicated to late Lebanese singer, songwriter, and oud player Farid al-Atrash.

www.Ilovearabicmusic.com. Site claiming to be the number-one Middle East music source.

www.rashid.com. A longtime distributor of Arabic music in the United States.

www.arabymusic.com. Site of Araby Music.

www.almazaj.com. Another Arabic music site for ordering Arabic CDs.

www.daleelaustralia.com/entertainment/artists.php. Australian site with a list of official Web sites for Arabic singers.

http://albawaba.com/entertainment/index.php3 Good site for Arabic entertainment news.

www.art-lb.com. Information on the arts, singers, and actors in Lebanon.

6

Theater

Arab Theater Develops in the Early Twentieth Century

Arab theater developed after the region's encounter with European theater in the nineteenth century, but as it did so it borrowed from a number of popular traditions. The result is a mainstream theater today dominated by a burlesque-like genre led by the Egyptians. The first modern Arabic-language play was shown in Beirut in 1948, an adaptation of Molière's *The Miser* by Maroun al-Naqqash. After that there was a movement of Lebanese and Syrians to Cairo that led to what's referred to as the modern Arab renaissance in arts and culture. Egypt became the center of a new Arab theater. Alongside Arabized versions of European material, mainly French, two main forms developed. One was dramas by the Egyptian literati such as Mahmoud Taymour, poet Ahmed Shawqi, and Tewfiq al-Hakim—who is often regarded today as the father of modern Arab theater, at least in terms of comedies (Sayed Darwish and Bairam al-Tunsi were pioneers in musicals).

The second form, comedy, was the more popular and continues to dominate to this day. Its origin lies in folk elements of popular culture—the traditional story-teller, or *hakawati;* comic scenes called *fasl mudhik* (comic break) performed at local festivals; poetry recitation that would involve dialogue read out loud by different people representing characters; and shadow plays. Bawdy humor plus subversive political comment was something that readily transferred from the shadow play tradition to modern

Egyptian playwright and short story writer Mahmoud Taymour, who died in 1974. (Condé Nast Archive/Corbis)

theater, and from theater to cinema. Many of the early theater stars went on to become stars of early cinema, such as Naguib al-Rihani, Ali al-Kassar, and Yousef Wahbi, and most of today's TV and cinema comics in Egypt began their life in theater and continue to move between the two (Adel Imam, Mohammed Sobhy, Samir Ghanem). Today's new crop of cinema stars in Egypt have turned to theater to maintain popularity between films.

When Arab countries achieved independence, theater took off. The spread of mass television culture in the 1960s and 1970s gave a boost to theater, as hugely successful Egyptian productions became known throughout the region and went on tour to further entrench their fame. Ghanem's *Musiqa fil-Hayy al-Sharqi* (*Music in the Eastern Quarter*), based on *The Sound of Music*, ran for four years in the 1970s, the decade that also saw the Imam-Sobhy play *Madrasat al-Mushaaghibeen* (*The School of Troublemakers*), Imam's *Shahid Maa Shafshi Haaga* (*A Witness Who Saw Nothing*), and later Ghanem's *al-Mutazawwigun* (*The Married*). Imam's *al-Wad Sayyid al-Shaghghal* (*The Boy Sayyid, the Cleaner*) opened in 1984 and ran for eight years, and his *al-Za'im* (*The Leader*) opened in 1993 after Imam built his own theater on Cairo's nightclub row, Pyramids Road. Later he showed his film *The Bodyguard* at the theater (a loose adaptation of the Whitney Houston film), which is still running today. Basing films and plays on Western originals is common in the Arab world (but rarely to the extent of acquiring rights). The Imam film *Ragab on a Hot Tin Roof* (*Ragab 'ala Safeeh Sakhin*) uses a Western play in its title but is based on the film *Midnight Cowboy*. Director Inas al-Degheidy claimed her *Istakoza* was based

on Shakespeare's *The Taming of the Shrew*.

The tradition of state-sponsored theater, which has been a prominent feature of theater in many of the nationalist, postindependence Arab states, is hallowed today as a means of preserving the intellectual traditions of the liberal renaissance period. In Egypt, state-sponsored theater is seen as a break from the excesses of commercial theater and lewd humor aimed at Gulf tourists in the summer season. A form of "new theater"—both political and experimental—has developed since the 1967 war, beginning in Syria, Tunisia, Morocco, and Egypt, by people who studied Western intellectual theater, and today Western and experimental theater has a place in the Arab theater pantheon. Cairo and other cities have annual experimental theater festivals that attract avant-garde groups and productions from around the world.

Intellectuals decry modern Arab theater in general, arguing that with the spread of lowbrow commercial productions and the emergence of the overly experimental, serious theater is on the point of extinction. As such, they say, today one cannot really talk about an "Arab theater" at all, because low culture has almost entirely crowded out high culture, which floats on the edges of a society from which it is cut off—the same argument used by cultural elites when bemoaning today's cinema. At the same time, experimental theater has its limits. An Egyptian gay activist who goes by the name of Horus wrote and directed a play in 1999 called *Harem* (referring to a harem of women, but also linked to the word *haraam*, meaning "forbidden"), dealing with taboos such as homosexuality. After heated debate, a culture ministry committee decided not to put it forward as an

Egyptian entry for a European theater festival. But theater remains an important part of popular culture and a gauge of what's happening in politics and society. This has been clear in Iraq, where theater has reflected the issues generated by the replacement of the old dictatorship with foreign occupation, and most recently the Western-backed rule. The first play staged examined the experience of censorship and theater under the old regime. *They Passed Here* was based on *Caligula*, the classic portrait of the Roman tyrant by Albert Camus, which was banned under Saddam Hussein.

Egyptian State-Funded Theater since 1952

When Egypt held celebrations in July 2002 to commemorate the fifty-year anniversary of the July 23 Revolution of 1952, the occasion afforded a chance for critical appraisal of the era of "the big state" on many areas of public life in Egypt, including theater. The verdict, in the cultural sphere, was surprisingly brutal. While the state didn't take control of cinema until 1961, theater was immediately touched by the revolution, partly because cinema had already ravaged popular theater by luring away most of its stars and partly because state theater troupes were riven with personal disputes. The revival came from 1956 onward, when the government appointed Ahmed Hamroush as director of its National Theater Department. A new era of writers came to the fore, expressing all the zeal and vitality unleashed by the revolutionary era, such as Alfred Farag (*Sawt Misr*, or *The Voice of Egypt*), Noeman Ashour (*Afareet al-Gabbana*, or *Graveyard Demons*), and Yousef Idris (*Gumhouriyat Farahat*, or *The Republic of Farahat*). After the Suez War,

state theater lowered its prices and moderated its admissions policy to allow the poor masses to watch plays that often had a clear jingoistic line (such as *Kifah Shaab*, or *A People's Struggle*). Performances traveled all over Egypt and other Arab countries, where similar state theaters were established (such as the Algerian National Theater) with similar nation-building goals. But by the mid-1960s the sector was riddled with overemployment and debts, scaring the state away from overpromoting theater ever since. And those directors and writers who tried to air criticisms, however well intended as friendly advice, such as Hamdy Ghaith and Abdel-Rahman al-Sharqawi, found themselves without theaters to present plays and they were barred from state radio. "Now we live in the era of commercial theater," Hamroush has said. "The guarantee of success for a play is the level of triviality and lack of substance, with only a few exceptions. This 'privatization' has even affected the behaviour of the actors as well" (*Akhbar al-Nugoum*, 20 July 2002).

Shakespeare has a hallowed place in Egyptian theater. He was first introduced to Egyptian audiences in the early twentieth century by veteran classical actor George Abyad, and treated, in translation and presentation, with a reverence that maintained an elitist distance between the text and the public and that for decades forestalled modern approaches to staging the play. This cultish view of Shakespeare continued throughout the 1960s, 1970s, and 1980s. Experimental versions by foreigners left Egypt's cultural establishment cold, but they did alert the more creative to the fact that there was a straitjacket to be broken out of. In 1991 director Mohammed Abdel-Hadi presented a version of *King*

Lear at an avant-garde theater, with six actors wearing garish masks and no set to speak of. At the same time, Egypt's National Theater produced *Macbeth* in the old standard format.

Then summer 2002 saw a version of *King Lear* by the National Theater that compromised between the two traditions and was hailed as a huge success. The main reason was the actor playing Lear, Yehya al-Fakharani, who has come in recent years to be regarded as Egypt's "best actor," and who through both stage and TV work has also managed to walk the tightrope of quality versus commercialism—though with his round, jolly visage, his casting was something of a novelty in Egypt and a break with classical tradition. The theater's director, Ahmed Abdel-Halim, is a graduate of London's Royal Academy of Dramatic Arts (RADA). According to Egyptian critic Nehad Selaiha, Abdel-Halim was influenced by the ideas of Peter Hall, the head of the Royal Shakespeare Company in England, who maintained that Shakespeare productions should be lively, be careful with the text, aim for social relevance, and maintain a coherent whole.

The result challenged audience expectations and still won them over, with various actors cast "out of type": impish colloquial poetry by leftist rascal Ahmed Fouad Nigm, the familiar melodramatic music of film composer Rageh Dawoud, and monologues from the evil Edmund confided with the audience in the cozy confines of the National Theater in central Cairo. The vision of filial impiety and lack of respect for elders struck a chord with Egyptians, as did the depiction of a corrupt and upside-down political order. Selaiha called the whole show something of a "Christmas pantomime," but it gave the state sector a

Egyptian scriptwriter Osama Anwar Okasha, whose material has been immensely successful on stage and screen. (Mohammed Mahjoub/ AFP/Getty Images)

new buzz all the same. The same year saw the acclaimed political satire *al-Nas Illi Fil-Talit* (*The People on the Third Floor*), by dramatist, soap writer, and columnist Osama Anwar Okasha, which was staged in the same theater.

A simultaneous presentation of *Othello* in another state theater, the avant-garde Hanager Center, was blessed with less success, however. A truncated Arabic text turned the work into a statement about racism against Arabs in post–September 11 Europe, with Shakespeare's "the Moor" continually rendered as "the Arab Moroccan," peppered with lines such as "these Arab Moroccans are known to have changeable characters." To further accentuate the theme of rough Arab otherness, lead actor Ahmed Maher wore a matted, bushy wig and spoke in a booming drone below his normal vocal pitch. Overattention to the set and costumes further added to the quaint, functional nature of the performance, which was panned in the press. Director Mohammed al-Kholi said in program notes that his aim was "to rehabilitate the negative image of the Arab male," not least from Shakespeare's representation of Othello as little more than "a Bedouin who has never known civilization." The play has seen a number of translations, including Lebanese poet Khalil Mutran's standard classical version from the early twentieth century, a colloquial Arabic version by Noeman Ashour (rejected to this day by many critics), and Hussein Ahmed Amin's midway house version of the 1990s. Kholi offered an amended version of Mutran. It was a disappointment for the Hanager, which usually presents works by respected writers such as Syrian Saadallah al-Wannous, Egyptian Salah Abdel-Sabour, and contemporary Egyptian and Iraqi playwrights.

Popular Commercial Theater in Egypt since the 1970s

Do-re-mi Fasulya (*Do-re-mi Fava Beans*) is a good example of the sort of theater that brings in the audiences in Cairo's hotly contested summer season. Largely a vehicle for comic Samir Ghanem, around whom much of the four hours of slapstick revolves, the play is heavy on bawdy, lowbrow humor. Plot matters little. A corrupt member of parliament wants to marry the daughter of a successful businesswoman, but the daughter is already engaged to a singer. After the marriage, the businesswoman schemes to persuade the singer to divorce her daughter by telling him he is really her father and he should try to get his new wife to divorce him. This he does by pretending to have an affair with the maid—a midget. The appearance of the midget makes for some twenty minutes of merciless, obscene jokes. "I'm meant to cheat on my wife with her?" Ghanem asks incredulously. "She doesn't even have the right bit on her for me to cheat on my wife."

Before it all ends with the corrupt member of parliament being exposed, an appearance by real-life singing star Shaaban Abdel-Rahim is woven into the plot—an addition sure to bring in bigger crowds. Though Abdel-Rahim is adored for his *I Hate Israel* hit song of 2001, he is something of a national joke because of his unabashedly lower-class, rural background, his gaudy suits and gold jewelry, and obvious lack of vocal talent. The jokes target his tasteless attire, his real-life past as an ironer of clothes, and his illiteracy. It seems Abdel-Rahim has no script as such, and is only there so that the cast can improvise jokes about him. "You were meant to say that at the end of the show," one character says to him, handing him a script. "Oh, I forgot, you can't read it." Cue howls of laughter from the audience. Shaaban's mobile phone rings, prompting the comment "It's the neighbors, they want you to hurry up with the ironing." The plot also manages to include a belly dancer, a psychiatrist, jokes against Israeli prime minister Ariel Sharon, and jokes involving the use of English words for comic effect.

Up to 50 percent of the audience is from the Gulf, including a fair amount of children and fully veiled women in black cloaks. Back home for the Saudis, adultery—the theme around which the show is based—could result in the death penalty, and theater is virtually an alien art form. While the winds of religious conservatism have blown over Egypt from Saudi Arabia since the 1970s, the fact is that Gulf tourists flock to Cairo every year to let their hair down. Egypt, Syria, Jordan, and Lebanon are receiving more Gulf visitors than normal because of fears of racism in the United States and Europe after the September 11 attacks. In Cairo they have plenty of entertainment options to choose from. A bratpack of popular young movie actors star in the heavily publicized *Kida Okay* (*That's Okay*), in-vogue comic Mohammed Heneidy has just opened his *Tara'i'o* (*Lunatics*), and veteran comedy actor Adel Imam stars in *The Bodyguard* in his own custom-built theater near the pyramids of Giza. The phenonemon of cheap comedy for affluent Gulf tourists was depicted in the 2001 film *Rashsha Garee'a* (*Go for It*).

Cairo's Experiment since 1988 in Arab Experimental Theater

The main forum for experimental theater in the region is the Cairo International Festival for Experimental Theater, set up in 1988 by Culture Minister Farouk Hosni. The festival's longevity is perhaps an achievement in itself, since it brings up issues plaguing cultural elites throughout the Arab world, including the problem of elitist highbrow culture and its distance from the popular culture of the masses. Disputes rage every year over the small audiences, the choice of jury, the often-cheesy opening ceremony, the selection committee and the plays it chooses, and whether the culture ministry should hand over the entire administration of the festival to an independent body. In *Al-Wasat* (the weekly magazine inside *al-Hayat*), columnist Pierre Abi-Saab wrote in August 2002 that "whoever talks about experimentation doubtless means contradicting the norm, looking for horizons beyond which it can be transcended and changed. This is why experimentation cannot be an instance of some conventional, conservative tendency, nor of the tendency to gloss over conflicts and differences by coating unmediated heritage in a thin modernist crust—theatre as decorative performance that combines folklore with official ceremonies." Eve Ensler's feminist play *The Vagina Monologues* was performed at a small theater of the American University in Cairo in February, but publicity was low-key to avoid attracting sensationalist media attention. Critics argue that intellectual theater began to fall away when commercial theater grew in Arab countries in the aftermath of state efforts to promote theater in the 1960s, primarily in Egypt. Anything vaguely serious—from the good to the bad—is considered "experimental" today, but with no hard tradition of Arab serious tradition to judge it against. The result, thinking goes, is a free-for-all that has little chance of saving the public from the lure of slapstick theater.

The most prominent effort to experiment in theater beyond the confines of the perennial dilemma of commercial-versus-intellectual theater has been the al-Warsha company, set up in Egypt by director Hassan el-Geretly, the only truly independent troupe in the country. Like Yousef Wahbi before him, Geretly sought to purify an art form that many perceived was bogged down in degenerate theater for the masses. But more than that, he wanted to rescue the sources of traditional theater—the shadow plays, the readings by *hakawatis* of epic tales, and other forms that have faced extinction amidst the cacophony of modern Arab culture. The result has been a new, controversial, elite form of theater that, like world music and Paris-based *rai*, dips into popular traditionals and then re-contextualizes them in an avant-garde format. As cinema critic Viola Shafik puts it: "Its 'intellectual' reappropriation of so-called popular and traditional culture sets it apart from the rather unconscious use of these elements in mainstream cinema" (Shafik 1998, 81). The same could be said for mainstream theater, with its caricatural performances that serve to clarify social roles rather than emphasize the psychological state of the character, an approach that has more immediate appeal with audiences that may be mostly illiterate.

After serving time as assistant director to Yousef Chahine and his protégé Yousry Nasrallah, Geretly brought together a group of writers, actors, and designers in the late 1980s to create a freewheeling outfit beyond the bureaucracy of state theater and the crassness of commercial theater. Geretly's stated aim was also to liberate intellectual Egyptian theater from Western forms. "The forms of our popular culture—music, shadow plays, saints' carnivals, story-telling—are now, at last, warmly familiar to me, like long lost friends," he said, and expressed determination to ditch "European techniques which have been developed for centuries to express an outlook so different from our own" (*al-Ahram Weekly*, 2 September 1999). Al-Warsha, as arts critic Youssef Rakha noted, has become "both a way of life and an intellectual statement" (*al-Ahram Weekly*, 2 September 1999). But the ultimate irony is that al-Warsha has found its audience with Egypt's Westernized elite and European and American audiences at avant-garde festivals around the world. The result is an eclectic mix: as the *Weekly* noted, university professors discuss folk psyche with illiterate storytellers after performances in restored Islamic monuments in Cairo. Purists freak, but they are resigned to the fact that some form of preservation is better than nothing.

The story of al-Warsha (lit., "the workshop") began in the early 1980s with theater lover Alfred Mikhail. During research at the Sorbonne in Paris, he traced some of the few living shadow puppeteers and pieced together some originals. It fit perfectly with al-Warsha's idea of bringing together Cairo's traditional street entertainers, magicians, and storytellers to keep the old tales and folklore alive. The puppeteers, Ahmed al-Komi, Hassan Khanoufa, and Hassan al-Farran, passed on their skills. Farran and al-Komi died in 1996 and 1998, respectively. Ironically, Khanoufa, now in his seventies, has said that when he was a child and his voice was used in the shadow plays, he always dreamed of "one day being in front of the screen, rather than forever hidden behind it, so that I could be seen" (Feeney, www.karaghiozis.net). The productions have included *Dayer Maydour* (*Revolving as It Will*), by Naguib and Khaled Guweili and based on Alfred Jarry's *Ubu* cycle, with the story taking place in Mameluke Egypt and incorporating traditional shadow puppet theater. It eventually became the play *Dayren Dayer* (*Spinning Around*). *Layali al-Warsha* (*al-Warsha Nights*) was a series of storytelling performances based on the classic series of epic tales known as *al-Sira al-Hilaliya*, about the exploits of Arab tribesman Abu Zeid al-Hilali of the North African Hilal tribe. *Ghazir al-Lail* (*Tide of the Night*) drew on the popular love story of Hassan and Naima; *Lu'bat al-Timsah* (*The Croco-dile's Game*) was based on a popular shadow play; and, most recently, *Ghazl al-A'maar* (*Spinning Lives*) was an attempt to dramatize the *al-Sira al-Hilaliya* epic.

Morocco's Halqa

Morocco's indigenous dramatic form connecting with modern theater is *halqa* ("circle"), a public gathering in a circle around a group of performers, storytellers, dancers, acrobats, dancers, and others. The performance usually centers on some mythical or religious story from the Arab-Islamic repertoire (from the life of the Prophet, for example). Writers have argued that the popularity of Brecht and his style since the 1960s is connected to similarities between Brecht and the *halqa* form. "As in Brechtian epic dramaturgy, *al-halqa* performers insist on historicizing their narratives, through comments and accompanying transitory devices," wrote anthropologist Khalid Amine (Amine 2001). As in Egypt, decades of appropriating Western theater into the local context gave way to efforts to merge it in some form with a revamped version of *halqa*—that is, merging the local version based on an oral culture with the foreign version tied up with a culture of literature. The pioneers were Tayeb Saddiki in 1965, with *Diwan Sidi Abdel-Rahman al-Maj-dub* (*The Court of Sidi Abdel-Rahman al-Majdub*), and Ahmed Laalaj in 1968, with *al-Qadi fil-Halqa* (*The Judge in the Circle*). After attempting together to create a "theater for the working classes" (*al-mas-rah al-'ummali*), Saddiki concluded that the "festive" traditions of Moroccan dramatic form, as seen in the *halqa*, were missing from the Western theater his generation was copying. The result was Moroccan *al-masrah al-ihtifaali*, or festive theater, after

realizing that pure Western theater "does not reflect the inner self of Moroccans"; in other words, *halqa* transferred to the stage.

The result has been a new theatrical form that mediates two sides of a debate about theater in Morocco: on the one hand, the notion that theater should be "decolonized" by rejecting Western forms and thereby return to an imaginary pure state before the influence of the West was felt; and on the other hand, the idea that indigenous theater was in fact "pre-theater"—inferior and not really theater at all (in the way that nationalist cinema critics say that much of Egypt's pre-1960s output wasn't really serious cinema). Saddiki merged another traditional form, called *labsat*, with *halqa* and modern Western theater, as best seen in his *al-Fil wal-Sarawil* (*The Elephant and the Trousers*). El-Meskini Sghir's *Hkayat Bou Jmaa al-Faruj* (*The Story of Bou Jmaa the Rooster*) demonstrates well the merging of illusion and reality. Storytellers relate a tale of villagers afflicted by an evil spirit and how they challenge it, but the plot is far from linear or conventional. The audience is engaged and confused by various devices: play-within-a-play, role-playing within a role, ceremony within play, references to literary and real-life figures and events, and characters that are played by different actors throughout the performance. The language used varies between the formal and the colloquially obscene, a mixed style that has been dubbed in Morocco *'arbadajiyya*.

Algeria: A Slower Development

Neighboring Algeria has seen less development. The state-sponsored Algerian National Theater (TNA) was modelled on Nasserist lines, but some critics have argued that by relying too much on translations of Western theater and on classical Arabic, the TNA failed to express Algeria's national identity and also failed to remodel it after the cultural ravages of French colonialism. In these attempts, the independence regimes were actually mimicking the policies of the French. "The behaviour of the TNA reflects the survival of the outlook which underlay the mainstream Algerian theater of the later colonial period, which refused to work in the linguistic medium of the majority of the population and reflected the debased image of native Algerian society which its colonial sponsors required," Kamal Salhi wrote (Salhi 2000). "It thereby established a tacit tradition of anti-national theatrical activity which, given a new lease of life by the cultural commissars of the post-colonial state, has persisted to this day." The exceptions to this rule have been celebrated authors such as Kateb Yacine and Abdelkader Alloula. At the same time, there has been no revival and reworking of indigenous theatrical forms such as Egypt and Morocco have witnessed. This is despite the fact that the same carnivalesque elements exist in Algerian indigenous culture, though perhaps they have been ignored because they are Berber customs. Liliane and Nordine el-Hachemi have pointed to the popular festival known as *forja*, which lasts to this day near the western city of Tlemcen to celebrate the Berber New Year (El-Hachemi 2000).

Arab Political Theater since the 1970s

Syria

The work of Syrian director Saadallah Wannous examined the relationship between the individual and authoritarian states in the Arab world. Originally a journalist, Wannous was instrumental in forming a new Arab political theater after the 1967 defeat, as shown in his 1968 work, *Night Party for June 5* (June 5 was the eve of the war). Wannous worked with other playwrights to found the Damascus-based Arab Festival for Theater Arts. Through this festival, he promoted his ideas that theater should be a tool for creating political awareness and developing society. He made strenuous attempts to avoid letting his experimental theater go the way of its European counterpart, via introducing some of the same traditional theatrical forms that Geretly later revived, such as the *hakawati*, and also using improvisation and forms of audience participation (such as 1969's *The Elephant* and *The King of All Times*, 1970's *The Adventure of Jaber's Head*, 1977's *The King Is the King*, and 1978's *Handala's Journey from Slumber to Consciousness*). He also helped set up the High Institute for Theater Arts in Damascus and the arts periodical *Theater Life*. Before his death from cancer in 1997, Wannous was asked to give the prestigious annual address at UNESCO's International Theater Day, the first time an Arab playwright had been given the honor. "Theater is not only an expression of civil society, but also a necessary condition for its establishment and growth," he said, but warned: "Theater is in decline" (Swairjo 1996).

The blows of the Arab-Israeli crisis took their toll on Wannous and other intellectuals. Egypt's Salah Jahine never recovered from the 1967 defeat, Arab nationalist Khalil al-Hawi committed suicide when the Israelis besieged Beirut, and Wannous ceased writing for a decade after the Lebanon invasion. In 1971, during the honeymoon period after Assad first took the helm in Syria, he was able to stage a play in Damascus that debunked the official version of the Six Day War. As government officials made triumphant statements of victory, actors shouted their complaints, comments, and more correct memories of what happened where during the debacle. The denouement of Israel's foray into Lebanon was in a sense a statement of failure for all of Wannous's efforts to use theater to modernize and strengthen Arab society. When he resumed work in the 1990s, the Arab-Israeli conflict was the direct and indirect object of his concern, as in 1990's *The Rape, Fragments from History*, and *Rituals of Signs and Transformations*; 1994's *Miserable Dreams*; 1995's *A Day of Our Time*; and 1996's *Mirage Epic*. *Fragments from History* portrays Damascus on the eve of its fall to the invading Central Asian ruler Tamerlane in 1400 and suggests that the social injustice, despotism, and corruption that permeated society from top to bottom weakened the Syrians and allowed Tamerlane to win. Celebrated Arab historian and religious scholar Ibn Khaldoun is shown being a party to the city's fall by seeking to promote himself with Tamerlane. Historians know the two men met in Damascus, but there is no record of what passed between them. The suggestion is that today's Arab intellectuals have been co-opted by the Arab regimes.

Iraq

Saadallah Wannous managed to maintain his intellectual integrity despite living through the authoritarian era of Baath rule in Syria that began in the early 1960s. Other theatrical traditions in the Arab world have not been so lucky. Iraq's intellectual classes who remained in the country during the Iran-Iraq war and after the UN sanc-

tions regime was imposed in 1990 have been severely compromised in their freedom. A play that opened in Baghdad in April 2002 starkly demonstrated the fate of cultural life in Iraq under Saddam Hussein. It was based on a novel, called *Zabiba and the King (Zabiba wal-Malik)*, which was published in 2001 and then adapted for theater by Palestinian-born poet Adib Nasir. The rapturous reception given by the Iraqi media to the book and a second novel by the same mysteriously unidentified author made it clear that Saddam Hussein himself was the author. The story has a king avenging the honor of a woman, Zabiba, after she is raped on the day that U.S.-led forces launched the 1991 Gulf War to oust Iraqi forces from Kuwait. The king, who is earlier spurned by the same woman, dies in the process. Zabiba (a name that means "raisin" in Arabic) is apparently meant to represent the Iraqi people, who come to realize eventually that the ruler is acting in their best interests and ready to make all sacrifices for them. The story harks back to the ancient Mesopotamian tale of King Gilgamesh, who is engaged in an epic battle of good versus evil and dares to challenge the gods. High government and Baath officials as well as much of Baghdad's intelligentsia turned out for the first performance, which offered an alternative to bawdy Egyptian productions with cheap entrance fees. An Egyptian skit on the Bill Clinton/Monica Lewinsky affair, *Ana wa Marati wa Monica (Me, My Wife and Monica)*, starring Samir Ghanem, was a big hit in summer 2001 when the cast traveled to Iraq especially to perform it.

One can contrast this with the experience of Iraqi directors abroad such as Awni Karoumi. A graduate from Baghdad University, Karoumi left Iraq for Berlin where

Issam Bou Khaled's *March*, a satire of U.S. military interventions in Iraq and elsewhere, at the Beirut Theater in March 2004. (Ramzi Haidar/AFP/Getty Images)

he pursued a doctorate, before lecturing in Jordan, Iraq, and Germany and directing some seventy plays over the last two decades. He has recently set up an international theater workshop in Berlin and directs the Ruhr Theater in Germany. He held a well-received theater workshop at Cairo's Hanager Center in 2002 focused on "people who light fires," that is, people who add fuel to already-smoking fires in any environment. He has staged plays at the Cairo experimental theater festival on several occasions.

Lebanon

Political theater has a long history in Lebanon, spearheaded in the 1960s by writers and directors like Rida Kabreet and Jalal Khoury. Roger Assaf and Nidal Ashqar founded the Beirut Theater in 1966, but the outbreak of war in 1975 ended the project. Those were the heady days of Arab nationalism, communism, and public debate about Lebanon's identity; now, post–civil war especially, things are different and playwrights bemoan the apolitical, directionless younger generation in Lebanon today. There are young directors attempting to deal with these issues, but there's no public for them anymore. Ashqar, who also set up the Arab Actors Group in Jordan, made a number of successful television drama serials and soaps in the 1990s, including *Zenoubia, Queen of Palmyra*

Kuwaiti director Sulayman al-Bassam stages *The Hamlet Summit* in London in March 2004, with actors Kifah al-Khous as Hamlet and Amana Wali as Gertrude. (Graeme Robertson/Getty Images)

(*Zenoubia, Malikat Tadmur*); *Shajarat al-Durr* (a famous Egyptian princess from the Islamic era); and *Women Lovers* (*Nisaa' 'Ashiqaat*).

Kuwait

Kuwait is the only country in the Gulf with a theatrical tradition. Since the 1960s there have been four main troupes: the Arabi Theater Group, the Arab Gulf Theater Group, the Kuwaiti Theater Group, and the Public Theater Group. They are semiprofessional groups receiving support from the Kuwaiti government. There are a number of private groups too, including the Kuwait Little Theatre. The Kuwaiti International Theatre Institute (ITI) is headed by director Sulayman al-Bassam, whose play *The Hamlet Summit* won critical acclaim at the 2002 Cairo experimental theater festival. The play relocated Shakespeare's tale in the contemporary Middle East and the Palestinian-Israeli conflict, in an attempt to expose the tyranny and moral bankruptcy of Arab regimes, Israeli brutality and oppression (of Palestinians), and the Islamist reaction to both. "We are living in an age of political charades, where the emphasis on spin, public opinion, focus groups and the so-called transparency of government hides a callous agenda of economic and political barbarism," he wrote in eloquent director's notes. "In the recent scramble to unite world opinion behind America's war on terrorism, the slogan mentality that pitches good against evil, crusade against *jihad*, presents us with a world split into two halves, each baying for the other's blood."

Sudan

The only modern theater in Sudan is explicitly political in outlook. The Kwoto

Popular Theater Group in Khartoum consciously gives expression to the cultural differences of southern Sudanese in the environment of the north. "Today we are displaced people, compelled by war to flee to the north. We have lost the security and tranquillity which we had in the south. We are now at the mercy of the cruel and brutal situation in the north. That is why we need the theater to accompany us in our quest for human communication as the means of social change. Therefore, we are looking for theater that solves the problems of the displaced," wrote Edward Ladu Terso in an essay on south Sudanese theater ("The Philosophy of Our Theatre," *Khartoum Monitor*, 21 August 2002). "The people of the south possess languages and rich styles of self-expression, such as dance, songs, educational and political jokes, idioms and poems. Thus, southern Sudanese through this kind of theater ought to rediscover themselves, their mentality, aesthetic appreciation, social norms, and the potential that lies in the myth, religious practices, rituals and celebrations." Rights campaigners are also using theater as a way of combatting the custom of female genital mutilation, which is spreading from northern society to southern refugee communities in Khartoum.

Saudi Arabia

The only indigenous theater to speak of in Saudi Arabia—apart from expatriate activity—is based on the religious passion plays of the Shi'ite community in the east. The Shia are a repressed minority in the Wahhabi state, which reserves particular revulsion for Shi'ite customs of veneration of the family of the Prophet. Suspicion that the Saudi Shia and revolutionary Iran would find each other made the situation worse, but a current rapprochement between the two countries has allowed the Shia new freedom to openly practice their rites. There were plays performed in the streets of Shi'ite towns like al-Qateef to mark Ashoura and the Arbaeen in March and April 2003. Crowds gathered to see a drama in which evil-looking soldiers of the Caliph Yezid whipped prisoners who refused to join the war against the Prophet's grandson Hussein, whose murder at the hands of the caliph's forces is a defining moment in early Islam that led to the Sunni-Shi'ite schism. After Hussein's brutal murder, an old man wails over this body. "They killed him, and they knew who he was," he cries. Then the spirit of Hussein appears to tell mourners not to be sad, but to spread Islam's message of peace and justice. Shi'ites say they have resigned themselves to working peaceably to improve their situation in the kingdom and that these plays help inculcate this message in the community. "Imam Hussein was an example for people today about how to act when people spread mean things about us. Hussein's brother gave up the caliphate to save people more suffering. It's an example of knowing how to let it go," one viewer said.

Egypt

One of Egypt's best-known political playwrights is Lenin al-Ramly, whose leftist critiques of Islamist groups have been turned into hit films, such as *al-Irhabi*, starring stage and movie actor Adel Imam. Ramly is unique in Egypt in that he has consecrated his efforts entirely to playwriting. Like Wannous, much of his work tries to examine the causes of the rise and fall of the Nasser generation, such as *Ahlan Ya Bakawaat* (*Welcome, Pachas*), *Afreet Li Kull Muwaatin* (*A Devil for Every Citizen*), and *Saadoun al-Magnoun* (*Saadoun*

The new Cairo Opera House opened in 1988. (Caroline Penn/CORBIS)

the Crazy). "We find the collapse of the Nasserist national project, and the effect of this collapse on our generation, the generation born into the tragedy of Palestine and which lived the dream of liberation and Arab nationalism, then was broken with the setback [1967], and found itself at the end of the century with the nationalist dream receded," Egyptian critic Nehad Selaiha has said of the latter work (Selaiha 2001, 130). In *Saadoun al-Magnoun*, Saadoun is one of those Egyptians who gave everything to the revolution and ends up in a lunatic asylum after it all falls apart in 1967. He emerges in the 1990s from his institutionalized years to a world that he discovers, through black comedy, to be as nonsensical and illogical as was that of the Nasserist dream, despite the stark contrast between those two realities. The play was staged in summer 2000 in a commercial theater—which shows that some producers, in this case director Shaker Abdel-Latif, are still prepared to take risks. Another political writer is Egyptian Alfred Farag, whose *Awdat al-Ard* (*Return of the Land*), presented after the 1973 war with Israel, tried to give a rare, positive spin on the political situation.

Most often these directors will present serious issues through comedy. Efforts continue to bridge the eternal gap between popular, lowbrow commercial theater and the state-subsidized intellectual theater, with little reach beyond a narrow intellectual elite. Actor Mohammed Sobhy is working on a Theatre for All project, where cheap ticket prices are intended to bring the public to didactic theater. "No technology can ever replace the theatre, because nothing can replace the live encounter between spectator and actor," he said (*al-Ahram Weekly*, 6 April 2000). He teaches his troupe, whose members are required to read Shakespeare and classical Greek drama, undergo vocal training, and learn how to carry themselves on stage. He gave up on cinema acting in 1991 after appearing in eighteen films, though he made a controversial comeback in 2002 with his anti-Zionist soap opera *Faris Bila Gawad* (*A Knight without a Horse*). His works are often critical of the political situation in Egypt, other Arab countries, and the rest of the world, with an Arab nationalist bent. He is building a "culture city" outside Cairo with an open-air theater, an opera house with a theater troupe, a ballet and orchestra, and a school for talented homeless children. "I believe that in our streets dwell geniuses who are neglected," he once said (*al-Ahram Weekly*, 6 April 2000). Despite his love for theater, he is best known today for his comic TV show, *Yawmiyat Wanis* (*Wanis' Diaries*).

A-to-Z:
Key People and Terms

AMMAN INDEPENDENT
THEATER FESTIVAL

Jordanian experimental festival that has become a fixture for theater troupes in Egypt and the Levant. It is held in the Jordanian capital Amman under the organization and administration of the al-Fawanees theater group. It is the only festival in the Middle East and North Africa that is organized by an independent theater group. Al-Fawanees was established in 1984 by a group of Jordanian dramatists and participated in several national and European festivals. The group organized the first Am-

man Independent Theater Festival in 1994. Initally it was with the participation of local theater groups only, but it has now expanded to include independent groups around the Arab region. It has become a focal point for alternative, nonstate theater in the Arab world.

ANA WA MARATI WA MONICA
(*ME, MY WIFE AND MONICA*)

A commercially successful play starring the Egyptian comic Samir Ghanem, which made heavy reference to American president Bill Clinton's affair with White House intern Monica Lewinsky, though this incident was not actually an integral part of the plot. The play went on tour around the Arab region. It is of the type of commercial comedy that dominates Egyptian and Arab theater at present. Egyptian critic Nehad Selaiha railed: "For two hours we were treated to a string of verbal exchanges at a vet's clinic consisting of scabrous jokes about the physical attributes of women and scurrilous references to the biological functions of both humans and animals, particularly dogs. More tedious than shocking, this avalanche of fetid humour did not seem to be leading anywhere or building up to anything" (*al-Ahram Weekly*, 27 October 1999).

BYE, BYE LONDON

A Kuwaiti play by actor-playwright Hussein Abdallah, which pokes fun at Kuwaitis and other Gulf Arabs who may be culturally out of place but are full of confidence all the same, living it up in London on trips to escape their wives. Kuwait had a thriving cultural scene before the Iraqi invasion in 1990.

CARACALLA

A stylish Lebanese theatrical dance troupe that plays around the world, founded by Abdel-Halim Caracalla in 1970. Caracalla, a choreographer who graduated from the London School of Contemporary Dance, merged the traditional Lebanese dance called *dabka* with classical and modern dance; it's also an attempt to merge Western dance with oriental. Marcel Khalife has often written the music for Caracalla's dance shows. The troupe tours the world and, with permission from the Lebanese government, performs in festivals alongside Israeli performers. Caracalla's themes are often Phoenician. In *Elyssa, the Queen of Carthage*, the dancers, led by the charismatic Tania Haroun in the title role, are energetic, moving with amazing speed in a fusion of ballet and modern dance. After Elyssa (Dido) immolates herself on stage, the dancers break into a Lebanese folk dance.

GHANEM, SAMIR (B. 1943)

Egypt's biggest modern stage comedian, who shot to fame with the early 1970s comedy *al-Mutazawwigun* (*The Married*), costarring his stage sidekick George Sidhum. His quick wit and improvisation skills have made him Egypt's prime theater star, while others of his generation such as Adel Imam went on to equal success in cinema. His string of hit shows since the early 1990s have included *Bahloul fi Istamboul*, *Ana, Marati wa Monica*, and *Do-ri-me Fasulya*. But his film career has melted away while contemporaries like Adel Imam have gone on to greater things. He is married to actress Dalal Abdel-Aziz. Their daughter Donia Abdel-Aziz is an actress and singer.

AL-HAKIM, TEWFIK (1902–1966)

The leading writer of plays in the Arab world, regarded as the father of modern Arab theater. Hakim was born in the Mediterranean city of Alexandria in 1902. He studied law in Cairo and Paris before working for a period in the government bureaucracy. He was one of the leading intellectual figures of the "liberal" era before the 1952 revolution, who looked to Europe for cultural inspiration. He remains a controversial figure to this day, since those views on many issues are hotly debated by Arab intellectuals. Though his works clearly had a dissident tone, Hakim initially had good relations with the Free Officers movement. Nasser cited *The Return of the Soul* as a key work influencing his revolutionary career. He was also attacked by liberals for failing to understand female psychology, and nationalists accused him of being soft on Zionism. He eventually turned against Nasser and became an early advocate of a peaceful resolution with Israel.

HAZZIMNI YA BABA (TIE THE DANCING BELT AROUND ME, OH FATHER)

A popular play in Cairo in the 1990s, starring the famous belly dancer Fifi Abdou. Censors changed its name to *Hazzimni Ya . . .* (*Tie the Dancing Belt Around Me, Oh . . .*), because the idea that a father would encourage his daughter to become a belly dancer was deemed as promiscuous and against public morals. It has been the most prominent of a series of plays with weak plots that offer an alternative forum for belly dancing, their main box-office draw.

IDRIS, YOUSEF (1927–1991)

An Egyptian playwright, novelist, and short story writer, whose plays were mainly comedies with political overtones written in colloquial language. Known as Arab literature's Chekhov, he has come to be regarded as the father of the Arab short story. Among his works, *Gomhouriyat Farahat* (*The Republic of Farahat*) stands out, and his *al-Haram* (*The Sin*) was turned into a famous film. *Al-Farafir*, Idris's theatrical landmark (in the published version of the play, the text is preceded by a seminal essay, "Towards an Egyptian Theatre"), spawned dozens of self-consciously Egyptian theatrical experiments that set out to fulfill his vision of a grassroots tradition of theater emerging independently in Egypt and liberated from the overriding influence of the Western model.

IMAM, ADEL (B. N.A.)

One of the biggest theater comics in Egypt, who gained fame in the 1970s. His works include *al-Wad Sayyid al-Shaghghal* (*The Boy Sayyid, the Cleaner*), *Shahid Maashafshi Haaga* (*A Witness Who Saw Nothing*), and *al-Za'im* (*The Leader*). His *al-Bodyguard* (*The Bodyguard*) began in 1998 and is still running in his custom-built theater house near the pyramids in Cairo. His film career overshadowed his theatrical beginnings during the 1990s with a string of soft political comedies such as *al-Irhabi* (*The Terrorist*) and *Tuyour al-Zalam* (*Birds of Darkness*). His box-office appeal has dwindled markedly since a new wave of comic actors appeared in the late 1990s.

KAGHAT, MOHAMMED (1942–2001)

One of the most prominent Moroccan dramatists, whose works in Arabic include *Manzila Bayn al-Hazimatayn* (*A Place between the Two Defeats*), *Dikrayat min al-Moustakbal* (*Memoirs from the Future*), *Mortajalat Fès* (*The Fes Improvisations/L'Impromptu de Fès*), and *Assatir Moâssira* (*Contemporary Myths/Légendes Contemporaines*). He also wrote a number of essays on Moroccan theater and played comic roles in several TV productions. He taught at the University of Fez.

KAROUMI, AWNI (B. 1945)

A respected Iraqi experimental theater director based in Germany, with a string of accolades gained in Germany, Iraq, and other Arab countries. Born in Mosul in north Iraq, he currently works at Theater der Ruhr in Muhlheim, Germany.

AL-KASSAR, ALI (1887–1957)

One of the stars of popular theater in prerevolutionary Egypt, whose black Nubian ethnicity gave him comic potential that he used to the full. This earlier generation of theater actors also moved into cinema, and Kassar starred in nine movies by director Togo Mizrahi, a Jewish director from an era that is largely ignored by the state television establishment in Egypt today. Kassar was one of the first actors to perfect the the puppet-theater character of the typically unlucky *karagoz*, who might eventually get his lucky break.

AL-LAILA AL-KABIRA

A famous Egyptian marionette opera in the 1960s with the lyrics of Salah Jahine and music of Sayed Mekkawi. It captures the atmosphere of the traditional *moulid*, or saint festival, and is often performed on stage as a dance/ballet. It reflects, too, the revolutionary optimism and dynamism of Egypt at the time.

MADRASAT AL-MUSHAAGHIBEEN (*THE SCHOOL OF TROUBLEMAKERS*)

A famous Egyptian play that ran for three straight years from 1971 to 1974, written by Ali Salem. It still does well with young audiences today, due to Adel Imam's career-making performance as the class troublemaker. It was a watershed in the now-common practice of comic ad-libbing, which directors and writers often complain of bitterly. Critics were never sure what to think of the show because of the way it uses slapstick, talented comic actors, and a clever script to mock education, one of the hallowed edifices of the modern state in Egypt.

AL-MUTAZAWWIGUN (*THE MARRIED*)

A classic comedy play starring a young Samir Ghanem, in which a woman from an upper-class family desperately tries to bond with the masses to make a success of her marriage to a downtown guy. Ghanem is Massoud, an educated but down-at-the-heels young opportunist who sought to marry money in the form of a rich girl called Lina. But the rich kid has a social conscience, and she takes to a life on the poor side, reveling in the struggle to make ends meet. The juxtaposition of middle-class values versus "the masses" forms the central comic element of the play. In one scene where Massoud watches how his wife cooks, he is speechless as she washes *molokhiya* (a green leaf vegetable popular in Egypt and Sudan, often known as "Jew's mallow") in detergent and soaks chicken in cement, thinking it's flour.

AL-RAMLY, LENIN (B. N.A.)

One of Egypt's best-known playwrights today, producing political commentary such as the famous *al-Irhabi* (*The Terrorist*), which was turned into a film starring comic actor-star Adel Imam. His *In Proper Arabic* (*Bil Arabi al-Fasih*), which opened in November 1991, set a new standard in political satire that drew a lot of attention outside the Arab world (it has been translated into several languages). When a Palestinian student in London disappears, his colleagues, fourteen Arab students each representing a different nationality, meet to decide what to do. The portrayal of their stereotypical national characteristics and attitudes throws a sharp light on the way Arabs see themselves and each other, and their posturing, squabbling, double standards, and inability to act together in the face of a common dilemma call into question the whole idea of "Arab unity." "Proper Arabic" is the formal language that brings all Arab nationalities together and the phrase is also used to mean "speak clearly," since the formal language is understood by everyone. With its theme of Arab-bashing, it attracted a lot of attention and praise in the West. Arab disunity was the theme at the time in the Arab world, due to the Iraqi occupation of Kuwait and an international effort led by the United States and including several Arab countries, among them Egypt, to remove Iraqi troops. The *International Her-*

ald Tribune called it "a milestone in the Arab world," and *Time* described it as "remarkable for its biting satire and rarely tolerated self-criticism."

REDA DANCE TROUPE

An internationally known Egyptian folkloric dance troupe that uses theatrical form. The original rush of enthusiasm for Mahmoud Reda's innovative work in the 1960s, and its endorsement by the government, fostered the growth of hundreds of troupes around the country over the past decades, as well as regular television coverage. As a result there's a certain apathy toward the troupe today. Aiming to preserve tradition, it can't easily develop new ideas, plus today's Egyptian youth are finding other interests besides visiting the troupe at its home in the Balloon Theater. Reda's troupe often performs with the National Folklore Troupe, which was founded at the same time. They were originally formed with the help of folkloric dance trainers from the Soviet Union, and their input gave a distinctly Russian flavor to much of the technique.

AL-RIHANI, NAGUIB (1892–1949)

An Iraqi-born comic actor who invented commercial theater in the early twentieth century to counter highbrow, Western-style theater by adapting French plays to Egyptian tastes, with the famous words: "We want an Egyptian theater with the smell of *taamiya* and *molokhiya*, not boiled potatoes and beef steak." He created the character of Kishkish Bey, a village mayor who embodies the contradictions between rural and city life. The plays in which Kishkish appeared were known as "Franco-Arab revues," a genre inspired by the French farce that was popular around the time of World War I. It offered a forum for satire against the British occupying authorities. Rihani's famous role in *Ghazal al-Banat* (*Girls' Flirtation*) alongside Laila Murad owed much to this genre of play.

SALEM, ALI (B. 1936)

An Egyptian playright famous for his 1970s classic *Madrasat al-Mushaaghibeen* (*School for Troublemakers*). He rose to prominence in the 1990s when he traveled to Israel and published his experiences in the 1994 book *Rihla Ila Isra'il* (*Journey to Israel*), bringing him problems with the staunchly anti-Israeli intellectual establishment in Egypt. He was turfed out of the Arab Writers Federation for his misdemeanor. He has since cast himself in the role of advocate of peace with Israel and critic of Arab governments for supporting the Intifada, and he openly associates with Israeli academics and writers. An outcast, since his 1994 visit he has not found a producer for two plays and a movie script is gathering dust. He sought more for his opinions on politics than for his theater.

SIKKAT AL-SALAMA (THE SALAMA ROAD)

One of Egypt's most popular contemporary plays is *Sikkat al-Salama*. First performed in 1964, it was written by Nasserist intellectual Saadeddin Wahba and directed by Saad Ardash. It was full of political innuendos tailored to fit the era, but has managed to win enduring popularity, possibly because the depiction of a corrupt society—made palatable by the comedy—still rings true today. In 2000 it was revisited by director Mahmoud al-Lozy and actor Mohammed Sobhy. A group of bus passengers lose their way on a trip to the city of Alexandria and end up stranded in the desert. Like a classic disaster movie, they are forced to confront their lives, their mistakes, and their sins, and they get a chance at redemption. But after vowing to right what is wrong in their lives, they all go back to their twisted ways the minute they see help on the horizon. Lozy offered deliberate parallels to William Golding's *Lord of the Flies* in his production.

SOBHY, MOHAMMED (B. 1948)

Egypt's intelligent comic actor, who has stuck to the stage more than to the big or small screen. His *Dastour, Ya Asyadna* (*Excuse Me, Sirs!*) was nixed by Egyptian censors in 1996 for the political content in Sobhy's improvised dialogues. Sobhy gained mass notoriety through his 1990s TV series *Wanis' Diaries* (*Yawmiyaat Wanis*), where he plays Wanis, a good-natured father of a five-member family—a U.S.-style family-values sitcom. He came to public attention around the Arab world and beyond in 2002 with his dramatic series *Faris Bila Gawad* (*A Knight without a Horse*), which was denounced by the U.S. administration and Israel as anti-Semitic. Sobhy tirelessly defended the show against the charges.

WAHBI, YOUSEF (1897–1982)

An actor, author, and director of plays and films in Egypt who saw his heyday in the 1930s and 1940s. Wahbi was the wayward son of an aristocratic family who found a passion for theater, setting up the Ramses Theater Company with inherited money.

But his racy autobiography, arrogant style, and onetime plan to depict the Prophet Mohammed on screen have marred his memory in the official nationalist canon of entertainment greats in Egypt. In Chahine's 1979 film *Iskandariya Leih?* (*Alexandria Why?*), he took the bold step—in the prevailing public atmosphere—of appearing as an Egyptian intellectual Jew, in an era when there were none left. Wahbi wrote the script and played the leading role in Egyptian cinema's first talkie, *Awlad al-Zawat* (*Children of the Aristocracy*), in 1932. He was the mentor of veteran Egyptian actress Amina Rizq, who died in 2003.

Bibliography

Print Resources

Abu Shanab, Adel. *Masrah Arabi Qadim: Karakuz.* Damascus: Culture Ministry, 1963.

Al-Raai, Ali. *al-Masrah fil-Watan al-Arabi* Kuwait: N.p., 1980.

Al-Shaarawi, Abdel-Mu'ti. *al-Masrah al-Misri al-Mu'aasir* (Contemporary Egyptian Theater). Cairo: General Egyptian Book Organization, 1986.

Amine, Khalid. "Crossing Borders: *al-Halqa* Performance in Morocco from the Open Space to the Theater Building." *The Drama Review* 45, no. 2 (Summer 2001): 55–69.

Aziza, Mohammed. *al-Islam wal-Masrah.* Cairo: N.p., 1990.

Badawi, M. M. *Early Arabic Drama.* Cambridge: Cambridge University Press, 1988.

———. *Modern Arabic Drama in Egypt.* Cambridge: Cambridge University Press, 1988.

El-Hachemi, Liliane and Nordine. "In Search of a Lost Heritage." *Journal of Algerian Studies* 5 (2000).

Farouk, Abdel Wahab, ed. *Modern Egyptian Drama: An Anthology.* Minneapolis: Bibliotheca Islamica, 1973.

Feeney, John. "The Shadows of Fancy: Demise and Birth." www.karaghiozis.net (a site hosted by karaghiozis.net, which is dedicated to the Greek shadow play).

Gharib, Lubna, and Richard Woffenden. "Should the Show Go On?" *Cairo Times*, 7–13 September 2000, vol. 4, no. 26.

Jayyusi, Salma, ed. *Short Arabic Plays*. Northampton, Mass.: Interlink, 2003.

Jayyusi, Salma, and Roger Allen, eds. *Modern Arabic Drama: An Anthology*. Bloomington: Indiana University Press, 1995.

Landau, Jacob. *Studies in the Arab Theater and Cinema*. Philadelphia: University of Pennsylvania Press, 1958.

Moreh, Shmuel, and Philip Sadgrove. *Jewish Contributions to Nineteenth-Century Arabic Theatre: Plays from Algeria and Syria*. Manchester, UK: University of Manchester, 1996.

"The Philosophy of Our Theatre." *Khartoum Monitor*, 21 August 2002.

Rakha, Youssef. "The Empty Stage." *al-Ahram Weekly*, 7–13 September 2000, no. 498.

———. "Hassan El-Geretly: Playing It Up." *al-Ahram Weekly*, 2–8 September 1999, no. 445.

Rubin, Don, ed. *World Encyclopedia of Contemporary Theater*. Vol. 4, *The Arab World*. London: Routledge, 1999.

Sadgrove, P. C. *The Egyptian Theatre in the Nineteenth Century: 1799–1882*. Reading, UK: Ithaca Press, 1996.

Salhi, Kamal. "Theatre, Politics and National Identity in Algeria: The Ambiguous Compromise." *Journal of Algerian Studies* 5 (2000).

Samaha, Hanan. "Burning the House Down." *Cairo Times*, 14–20 February 2002, vol. 5, no. 48.

Selaiha, Nehad. *Wamdaat Masrahiya (Theatrical Flashes)*. Cairo: General Egyptian Book Organization, 2001.

———. "Put Out the Light." *al-Ahram Weekly*, 11–17 July 2002, no. 594.

———. "Royal Buffoonery." *al-Ahram Weekly*, 4–10 April 2002, no. 580.

Shafik, Viola. *Arab Cinema: History and Cultural Identity*. Cairo: American University in Cairo Press, 1998.

Shahine, Gihan. "Samir Ghanem: A Natural." *al-Ahram Weekly*, 21–27 February 2002, no. 574.

Swairjo, Manal A. "Sa'dallah Wannous: A Life in Theater." *Al Jadid Magazine* (Los Angeles), June 1996, vol. 2, no. 8.

Wahish, Niveen. "Mohamed Sobhi: The World, the Stage." *al-Ahram Weekly*, 6–12 April 2000, no. 476.

Zuhur, Sherifa, ed. *Colors of Enchantment: Theater, Dance, Music and the Visual Arts of the Middle East*. Cairo: American University in Cairo Press, 2002.

Web Sites

www.masraheon.com. Site in Arabic about theater in the Arab world; a forum for intellectuals involved in theater.

7

Popular Religion

Islam: Home to a Thousand-and-One Traditions

Islam as a religion is more than a theology or moral code. It entails an elaborate body of rules and regulations (codified in more than one school of law) that seek to cover almost every aspect of human behavior, from bodily functions and acts of worship to property and commerce. These rules are part of Islam's literate Great Tradition. As kept by urban scholars, this tradition has existed side by side with more emotive folk traditions, which are in the keeping of holy lineages, religious brotherhoods, and freelance saints. Although there is no formal body codifying orthodoxy in Islam, as commentators often point out, there are in fact a variety of institutions that come close to doing so. Many Arab countries have an official mufti, a government-appointed cleric who is responsible for issuing fatwas on various issues. There are also bodies with a wider influence, such as the al-Azhar in Cairo, whose opinions are respected beyond national boundaries, as well as freelance clerics who have acquired positions of respect and who make effective use of television. But orthodox Islam and its official religious establishments have always ex-

Thousands of Cairenes perform the dawn prayers on the first day of the Islamic feast of Eid al-Fitr, marking the end of Ramadan. (Aladin Abdel Naby/Reuters/Corbis)

Hundreds of thousands of Muslims at Friday prayers in Mecca before the hajj season in January 2004. (Suhaib Salem/Reuters/Corbis)

isted in varying degrees of harmony with a multitude of smaller traditions in the region's rich cultures, many of whom predate the Arab-Islamic dispensation. These local customs, frowned upon by the authorities in some countries and banned in others, have often been the historical conduit through which Islam took hold in some areas—for example, Sufism in North Africa. The pilgrimage to Mecca appears to merge into a number of customs and practices of ancient Arabia—circling the *Kaaba*, rain-making cults—in an affirmation of the unitary vision of monotheism. Scholar Malise Ruthven wrote: "The central ritual of Islam, the Hajj, was arranged out of existing cultic practices. The actions themselves were almost unchanged, but their meaning was transformed to fit a new, vastly expanded, cosmic vision. The result was a religious and ideological *tour de force*" (Ruthven 2000, 48). The genius of

the religion—and a key reason for its survival and expansion—lies in its ability to absorb this mosaic of ancient customs, traditions, and identities.

The Popularity of Sufism across North Africa

Sufism (often termed Islamic mysticism) historically played a great role in spreading Islam in Sudan, imposing Sunni orthodoxy on medieval Egypt, and offering Berber communities in North Africa a means of preserving their identity as Arab tribes swept through the region during the eleventh century. In the long term, Berbers slowly disappeared as whole villages converted to the Arabic language or tribes migrated to Arab cities. The Berbers initially turned to Ibadism, a puritanical legal and theocratic creed of Islam. The central idea

The *Moulid*

The *moulid*, or celebration of a deceased holy figure's birthday, is a colorful element of popular culture in North Africa. This event is also strangely controversial. In most Gulf countries, major moulids—such as one that celebrates the Prophet's birthday—are not marked at all, while in North African countries the occasion warrants a public holiday. Strict Sunni Islam in the Gulf frowns upon the moulid, viewing it as a form of idol worship that runs against Islam's defining tenet of monotheism. In North Africa, the moulid is in some respects a repackaging in Islamic guise of Berber and Pharaonic customs of public celebration. Today's version of the moulid is an infamously noisy affair, and the term "moulid" has become a byword in everyday speech for chaos and crowds. Moulids are associated with Shi'ite and Sufi customs—Shi'ite veneration of the Prophet's family, with moulids of Hussein, Fatima, Nafisa, Aisha, and others, and Sufi veneration of hundreds of local saintly figures across the centuries in different parts of the region.

The biggest moulid of them all is the Sayed al-Badawi moulid, held for a week very autumn in the town of Tanta in the middle of the Nile Delta in northern Egypt, which is visited by

Men play with snakes at a moulid. The authorities have cracked down on some of the wilder displays at moulids. (Norbert Schiller/Focus MidEast)

A boy, wearing a hat that says "Jerusalem is Islamic," indulges in face-piercing at a Cairo moulid. (Norbert Schiller/Focus MidEast)

some one million people. The sacred meets the profane, as carnival rides and other attractions vie for the attention of the masses. There is tent after tent of Sufi incantation and trance dancing, food stalls and street restaurants, theatrical storytelling of the days of the Prophet, and bizarre shows that promise passersby the chance to gawk at freaks of nature such as cows with two heads, deformed midgets, or magic tricks where women are carved in two. Amid the cacophony of noise and neon lights, whole families lounge the night away under the tent awnings, munching on sugarcane, drinking tea, smoking *shisha* (a flavored tabacco water pipe), or even sleeping. Moulids were once even stranger affairs, featuring gypsy women who performed erotic dances or stunts such as horses riding over prostrate men, but since the

A scene from the moulid of Hussein, the Prophet's grandson, in Cairo. (Thomas Hartwell/ Corbis)

early twentieth century the modern state has stopped such colorful events.

In October 2002, crowds of young men fought to get tickets to one ten-minute show that was advertised over a microphone with the following pitch: "The age of technology—here it is. The age of miracles—here it is. You've heard of the internet? It's the age of miracles—here it is! Last year we had a cow with five legs. This year we'll have something more amazing—so pray to the Prophet!" Inside the large tent there was a ventriloquist show, featuring bawdy language, a juggler, a peasant girl who emerged unscathed from a wooden box sliced with swords, and a young boy whose body was contorted inside a pyramid, with only his head appearing on top. The youthful rabble left disappointed. Stories abound of sexual favors varying in magnitude occuring at some moulids, but these tales are perhaps best consigned to the realm of urban legends.

of this sect was that you didn't have to be an Arab to lead a Muslim community, and the important thing was to follow the rules for being a sinless, good Muslim. The idea of Ibadism was attractive to Berber North Africa in the early days after the stunning successes of the Arab conquests, when, as with Judaism, the religion was cast as the preserve of a particular people (the Arabs). Later, in the "medieval period," mainstream Sunni Islam made inroads among the Berbers, effectively Arabizing them in the process. The Ibadi groups that survive (the Mzab in the Algerian Sahara, the Jebel Nafousa in Libya, and a few communities in southern Tunisia) retain their Berber identity, "the last heroic remnant of the original attempt to transform the Islam of the Berbers into the Islam of the world," as Brett put it (Brett and Fentress 1996, 151).

Change is also coming to Sudan, where tribes who retained their non-Arab traditions through Sufism or other means are finally giving in to Arabism. Among a number of languages that have died out in the five decades since independence in 1956 is the Gule language, spoken by the Gule people, who reside in a mountainous area southeast of Khartoum. Ironically, the Gule played a central role in the creation of the Arabic-speaking Funj Sultanate in the Sennar region, which lasted some three hundred years until the early nineteenth century. "Now they say they are Arabs. It's a social aspiration to be from the Arabs and the Prophet's house," Sudanese linguist Amin Abu-Manqa said (interview with author, August 2002).

The battle to "purify" Islamic communities of these traditions rages to this day. The central force behind this movement is a "back-to-basics" puritanical ideology, which has dominated Sunni Islam over the last one hundred years. It is referred to by various names in different regions of the Middle East, but the most prominent and all-encompassing movement is Salafism, which designates a return to the way, or *sunna*, of "the ancestors" *(al-aslaaf)*, meaning the Prophet and early Muslims. The movement developed throughout the twentieth century, with two major fillips being the establishment in 1928 of the Muslim Brotherhood in Egypt and the simultaneous emergence of modern Saudi Arabia with its petroleum-based wealth. This conservative trend is at its most austere in Saudi Arabia, where it takes the name of Wahhabism. Popular saints, who were promoted by the Sufi brotherhoods that spread there from Morocco, were a main target of the Wahhabi movement. Shi'ite tombs and graveyards of the Zaydi sect in

Yemen have been desecrated by Wahhabis in recent decades. To this day Sufis must practice in private in the Hejaz region on the Red Sea, where they were most popular, and tombs that Saudi religious police suspect of attracting pilgrims are often destroyed.

In Egypt, too, the leaders of the sects (sing. *tariqa*, or "path"), who descend from the holy man who gave his name to the order, keep a low profile and rarely put their names on the mosques or religious foundations that they own. This is partly in keeping with the inward-looking nature of Sufism, but it is also a reaction to Wahhabi influence on thinking about this medieval innovation (or *bid'a*, as it is known derogatively), which deviates from the Islam of the Prophet. In Egypt, state-owned religious publications such as *al-Liwa al-Islami* (*The Islamic Banner*) and *Aqidati* (*My Conviction*) don't attack Sufism as such, just local practices their writers happen to observe. The government maintains a High Sufi Council (an attempt to control the seventy-two Sufi orders in the country). The council publishes *al-Tasawwuf al-Islami* (*Islamic Sufism*), which bans music and drumming to the *zikr*, the trancelike dancing of Sufis that they perform while uttering any of the ninety-nine adjectives ascribed to God in the classical Arabic language. The publication also attempts to regulate *moulids* and bans some practices that were rife until the nineteenth century, such as riding horses over human carpets of followers, though body-piercing, snake-handling, and fire-walking are still alive and well. Senior religious officials sometimes turn up at major festivals, such as that of al-Sayed Ahmed al-Badawi, a thirteenth-century holy man and spiritual father of the Ahmediya, Egypt's largest brotherhood (Sadat used to attend, but Mubarak never has). Hassan al-Banna, the founder of the Muslim Brotherhood, was himself a devotee of a Sufi order, from which he derived his vision of the Brotherhood as a super-Sufi sect, covering the entire nation with charity, education, and paramilitary activity along with the traditional devotional activities. In today's popular culture, Sufism has acquired a certain élan, as has its Jewish mystical cousin Kabbala, of which pop icon Madonna is a devotee (both involve focus on the names of God, in one case in Hebrew, in the other Arabic, as a means of getting closer to and understanding the Divinity). The Paris-based Tunisian pop singer Amina al-Nabawi used Sudanese Sufi chants and rhythms on her 2000 album *Amina*, as did Egyptian singer Mohammed Mounir in his 2002 album *Earth, Peace (al-Ard, al-Salam)*. Algerian pop stars Cheb Khaled, Faudel, and Rachid Taha sang for the intercession of a Sufi holy man in their 1998 hit *Abdel-Qadir*, and Tunisian Saber Rubai sang for the help of Sidi Mansour in his 2001 hit of the same name. A current trend in the Arabic novel is to highlight Sufi traditions (for example, the works of Egyptians Khairy Abdel-Gawad, Gamal al-Ghitani, and Mohammed Gibreel).

Belief in the *Jinn* across the Arab World

A major discussion currently taking place in the centuries-long debate over popular religion and official Islam concerns the belief in spirits, or the *jinn* (the English word "genie" is derived from *jinn*). The orthodoxy, as propagated by Sunni institutions such as al-Azhar, acknowledges the existence of *jinn*, or spirits, but says they belong to the other world, have no contact with this world, and thus cannot "possess" the living. The concept of contact with the nonhuman world is a sensitive one in Islam. The state of trance and possession is connected with the moment when prophets received divine messages or inspiration (*wahy*) from God. So questioning the existence of the *jinn* has proved to be a risky enterprise for some. A literal reading of the Quran makes plain that the *jinn* exist. Indeed, denial of the *jinn* was one of the ideas taught by an Egyptian professor of Islamic history, Nasr Abu Zeid. As a result of his teachings, he was given a court sentence in 1996 that forcibly divorced him from his wife. A group of conservative religious scholars and lawyers argued that Abu Zeid's ideas proved he was no longer a Muslim, and so he could not remain married to one. Popular culture, however, goes further and assumes that the spirits—either of the dead or any of a range of entities (such as *'afreet* and *ghoul*)—visit the world of the living. Numerous other words are used to specify spirit possession. The most common is *majnoun*, which literally means "occupied by a genie/spirit (*jinni*)," translated in English as "crazy" or "mad." *Majnoun* can be negative or positive—someone touched by crazy genius, for example, can be *majnoun*. Other words with a more negative connotation are *maskoun* (lit., "lived in") and *malbous* (lit., "clothed," as in "clothed by the *jinn*").

The medical profession in most Arab countries makes strenuous efforts to combat these ideas insofar as they affect beliefs in modern medicine, though until recent years this has been a losing battle due to the phenomenon of televangelists. The issue is complicated by the political and economic makeup of Arab societies. The millions who believe in the meeting of "man and spirit" are sniffingly referred to by religious scholars and modern doctors as *al-naas al-busataa,'* or "simple, ordinary people"—people of limited economic means or access to knowledge and technology, with little political power to change their situation. Experts who appear on television—whether religious, medical, or psychological, all of whom are backed by the state and spout the opinions of ruling establishments—come across as "talking down" to the masses, presumed to be hopelessly lost. For ordinary folks, time-honored traditions help them make sense of their daily lives, and they resent having these beliefs taken away by an authoritarian state, which has yet to prove that modernity can offer a viable alternative. The strident secular-national Arab states (such as Egypt, Iraq, and Syria) assume that removing superstitions is a prerequisite for the economic and technological advancement of the nations. But a valid argument can be made that people will give up their traditional beliefs and practices only if they are presented with convincing models of economic and political change (if stamping out traditions is even to be considered a worthwhile project in the first place).

The medical profession in some countries also objects to a practice known as *hejama*, which involves evacuating air from cups placed on areas of the body, mainly on the back, to suck tissue and stimulate blood flow. The treatment is cited several times in hadiths about the deeds and sayings of Mohammed, though it could date back to pre-Islamic times. *Hejama* is opposed by the medical profession in Egypt, where the Doctors' Syndicate has threatened to discipline members practic-

ing "the Prophet's medicine," as its supporters dub it, and police have closed down clinics. But the practice is legal in Lebanon, Syria, and Saudi Arabia. Interest in alternative medicines sanctioned by Islam is increasing, and these practices often are cheaper than modern medicines.

In post-Saddam Iraq, modern psychiatry is battling with traditional forms of treatment that are lodged in Iraq's popular religious culture. "Ninety-five percent of my patients went first to a sheikh who did some ceremony to try and remove the *jinn*. When that fails, they come to me," said renowned Iraqi psychiatrist Harith Hassan (interview with author, Reuters, 7 December 2003). There are approximately sixty-four practicing psychiatrists in a country of 26 million, but hundreds more who trade in exorcising the *jinn* via Quranic recitation or the Sufi *zikr* or *zaar*, a cultic trance-dance ceremony found all over the Arab world (called *dirbasha* in Iraq). "There are thousands of them. In 1998 we studied this and found that in Baghdad alone there were 474 offering healing services using the Quran," Hassan said (interview with author, Reuters, 7 December 2003). "It's all sorcery and nonsense, though I wouldn't reject the value of using the Quran to make people feel happy and peaceful. But the Quran is not a drug or remedy. It's a book to make people do good things, not to help people get rid of an illness." Practitioners of both modern and ancient methods are doing a roaring trade in Iraq today. According to Hassan, Iraqis are afflicted with "frustration, depression and aggression" after four eventful decades of military coups, wars, brutal one-party rule, and a crushing international embargo.

Although the belief in exorcising the *jinn* is widespread among the *busataa* (the

An Iraqi woman at a psychiatric hospital in Baghdad in July 2003. Most Iraqis first turn to traditional forms of treatment embedded in the culture of popular religion. (Marwan Naamani/AFP/Getty Images)

simple, ordinary people), it is also the simple, ordinary folk who come to psychiatrists. "Most of the patients come from faraway rural areas. They may be illiterate and uneducated, but they are more tuned in psychiatrically than educated people. It's very strange. People will travel up to ten hours from places like Samawa and Meisan [in the south] and will stay in hotels overnight if they don't find me. Educated people won't even bother to stick to an appointment," Hassan said (interview with author, Reuters, 7 December 2003). And it's not as if the city folk couldn't do with a bit of therapy, Hassan said: "Do you ever see people smiling on the streets? Never! It's because of the frustration, depression, and aggression all Iraqis had during the last forty-five years. If you don't deal with de-

pression it turns into aggression, like religious fanaticism, quarrels, and looting," Hassan said. He traces many problems of national psychology back to the 1958 revolution. "It was not only Saddam Hussein's regime that was bloody but the 1958 revolution. It was very violent and it was at that time that people started to learn strange new meanings for 'democracy' and 'freedom.' I remember how they [the new regime] brought the leg of Noury al-Said [the leading pro-British politician of the pre-1958 period] to our school. We were expected to drag it around or spit on it," he said. "The characteristic in Iraq is for these things to repeat themselves. It's not just the problem of who rules Iraq, it's how can we build a new self-esteem for Iraqis and fulfil their needs. We are trying to build a decent society" (interview with author, Reuters, 7 December 2003).

Healing by Quran, *Zaar,* and Sorcery

Healing from spirit possession takes three main forms, in descending order of social acceptability: healing by Quran, the cult of *zaar,* and black magic (*sha'waza*). Quran healing has gone a ways toward achieving respectability in a huge city like Cairo, which has some thirty official practitioners. One of them, Hosni Rashwan, has published a book on his increasingly popular work. He treats his patients in small groups, and their complaints range from nervousness, nightmares, headaches, and depression to the inability to say yes to a marriage suitor. Rashwan may begin by reciting some Quranic verses, such as *Surat al-Sifaat,* invoking the majesty of God and the grandeur of creation. The patients are quickly affected. They might start screaming, howling, or trembling. The sheikh will point to them, one after another, and recite: "Oh genies and devils who worship the Merciful, I employ you in the name of the covenant between you and Soliman, son of David, to leave our homes and to appear not unto us, nor to harm us" (*Cairo Times,* 25 December 1997). The spirits are usually assumed to be misguided but benign forces who don't realize the harm they cause to the living. Patients are instructed to keep reading and reciting specific Quranic verses to make sure the *jinn* don't come back. The medical establishment is coming around to the idea that therapy-by-Quran might be a good thing, since as long as people believe in the power of the holy book to heal them, whether the *jinn* exist or not is academic.

Psychiatrist Gamal Abul-Azayem, who runs the Cairo-based International Islamic Society for Psychological Health, devoted a whole chapter of a recent book on psychological health to the phenomenon of Quran therapy. He employs sheikhs in his clinic for treating drug addicts, who come to the clinic only after conventional treatments have failed. "Diseases have to be treated in their own context," he wrote (*Cairo Times,* 25 December 1997). Among the religious establishment, most frown on what they consider a mundane use of the word of God, while there are some populists who see the therapy as an ultimate vindication of the relevance of Islam to the everyday lives of the faithful.

The healing cult of *zaar* is found mainly in Egypt, Sudan, Ethiopia, and Somalia. It has attracted a lot of attention from anthropologists, partly because the participants are mainly women, the possessing spirits are usually characterized as male, and the trance ceremony appears to operate as a unique form of psychological relief for women in strictly patriarchal communities. Men sometimes help with drumming, slaughter of ritual animals (such as a chicken, whose blood is dripped over the possessed woman in her dance-trance state), or even playing the role of *zaar* leader (*sheikha* or *kodia*). In Egypt it is, like female circumcision, an ancient custom dating from Pharaonic times that today is practiced by the *fellahin* peasant communities, mainly in the south where the reach of religious authorities is weaker. Sudan's Islamist governments have actively sought to stamp *zaar* out, officially banning it in 1992.

The central idea of *zaar* is not exorcising spirits, but placating them—akin to the modern Western idea of "dealing with your demons." The leader is herself possessed, but considered as having come to terms with her *jinn* and so in a position to help others. She has her *'ilba*, or box, with the tools of her trade and symbols of her knowledge, and this box will often be passed on from teacher to teacher. Guests at the ceremonies pay money to the leader, allowing the ritual to function as a kind of charitable society. Incense is offered to the spirit, along with a sacrificed animal and other food and drink. The leader sings songs for various spirits, each with its own rhythms. The ritual offers a context in which women can indulge in drinking, smoking, dancing, and rambunctious behavior, without having society question their morals or feminity. It also spills over into Sufi practices, with its use of trance-like dance movements. In Tunisia, a version called *stambali* is connected with holy men and their shrines. A "non-Muslim" spirit can require an alcoholic drink, which will be consumed by the guests, or a female spirit might want a sweet soft drink.

Zaar music has been identified and packaged by the West, and it is featured on any number of world music albums, including Hossam Ramzy's *Introduction to Egyptian Rhythms* and Peter Gabriel's *Passion*. It was also featured in the movie *Ta'wiza* (*Talisman*), an Egyptian attempt at a supernatural thriller. The movie stars Yousra and Mahmoud Yassin are participants in *zaar* ceremonies and gay discos.

The belief in sorcery, or *sha'waza*, is also strong. Conservatively inclined Muslims might denounce *zaar*, Quran healing, and the practices of Sufi holy men and their followers as *sha'waza*. The holy men of North Africa, around whom Sufi sects developed, were all regarded as having God's blessing, or *baraka*, and were seen as people close to God through whom God worked his power (*awliyaa'*). In North Africa they are known as *marabouts*, or *muraabiteen* (sing., *muraabit*), holy men "bound together" or "connected" spiritually, as the name implies, as the force to spread Islam in the region. The Almoravid Islamic empire was founded in Marrakech in 1070 by Berber Tuareg tribes fired by such holy men. This empire was the first major attestation of the concept of the Muslim saint in North Africa, after which the idea merged with a strain of mysticism from the Middle East to form the peculiar Sufism of North Africa. The idea seems to have developed through Berber customs of ancestor veneration, but also became entwined with indigenous North African traditions of magic. The *marabouts* were seen as having miraculous powers, including second sight. In the famed repository of Arabic tales *1,001 Nights*, Morocco is referred to in the story of Aladdin and his magic lamp as a "hotbed of evil sorcerers." To this day, Moroccan women are renowned in the Arab East for dabbling in magic. A favorite is for a jilted woman to have an expert in the black arts summon a spirit to possess her former lover or his new attraction. The tabloid press in most Arab countries regularly features stories about charlatans (*dajjaleen*) who practice magic for a hefty price; they often have famous actresses as their customers, and their rituals involve clothes being taken off. The Quran acknowledges the existence of magic (*sihr*), so the power to bring ill to others is taken seriously.

In recent years, an obsession with maintaining Islamic orthodoxy against these practices has led to a stream of court cases in Egypt against individuals. They are usually groups of around twenty people from all walks of life, regularly congregating at the home of a sheikh figure who propagates alternative ideas about Muslim pilgrimage, prayer, and fasting—for example, that one should face toward somewhere other than Mecca when praying, forgo pilgrimage to Mecca or make pilgrimage somewhere else, or not bother with fasting during Ramadan. The charge is usually of "abusing the Islamic religion, propagating extremist ideas with the aim of provoking dissent, and scorning the Islamic religion by advancing ideas and beliefs contrary to fixed religious tenets." In one celebrated case in 2000, a woman known as Sheikha Manal received a five-year jail term for claiming she was a prophet and arguing that daily prayer and the pilgrimage were not necessary ("Egypt Court Says Sufi Group Denigrated Islam," Reuters, 5 September 2000). Most Islamic legal schools maintain five central pillars that include prayer five times a day, fasting, pilgrimage to Mecca, paying alms, and saying the *shehada* in Arabic ("there is no god but God and Mohammed is His prophet"). In Islam, Mohammed is the last of the line of the biblical prophets, and Jesus is conceived of as the second to last, before Mohammed. Sheikha's defense was that she received visions from her deceased uncle, the founder of a Sufi sect, that contained instructions to her followers.

Tied up with these ideas—of the power of the Quran, the power of people blessed by God, bad magic, and the *jinn*—is the belief in the "evil eye." Religious scholars consider that prayer five times a day and reading the Quran are enough to ward off the envy of others. But in society it doesn't stop there. People will visit the shrines of holy men and follow an elaborate list of rit-

uals to defend themselves from the malevolent power of others. In this world, fate and earthly powers are seen as playing a greater role in the course of one's life than any efforts made by individuals. Some have seen in these beliefs a link to the prevalence of the conspiracy theory at the level of national politics—a sense that the state itself is the target of bad karma from those who wish it harm. In both cases, the subject—the state, the individual—doesn't "do" but is "done to," as Egyptian sociologist Saadeddin Ibrahim has written (*al-Ahram*, 8 September, 1997). Warding off "the eye" can involve burning special types of incense; painting walls blue; or hanging near the front door of the home small or large broomsticks, pendants in the shape of an eye or a chili pepper, and other objects containing Quranic verse (usually a particular line, called *ayat il-kursiyy*, from *Surat al-Baqara*). These pendants will often involve the eye or hand of Fatima, a daughter of the Prophet, and people wear them around their necks too. According to a story in Islamic tradition, the Prophet had a bad feeling about a lady who once visited him while Fatima's children Hussein and Hassan were in the house, so he hid the babies and replaced them with stones wrapped in blankets. After the woman left, he found the stones had broken, vindicating his decision to remove the babies. Women in poor districts will go even further to avoid attracting the wrong attention, particularly if they have given birth to boys: they give them odd names, dress up boys as girls, or grow the boys' hair long or have them wear earrings. These beliefs extend to other areas. For example, women wear amulets and visit shrines to encourage fertility, based on ideas inherited from pre-Arab/Islamic

Berber, Egyptian and Phoenician times. Also, moths are said to be the spirits of dead people come to visit the living.

The Growth of TV Evangelists since the 1970s

When the culture of audiocassette tapes spread in the 1970s, it created modern pop stars such as Ahmed Adawiya and offered minority groups such as the Berbers a new means of expressing their own culture. More importantly, it allowed religious preachers to take their message to a new, vast public. The phenomenon has often been noted regarding Iran, where it laid the ground for Ayatollah Khomeini's Islamic revolution. But the videocassette also revolutionized religious politics in the Arab countries. Television revolutionized politics as well, though state control prescribed a different set of rules for TV preachers. In Egypt in the late 1970s, there were a number of sheikhs whose popularity spread far and wide. The biggest of them was Sheikh Kishk, whose fame spread from one end of the Arab world to the other and even into immigrant communities in Europe. Blind from a young age— as have been a number of famous preachers in recent decades—he was imprisoned for two years in the 1960s on suspicion of sympathy with the Muslim Brotherhood, during which time he was tortured. But he emerged from these experiences in the early 1970s as the biggest phenomenon in a new era of preachers, whose ninety-minute sermons in Cairo suburbs were recorded and sold on the spot. Articulating a major Islamist theory of recent decades, Kishk argued that the modern, secular Arab state

was a failure. He argued that the secularism that had replaced the educational and legal systems, ending the independence of the religious establishment—such as Nasser's state control over al-Azhar in 1962—amounted to nothing more than dictatorship. Kishk was arrested during Sadat's sweep of all opposition figures in September 1981, but when he was released after Sadat's death he chose to maintain a lower profile.

Religion-by-cassette is still an important factor of religious culture in Arab countries today. Kishk remains the most popular choice for taped sermons; Upper Egyptian reciter Abdel-Basit Abdel-Samad is the most popular Quran reader; and Sheikh Shaarawi is number one in the third genre of religious tapes, called *tafsir*, or explanations of the meaning of Quranic verse. All three figures are now deceased, but their fame lives on. Cairo has three music companies that deal in religious tapes, two of them exclusively dedicated to the genre, and they export tapes to France, Britain, and the United States.

Sheikh Shaarawi's nonconfrontational style with authorities perhaps explains why his influence has been more profound in the long term. When he passed away in the early morning of 17 June 1998, Egypt lost one of its most controversial figures. Over a million people crammed into the small northern town of Daqadous to say goodbye to Shaarawi. News of his death wasn't announced until the interior ministry made sure his body had safely traveled from Cairo to his home in the Nile Delta. The capital would have been completely paralyzed had the funeral been held there. Shaarawi was 87 when he died. He really made his mark in the last decades of his life, with a twenty-year television career

Islam and Music

Music is one sphere where "orthodoxy" has negotiated with tradition. Debate rages to this day about the musical quality of Quranic recitation and the permissibility of music in general under Islam. Many prominent reciters have written essays and articles on how melodic recitation of the Quran should or should not be seen as part of the debate on *samaa'* (listening to music). Scholars have always been uneasy about the power of music on the emotions (a concept celebrated by the Arabic word for musical enjoyment, *tarab*), suspecting that it disturbs and interferes with the believer's ability to act according to God's will. Music is seen as a rival of Islam in a battle for souls. Islamic tradition believes music is of human origin, and it maintains a strict divide between music and the Quran. But since the early centuries of Islam, Sufism has played a major role in gaining acceptability for music, as well as dance, arguing that they are neutral forces that can be channeled and regulated, therefore having the ability to lead the believer toward God and not away from Him. So although recitation is not associated with musical art in any way, there are acceptable limits for the use of melody. Indeed, much of the terminology in music concerns the Quran (though the line is drawn at *tarab*). But it is an ongoing debate. Egypt traditionally has a melodic style of recitation, as does the Hejaz area on the western coast of Saudi Arabia, which causes no end of trouble with the strict Sunni religious establishment.

Those who enter into the melodic tradition of recitation skillfully move among the scales of Arabic music, known as *maqamaat* (sing., *maqaam*), accentuating the emotions associated with the text. *Maqams* engender a range of emotions, including sadness and joy. One of the most renowned reciters in this regard was the Egyptian sheikh Rif'at, who could bring his listeners to tears. Other reciters have had their knuckles rapped for straying into *tarab* territory. Quranic recitation uses the same melodic system as secular music but not its rhythmic systems. Some singers in fact began their careers as reciters of the Quran, including Umm Kalthoum and Sayed Darwish. Some forms of

---

that made him beloved of millions and arguably more influential than the overtly political Islamists of the Muslim Brotherhood or the radical groups who launched war against the state in the 1990s. Shaarawi was the soft face of the Islamist crusade for a return to faith and traditional values in the aftermath of the crushing Arab defeat in the 1967 war with Israel and the demise of the secular-nationalist revolution. Amidst the chaos of post-1967 Egypt—urban expansion, mushrooming slums, numbing bureaucracy, politicized religion—Shaarawi came to be seen as a symbol of integrity and humility, giving people a sense of reality in an increasingly surreal world. Neither a fiery Omar Abdel-Rahman (the radical Egyptian sheikh convicted of trying to blow up the World Trade Center in 1993) nor a cautious Sheikh Tantawi (the head of al-Azhar), Shaarawi was the hero of the silent millions who don't like rebellion and certainly don't vote in elections, but who watch lots and lots of TV.

Shaarawi's rise to preeminence offers an insight into the machinations of Arab politics in the 1970s, when Islamic fundamentalism became the paradigm of anti-Western struggle in the Arab region. Nasser's successor, Anwar Sadat, made a conscious

A Turkish man at prayers in Istanbul in February 2003. Many Arabs think Turkey's model of secular democracy is worth emulating, while others think they have gone too far with imitating secular Western mores and ditching Islamic public morals. (Chris Hondros/Getty Images)

music bridge the divide between religious and secular singing, such as *tawashih* (a form of poetry) and *ibtihalaat* (hymns). Recitation, like music, is big business. Reciters command big fees and the atmosphere at their performances can be similar to that at pop concerts.

decision to set up Shaarawi as a TV sheikh. Sadat and Shaarawi created a coalition of interests: both of them feared the influence of leftists and communists. Before Egypt's 1973 war with Israel, Sadat dispatched Shaarawi to Saudi Arabia to persuade the wealthy regime to bankroll his coming war, arguing that this war would be fought by a nation that had rediscovered its faith after the godless years of Nasser. Shaarawi was like Rasputin to Sadat's czar. After Shaarawi's death, leftist publications in Egypt came out with revelations about Shaarawi's supposedly nefarious influence on the impressionable president. In one tale, it was reported that Shaarawi would reduce Sadat to tears through the power of his rhetoric in private meetings. Sadat made Shaarawi a government minister. He also had him appear on national television after bread riots in 1977, where he denounced the unrest as a "rebellion of thieves" led by communists (*Cairo Times*, 25 June 1998).

It was after the riots of 1977 that Sadat gave Shaarawi a weekly television program. Every Friday for twenty years, until his death in June 1998—and well beyond Sadat's death in 1981—"Khawater al-Shaarawi" (The Thoughts of Shaarawi) was broadcast from a mosque in Daqadous,

Iraqi Communists Ride the Religious Wave

In the new Iraq, even communists are promoting religion as a central part of the national fabric. Iraqis in general are still mild in their observance of religious occasions, at least in Baghdad, where eating or smoking in public during Ramadan remains acceptable behavior. But for more and more Sunnis and Shia alike, religious background has become their primary mark of identity and a source of pride and self-respect. Whereas before it was Arabism that had been the glue used to hold the country together, now it is Islam. According to Iraq's communist culture minister Moufid al-Jazairy, Iraq could be a secular model for the Arab region, "but with full respect for the different religious groups so that they have absolute freedom just like all other political and social groups" (interview with author, November 2003).

Gradually since the defeat of the secular-nation project in 1967, "secularism" has become a dirty word in the Arab world, even in traditionally secular, Arab nationalist Iraq. "Communist" has come to mean "atheist," or at least the Islamists who have been in the ascendancy since 1967 have succeeded in giving that impression. Communists are officially banned in Egypt, and no one anywhere else in the Arab world would publicly take on the mantle of "communist." But in Iraq, communists have a long history and an important place in the narrative of the emergence of the modern nation-state. Their posi-

tion is so important that, after the invasion of 2003, there was a communist on the governing council appointed by Washington, D.C., and a communist in the cabinet was subsequently chosen by that council. "At the street level the word 'secular' is not understood, but people try to say that it means being an infidel," said Abdel-Latif al-Saadi, an editor of the communist weekly *Tariq al-Shaab* (interview with author, November 2003). "We consider that praying and fasting is a personal issue. We use the word 'secular' all the time in our paper. Our society was more secular than other Arab societies. We didn't have religious extremism, but then Saddam Hussein exploited religion. I used to be able to discuss the existence of God with Muslim brothers, now I couldn't do that" (interview with author, November 2003).

During the period of the United Nations sanctions in the 1990s, hundreds of thousands of Iraqis sought refuge in God with the state's encouragement. In 1998 Saddam Hussein announced a "faith campaign," which aimed to keep the masses on a straight and narrow path during difficult times. The campaign established dozens of mosques and religious schools, a radio station dedicated to Quranic recitation, and independent newspapers specializing in religious affairs. The faith campaign also performed a favor for America and its allies, since it aimed to check the attempts of

with Shaarawi interpreting the Quran before a captivated audience of ordinary Egyptians—mainly the rural and urban poor. Via his show, the TV sheikh won the hearts of millions of Egyptians and other Arabs with his grasp of Quranic Arabic and also his ability to create pithy homilies in colloquial language, which made the seemingly incomprehensible in scripture appear

relevant to modern life. His aim was to maintain traditional religious values in society. In one example of his influence in everyday affairs, an Egyptian newspaper reported in 1997 that it had sought his opinion over three zucchinis discovered in north Egypt that appeared to have the phrases "there is no god but God," "have faith in God," and "God" embossed on them

The Iraqi Communist Party jubilant in post-Saddam Iraq at May Day celebrations in 2003. (Wathiq Khuzaie/Getty Images)

radical groups (such as Shi'ite Iran, Wahhabi Saudi Arabia, and al-Qa'ida) to influence Iraqis during a difficult decade.

The communists and other secular forces in Iraq hope they can ride the wave of religious feeling and prevent it from going too far. "We are trying to create the conditions for a new democratic Iraq. We are not afraid of religious groups because they are religious, we are afraid of extremists," Moufid al-Jazairy said (interview with author, November 2003). "Iraq as a country is a country of natural plurality; there are many nations, of religious plurality; and political plurality, although the old regime didn't want to recognize it. Sometimes there are extremists, but when you put them aside you see that for the main part there is coexistence, acceptance, and respect."

(*al-Osboa*, 11 August 1997). Shaarawi confirmed to newspapers that they were a miraculous sign. "Indeed, they are a message from God to the Islamic community in every corner of the Earth in answer to the filthy Israeli who insulted the Prophet of the Muslims and the holy Quran, which is the constitution of Muslims," he said, referring to an Israeli settler girl who achieved media notoriety earlier that year for distributing a sketch of a pig with the Prophet's name on it around Hebron in the West Bank (*al-Osboa*, 11 August 1997).

As the state under Mubarak more openly embraced a Western development agenda in the 1990s, it came to regret creating the TV sheikhs. When Shaarawi died, Egypt's state television devoted barely fifteen minutes to covering his funeral—coverage that one religious-leaning Egyptian opposition paper described as "the farce of the century." Having survived the Islamist insurgency of the 1990s, the government clearly regretted Sadat's creation. Shaarawi had come up against the authorities on a number of occasions. He defied the government in the late 1990s by pronouncing repeatedly that female circumcision was religiously sanctioned. He famously justified this belief in one interview by saying: "If a woman rides a horse she will become sexually excited, so this excitement must be reduced" (*Cairo Times*, 25 June 1998). He seemed to confirm prejudices against women in the workplace by declaring that "what women lack in the mind, they make up for in emotion" and spoke out against the 1994 United Nations population and development conference in Cairo, believing that Western-pushed ideas of family planning and birth control were un-Islamic. By the late 1990s, these opinions had come to be seen by the Egyptian state as an embarrassment before the world.

It didn't stop there. Shaarawi was an outright opponent of organ transplants, causing enormous problems for the official medical establishment. A year before his death, he reduced a young man to tears on national television by telling his mother that she should not donate her kidney to her son because if God has decided his time is his time, then his time is up. The next day, Cairo's National Kidney Centre reported that operations were paralyzed as doctors and patients failed to turn up. Many secularists in Algeria have bitter memories of Shaarawi from when he spent time there in the early 1970s. They in part attribute to him and other Egyptian preachers who resided there the rise of religious conservatism in

Algerian society, which played a role in the Islamist insurgency that erupted there in 1992. Secularists in Egypt consider that the radical Islamist groups that declared open war on the state in 1992 found fertile ground in the 1980s and 1990s because of the fundamentalist influence of Shaarawi and others. Shaarawi also comprised a multimillion-dollar multimedia industry. The biggest selling CD-ROM at the annual Cairo Book Fair in recent years was the preachings of the first TV sheikh. The bestselling books in Egypt throughout the 1990s were cheap paperbacks sold on street corners, bearing the wisdom of Shaarawi and other TV religious personalities, such as mosque preacher Mustafa Mahmoud. Even today he remains a best-seller and his sermons are regular fare on various television stations. It's as if he never died at all.

Today, although TV is full of the regular faces of the official religious establishment, they don't stir the public's heart in the way Shaarawi did. But there are a few pretenders who could perhaps one day fill their shoes. These are preachers who reach out to untapped, niche markets. One is the Egyptian "society sheikh," Amr Khaled. Another rising star, astronomist Zaghloul al-Naggar, regularly appears on state television and in a weekly column in the Egyptian main national daily *al-Ahram*, offering interpretations of Quranic verses and hadiths with references to the discoveries of modern physics, chemistry, and biology. Naggar sees himself as reconciling science with Islamic tradition. In one example, he argued that a particular saying of the Prophet referred to the forces of gravity, nuclear reactions, and electromagnetic activity that hold bodies of matter in space. "These truths were arrived at by man in the 20th century, but the Prophet spoke them

Amr Khaled: Modern, Sharply Dressed "Preacher Man"

The newest phenomenon in Arab TV evangelism is a thirtysomething, self-made Egyptian preacher named Amr Khaled. Though he lacks the proper qualifications and doesn't sport a beard or wear clerical robes, Khaled has become well-known through regular appearances on numerous Arab satellite channels and Internet sites. The Egyptian government's efforts to silence him have only added to his fame. He left Egypt in October 2002 after government authorities, miffed at his popularity among the middle classes, hounded him out of every mosque he preached in. He was disturbing to the government because, unlike most preachers who set out to appeal to the common man, Khaled managed to get to the moneyed elite. He consciously focused his attention on persuading their Westernized daughters—working in public relations firms, driving cars bought for them by their business tycoon fathers, dressing in tight-fitting clothes, and hanging out in trendy bars—to take the veil and repent of their liberal ways. Young people had the sense that Khaled was one of them and their generation, someone who understood their problems. He seemed to speak to their guilt about a life of conspicuous consumption in the midst of the images of suffering from around the region that the media showered upon them.

Khaled was born into a middle-class family and trained as an accountant. He became a preacher at "Islamic salons," organized among high-society women by former singer Yasmine Khayyam, who took the dapper young man under her wing. "Khaled has simultaneously the hipness of Amr Diab, the persuasion power of evangelist Billy Graham, and the unsubtle therapy of Dr. Phil, an American popular talk show host," said sociologist Asef Bayat (al-Ahram Weekly, 22–28 May 2003). "Unlike more orthodox preachers known for their joyless moralizing and austere methods, Khaled articulates a marriage of faith and fun. It seems to be a globalized form for preaching that is very similar to American evangelists in terms of presentation." Some see him as a post-Islamist Islamist, not out to modernize Islam, politicize it, or establish a new social order, but simply to influence a sector of society, whose lifestyles lack outward piety, to think again. On his Web site (www.forislam.com) one can listen to his sermons, read his articles, send him e-mail, schedule a chat, and check out his satellite TV broadcasts (he is on the Iqra religious channel almost daily). Notably, the poorer classes don't respond to Khaled; they are turned off by his slick image and odd, high-pitched voice. The secularist-government press attacks him as a fraud who sells opium to the masses. Khaled steers clear of the Muslim Brotherhood, but the Brotherhood has spoken out against his eviction from mosques and state TV. The Amr Khaled phenomenon is paralleled by a trend that features young actresses and singers publicly shunning the limelight for a life of religion—though many of them eventually make very public returns.

over 1,400 years ago with this scientific precision when the world was full of superstitions and myths. It is indeed a miracle and there can be no explanation for it other than the link to the Creator by way of the revelation [the Quran]," Naggar wrote (al-Ahram, December 2002). "These noble understandings have been distorted in the minds of people who have become infatuated with science and its precepts. But if we show them knowledge such as that in the hadith, it would convince them more to take stock of the book of God and the way of his Prophet."

These ideas have been around in Egypt since the wave of religious conservatism swept Arab and Islamic societies throughout the twentieth century, but they have gained popular currency in recent years as political Islam gained ground. Naggar was actually "discovered" by TV presenter Ahmed Farrag, the man who first brought Shaarawi to state television some thirty years ago. Some of his assets in an Islamic bank were frozen in November 2002 after the bank appeared on a list of groups that the American government said might be supporting radical groups linked to Osama bin Laden's al-Qa'ida. Another popular figure is Yousef al-Qaradawi, an Egyptian cleric based in Qatar who regularly appears on an al-Jazeera show (*Islamic Law and Life*, or *al-Sharia wal-Hayat*) dedicated to his opinions. His views are popular around the region, and probably reflect the mainstream belief among Arabs—that the United States is admired for its democracy but despised for misguided pro-Israeli policies; that Palestinian suicide bomb attacks are the weapons of the weak and oppressed; and that Israel is a militarized society, so that the distinction between "civilian" and "military" is a blurry one. He is able to express these popular views because he is independent of any Arab regime and has his pulpit on satellite television, to the extent that he has almost come to be seen as the "Mufti of al-Jazeera." Many religious hardliners, especially in Saudi Arabia, think he is far too liberal, from his calls for women to vote in elections to his publicly stated penchant for listening to the female voice in song (specifically, Umm Kalthoum). On television he legitimized American Muslims fighting in the U.S. Army in Afghanistan—which didn't go down well with most of his audi-

ence—and condemned bin Laden for masterminding the September 11 attacks at a time when many still questioned bin Laden's complicity.

Wahhabism in Saudi Arabia: A Strident Form of Islamic Orthodoxy

When the Saudi royal family carved out their kingdom in the Arabian Peninsula in the early decades of the nineteenth century, they used the fundamentalist ideas of a religious reformer called Mohammed ibn Abdel-Wahhab to fire up the Bedouin tribes who formed their fighting force. Abdel-Wahhab was a pious man from an isolated desert town near modern-day Riyadh who thought that the urban ways of Muslims in the West Coast cities of Mecca, Medina, and others—such as venerating holy men through visiting their graves, and celebrating the birth of the Prophet and other figures from early Islam—were heretical. He even said that using rosary prayer was against the monotheistic spirit of the religion. The Bedouins in the central plains where he came from didn't have any religion at all, as far as he could see. One local tribal grouping, the Al Saud family, made an alliance with Abdel-Wahhab and his followers in 1745 to unite the Bedouins of this area, known as the Nejd. But Bedouin tribes fired up with a religious zeal weren't going to stop there, and they went on to invade the cities in the West—then under Ottoman Turkish control—sacking the Prophet's grandson Hussein's tomb in Kerbala, Iraq. This first Saudi state collapsed under internal and external pressure, but the Saud family plotted its return. They came and went again in the mid-nineteenth century. But in 1902 they were back for a

An Anthropologist's View: Religion Holds Saudi Arabia Together

Saad Sowayan is a postmodern man in a premodern land. An internationally respected academic abroad, in his native Saudi Arabia he's a loose cannon who skirts the boundaries of what can and can't be said in public. Just being an anthropologist in itself can court suspicion in Saudi Arabia's closed society, where social divisions and political fissures are the stuff of purely private discussion. "I have a great deal of trouble teaching anthropology at the university [or anything] that seems to be in contradiction to the teachings of the Quran. Freud and Marx cannot be taught," Sowayan said (interview with author, April 2003). "If you write books on pre-Saudi history or Marxism it won't pass the censorship. Most of my books I publish outside and then bring in because I could never publish them here. One of your students can easily file a complaint against you on religious grounds. I always get notifications and letters. That's fine if you're happy where you are and don't want to be promoted to the Shura Council [Saudi's unelected parliament] or be a minister."

Saudi Arabia is currently in the throes of a bitter debate over political and economic reforms, as proliberal activists come up against the clerical establishment, which runs the country in alliance with the Saudi royal family. But Sowayan argues that intellectual reform is needed first. "The country doesn't need political reform, it needs scientific and intellectual reform. If you improve, your rulers will improve," he said (interview with author, April 2003).

Sowayan argues that key, powerful members of the royal family are reluctant to move quickly on reform for fear of breaking up the Saudi state—a perennial fear of the Al Saud since they established the third Saudi state in 1902. "It's almost like four countries," Sowayan said, referring to the Nejd, the Hejaz, Jizan, and the Eastern Province (which has a Shi'ite majority). "That's why people are wary of change, because it could all deconstruct. They say we need more time to let it all weld together. The wealth is somehow expected to make it a melting pot, like America, but it's based on one product, oil, which is concentrated in one region, the East. In the Eastern region people could say, 'it's ours and we're going away.' The Hejaz could easily say, 'we want to be alone,' along with the Eastern region, and the rest will be left with poor resources" (interview with author, April 2003).

This regionalism is compounded by the Bedouin tribes who characterize much of the nation. Sowayan estimates the Bedouins comprise about 60 percent of the Saudi population today (although urbanization is weakening tribal affiliations). "There is strong suppression of discussing these regional differences in the open in case old tribal wars are opened up. You can't discuss tribal histories for fear that all these conflicts will crop up," Sowayan said (interview with author, April 2003). "The best way to weld this country together is through big businesses. Being politically united under one ruler is not enough. The country has to be economically integrated. Interests need to become enmeshed." But the power of religion is so pervasive in Saudi Arabia that reforms will have to be framed in religious discourse, Sowayan argues, which is what the regime did in the 1970s to promote women's education, the introduction of television, and other Western technology.

third time, and by 1932, after following the same tactics of firing up Bedouin tribes against urban Muslims considered unworthy of their religion, they had united most of the peninsula and secured United Nations recognition (the defeated Hejaz rulers in the West survive in Jordan's Hashemite monarchy). All the Saudi family failed to take were the mountainous territories of Yemen and Oman in the south and some coastal areas where colonial Britain propped up local rulers.

Wahhabism today means religious police patrolling Saudi cities to enforce strict dress codes and gender segregation, the absence of female singers on Saudi television, and implementation of controversial punishments such as death by public beheading. It has been identified by many writers in Saudi Arabia as central to an Islamic religious zealotry, which explains why fifteeen of the nineteen suicide hijackers in the September 11 attacks were Saudi nationals, why al-Qa'ida is run by a Saudi, and why so many of its foot soldiers are Saudi citizens. It's also regarded by secularist liberal intellectuals in countries like Egypt, Syria, Morocco, and Algeria as one of the driving forces behind the "fundamentalization" of Arab societies since the 1970s, when Saudi oil wealth financed an aggressive expansion of Wahhabism throughout the Islamic world, through funding of mosques, preachers, charities, and Islamist groups. Millions of workers from all over the Arab and Islamic world went to Saudi to work and came back with a new religion. Within Saudi Arabia, too, Wahhabism has stamped out other forms of Islam. The Wahhabi religious authorities in Riyadh maintain strict control over the beliefs of clerics who preach in the Hejaz, marginalizing the schools of Sunni Islam

that were once prevalent in Mecca and Medina. So, for example, visiting the graves of holy men and the promotion of more liberal schools of Islamic law are officially prohibited. Saudi religious scholars actually shun the word "Wahhabi," which almost elevates Sheikh Abdel-Wahhab as a founder of a new school of Islamic law—an instance of the idol worship they so abhor. They prefer the term "Salafi," a general term covering fundamentalist movements seeking a return to early Islam. Technically, the kingdom enforces a strict form of Hanbali law, one of the four legal traditions of mainstream Sunni Islam.

The centuries-old alliance of convenience between the Saud family and Wahhabi clerics is being stretched perhaps to the breaking point. But the Wahhabis are strong. The family of Abdel-Wahhab is tied to the House of Saud through a long process of intermarriage. The Saudi minister of religious affairs is always a member of the Al Sheikh family, descendants of Abdel-Wahhab. The Wahhabis run the religious police, or "authority for forbidding undesirable practices and encouraging accepted behaviour."

In the aftermath of the September 11 attacks there has emerged for the first time a public debate in Saudi Arabia about the efficacy of this unique body, which answers only to the king. Yet Saudi Arabia's wealth has managed to distance some elements of Saudi society from the Wahhabi vision of the world. The wealth brought an alliance with the United States that led many Saudis to live, study, and work in America. The ruling family itself is cosmopolitan and the population includes a powerful business class and a Westernized middle class with a similar outlook. When one also takes into consideration the Hejazis and

Shia and their different religious outlooks, this means that a considerable portion of Saudi society today is in a position to turn against Wahhabism. Suicide bombings in Riyadh in May and November 2003—probably carried out by al-Qa'ida or its sympathizers—have brought these tensions to the fore. The attacks gave liberals the upper hand in their campaign for democratic reforms that they believe will allow people to express resentment about Saudi Arabia's conservative Islamic society. A certain portion of the population—perhaps most of them in the central Nejd area—sympathize with the goals of the attackers and are happy with their Wahhabism.

"Islam under Attack" since the September 11 Attacks

Since the events of September 11, 2001, in the United States, mainstream Islam has been under attack. The idea that the West is making war on Islam has been around since the Middle Ages, but it received a boost with U.S. political scientist Samuel Huntington's thesis of a "clash of civilizations" (Huntington 1996) and has reached its zenith with America's "war on terror." Huntington argued that in the post–Cold War world the coming struggle would be between ethnic and religious civilizational blocs, as opposed to ideologies as such, and the main challenge to the predominance of liberal Western democracies would come from Islamic and Chinese cultures. September 11 clerics, academics, and journalists in the Arab world almost unanimously give credence to the view in public space that it is a "war on Islam." The Arab League even set up a special unit to deal with "dialogue between civilizations"

after the September 11 attacks to challenge the idea that a confrontation between the Arab world and the West was just around the corner. The media throughout the region has been full of horror stories of arbitrary detention and harassment of Arab nationals and Arab Americans in the United States, alongside reports of official news about the trial of suspects in the attacks, detention of suspected al-Qa'ida operatives at Guantanamo Bay, and tales of pilots refusing to take off because Arabs were on the plane. Anti-Islamic comments by figures from the American religious right further the conviction among many that there is a war on Islam. Some Israelis are openly promoting these ideas. "What we are now seeing across the Muslim world is not a powerful surge of faith but the dying embers of Islam," Israeli tourism minister

Saudi Arabia's King Faisal in prayer. He was assassinated in 1975 by a disaffected royal amid protests against modernization. He is well remembered among Arab nationalists for his use of the oil embargo during the 1973 Arab-Israeli War. (TRIP/Art Directors)

Saudi Arabia's King Faisal who was assassinated in 1975. (TRIP/Art Directors)

Benny Alon said in 2003 (*Ha'aretz*, May 2003). "Within a few years a Christian crusade against Islam will be launched, which will be the major event of this millennium."

Refuting Samuel Huntington's thesis has become an obsession in the region. The main line of response has been that the two civilizations have fed each other throughout most of recorded history—that it was the Arabs who, in the Middle Ages, passed on to Europe the knowledge of the Greeks, leading to Europe's Renaissance—and that Arab-Islamic society has always been characterized by a tolerance unknown in Europe, where, since the nineteenth century, ethnic nationalism has been the order of the day. Arab commentators say the thesis is too vague and general to be meaningful. For a long time there has been an internal clash between political Islam and Arab secular-national regimes, and now, since September 11, Western governments are also clashing with political Islam.

But Huntington's idea presumes that the current standoff between the democratic West and undemocratic Islam is an inevitable state of affairs. It does not acknowledge any historical process that led to Western and other states becoming democratic, and that, by extension, would warrant viewing nondemocratic states as nascent democracies. "The survival of the West depends on Americans reaffirming their Western identity and Westerners accepting their civilization as unique, not universal, and uniting to renew and preserve it against challenges from non-Western societies," he said (Huntington 1996). Huntington's thesis implies that Islamic countries are not democratic because of a fundamental cultural reality that has kept them undemocratic since the beginning of time. Or, as sociologist Fred Halliday argues, Huntington fails to realize that an adequate analysis of international relations requires as its prime task the "disaggregation and explanation, rather than invocations of the timeless essence of cultures" (Halliday 2002). A more cynical viewpoint is that ideas like Huntington's are intended as self-fulfilling prophecies, and that the democratic West has an interest in perpetuating autocracy and conflict among the Arabs. Arab commentators also note that Arab moderation regarding Israel has come hand in hand with crucial American backing for undemocratic regimes. Huntington appears to gloss over this to simply present Islamic-Arab peoples as forever troublesome, unbalanced, undemocratic, and given to forming "failed states." From this standpoint, the "clash of civilizations" is a lazy alternative to the far more difficult task of analyzing and ironing out colonial legacies and helping other peoples of the world attain the wealth of the West.

Arab commentators see similar problems in the much-hyped writings of historian Bernard Lewis (who in fact preceded Huntington in coining the phrase "clash of civilizations" in a September 1990 article in *Atlantic Monthly*, "The Roots of Muslim Rage"). In his post–September 11 best-seller *What Went Wrong?* Lewis further promotes the idea of eternal, deep-seated differences between the East and the West. Israel is listed a mere three times in the index of a book with the grand aim of answering the question "what went wrong?" in Arab-Islamic societies today that prevented them from developing modern societies like those in the West. The idea of excepting the Zionist project from such a discussion would appear ludicrous to many scholars in the West as well as the Arab world. In his 1990 article (and elsewhere) Lewis contends that the origins of anti-Americanism do not lie in support for the State of Israel or U.S. support for tyrannical regimes, but in pent-up anger and humiliation over the power of the "Christian West." Concerning Israel, Lewis says the Arabs' Soviet ally was one of the early supporters of Israel, while it was the United States that acted to force the tripartite alliance of Britain, France, and Israel to withdraw from Egypt during the Suez crisis of 1956.

In the face of this, Israel is today almost unanimously the main reason posited by the Arab intellectual and political class for the strength of anti-U.S. sentiment, to the extent that the Iraq invasion is seen as launched in part to protect Israeli interests.

Bernard Lewis, emeritus professor of Near Eastern Studies at Princeton University, pictured in 2003. A dominant figure in academic writing on the Arab world in recent decades, Lewis is regarded as a prominent influence on U.S. foreign policy-makers. (Princeton University, Princeton New Jersey; photo: Denise Applewhite, 1993)

Further, in 1948 no one in the region imagined that fifty years later the Palestinian refugees would not have returned to their homeland, or that Jerusalem and the rest of the occupied territories would fall into Israeli hands nineteen years later. Neither was there the vigorous Arab satellite media that has today helped create a clear and present Arab public opinion on these issues. Lewis also joined with Republican right-wingers Donald Rumsfeld and Paul Wolfowitz in writing a letter to former U.S. president Clinton in February 1998 calling for the invasion of Iraq, a stunning example of Edward Said's vision of imperialist collusion between academia and politics ("Orientalism Is Alive and Well in Iraq." *The Daily Star*, 20 October 2003).

Certain image-improvement tactics have been adopted by Arab governments, intellectuals, and media commentators to counter this perceived attack on their religion and culture. Sometimes they argue that the West and Islam actually have the same values, sometimes they point out that it was Islam that passed on Greek knowledge to medieval Europe, and other times they engage in verbal excommunication of critics of the West for not being true Muslims. There are nationalists who say all three approaches are demeaning. Opponents of Arab nationalism argue that the Arabs were never anything but transferors, not innovators. "Islam is our creed, and we cannot engage in self-abasement over its tenets. We cannot apologise for Islam to politicians who have never made the slightest gesture toward civility," Egyptian nationalist writer and economist Galal Amin wrote in one commentary (*al-Ahram Weekly*, 28 February 2002). "We cannot excuse Islam to people whose claim to civilisation is questionable, to say the least. We cannot revise our values and way of life for the sake of people who have never acted fairly toward their opponents, shown magnanimity in victory, kept their temper under duress, or forgiven their enemies—all of which, I recall, are perfectly Muslim values." Secular intellectuals argue that Islam has developed as the "rebel call" of the era simply because the regimes have been so successful in quashing dissent, particularly among followers of respectable political Islam who want a place at the table of government. Bin Laden's challenges to America in videos shot in mountain hideaways in Afghanistan, while Bush addresses Ameri-

cans from the comfort of the White House, have appealed to more than just Islamists, touching anticapitalist and antiglobalization chords in the Middle East and casting him as a Robin Hood–like hero in the eyes of the ordinary man on the street. Islam has become part of a dialectic of opposition to occupation and oppression. Some Arab scholars have argued that the Western emphasis on Islam itself as a practice is misplaced, as if Islamic societies are uniquely religious, as opposed to Europe where religion is just one element of culture and not *the* influencing factor. Egyptian Islamic historian Nasr Abu Zeid writes: "Islamic societies are like any other, in that they are not only moved by the logic of religion, but also the laws of the community, politics, economy and culture" (*al-Arabi*, 4 August 2002).

The United States is now perceived as intervening to force some form of change and reduction in the role of religion in society, particularly in Egypt and Saudi Arabia. Both countries attracted attention in the West for having spawned the men at the core of the al-Qa'ida group that carried out the September 11 attacks. Mainstream American publications accused these two countries of running dysfunctional undemocratic states, which permitted religious extremism to spread like cancer through society. Within two weeks of the attacks, the American weekly *Newsweek* was saying the Bush administration needed to push Egypt and Saudi Arabia to "actively fight the virulent currents that are capturing Arab culture" because both countries had "resisted economic and political modernization" (Fareed Zakaria, *Newsweek*, 1 October 2001). *New York Times* columnist Thomas Friedman said, "U.S. policymakers and analysts now believe that the West is not fighting to eradicate terrorism. Terrorism is just a tool. It is fighting to defeat an ideology: religious totalitarianism" (*New York Times*, 27 November 2001).

Now newspaper columnists in the region are saying Arabs need to reform their Islam or else they will find the Americans reformulating it for them. They also say they should democratize, in line with stated White House goals of creating stronger legal, judicial, and political systems in the Arab world. "If we don't change ourselves and correct our mistakes we'll find people imposing change on us, and in a way that suits their own aims and interests," Egyptian Islamist writer Fahmy Howeidy wrote (*al-Arabi*, 13 January 2002). He argued that removing the concept of *jihad* (meaning "holy struggle," military or otherwise, for the betterment of Islamic society) from the state school and religious curricula was not the answer: "Weakening religiosity is not the solution to the problem of terrorism. . . . Removing *jihad* from religious studies will not remove it from the Muslim mind; if *jihad* is put in the right context the idea will not be abused. The Iranian experience is a good example. A special ministry for rural development promotes 'the *jihad* of development.'" In January 2002 Egypt's parliament was debating government proposals to moderate the religious rhetoric of the country's thousands of mosque preachers, and the country's main Muslim and Christian leaders gave public support to the moves. In effect, the state is tacitly acknowledging that some elements of the religious establishment have continued to promote extremist thought, despite government efforts since the mid-1990s to reduce their influence.

A similar situation exists in Saudi Arabia. After the September 11 attacks, reform of state education became a pressing need.

Saudi officials say that up to 40 percent of education in state schools concerned religion, and much of it is harsh, desecrating other religions and sects of Islam frowned upon by the official creed in the kingdom (the Shia are termed *al-Rafida*, "the rejectionists"). Theology texts used by thirteen- and fourteen-year-olds formerly enjoined Muslims not to befriend Christians and Jews because "emulation of the infidels leads to loving them." "It is the duty of a Muslim to be loyal to the believers (Muslims) and be the enemy of the infidels. One of the duties of affirming the oneness of God is to have nothing to do with his idolatrous and polytheist enemies," textbooks said (Samia Nakhoul, Reuters, 15 October 2003). "Muslims should not imitate the infidels in music and art or frequenting theatres and cinemas. All these are frequented by the wayward and those who have strayed from earnest life." The Saudis say many mosque preachers have been sacked for using extreme language in Friday prayers. But the Saudi rulers have taken exception to the Western media attacks on their guiding Wahhabi ideology. "Wahhabism is not an Islamic school (of law), it is a call for reform made by a reformist who worked to purify the Islamic religion from the rubbish that some simple Muslims believed in," Interior Minister Prince Nayef said in one of his many public comments in defense of Wahhabism (*al-Hayat*, 28 January 2002). "Those who accuse us of Wahhabism don't know what it is, and don't know that it is simply an attempt at correction and not a school." Prince Nayef, who often talks of maintaining "ideological security" in the kingdom, is seen as one of a group within the ruling family who are loathe to accept that the Saudi state religion could be at fault.

Political Islam was born in Egypt and Saudi Arabia. The Muslim Brotherhood was set up in Egypt in 1928, and the Wahhabi State of Saudi Arabia achieved United Nations status in 1932. The two have coalesced since the 1970s, when Brotherhood cadres worked in the oil-rich kingdom, and with the brains of the Brotherhood's thinkers and the brawn of Saudi capital they have made Islamic "fundamentalism" the powerful force it has been in Arab politics and society over the last three decades. ("Fundamentalism" is probably the best term to describe their movement to promote *al-Salafiyya* [going back to the ways of the early Muslims].) The interesting thing about *al-Salafiyya*, or Salafism, is that it represents a radical shift in the centuries-old balance between Islam's greater and lesser traditions. Salafism is the contemporary dominance of the Islam of rules and "orthodoxy" over its folkloric and populist elements. Thus, varying degrees of scorn are reserved for Sufism in Arab countries, from bans in Saudi Arabia, where political Islam rules the roost, to periodic attempts to stamp on Sufism in Sudan, where the regime since 1989 has tried to impose the Saudi model, to disdain in Egypt, where political Islam holds sway in public life despite being shut out of government. The reasons why greater Islam rears its head so strongly lie, as sociologist Ernest Gellner argued in his 1979 study *Muslim Society*, in the impact of the modern world and in the way colonialism and industrialization upset a once-stable balance.

Concerning radicalism, the Islamic groups that promote violence are offshoots of this Salafi mainstream in Egypt and Saudi Arabia. It began in Egypt with the radical theorizing of Brotherhood ideologue Sayed Qutb, who first made use of the argument that Arab regimes had created godless societies. "The world was not cleansed of the Byzantines and the Persians to pave the way for the authority of the Arabs—it was for the sake of the authority of God . . . Infidel societies include those which claim to be Muslim but give authority to other than God," he wrote, in a clear attack on secular Arab nationalism (Qutb 1979, 29–91). Since Qutb was put to death by Nasser's regime in 1966, this use of *takfir*, or deeming nominal Muslims as apostates from Islam, has developed into a whole complex ideology of its own at the hands of myriad radical groups, including today's al-Qa'ida. Their sympathizers justify killing Muslims in attacks on Western targets—for example, as happened when foreign residential compounds were bombed in Riyadh in 2003, killing Westerners as well as Arab Muslims. They say that God must have chosen them as unwitting martyrs to a cause and that they will have a place in heaven. This was the justification given by Egyptian Islamist Hani al-Sibai on the Arabic television channel al-Arabiya (May 2003). Commentators such as Salah Issa, who has researched the growth of Islamist movements in the Nasserist period, say it was the systematic brutality of Nasser's secular-national regime toward the Islamists that nudged Qutb and his acolytes into radicalizing their ideology. Arab commentators also point to the support that this Islamic fringe received from the United States in the Soviet era, unleashing a genie from the bottle that came back to haunt them. Now the rallying cry of radicals fighting the Saudi monarchy since 2003 has been a commonly cited saying of the Prophet, "get the polytheists (*mushrikeen*) out of the Arabian peninsula" (for example Bukhari's collection *Sahih al-*

Bukhari, No. 3090, *al-Jihad*). This refers to making war on the Americans and other Westerners whose presence in the kingdom, as civilians or military, is perceived by the radicals as supporting a corrupt monarchy that is complicitous in American and Israeli actions in the region.

Now an elusive search is on for the "true Islam," a phrase that consistently pops up in public discourse concerning the region and its relations with the rest of the world. The Arab world is awash with endless conferences and other projects to correct the perceived distorted image of Islam in the eyes of the West. These campaigns are promoted by various competing groups, from al-Qa'ida and radical groups, to the Muslim Brotherhood, to official state-sponsored religious establishments in influential countries like Saudi Arabia and Egypt. The result is a cacophony of Islams, including satellite channels, Internet Web sites, newspapers, national religious bodies, supranational Islamic institutions, and local mosque preachers. They are all working to promote a purported "real Islam." Secular intellectuals note that because of the alliances that the Arab regimes seek to establish with religion, none of these official bodies talk much about open government, fighting corruption, promoting meritocracy, or checking abusive security apparatuses. (They would also argue that Saudi human rights issues, such as chopping the heads off of murderers, rapists, and drug dealers, are mirrored by America's electric chairs and other forms of the death penalty that make more creative use of modern technology.) Perhaps the key issue in the quest to discover the origins of today's religious violence is the authoritarian rule and arbitrary justice prevalent in the Arab world, which denude the state of any moral value in the eyes of the citizen. In Saudi Arabia, the citizen belongs to a state defined as the exclusive preserve of one huge, extended family. In Egypt, the citizen is essentially powerless in the face of a polity that defines his/her raison d'être as serving the interests of the military state. In both cases there are no "rights" independent of the state at all, or rather they exist more on paper than in reality. These situations pertain in one form or another and to one degree or another throughout the Arab region. This includes Israel, where a state that controls the lives of more than nine million people (in Israel proper and the occupied territories) assigns full rights to five million Jews, incomplete rights to one million Arabs, and heavily depleted rights to the remaining three million Arabs who reside in the Gaza Strip, the West Bank, and East Jerusalem. As far as the link between all this and Islam is concerned, perhaps—as Patricia Crone and Martin Hinds suggested in their groundbreaking scholarly study, *God's Caliph* (1986)—Islam is only "the problem" in the sense that Islam in its formative period consecrated a political system whereby the ruler's job was primarily to maintain Islam as the faith of the nation and to ensure the application of its schools of law and theology and its unfettered practice in society. Apart from that, the ruler has a free hand to do much as he pleases. So the issue of Islam and politics—the much-cited merging of the two since the time of the Prophet—is a red herring. The solution, then, is not how to prize religion out of the state or the state out of Islam, or even to change the religion; it is to create a consensus that government is responsible for more than just maintaining Islam as the state religion. Abetted by the removal of a brutal dictatorship in Iraq, such a debate is showing signs of entering the public domain with more force than before. Egyptian preacher Yousef Qaradawi has said that after a hundred years of advocating Sharia law, "freedom" must now be the number-one priority. "Anyone who asks for freedom is actually asking for part of the Sharia, in all its richness," leading Saudi cleric Salman al-Awda said in apparent acknowledgment of Qaradawi's claim (al-Jazeera, October 2003). It won't be an easy task. The Saudi religious police states bluntly in an article on their Web site that there is no such as thing as "personal freedom" in Islam (Fadl Alha, www.hesbah.com), and the fear grips Islamists and even some secularists that democracy could lead to legislation (for gay rights, rights for single mothers, etc.) that is contrary to the general tenor of morality reflected in Sharia law.

A-to-Z:
Key People and Terms

ABDEL-KARIM, KHALIL (D. 2002)

The "Red Sheikh" and a former member of the Muslim Brotherhood, who felt that the group's leaders of the 1970s were more into applying Sharia and promoting Saudi versions of Islam than into applying the social justice of Brotherhood founder Hassan al-Banna. He wrote left-leaning columns in Egypt's opposition paper *al-Ahali* (for example, one of his statements was "If a man dies of hunger, all the people of the district are responsible for his death"). In general, the left never made better use of the Red Sheikh. His religious credentials were never in question, so if he argued in favor of organ transplants, against female cir-

cumcision, and calling people apostates (he led Abu Zeid's defense), his message would get through to the masses. He was a member of a reformist group of publishers called the Dar al-Sima group.

ABDEL-RAHMAN, OMAR (B. 1938)

Egyptian cleric, referred to as Sheikh Omar, convicted in U.S. courts in 1995 of being part of a conspiracy to bomb the World Trade Center in New York and other American landmarks. He was sentenced in 1996 to life in prison. Abdel-Rahman, with his blindness and fierce preaching, was a notorious figure in Egypt, who the state media succeeded in presenting as the archetypal image of terrorist cleric. He was the spiritual leader of the radical group al-Gamaa al-Islamiya, which waged an insurgency campaign against the Egyptian government from 1992 to 1997. Abdel-Rahman was convicted by an Egyptian court in 1993 of mobilizing to overthrow the government, but had already left Egypt for Sudan in 1990, where he obtained a visa for the United States. Washington maintained contacts with many Egyptian Islamists in the early 1990s, in case Egypt's regime should fall to the Islamist movement, as Iran did in 1979.

AL-AWDA, SALMAN (B. 1955)

Leading sheikh of a group of Saudi clerics who were jailed from 1994 to 1999 for criticizing the Saudi royal family and their alliance with American troops, which, since the 1990–1991 Gulf War crisis, were permanently based in the kingdom. The controversial troop presence was virtually ended in 2003, after the war to topple the regime of Saddam Hussein in Iraq, with the American military refocusing its military presence in the Gulf to Bahrain, Qatar, and Kuwait. The other major figures jailed were Safar al-Hawali and Nasser al-Omar. Al-Awda was prominent in his backing of the Saudi government's position vis-à-vis the 2003 Iraq war, arguing in public that there was no cause for Muslims to head to Iraq for a *jihad* against the foreign troops. He is based in the town of Buraida in the Wahhabi heartland of Saudi Arabia, the northern area of Nejd. The last of the jailed clerics, Sheikh Zuair, was released in March 2003.

AL-AZHAR

A mosque and religious education institution based in Cairo, established over a thousand years ago and seen as one of the highest authorities for the world's majority of Sunni Muslims. Al-Azhar runs its own religious school system, separate from Egypt's state education system, with secondary schools and university branches throughout Egypt, attended by Muslims from around the world. Since 1961 the institution has been officially an arm of the state, its sheikh nominated by the president and in the pay of government. The idea behind this was to limit the independence of the powerful religious establishment. Today the opinions of the sheikh are still sought in areas where faith touches social and political issues—from the legitimacy of armed resistance to Israeli occupation, to bank interest, to TV game shows. Though Arab countries have their own state-sponsored religious figures, known as muftis—a *mufti* is "someone who gives a religious opinion"—most of them would take their cue from Egypt's al-Azhar sheikh. Saudi Arabia's official mufti carries

influence, as do some of the preachers at the main mosque in Mecca. In Egypt there is also a separate government mufti. Shi'ite communities in the Middle East have their own religious figures whom they look to for guidance. There is no official orthodoxy in Sunni or Shi'ite Islam.

BAHR AL-ULOUM, MOHAMMED (B. 1923)

A highly respected Shi'ite cleric seen as a liberal, who returned from London where he headed the Ahl al-Bayt charitable center. He was elected as the Shi'ite member of a leadership triumvirate by the Iraqi opposition after the 1991 Gulf War. He was appointed as a member of the Governing Council set up by the coalition authority after the Iraq invasion in 2003.

BIN LADEN, OSAMA (B. 1957)

Saudi Islamist dissident who used money he inherited from his wealthy business family to set up an Islamist guerrilla movement, based in Afghanistan, which is being pursued globally for carrying out the September 11 attacks. Bin Laden was born in Saudi Arabia to a Yemeni family that had established a successful construction business in Saudi Arabia, but he left all that behind in 1979 to fight against the Soviet invasion of Afghanistan. After the Soviet withdrawal, the "Arab Afghans," as bin Laden's faction came to be called, turned their fire against the United States and its allies in the Middle East. Bin Laden returned to Saudi Arabia to work in the family business, but was expelled in 1991 because of his antigovernment activities there. He spent the next five years in Sudan until U.S. pressure prompted the Sudanese government to expel him, whereupon bin Laden returned to Afghanistan. Since the October–November U.S.-led war to topple the Taliban government that sheltered bin Laden and his fighters, a network referred to as al-Qa'ida (The Base) for short, bin Laden and his Egyptian number-two man, Ayman al-Zawahiri, have been in hiding. His al-Qa'ida has since launched open warfare on the Saudi regime.

GHANNOUCHI, RACHED (B. 1941)

Preacher and leader of the Tunisian Islamist movement called al-Nahda (the Renaissance). He argues that the Tunisian regime destroyed al-Nahda because it offered a successful model of Islamic moderation and coexistence with secular forces that was capable of creating a new Islamist Tunisia—a similar argument made by Egyptian Islamists to explain the violence that ensued between the radical groups and the state (see Egyptian lawyer Montasser Zayat's *Hiwarat Mamnua*, or *Forbidden Dialogues*). Initially a Nasserist, he studied in Egypt and Syria before settling in Paris, where he turned to political Islam while studying at the Sorbonne. He was sentenced to life imprisonment in 1987 under the regime of Bourguiba, a verdict that was affirmed twice again under Ben Ali in 1991 and in 1998 for activities aimed at overthrowing the state. He has been living in London since 1991, where he has established a reputation as a moderate Islamist intellectual.

GHAZALI, MOHAMMED (D. 1996)

Popular and controversial religious scholar who died in 1996. A major intellectual figure of the "return to faith" after 1967, though he never sought the bright lights of Sheikh Shaarawi through television. He was one of the first to challenge the modern secular state with his 1950 response to leftist Khaled Mohammad Khaled's *From Here We Begin* with *From Here We Know*, in which he argued vehemently that a non-secular Islamic state is capable of achieving the "progress" secular-nationalists dreamed of (Khaled later became part of the movement of leftists who turned to Islam). Ghazali turned his back on the Muslim Brotherhood, arguing it had no right to imply it was an organization that spoke in the name of all Muslims. This independence made him the darling of Islamist intellectuals. When he was called to testify at the trial of the assassins of secular writer Farag Foda, killed in Cairo in 1992, he said the penalty in Islam for apostasy is death. That opinion, which caused major embarrassment to the government, increased his reputation among Islamists. He had a regular column called *This Is Our Islam* that appeared in the popular Islamist newspaper *al-Shaab*.

AL-HAKIM, ABDEL-AZIZ (B. N.A.)

The head of Iraq's largest Shi'ite political party, the Supreme Council for the Islamic Revolution in Iraq (SCIRI), which was based in Tehran during the years of Baath rule. He became its leader in September 2003 after his brother, Mohammed Baqir al-Hakim, was murdered in a suicide-bomb blast in the Iraqi holy city of Najaf in August 2003. Abdel-Aziz al-Hakim was one of the Shi'ite members appointed by the U.S. coalition authorities to the Interim Governing Council set up in July 2002. Hakim emerged as the Shi'ite figure closest to the highest Shi'ite authority in Iraq, Ali al-Sis-

A portrait of Iraqi Shi'ite leader Ayatollah Mohammed Baqir al-Hakim after he was assassinated in August 2003 in the holy Shi'ite city of Najaf. (Scott Peterson/Getty Images)

tani, who himself keeps a distance from politics.

AL-JAAFARI, IBRAHIM (B. N.A.)

A Shi'ite and the main spokesman for the Islamic Daawa Party. The party, once based in Iran, launched a bloody campaign against Saddam's regime in the late 1970s, but it was crushed in 1982. The group said it lost 77,000 members in its war against Saddam. Born in Karbala, Jaafari was educated at Mosul University as a medical doctor.

KAIRAWAN (KAIROUAN)

Holy city in central Tunisia that is tied to the Arabian Peninsula through two parallel legends that foster the notion of Kairawan and by extension Tunisia as holy Arab territory. The first one tells that the conqueror Uqba bin Nafi put his stick into the ground

and struck water. This place is still there, and is known as *bi'r baruta*. The other story says that the well already was there, but that Uqba found a cup of gold that he had lost in the well of Mekka. This was interpreted as proof of a direct connection between Mecca and Kairawan, through the water.

KHALED, AMR (B. 1967)

Young Egyptian preacher who shot to fame in the late 1990s with a new style of rhetoric that appealed to young people in affluent society. He is credited with having caused a wave of young women, including actresses and singers, to take the veil, which prompted the government to take steps against him, such as preventing him from leading Friday prayers in some mosques and keeping him off state television. In 2002 he left the country, but his presence is still felt in Egypt and beyond through his regular appearances on satellite television channels and his Web sites. Previously sidelined preachers in Egypt include Omar Abdel-Kafi, who made comments suggesting that Muslims should not greet Copts on holy Christian days. Abdel-Kafi has recently resurfaced as a guest on religious shows on Arabic satellite channels.

AL-KISHK, ABDEL-HAMID (1933–1996)

Radical, blind preacher who rose to prominence during the 1970s in Egypt after suffering two years in prison during President Gamal Abdel Nasser's crackdown on the Muslim Brotherhood in 1966. Known as Sheikh Kishk, he was the first preacher in the Arab world to make a huge impact through selling his sermons on cassette tapes, which offered a stunning critique of capitalist and consumerist society in the making during the 1970s. Unlike his Egyptian contemporary Sheikh Shaarawi, he avoided being co-opted by the state and was among over one thousand opposition personalities arrested by Sadat's regime in September 1981, a month before Islamist radicals assassinated Sadat. Since then he has renounced extremist politics, sometimes writing in Islamist newspapers.

MADANI, ABBASI (B. 1931)

Leader of the Islamic Salvation Front (FIS), which was poised to win parliamentary elections in Algeria in 1992. Madani and his deputy Ali Belhadj were held for twelve years for threatening state security and released in 2003 with a bar on any political activity. Madani agreed to the terms but Belhadj refused and has been detained on occasion for making public statements and unauthorized movements. Madani is now in his seventies, based in Qatar, and is seen as the more moderate of the two.

MUSLIM BROTHERHOOD

The godfather of Islamist movements in the Arab world, set up by a schoolteacher called Hassan al-Banna in the Suez Canal town of Ismailiya in 1928. The group saw its role as reestablishing an Islamic order after Turkey, under European influence, did away with the caliphate in 1924. It played an instrumental role in promoting Arab nationalism through its lobbying in favor of Palestinians against the Zionist movement in the 1930s and the militia force it put into the field in the 1948 Arab-Israeli war. Though Gamal Abdel Nasser was once a Brotherhood member, he turned against the group in 1954, saying it was behind an assassination attempt against him. Banna himself was murdered in Cairo in 1949 after the Brotherhood's military wing was implicated in the killing of Egyptian prime minister Noqrashi Basha in 1948. The group was violently suppressed by Nasser's regime, giving rise to a series of radical Islamic groups around the Arab world in the 1970s, while the Brotherhood itself set a path for mainstream moderation and respectability. It seeks status as a political party in Egypt today.

NASRALLAH, HASSAN (B. 1960)

Secretary-general of Hizbollah, the Lebanese Shi'ite group set up in 1982 to fight the Israeli occupation of the country. His power base consists of the Shi'ite communities in the Bekaa Valley and the south, and his prestige in Lebanese society rose after the Israeli withdrawal in 2000. He has redirected Hizbollah toward ending the Israeli occupation of the Shebaa Farms area (which the United Nations has said is Syrian, not Lebanese), freeing Lebanese in Israeli prisons, and backing the Palestinian uprising that began in 2000, several months after the Israeli exit from Lebanon. He was born in a poor neighborhood of East Beirut, and left for the south when the civil war broke out in 1975. He studied in Iraq for two years in the Shi'ite holy city of Najaf at the same time as Ayatollah Khomeini lived there in the years before the 1979 revolution in Iran. He has led Hizbollah since 1992.

AL-QADIRIYYA

A major Sufi order that has spread throughout the Arab and Muslim countries. It is named for an eminent Baghdadi jurist of the Hanbali school of Islamic law called Abdel-Qadir al-Jailani (1077–1166). Referred to as *al-ghawth al-a'zam* (the great help), he has many miracles attributed to him, including the gift of guidance through words that led thousands to convert to Islam. The Qadiriyya were instrumental in organizing resistance to Turk and then French overlords in ninteenth-century Algeria. In many cases the Qadiriyya have united with an Egypt-based order called the Rifaiya, after Sheikh Ahmed al-Rifai (1118–1181).

QARADAWI, YOUSEF (B. 1926)

An Egyptian preacher who regularly appears on the al-Jazeera satellite channel from his base in Qatar. He is associated with Egypt's Muslim Brotherhood and talks about political issues affecting Arab and Muslim countries as well as Islam in modern Arab life. Qaradawi memorized the Quran by the age of ten and has written dozens of books on Islam that are best-sellers in Muslim countries. He has said that anyone killed while fighting the U.S. occupation forces in Iraq or other Gulf countries is a martyr, but that there is a difference between American civilians and the country's government and military. He has attacked the current effort, prompted by Washington, to change education curricula in some Arab countries so that Islamic religion features less prominently. But in general his line is that Muslims must find a way to coexist with the West and within the West, stances that have earned him considerable ire among the strict religious establishment in Saudi Arabia.

QUTB, SAYED (1906–1966)

Egyptian Islamist pioneer put to death by Nasser in 1966, but whose controversial ideas had a profound influence on the course of politics in the Arab world for the next three decades. Initially somewhat secular, Qutb began to write in the late 1920s as a poet and literary critic, but by the late 1940s he began to write from a more Islamic perspective. His first Islamic book, *al-Adala al-Ijtima'iya* (*Social Justice*), was published in 1949. Coming from a traditional background in a village of south Egypt, he found the ways of the West and the modern world shocking feelings that intensified after a two-year stint in the United States. He joined the Muslim Brotherhood upon his return in 1950 and spent most of the period from 1954 to 1966 in prison, before being sentenced to death for treason. But his writings in prison, foremost among them *Ma'alim Fil-Tareeq* (*Milestones*), contained a revolutionary ideology that argued that Arab-

Muslim societies, from top to bottom, including their governments, were themselves infidel. Debate rages over how much the brutal treatment of the Brotherhood by Nasser's regime contributed to this belief.

AL-SADR, MOUSSA (B. 1928)

Charismatic Shi'ite cleric born in Iran who moved to Tyre in Shi'ite south Lebanon in 1960. He became head of the Higher Islamic Shi'ite Council upon its founding in 1969 and acquired mythical status through his work with Christian clerics in a campaign against poverty in rural south Lebanon during the 1970s. During the civil war he founded the Amal Movement, headed today by Lebanon's parliament speaker Nabih Berri. In August 1978 he mysteriously disappeared with two of his companions during an official visit to Libya. A group affiliated with Amal in 2002 publicly accused Gaddafi's regime of murdering Sadr. Libya has long said Sadr left Libya for Italy, while Italy says he never arrived there. Sadr had gone to Libya to mend strained relations with Gaddafi.

AL-SADR, MUQTADA (B. CA. 1973)

The youngest son of Mohammed Sadeq al-Sadr, a revered Iraqi Shi'ite leader who died in a car crash in 1999. Thought to be in his early thirties, Muqtada was little known in Iraq before the U.S.-led invasion of 2003 but quickly rose to prominence through a power base in the poor Shi'ite neighborhoods of Baghdad with a network of charitable institutions set up by his father. In contrast to quietist clerics, Sadr calls on Shia spiritual leaders to play an active role in shaping Iraq's political future. Unlike the former exiles who head the Supreme Council for the Islamic Revolution in Iraq (SCIRI), he opposes cooperation with the United States, saying it does not really intend to leave or allow Iraq true sovereignty. He has his own militia, the Mahdi Army, and moves between Kufa, where his followers control important mosques and their revenue, and Sadr City, a huge Shi'ite slum in Baghdad, which was named after his father once Baghdad fell from its previous designation as Saddam City. Many regard him as little more than an uneducated firebrand cut from a different cloth from his father.

AL-SAFFAR, HASSAN (B. 1957)

Senior Shi'ite cleric in Saudi Arabia, who is a leading reformer and proponent of Shi'ite rights among the Shi'ite minority community. He was involved in antigovernment disturbances in the Shi'ite-dominated Eastern Province following the Iranian revolution in 1979, after which he fled abroad to Syria and the United States. Since his return he has acquired a status as the Shi'ite community's number-one interlocutor with the authorities—the head of the Shi'ite Reform Movement from his base in the Shi'ite town of al-Qatif—and he has a weekly column in the newspaper *al-Yaum*. He has published a number of books that promote civil rights, including women's rights, and he spearheaded a movement for Shi'ites to give blood during annual holy festivals, rather than inducing bleeding with razors and knives, as many Shi'ite men do in processions.

SHAARAWI, MOHAMMED (1911–1998)

Popular religious preacher in Egypt, who achieved immense fame and influence from the 1970s onward via his appearances on Egyptian state television, making him the first and the biggest Arab "TV sheikh." When Sheikh Shaarawi, as he was known, died in 1998, many in Egypt's government and civil society heaved a sigh of relief. Through his close relations with the authorities—he served as minister of religious endowments during the 1970s—he outblasted most of his peers in influence and arguably did more to "Islamicize" society than dissident preachers, most of whom ended up in jail, or politician preachers who associated with the Muslim Brotherhood. He was around long enough to corner the market in religious CD-ROMs when they first came out. His books are bestsellers in Arab countries and his sermons are still shown on television as if he were alive today.

SHAZLIYYA

Major Sufi order in Arab countries, named after Abul-Hassan al-Shazli (d. 1258 C.E.), whose tomb is at Abu Humaithra on Egypt's Red Sea coast. The Shazliyya actually derives from an earlier figure, Abu Madyan Shu'ayb (d. 1198), whose tomb is in Tlemcen, Algeria. One of Abu Madyan's disciples was Mohammed Ali Ba-Alawi, from whom the Alawiya Order derives. It has a branch called the Attasiya based in Yemen.

AL-SHEIKH, ABDEL-AZIZ BIN ABDULLAH (B. N.A.)

State mufti of Saudi Arabia who, in the tradition of occupants of state religious posts, is a descendant of Mohammed ibn Abdel-Wahhab, the eighteenth-century Sunni radical whose ideas are the theological base of the Saudi state. As the state-appointed authority on religious issues, his opinions always coalesce with those of the royal family, but he is using his position to make sure that reforms pursued by the Saudi government do not go further than the religious establishment would like and curb its influence. After the May 2003 bombings on foreign residential compounds in Riyadh, Al-Sheikh told al-Arabiya TV: "It's not possible to imagine that what happened is because of shortcomings among clerics, preachers, and religious people. The Islamic establishment was not negligent, thank God, and has not been going too far in raising religious awareness in society." He went on to say there was no need to dismantle the Saudi religious police force and played down calls for reforms, including elections and women's participation in political life.

SISTANI, ALI (B. 1930)

The Shi'ite figure who has emerged as the most powerful Shi'ite cleric in postwar Iraq. Grand Ayatollah Sistani, who rarely emerges from his residence in the holy city of Najaf, was considered to be one of the quietist Shi'ites, who would go along with the U.S. plans for Iraq once Saddam was gone, but showed his teeth in December 2003 when he let it be known that no Iraqi government could call itself sovereign and independent unless it was chosen via popular election. His demand for direct elections threw a wrench in the works of the American plan for local leaders to select delegates to a transitional government by July 2003. Earlier he had declared "fundamentally unacceptable" any effort to write a constitution without directly electing its drafters. Sistani's opinions signaled that the Shi'ite community was eager to flex its muscles and was concerned that the Americans would cut deals with Sunnis and Kurds and seek to limit the influence of the majority Shi'ites. The death of his more

Shi'ite Iconography Spreads in Post-Saddam Iraq

Repressed under three decades of secular, Arab nationalist rule, Iraq's majority of Shi'ite Muslims are enjoying a newfound freedom to practice their Shi'ism with impunity. An obvious expression of this freedom is the devotional images of the first two Shi'ite imams, Ali and Hussein, which are now spread all over Iraq. One of the most prominent portrait painters of these Shi'ite heroes is Haidar Dahlouz. Shi'ites revere the family members of the Prophet Mohammed as the true leaders of the Islamic community, and Dahlouz has no compunction about glorifying them with his unabashedly naturalistic brushstrokes. "The family of the Prophet are people we have learned to love since childhood," he said (interview with author, December 2003). "Under the former regime it was completely forbidden to draw these pictures or even to pass them around, but since the regime fell we're able to do this freely. Now there is demand and people are asking for this stuff." Sunni Muslim clerics frown on the devotional images but they have not dared to object. In Baghdad, in the Sunni Muslim heart of the country, Shi'ites adorn cars and shops with the small posters and postcards that fill the capital's street markets.

It is hard to exaggerate the oddity of this phenomenon in the Arab world. In neighboring Saudi Arabia, Shi'ite veneration of holy figures, through pictures or visits to shrines, is seen as a form of idol worship, just one step away from heresy. Even Shi'ites in Lebanon are shy about venerating the early imams in this manner. Iraq's staunchly secular artistic community is also aghast over the practice. "These are the same people who used to do portaits of Saddam Hussein. Now they're doing the imams," said Qasim al-Sabti (interview with author, December 2003). "This is a big lie and has nothing to do with a holy figure like Ali [the fourth caliph] . . . They make him look like a film star, with white skin, beautiful eyes, and a striking pose. But we know what he looked like because it's written in history and it's more like this guy here," al-Sabti said, pointing to a squat, dark-skinned man entering the gallery. "He was brown, fat, short, and bald." The images of Ali and his son Hussein, whose martyrdom at Kerbala is a defining moment in Shi'ite history, are based on Iranian depictions that have been extant for at least a hundred years. With flowing brown hair and beards, the figures do not look dissimilar to Catholic images of Christ. One common image shows Hussein as a baby in the arms of Ali, riding on a horse, and the heads of both are surrounded by shining white halos— like the Madonna and child.

According to Dahlouz, the Iranian input only slightly altered the true visage of the Shi'ite imams. "The imams, peace be upon them, were first depicted by Iranians, so they always make the nose straight, while the Arab nose isn't straight. I don't like to make the eyes so femi-

radical great rival, Mohammed Sadiq al-Sadr, in 1999, most likely a Baathist assassination, left the way open for the aged Sistani to dominate Shi'ite politics.

TANTAWI, MOHAMMED (B. 1928)

Appointed by Egypt's President Mubarak in 1996 to the position of Sheikh of al-Azhar—

the forty-third since the institution was established over a thousand years ago—making him technically the highest authority in Sunni Islam. A quiet moderate, the government chose him to counter the influence of his predecessor, Gad al-Haqq, who had stymied the efforts of social reformers inside and outside government to improve women's marriage rights and fight the prac-

Shi'ite iconography showing Ali, the fourth caliph and cousin of the Prophet Mohammed, on the streets of Baghdad after the end of Saddam Hussein's rule. (Reuters/Corbis)

nine and I try to make the nose round," said Dahlouz. "Most of the Iranian artists tend to idealize and beautify them. They make the eyes dreamy and sleepy. I prefer eyes like a hawk. But I've had visions of the 'commander of the faithful' [Ali] myself so often and I see him as something more close to this Iranian image. All the history books show that all of the imams were beautiful and shining, and they got this light and beauty from the Prophet" (interview with author, December 2003). Dahlouz hopes some Sunnis will eventually come to appreciate the images: "They respect the family of the Prophet and love them, but they need more knowledge about them. The past regime spent thirty-five years sidelining the role of the Prophet's family. We Shia read books about them and visit their shrines, but the Sunnis are a bit distant from them" (interview with author, December 2003).

tice of circumcision of young girls. Tantawi is regarded by many Muslims as being so compliant with the state's wishes as to make a mockery of al-Azhar's traditional role in society. In one of his most infamous opinions, he wrote off the Islamic condemnation of usury with a neat wordplay in Arabic—bank interest was not *riba* (usury) but *ribh* (profit), he said. Since his appointment he has sanctioned government efforts to promote peace with Israel in the face of rabid opposition among the intelligentsia as a whole, who always resented Sadat's almost-overnight imposition of his very personal peace with Israel over two decades ago. He introduced reforms of al-Azhar's education curriculum that reduced study of concepts of *jihad* and of religious education in general and allowed foreigners to study in their own language, not Arabic—all to accusations that he was trying to "secularize" Islam. Civil rights activists note that neither Haqq nor Tantawi, nor any other religious figure of stature, speaks out against authoritarian rule, police brutality, or corruption.

AL-TIJANIYYA

Important Sufi order in Africa, named after holy man Sheikh Ahmed al-Tijani (1737–1815). Like many other Sufi paths, the Tijani order has its origins in Morocco. The Tijaniyya practiced intellectual severity and spread into Sudan. Tijani was an Algerian from the town of Tijan who memorized the Quran at the age of seven. Tradition says that at the age of forty, Tijani had a vision of the Prophet in broad daylight. It strictly advocates following the Quran and the Sunna, or way, of the Prophet.

WAHHABISM

School of mainstream Sunni Islam established by a Saudi radical reformer named Mohammed ibn Abdel-Wahhab (1703–1792) in the eighteenth century, whose idea of returning to a pure monotheistic Islam and stamping out Shi'ite and Sufi traditions was taken up by the Saudi family. The Saudis used his teaching as the ideological glue that held together three Saudi states, including the third one, founded in 1902 by King Fahd's father, Abdel-Aziz ibn Saud. But the austere Sunni Islam of Wahhabism has come under unprecedented criticism since the September 11 attacks, with many Saudis arguing it has bred a fanatical view of Islam that is now threatening Saudi society itself as followers of bin Laden's al-

Qa'ida fight a campaign to bring down the House of Saud. These critics have been shocked by al-Qa'ida's readiness to kill Saudis and other Muslims in their attempt to strike at foreigners and symbols of the Saudi state.

WILAYAT AL-FAQEEH

The Shi'ite doctrine of "rule by religious scholars/jurists." The idea was an innovation developed by Ayatollah Khomeini and put into practice after the Iranian revolution in 1979. Shi'ite political theory normally blocks clerical rule, since the twelfth imam is considered to be in occultation and only upon his return could clerics take over and institute a reign of justice through direct governance, that of the twelfth imam himself. Saudi dissident reformer Saad al-Faqih has come close to advocating a Sunni version of *wilayat al-faqeeh* in Saudi Arabia, with his argument that the clerics are the only sector of society who would be in a position to take control of Saudi Arabia in the event of Saudi rule collapsing (Al-Rasheed 2002, 182).

AL-ZAWAHIRI, AYMAN (B. 1951)

The Egyptian number-two man to Osama bin Laden in Afghanistan, who joined the Islamic Jihad organization that carried out the assassination of Anwar Sadat. A surgeon and prominent Islamist as a student at Cairo University, he served three years in prison for a minor role in the operation to kill Sadat and carry out a coup, but eventually came to head Jihad. He officially merged the group with bin Laden's followers in 1998 in Afghanistan. Zawahiri hails from a prominent family and grew up in an upper-class neighborhood of Cairo; his relatives included a sheikh of al-Azhar and a secretary-general of the Arab League. He left Egypt in 1985 and lived in Pakistan as well as Afghanistan, where he committed himself to the fight against Soviet-backed forces. Like bin Laden, he has been on the run since the Taliban regime fell, but has issued a number of taped messages to Arabic satellite channels, enjoining Muslims to fight the United States and its allies over what he said is a prolonged war on Islam.

Bibliography

Print Resources

Abdul-Jabar, Faleh, ed. *Ayatollahs, Sufis, and Ideologues*. London: Saqi Books, 2002.

Al-Faqih, Saad. *Kayfa Yufakkir Al-Saud: Dirasa Nafsiyya* (How the Saudi Family Thinks: A Psychological Study). London: Movement for Islamic Reform in Arabia, n.d.

Al-Rasheed, Madawi. *A History of Saudi Arabia*. Cambridge: Cambridge University Press, 2002.

Bayat, Asef. "Piety, Privilege and Egyptian Youth." *Isim Newsletter*, no. 10 (July 2002).

———. "From Amr Diab to Amr Khaled." *Al-Ahram Weekly*, 22–28 May 2003, no. 639.

Boddy, J. *Wombs and Alien Spirits: Women, Men and the Zar Cult in Northern Sudan*. Madison: University of Wisconsin Press, 1989.

Brett, M., and E. Fentress. *The Berbers*. Oxford: Blackwell Publishers, 1996.

Bulliet, Richard W. *The Case for Islamo-Christian Civilization*. New York: Columbia University Press, 2004.

Chomsky, Noam. *Power and Terror: Post 9-11 Talks and Interviews*. New York: Seven Stories Press, 2003.

Cole, Juan. *Sacred Space and Holy War: The Politics, Culture, and History of Shi'ite Islam*. London: I. B. Tauris, 2002.

Cole, Juan, and Nikki Keddie, eds. *Shi'ism and Social Protest*. New Haven, Conn.: Yale University Press, 1986.

Crone, Patricia, and Martin Hinds. *God's Caliph: Religious Authority in the First Centuries of Islam*. Cambridge: Cambridge University Press, 1986.

El-Affendi, Abdelwahab. "Orientalism Is Alive and Well in Iraq." *The Daily Star*, 20 October 2003.

El-Shamy, Hasan M. *Folktales of Egypt*. Chicago: University of Chicago Press, 1980.

Fandy, Mamoun. *Saudi Arabia and the Politics of Dissent*. New York: St. Martin's Press, 1999.

Farrah, Ibrahim. "Zar Dance." *Arabesque* 3, nos. 3–4 and 4, no. 1 (1978).

Gellner, Ernest. *Muslim Society*. Cambridge: Cambridge University Press, 1979.

Gilsenan, Michael. *Saint and Sufi in Modern Egypt*. Oxford: Oxford University Press, 1973.

———. *Recognizing Islam: Religion and Society in the Modern World*. New York: Pantheon Books, 1983.

Halliday, Fred. *Two Hours That Shook the World*. London: Saqi, 2002.

———. *Islam and the Myth of Confrontation*. London: I. B. Tauris, 2003.

Huntington, Samuel P. *The Clash of Civilizations and the Remaking of the World Order*. London: Simon and Schuster, 1996.

Keddie, N. R., ed. *Scholars, Saints and Sufis: Muslim Religious Institutions since 1500*. Berkeley: University of California Press, 1972.

Kepel, Gilles. *Muslim Extremism in Egypt: The Prophet and Pharaoh*. Berkeley: University of California Press, 1985.

———. *Jihad: The Trail of Political Islam*. Cambridge, Mass.: Harvard University Press, 2002.

———. *Bad Moon Rising*. London: Saqi Books, 2003.

Kienle, Eberhard. *A Grand Delusion: Democracy and Economic Reform in Egypt*. London/New York: I. B. Tauris, 2000.

Natvig, Richard Johan. "Arabic Writings on Zar." *Sudanic Africa* 9 (1998): 163–178.

Negus, Steve. "Sufis Just Want to *Zikr*" (on Egyptian Sufism). *Cairo Times* 1, no. 19 (16–29 October 1997).

———. "Brother of Another Color" (on Khalil Abdel-Karim). *Cairo Times* 2, no. 2 (19 March–1 April 1998).

Nelson, Kristina. *The Art of Reciting the Qur'an.* Austin: University of Texas Press, 1985.

Qutb, Sayed. *Ma'alim Fil-Tareeq* (Milestones). 1965. Reprint. Beirut: Dar al-Shurouq, 1979.

Ruthven, Malise. *Cairo.* Amsterdam: Time Life Books, 1980.

———. *Islam in the World.* London: Penguin, 2000.

Sells, Michael. *Approaching the Qu'ran.* Ashland, OR: White Cloud Press, 1999.

Vidal, Gore. *Dreaming War: Blood for Oil and the Cheney-Bush Junta.* New York: Thuder's Mouth Press/Nation Books, 2002.

———. *Perpetual War for Perpetual Peace.* New York: Thuder's Mouth Press/Nation Books, 2002.

Waguih, Asmaa. "Where Genies Fear to Tread." *Cairo Times* 1, no. 11 (25 December–7 January 1998).

Walker, John. *Folk Medicine in Modern Egypt.* London: Luzac & Co., 1934.

Web Sites

www.islammemo.com. A compendium of Islamic Web sites.

www.azfalrasas.com. An Arabic site that advocates *jihad* against Americans. There have been many such sites closed down or hacked by the U.S. authorities.

www.forislam.com. Web site of leading Egyptian preacher Amr Khaled.

www.islamtoday.net. Saudi-based site of leading Saudi cleric Salman al-Awda.

www.islam-online.net. Site of Qatar-based IslamOnline, one of the most popular Islamic Web sites.

cgi.sociologyonline.co.uk. British site offering useful discussions on September 11–related issues.

www.alazharonline.org. The official Web site of the al-Azhar Islamic institute in Egypt.

www.qaradawi.net. The Web site of leading Arab cleric Yousef al-Qaradawi, who appears regularly on al-Jazeera.

www.saffar.org. The Web site of Sheikh Hassan al-Saffar, the leading Shi'ite cleric in Saudi Arabia.

www.zawaj.com. A popular Muslim dating site and forum on Muslim marital issues.

www.MuslimMatch.com. Another matchmaking site for Muslims.

www.islamicfinder.com. A Web site that translates dates between the Islamic and Julian calendar.

www.muhaddith.org. Islamic Web site in Arabic and English called Al Muhaddith, with Islamic software, Islamic books, and Quranic recitation.

www.atrueword.com. Islamic site in English run by prominent Australian Muslims.

www.reason.com. Web site that deals with issues of religious history and theology relevant to the region.

http://www.arches.uga.edu/~godlas/ sufismorders.html. Site run by the University of Georgia with useful outline of Sufism and its many orders around the world.

http://www.tijaniyya.com. Web site run by a Tijani Sufi order.

www.hesbah.com. Site of the Saudi religious police.

www.sistani.org. Site of Iraq's main Shi'ite cleric Ali al-Sistani.

www.moubadara.net. Site of Algerian Islamist leader Abbasi Madani.

www.alazhr.org. Site of Egypt's al-Azhar, with a comprehensive hadith search facility in Arabic.

www.yaislah.net. Saudi opposition site with Islamic leanings that often carries al-Qa'ida linked material in its chatrooms (as do www.qal3ati.net and www.alsaha.net).

8
Belly Dancing

The Origins of the Dance

In his *Histories* written in 440 B.C., the Greek historian Herodotus related the remarkable ability of Egyptians to create for themselves spontaneous fun, singing, clapping, and dancing in boats on the Nile during numerous religious festivals. It's from somewhere in this great, ancient tradition of gaiety that the belly dance emerged. Researchers cite Pharaonic religious worship and fertility rites, as well as Bedouin traditions and the great mixing of cultures engendered by the Ottoman Empire, whose court elevated the belly dance in particular—just one of a range of dance forms referred to today as belly dancing or oriental dance. But practitioners of the art form uniformly agree that its soul is lodged imperceptibly in Arab cultures, especially Egyptian, and in the way that Arabs walk, talk, laugh, pout, and flirt with each other. In recent decades belly dancing has become a global dance cult. Since the 1960s instructors from the region, such as Yousry Shant and Bobby Farra, have been teaching *raqs sharqi*, or oriental dance, in the United States, from where it spread to Europe. In 2002, the top names in belly dancing put out a dance video (*Amiraat al-Raqs al-Sharqi*, *Princesses of Eastern Dance*), confirming the current élan surrounding belly dance in the West. Cairo's colony of dancers talk of special performances they have done for Henry Kissinger, Presidents Carter and George Bush, as well as Prince Charles and Camilla Parker-Bowles. In an earlier age Hikmat Fahmy danced for Hitler and Mussolini.

In the 1990s, Egypt saw foreign dancers take up a considerable slice of the market—while conservative society saw local interest decline—but the consensus of opinion among Egyptian dancers, foreign dancers, and the punters themselves is that technique is one thing, but only Arabs have the ability to "make their bodies sing," as high-culture singer Umm Kalthoum once said of belly-dancing star Tahiya Carioca. The gentle hip movement of belly dance reflects the quarter note unique to Arabic music, and even modern Arabic pop music developed around a rhythm, called *taqseem*, that matches the hip swing of a dancer. It is something

Belly dancer Ziz Mustapha dancing in Cairo for Jackie Onassis (seen third from left) and Aristotle Onassis (in dark glasses on right) during a visit to Egypt. (Bettmann/Corbis)

passed on from mothers to daughters, often in secluded feminine society where it is learned by young girls before they are exposed to the world of men. Different forms of belly dance are involved in rites of passage for women in Arab countries, from birth, to menstruation, to marriage, and some Bedouin communities even know of a menstruation dance called *raheel* ("departure"). Its practitioners surmise that the pelvic wave mimics the stomach's contractions in child labor. Whereas in most Western dance, the trunk of the body is still while the limbs do the moving, in belly dance it is the other way around. There is a connection between belly dance and the ability of Arab women to carry things on their heads—the pelvis moves freely while the head and the burden never move. As a result, when most foreigners practice belly

dance "you feel it's a toy, a doll or a puppet dancing, not a person," as Egyptian actress Rola Mahmoud puts it (interview with author, October 2003).

Arab society currently has a number of conflicting trends concerning belly dancing. The biggest stars have become immensely rich women and are attacked by religious and nationalist elites as signs of the corruption of the times and of a decadent modern Arab society where oil-rich Gulf Arabs will spend a fortune at a nightclub while Palestine cries in pain. *The Age of Fifi Abdo* (*Zaman Fifi Abdo*) was the title of a recent popular paperback attacking the empty capitalist times of modern Egypt, taking the country's top-earning dancer Fifi Abdo as a symbol of all that's wrong with today's Egypt. In the traditionalist viewpoint, dancing tops a list including singing and acting of disrespected professions a woman should not engage in, since these professions are associated with loose morals and prostitution. The most famous dancer in the Levant is an Iraqi who goes by the name of Samara. She revealed on Lebanon's LBC television that her real name is in fact Tahira, a name that means "morally pure." Iraqi dancers and other entertainers in "impure" professions, who were also considered to be close to the ruling clique of Saddam Hussein, were murdered after his regime collapsed in 2003. From the fall of *al-Andalus* (Arab Andalusia) to the debacle of the 1967 Arab-Israeli war, dancers are depicted in Arab lore as the critical distraction for political leaders that caused the demise of Arab glory. At the same time, there is a trend to idolize the entertainers of the past as examples of strong, independent Arab women: the 1998 television serial *Zizinia* (the name of an old quarter of Alexandria) cast belly-

Infamous Egyptian belly dancer Fifi Abdo performing for handicapped sports champions in Cairo in August 2003. (Amro Marghi/AFP/Getty Images)

involved in the entertainment business, Mohammed Ali Street—ironically named after the Egyptian ruler who once banished belly dancers and prostitutes to southern Egypt in 1834—hosts only a few aging artists now, repositories of an entire culture (including the old trade argot of entertainers, known as *sim*). Fifi Abdo was the last of the generation that lived and trained there, but with fame and money she moved out, and now lives in an exclusive, luxurious tower bloc by the Nile in central Cairo. The authorities limit dancing at *moulids*, sometimes preventing it altogether in major festivals such as the Tanta *moulid*. Professionalization of the entertainment professions in the modern era has eroded the prestige of belly dancing. Traditionally, performers sang, danced, joked, and performed music. Now acting, singing, and music are separate art forms with their own academies, which affords access to the state media. Only ballet and folk dancers are accorded union status. Techniques of belly dancing are not taught on any television programming. Belly dancing experiences public denunciation, as a shameful practice, but the shame does not affect those who are entertained by it, and it is still a national obsession. According to van Nieuwkerk, belly dancers "mainly differ from 'decent' women because they use their bodies instead of hiding their shame as much as possible. They publicly employ the power of their bodies" (van Nieuwkerk 1996).

Golden Age of Dancing in Pre-1952 Egypt

Egyptian dancing was popularized and commercialized throughout the nineteenth century after Egypt's first great modern

dancing star Nagwa Fouad as the pioneering dancer and club owner from the early twentieth century, Badia Masabni.

Meanwhile, the trade has actually shrunk, because of the increasing religiosity in society since 1967, because economic pressures often prevent people in poorer districts from hiring dancers for their weddings, and because the discos and nightclubs have become more Westernized, often forgoing the belly dancer for a floor show by a group of Russian dancers or a DJ and dance floor (though to combat local unemployment Egypt stopped licensing non-Egyptian dancers in 2004). The traditional quarter for dancers, musicians, and others contact with the West, when Napoleon invaded in 1798—so that by the time the British occupation began in 1882, belly dancing was a fixture of the Western-style entertainment industry based around cabaret acts that had taken root, and it went on to play a central narrative role in emerging theater and film. In Morocco and Algeria, too, the Europeans came to know of a tribe called the Awlad Nayel, who performed a pelvic dance. Before the advent of foreigners, the dance was mainly for private audiences with women, by women in normal garb: it was the Westerners who recontextualized it as eroticism, with the designation *danse du ventre*. The Orientalist depiction of the belly-dancing East was an interpretation born of a particular historical moment—the natural sciences were changing the European world, the industrial revolution was taking over from the agricultural revolution, and life was regimented by the spread of clocks. The belly dance typified the supposed fundamental differences between the rational West and the backward, emotional, and self-indulgent culture of the East. From 1851, dancers were exported to world exhibitions in Britain, France, and America. There the dance was modified to conform to Western ideas in general about the Orient, with risqué performances and exotic costumes—images perpetuated by Hollywood (such as the early movies *Intolerance* in 1916 and *Salome* in 1918)—before it came back to Cairo in a different form entirely.

With the advent of entertainment establishments came the gradual disappearance of the traditional contexts for dancing, namely the traveling groups of dancers in the countryside known as *ghawazi* (and thought to be of Gypsy origin), who performed at *moulids*, and the more

A Moroccan belly dancer performing before tourists. (TRIP/Art Directors)

respected urban dancers—who populated Mohammed Ali Street—known as *awaalim*, who came with their own musical bands, and moved from performing exclusively for women to working-class street weddings. Morocco also had women who performed for women and were accorded reasonable status in society. The last of the known *awaalim* were Bamba Kashar, Dalal al-Misriyya, and Shafiqa al-Misriyya, all three of whom have been depicted on film by modern actresses Nadia al-Gindy, Magda al-Khatib, and Safiya al-Emary, respectively. The era of the famous dancers began in the 1920s, when Qibtiyya and Syrian dancer Badia Masabni set up their own clubs in downtown Cairo. Masabni modernized the dance, adding arm movements, chest-shaking, and the use of veils, as well as dance movements that made full use of the stage.

Ouled Nayel: The Infamous Dancers of Algeria

The Ouled Nayel, whose dancing so tititlated French travelers in the late nineteenth and early twentieth centuries, were in fact an Arabic-speaking Berber tribe—possibly racially mixed with Arab Bedouins. The tribe had settled in the Ouled Nayel mountains of southeast Algeria near Tunisia and developed a ritual of women dancing for money. By tribal custom, the Ouled Nayel sent young women at the onset of puberty to oases, where they would acquire their dowries by dancing at public festivals and in cafés, where they would establish relationships with their admirers. When they had enough money, they would return to the mountain villages with the dowries they needed to marry within the tribe. They might spend up to fifteen years in the oases. At the same time, they fasted during Ramadan and visited the shrines of Muslim saint figures (*Nayel* probably refers to such a Sufi holy figure). The French colonial authorities thought of them as little more than prostitutes, and the destruction of rural society that followed the French conquest and colonization of Algeria drove many of the women into the brothels of Algiers and Tunis. The women of the Ouled Nayel (or Awlaad Naa'il) "were an ancient geisha caste of North Africa in a pre-modern context that could tolerate within the social rituals of tribal sanctity the profane as well as the sacred," according to Professor Abdallah Schleifer of the AUC in Cairo (catalog essay, "L'Orient: The Photographs of Lehnert and Landrock," Cairo exhibition, 1999). Lehnert and Landrock, famous photographers of the region during the colonial period, took pictures of the Ouled Nayel women at the oasis of Bou Saada between 1904 and 1930. They captured a society, indeed an entire culture, on the cusp of radical, destructive change. In their photographs, the women wore costumes that they danced in, as described by many chroniclers of the time (though they would often end their dances naked). They wore *kohl* on their eyes; a profusion of jewelry, including large earrings, bracelets, and coin necklaces; elaborate headdresses, sometimes topped with ostrich feathers; and voluminous skirts. They were also elaborately tattooed on their faces, arms, hands, and fingers, and sometimes on their breasts and pelvic areas. Their dancing, in Maghrebi fashion, centered on the top half of the body, with upward pelvic thrusts, chest held out, undulations, and snaking arms.

Choreography, costumes, shoes, and castanets now featured as part of the show. The result was the classic "belly dance" that is so popular today—referred to simply as *raqs sharqi*, or oriental dancing—and it was this new, consolidated style that went on to conquer the region through the burgeoning Egyptian cinema industry. The term "belly dancing" doesn't really translate into Arabic: those who respect it use the term *raqs sharqi*, and the local Egyptian dancing from which it is mainly derived is referred to as *raqs baladi*, or "local dance." *Raqs sharqi* is probably the most accurate: a made-up name for a made-up dance. Two of the most famous dancers, Tahiya Carioca and Samia Gamal, trained with Masabni. Other greats of the era were Na'ima Akef, Laila al-Gazairiyya, Nelly Mazloum, and Kitty. Egypt's Nobel-winning novelist Naguib Mahfouz immortalized this era in his Cairo Trilogy. It came to a sort of coda with the great riot of Cairo in 1952, during which Masabni's infamous club was burned down by mobs who associated it with British colonial power, and Masabni fled the country. The club had been more than just a music hall. During World War II, officers and spies mingled there, and when she turned down Hitler's overtures to work for the Germans, Madame Badia was accused of being a British secret agent in German propaganda.

In the Middle Ages, most Islamic law schools came down against the lawfulness of music and singing, with the exception of religious chanting for men, because they were seen as distracting the believer's attention from devotion to God and invoking temptation. But these arts still flourished in the courts of rulers and in society at large. But as the dance changed through contact with the West, so did local attitudes toward dancing. The idea that dancing was sinful continued and developed in

A Bulgarian belly dancer. In recent years there has been an influx of dancers from outside the Middle East. (TRIP/Art Directors)

the Nasserist era, not least because the former King Farouk, associated with the era of subservience to foreigners, had been a great fan of the club scene. The naked midriff was banned, with skin-colored material or chiffon used as coverups, as were various forms of dance involving sitting on the ground. The ministry of culture encouraged Western arts such as ballet, opera, and classical music, as well as the Arabic heritage of music and folklore. Previously, even the big composers would write for the dancers in their cinema roles, during an era when there was an aristocratic upper class of reasonable size with different cultural values from the masses. But the dance went on—only now it was mainly centered on a certain area on the outskirts of the capital: Pyramids Road.

The Historic Role of the Pyramids Road in Cairo

The Pyramids Road, an area of nightclubs, cabarets, and casinos, has birthed millionaire belly-dancing stars, has fired up popular fantasies and moral crusades, and was the scene of many a riot against the established order. It was originally built in 1867 by Khedive Ismail, on agricultural land extending all the way up to the pyramids. It was intended to be a showpiece boulevard, but as the atmosphere against foreigners and their habits intensified in the 1940s, clubs began appearing along the Pyramids Road strip. In the 1960s the social profile of the area changed as rural migrants created poor suburbs all around and along the road. When riots broke out in the vicinity in 1977, twelve of the fourteen clubs there were attacked, and when the security forces rioted in 1986, the clubs were again targeted.

Throughout this period and up to today, calls from the religious lobby increased for the clubs to be closed down or moved away. As the clubs found themselves in the midst of Egypt's burgeoning poor, residents agreed with the religious rhetoric and complained that women weren't safe from harassment by the drunken club clientele and wealthy Gulf tourists pushing up rent prices, and locals even raised legal action to force removal of the clubs. "They say the presence of these nightclubs is necessary to stimulate tourism and attract male and female visitors, even if they're naked. They say we need their dollars, francs and shekels. But our ethical values must govern our economic demands, not the other way round," prominent cleric Abdel-Maqsoud al-Askar once wrote (*Cairo Times*, 17 September 1998). Popular preacher Sheikh Shaarawi said on television in 1988 that the only permissible entertainment was music that does not "tickle the nerves" (Nelson 1985). In a 1996 street paperback called *Secret Confessions: A Journalist Infiltrates the Nightlife* (*I'tiraafaat Sirriyya: Sahafi Yaqtahim Aalam al-Lail*), Emad Nassef claimed to have come across decadent bars where dancers "did things" with melted chocolate. When open warfare finally broke out in the 1990s between the radical Islamist groups and the government, tourists in general were a target. But in one incident in 1996, Gamaa Islamiya activists shot eighteen Greeks outside the Europa Hotel, mistaking them as Israelis. Since the late 1990s the tourist ministry has worked to make the area more in tune with "family values," encouraging more fast-food restaurants, while the government and local police have kept up pressure on the nightclubs that remain, with constant enforcement of regulations keeping women performers away from customers and concerning dancers' costumes, and the occasional shutdown on suspicion of prostitution. Since the mid-1990s, the government has forced dancers to add a lace net between the top and bottom of the bikini so that the belly button and hip movements are partly obscured, but they also scrutinize the dancers' music and the lyrics. Ironically, Egypt's President Hosni Mubarak once sought to insult Islamic extremists in an angry interview, calling them "sons of bellydancers and drummers" (Weaver 1999)—he borrowed the phrase from the 1984 film *al-Raqisa wal-Tabbal* (*The Belly Dancer and the Drummer*), starring Nabila Ebeid and Ahmed Zaki. Preachers have even said belly dancers are not fit to make pilgrimage to Mecca.

The stomping ground of today's big dancers is the five-star hotels, though Pyramids Road still has its attractions, while a few clubs have even reopened in downtown Cairo again—one, ironically, on the street where the Muslim Brotherhood's head offices were located, until police closed them down in 1995. Called the New Arizona, it's named after the first dancing club to open on Pyramids Road in 1946. But the face of traditional nightlife is changing. The fees of the biggest dancers have become huge, and most five-star hotels keep them on only because of the prestige of having a dancer in their special belly-dancing club. Western-style bars, often with lounge singers, are attracting the new middle class, especially businessmen who don't want to sit up until five or six in the morning, as is the custom in belly-dancing clubs—a change in work practices brought on by economic liberalization. There were some 5,000 registered dancers in 1957; today there are only around 300, with perhaps around 200 unregistered. Many people in the entertainment industry fear that the clubs are dying and that belly dancing is fast being relegated to a gimmicky art preserved for foreigners, tourists, and locals with a penchant for Orientalist folklore—a sad fate for a rich subculture that was once, to quote the title of van Nieuwkerk's classic study, "a trade like any other." The Egyptian government in 2004 issued a ban on foreign dancers—more out of concern for unemployment in general than out of a newly discovered love of the native art form. Lebanon has also stopped licensing foreigners, and as a result many foreign (and Arab) dancers are heading to the United Arab Emirates, where tourism is booming and dancers are welcome. The belly-dancing industry in Egypt fears these moves could backfire. "We are not even able to open a formal institute to teach in Egypt, so how will our heritage survive?" leading promoter of belly dancing Raqia Hassan has said (*al-Ahram Weekly*, 4–10 March 2004).

On the other hand, there are currently renewed efforts to set up a professional syndicate, which would offer financial help and legal protection for belly dancers, as well as regulation and perhaps more respect. Several years ago dancers were thrown out of the actors' syndicate after the religiously inclined members argued that the money of dancers taken by the syndicate in subscriptions was *haram*, or deemed unlawful by Islam, though oddly enough Russian dancers are still accepted as members. At present dancers get licenses from the same arts censorship office that approves films and music. The press scorns the idea, saying it would be a "shake-your-hips syndicate," but it's likely to happen eventually. Dancers are using the smart argument that a syndicate will "clean up" the profession, removing the immorality it is accused of by the public. "At the moment any girl can go to the arts censors and get a licence to dance, then abuse this to do other things," Dina, a likely head of the syndicate if it comes about, told the Egyptian press (*Rose al-Youssef*, 27 September 2002). "When there's a syndicate there will be committees to examine dancers and only those who really can dance will be licenced." When the syndicate finally comes into being, it will mark the final coming-of-age of oriental dancing, from disparate traditions two centuries ago to a new art form today, celebrated abroad and now given full recognition in its homeland, and more respect in the Arab world will surely follow. "Society's view of dancing could change, but it will take at least 20 years. The beginning could be to set up some sort of body," Lucy has said (*Rose al-Youssef*, 27 September 2002).

Today's Mega Belly-Dancing Stars in Egypt

Despite all that, television exposure has led to Hollywood-style cult status around the top belly dancers—namely, Fifi Abdo, Lucy, and Dina. Their travels, tiffs, amours, and astronomical wealth are the stuff of gossip columns in the press. Only about the top ten make huge amounts of money. On a big night like New Year's Eve, a major artist can rake in 200,000 Egyptian pounds (around $33,000) from playing at several venues. The biggest singers do the same—playing several weddings or concert venues in an evening—but they make a lot more than the dancers do. Abdo and Lucy are charging around 12,000 Egyptian pounds (about

Egyptian dancer Dina appears for the first time in public in January 2004 after her involvement in a sex scandal. (Amro Marghi/AFP/Getty Images)

$2,000) for a wedding appearance, Dina charges about 7,000 Egyptian pounds (around $1,200), followed by Argentinian Asmahan, the Russian Nour, and Egypt's Safwa ("Open Buffet," *al-Ahram Weekly*, 4–10 January 2001). This compares with about $35,000 for Nawal al-Zoghby or Kazem al-Saher (though they perform for much longer). In one year alone the state will gather about $250 million from the dancers' earnings. Like all others in public space, they have been sucked into the debate over normalization with Israel—the press regularly reports that Israel has offered huge sums of money to bring Fifi Abdo to dance in the Jewish State, and the

dancers regularly respond in shocked denial that they take offense at such disrespectful propositions. The dancers also report numerous offers to train Israeli dancers. The idea underpinning this press theme is that today's rich made their money in a fast and immoral manner, so a hop over the border is but one small step further on the road to perdition.

Abdo has become a living legend, a rags-to-riches story of a girl from the Cairo poor district of Boulaq al-Dakrour who went on to become Egypt's biggest taxpayer and the most famous woman in the Arab world, detested by millions as symbolic of a world with no values or morals, and idolized by millions as a woman who battled through a male-dominated world to make it to the top. Her famed illiteracy is proof to her detractors that education counts for nothing these days; her achievement in learning how to read and write at the height of her fame is proof to her admirers that she is a worthy example for today's women. Her Arabic Web site, which offers advice to aspiring dancers, is reportedly one of the most popular sites in Egypt. Her popularity was at its highest throughout the 1990s, when she began a film and theater career, which was intended in part to offset the fact that she was in her fifties and couldn't stay on top of the dancing profession forever. European papers dubbed her "the fourth pyramid." Between 1993 and 1996 she earned 1.1 million euros, according to the Egyptian weekly *al-Mussawar*. She owns around 5,000 costumes, which cost up to $1,500 apiece. As well as being a dancer par excellence, Abdo has been an adept publicist who has actively projected an image of dangerous glamour. A team of bodyguards is in tow wherever she goes, and in 1997 she reportedly assaulted stand-up comedian Adel al-Far over his onstage impersonation of her. But she has also noted wryly that she's become so used to being in gossip columns that she gets uneasy if she doesn't get mentioned.

Abdo first came to public attention in 1979, when an infatuated TV interviewer said that her ancestral home of Shibeen al-Kom, a poor peasant town in north Egypt, "clearly has a lot of nice talent!" The comment, considered too risqué at the time, caused such a fuss that the interviewer disappeared from television screens for some five years, but it made Abdo a household name. The grandees of the profession at that time, such as Tahiya Carioca and So-

heir Zaki, singled her out as the best of a new generation of dancers. Abdo's films have included 1992's *al-Qatila* (*The Killer*), 1994's *Lailat al-Qatl* (*The Night of the Murder*), and 2001's *Yamin Talaq* (*Divorce Oath*), all of them tawdry works of commercial cinema. Her plays have included the successful *Hazzimni Ya Baba* and the not-so-successful *Iddallai Ya Dosa*, which both highlighted her dancing. She once admitted on television to having married five times by an Egyptian marriage contract called *urfi*, which is widely seen as an easy marriage of convenience that doesn't last and isn't serious, and which comes in various forms and under various names all over the Arab world and beyond. During the month of Ramadan she sponsors street tables of free food for the poor—an old tradition in Egypt—and has put up with preachers saying that eating of her food is *haram*. Her belly-dancing act astonishes by its sheer energy: she and her band of players and singers go through various set-pieces reflecting the old days when the Mohammed Ali Street entertainment culture was alive and respected, and the audience is even treated to the sight of Abdo snorting shisha-pipe smoke through each of her nostrils. She also raps, chews gum in a provocative manner, performs the stick dance, and mimics behavior taken by most Egyptians to be vulgar, knowing, of course, that vulgar is what most of the audience consider her to be. The entire show is testament to the power women had over their own lives in the entertainment days of old, offering a tamer version of Madonna's provocative *Blonde Ambition* stage show.

Dina, on the other hand, oozes sexuality in the manner of the Orientalist fantasies that transformed local dance traditions into the belly-dancing phenomenon of today. She has, as one reviewer once put it, a "mane of jet black ringlets down her back and a cleavage virtually bursting out of her bustier" ("Beauty and the Beat," *al-Ahram Weekly*, 6 July 2000). She has even done away with the prescribed costume with fabric covering the navel, dancing in a straightforward bikini. Consequently, she has had more trouble with the morals inspectors who often attend her shows. Against type, she comes from a well-to-do family and completed a degree in philosophy to please her father, while pursuing a career in dancing with the Reda Dance Troupe in the early 1970s.

She has been outspoken in her defense of dancing and outspoken about her private life. For three months she was secretly married to an Egyptian high-society louche who gave her a hard time about her profession, while he carried on behind her back during his nights on the town in Cairo's elite hot spots. She broke up the marriage, then revealed all to the media after four depressed days when she took the veil and renounced dancing. That was in 1998. A year later she was married to film director Sameh Bahgoury and had his child shortly before his death in 2001. In 2002 she suffered further embarrassment when papers publicized a videotape of her with a well-known businessman, and she subsequently revealed that she had been secretly married to him for some years. She has ventured into films, but not with the success of Abdo, and most of her roles have presented her as a bimbo figure. In interviews she has said she feels what she does for a living is wrong, but no worse than the sins of anyone else in an imperfect world. She doesn't mind being called *raqqasa*, the colloquial term for belly dancer that is also used as an insult, as opposed to others who

insist on being referred to as *raaqisa*, the formal word for a woman who dances.

Lucy is the less enigmatic of the three, but perhaps the most talented. She began a movie career in the late 1980s, and was hailed as one of the country's best actresses after her role as a dancer in the 1993 soap opera *Layali Hilmiya* (*Hilmiya Nights*). The Alexandria Film Festival gave her the best actress award in 1996 for her role in the obscure but engaging *Romantika*. She continued to act in a few art-house films, while her reputation as the most technically proficient of Egypt's dancers has grown. She isn't the type to engage the audience in flirtatious eye contact, risqué dramatics, or any of the other aspects of modern performance that society perceives as edging over the boundaries into vulgarity. And her wardrobe, by her own admission, includes only about 500 outfits, considered modest for an entertainer. She is a dancer's dancer and in fact trained as a ballet dancer as a child in Alexandria, but she moved into belly dancing to make ends meet after her parents' death. Other dancers of the 1970s, who often appeared in films, include Hayatem, Zizi Mustapha, Nadia Fouad, and Hala al-Safi. Dancers of the 1960s include Ne'mat Mokhtar and Zinat Ulwi.

Many argue that the 1970s marked the end of an era in belly dancing. It was not just that society's view of the art changed, the art itself changed, with dancing beccoming more sexual, more commercial, and less individual. For the most part, belly dancing today has become the sort of erotic, sleazy art that foreigners fantasized it to be over a hundred years ago, a self-fulfilling prophecy coming full circle. Said described "Orientalism" as a mode of thinking and representation of the Orient that saw the East as stagnant, sensual, passive, and irrational, in opposition to the West as changing, logical, active, and rational. By one reading, the belly dance has been forged in this Western image of the East. Dancers in most nightclubs and at weddings rely on flirtation and innuendo to entice tips out of drunken customers infatuated by the idea of sleeping with them. Until the 1970s, the dancers were allowed to sit with customers at their tables, an action known as "opening," in order to encourage them to buy more. Since this practice has been banned and enforced by special morals police, the dancers are expected to engage in "bewitching" (sha'waza) from the stage. This can involve fixing a guest with their eyes and moving their eyebrows and pelvis suggestively with a hand on their hip. In many of the nightclubs the guests—often Gulf Arab tourists—are allowed to get up and dance and shower the dancer with money, sometimes placing it in her brassiere. On a busy night in a small venue, the atmosphere can be charged and steamy, the equivalent of a strip joint in other parts of the world. Fifi Abdo graduated from this world to the top end of the trade in five-star hotels, where it is a much more sanitized artistic affair. But most of the top dancers have trained in folkloric dance, are well educated, and do not come from a traditional entertainment background—reflecting the fact that today's belly dancing is essentially an invention. The dancers who still perform at popular weddings are those with the closest links to the traditions of the past. They often come from lower-class backgrounds, had parents who worked in the same area, and had more corpulent frames, reflecting working-class preferences in a woman.

Today's clubs reveal a clash of cultures. Westerners, often tourists, sit in the audience in awe at what seems a thoroughly bizarre, dated, and even debased custom, rounding off a night out with a bit of outlandish popular culture. Some of the girls—who appear at the early shows—can hardly dance, and some look thoroughly embarrassed, though the players in the small music troupes and the shaabi singers are all rather adept. At the Palmyra, for example, the retro 1960s décor has unusual additions: mini Santa Clauses hang from above; colorful, giant leaves spread out over the ceiling from the bar; and golden party decorations twirl in the smoky air. It could be the set of a music video. The music is raucous as the singers belt out numbers by Adawiya and Hakim, but the band sits in silence, only occasionally allowing a wry smile to break their stony stares. They know the dancer's every move, including the repartee with her audience. Greetings are declared to the tables of people from different parts of Egypt and Arab countries. The more professional will pull off the cheeky but good-humored dig with aplomb. The foreigners are treated cordially but left out of the jokes. One might encounter scenes of deliriously happy wedding parties from Cairo's poor districts dancing madly on the stage, or priceless images such as a drunken, one-legged Kuwaiti who whirls his crutch around while dancing and gyrating furiously on one leg.

Traditional Dances Still Found in the Arab World

Modern belly dancing centered on Cairo is a hybrid of just some of the myriad local dance styles found in Egypt and beyond. Most dances involve men and are per-

Palestinians in the Gaza Strip dancing the traditional Levantine dance known as the *dabka* on 1 January 2004. (Abid Katib/Getty Images)

formed in groups. The Alexandrian "chandelier dance" (*raqsat al-shama'daan*), where dancers perform various moves with chandeliers on their heads, was incorporated into mass-culture belly dancing in 1920s Cairo. Those other dances still exist. The Egyptian dances are preserved via dance troupes such as the Reda Folkloric Troupe, but there are folklore dance festivals throughout the Arab world fulfilling the same function of preservation. The Suez Canal area on the edge of the Sinai Peninsula has its own *simsimiya* dance, named after the *simsimiya* instrument it is performed to, which mixes the Gypsy dancing of north Egypt (which developed into today's "baladi/belly dance") with the *dabka* of the Levant and is performed in groups. The Nubians of southern Egypt and northern Sudan have their own dance, performed to the distinctive pentatonic music of Nubia. The Bedouins of North Africa have the *haggala* dance, performed in groups wearing the fez. In Saudi Arabia only men dance, and in other Gulf countries, though women take part, head moves are central because of prohibitions on moving the rest of their bodies. Male Bedouin communities in the Gulf also dance with swords and other weapons. Iraq has a Bedouin war dance called *al-dahha*, where a woman brandishing a sword dances inside a ring of men. During the *al-hossa*, a poet stands in the middle of a crowd chanting war verse. Black African immigrants to southern Iraq dance the *al-haiwa*. Iraq also has Gypsy communities (thought to be of Arab or Indian origin) who dance the *al-hasha'a*. In Moroccan dancing, women move only their waists and have a more relaxed way of holding their backs, allowing certain nuances that are missing from the Egyptian forms. It is more simple and less theatrical than Egyptian dance, which some argue allows the dancer to develop more self-expression in her dance. In Egypt, before it developed into today's sophisticated art form with its Western, Turkish, Indian, and Persian accretions using all of the body, the dance mainly involved the pelvis. There is also a classical form of dancing named after the Arab-Islamic rule in Andalusia, called the *andalousi* (Andalusian) dance, performed to distinctive poetic songs and music of Arab Andalusia (known as *muwashshahaat andalousiyya*). The music, which is less rhythm-based and sung to classical Arabic, is known throughout the Arab world.

Recently there have been attempts by a number of writers and enthusiasts to cast the belly dance as part of today's pantheon of femininity cults, and it's almost become a fad in the manner of the Spice Girls' "girl power" or green tea. "Why should one learn to belly dance?" says a blurb on the home page of the Web site www.learn-to-belly-dance.com. "For physical, emotional, spiritual, and intellectual expansion," it answers, as if belly dancing were a new Sufi order. "The swings, circles, and spirals used in belly dancing stimulate gently and gradually dormant energies, which are then picked up by the body. So belly dancing refines energy and consciousness progressively and playfully, in perfect harmony without any risk of trauma," writes al-Rawi in her *Belly Dancing: Unlock the Secret Power of an Ancient Dance*. "This dance form is more than just a dance. Only a woman's life experience and sensuality can lend it both meaning and a true depth." According to al-Rawi, Arab women are more aware of their femininity—even if its space is carefully proscribed in Arab societies—while Western women feel obliged to play down their femininity in an attempt to be taken seriously in the post-1960s world. Thus, belly dancing seems to offer all women a chance to reconnect with themselves. "Expressing her personality through belly dancing, at times alone, at times with others, enables a woman to take a new look at her sometimes negative self-image, in a supportive and strengthening atmosphere. This uniting of earth and spirit, strength and grace, intensity and inner peace, sensuality and poetry, enables many a woman to reach inner freedom," al-Rawi says. Ironically, Western dance as it developed in the twentieth century became an expression of disintegrating social hierarchies and a means in itself toward freeing young people—a movement that saw its culmination in the 1960s. But, at least up to now, that has not happened with the belly dance of the Arabs. If the dance has liberated any women (or men), it's only the few who dare to dance it. Al-Rawi offers perhaps the most appropriate coda to the story of the dance so far: "A dance such as belly dance, which is carried by women's sexual force, life experience, and self-confidence, will always raise objections and discussions, at least until such time when feminine wisdom and maturity are fully accepted and seen as an existential balance to masculinity and a precondition for harmony on earth."

A-to-Z: Key People

ABDO, FIFI (B. N.A.)

Egypt's best-known dancer, who dominated the profession in the 1980s and

1990s. She is seen as typifying a new style of dancing that is much more brusquely sexual and less graceful than the greats of the earlier era, such as Tahiya Carioca, Samia Gamal, and Soheir Zaki. But many admire her for her tough personality, determination, and a charisma that few in the entertainment industry can match. She transferred her dancing skills to theater and cinema and was reputed in the 1990s to be one of the wealthiest people in Egypt. Hailing from the Cairo slum district of Boulaq—she worked as a housemaid before turning to dancing—she has always been viewed as coarse and uncultured, a symbol of the savage consumer culture that has gripped Egypt and other Arab countries since the 1970s.

AKEF, NA'IMA (1929–1966)

One of the star dancers to emerge from the Badia Masabni club, Akef had her own particular style that borrowed much from her training as a trapeze artist in her father's circus. In the late 1940s she began a film career that ended with her death at thirty-seven in 1966. Her most successful films were the fourteen comedy musicals she made with her director-screenwriter husband Hussein Fawzy. Her dancing was viewed as highly expressive and dramatic, as if she were acting.

CARIOCA, TAHIYA (1915–1999)

A famous belly dancer, who usually played wily women who knew men would fall for her, and indeed she married a ridiculous number of times in real life. She ran away from home as a teenager for a life on the stage in Cairo. In her later years, she put on weight and became known for roles as a traditional, large, old woman. She took her stage name from the Brazilian Carioca dance that swept the world in 1933 and that Fred Astaire and Ginger Rogers immortalized in the film *Flying down to Rio*. She is remembered fondly as one of the most innovative dancers of the twentieth century and a classic dancer from the liberal age before dancing lost its reputation.

DINA (B. N.A.)

The biggest, most talked-about Arab belly dancer of the moment. She has played roles in a number of films, but her film career has not really taken off. Her life has been something of a drama, though, as she talks openly on television about her love life and her views on dancing and the surrounding controversy. She achieved unfortunate notoriety in 2003 when videos suddenly appeared on the market showing her in bed with a prominent Egyptian businessman, Hossam Aboul-Futouh, and she subsequently told the Egyptian press she had been married to him at the time. She then made pilgrimage to Mecca. She has been a strong campaigner for a professional syndicate to represent dancers and often teaches dance courses in the United States.

FAHMY, HIKMAT (D. N.A.)

Dancer who worked at the famous Casino Badia and in Europe. She then went on to spy on British officers for the Germans during World War II, in a plot involving a young Anwar Sadat, when British fear of German infiltration in Egypt was high. She and Sadat were imprisoned over the plot, but despite the amateurish nature of the scheme, it has spawned two English films (*Fox Hole in Cairo* and *The Key to Re-*

Brazilian Spice: Famed Dancer Tahiya Carioca

Born in 1915 with the name Badawiya, Carioca became one of the legends of oriental dance. She studied at the Ivanova Dancing School before moving to Mohammed Ali Street, Cairo's equivalent of Broadway. She adopted her stage surname "Carioca" after the Brazilian samba dance (popularized in the 1933 American film *Flying down to Rio*), which she used to perform at the famous Badia Masabni Club in Cairo, and the name stayed with her throughout her life. Her percussionist Zaki became known as Zaki Carioca after his Brazilian beats. Her fierce choreography spectacularly merged the elements of Egypt's localized *baladi* dance with modern cabaret. This fusion of styles was her own innovation, and through it she created a dance vocabulary of curves, arm movements, and resonating hip movements that became the dominant force in oriental dance for decades. Along with Samia Gamal, she is considered to be the dancer to have had the biggest influence on oriental dance in the twentieth century. The two of them were major dancing rivals in the 1940s. During the 1950s, Carioca went on to have considerable success in the film industry, acting in 200 films and marrying no less than fourteen times, including marriages to an American and also to actor Rushdie Abaza. In her heyday she usually acted the part of the femme fatale (in classics such as *Li'bat al-Sitt* (*Women's Games*) and *Shabab Imra'a* (*A Woman's Youth*), but in later years, after she put on considerable weight, she managed to reinvent herself as a matronly figure in TV soap operas. She also

Classic Egyptian belly dancer and actress Tahiya Carioca in the 1960s. (AP Photo/ Reproduction)

stood out for having danced in King Farouk's wedding procession in 1936, and in 1953 she was jailed for three months for supporting a return to constitutional democracy. On her death in 1999, Palestinian American academic Edward Said paid tribute to Carioca as a woman of disarming honesty, on politics as well as in her failed relationships with men, and as someone who managed to be seductive without recourse to excessive physical effort or sinking into vulgarity.

becca), based on two novels, as well as an Egyptian film, the 1994 film *Hikmat Fahmy* starring Nadia al-Gindy. Fahmy was said to have danced for Hitler and Mussolini while performing in European cabarets.

FOUAD, NAGWA (B. 1943)

As a child, she and her family were forced to flee from fighting in Palestine in 1948, and Fouad grew up in the Egyptian coastal city of Alexandria. In 1958 she ran away to Cairo where she found work as a receptionist with an agency for acting, singing, and dancing stars. Her dancing talent was noticed and soon she was performing in a club near the pyramids. Fouad managed to maintain respectability, mixing different belly-dancing styles with more respected folkloric dance, choreography, and drama—a good example is her 1976 stage show *Qamar Arbatashar* (*Blue Moon*), written for her by classical composer Mohammed Abdel-Wahhab. The musical transformed Fouad's career, and music was always a major part of her act.

GAMAL, SAMIA (1924–1994)

Born in 1924 as Zeinab Ibrahim Mahfouz, she joined the Badia Masabni dance company and went on to develop her own distinctive style with elements of classical ballet, Latin American dance, and new improvisations, such as wearing high-heeled shoes on the stage. She later became known for dancing without shoes and making full use of the stage. Like her nemesis Tahiya Carioca, she came from a lower-class background and left home while in her teenage years to work with the Masabni troupe in Cairo. Gamal was declared by King Farouk in 1949 as "the national dancer of Egypt." She starred in a number of films with oud player Farid al-Atrash, including *Valley of the Kings* (1954), and then married Texas oil millionaire Sheppard King. She also starred in the French film *Ali Baba et les Quarante Voleurs* (*Ali Baba and the Forty Thieves*), and married the top Egyptian actor Rushdie Abaza in 1958. She kept dancing in the 1980s when she was in her sixties, and she always said she would dance until she died.

HASSAN, RAQIA (B. N.A.)

Organizer of an annual belly-dancing festival/teaching course in Egypt, where the instructors include Dina, Lucy, and Nagwa Fouad. Attendees come from as far afield as the United States, Finland, Japan, and Singapore, including dance teachers abroad who want to pick up tips from the goddesses of the trade in Cairo, the "navel" of belly dancing. Top dancer Fifi Abdo very publicly has nothing to do with the festival—she says she boycotts it; Hassan says she's not invited. Abdo accuses Hassan of overcommercializing the profession through her lucrative business, which offers five-star courses for foreigners.

LUCY (B. N.A.)

One of Egypt's biggest belly-dancing stars today. She is currently one of the top earners in dancing. Her acting has also received praise from critics, including the TV drama *Layali Helmiya* (*Helmiya Nights*, 1993) and movies *Leih Ya Banafsig* (*Violets Are Blue*, 1991) and *Romantika* (1997). She has taught belly dancing in the United States and takes part in Raqia Hassan's annual belly-dancing school in Cairo. Lucy (her real name is In'am) has a good reputation in the business for her no-frills, technically adept style, and she minimally uses techniques that invoke a coquettish rapport with men in the audience. Her husband, Sultan al-Kashef, is a film director who has given her lead roles in some of his films.

MASABNI, BADIA (1878–1970)

The godmother of today's oriental dance, Lebanese-born Masabni opened Madame Badia's Club in central Cairo in 1926, modelled after European cabarets in order to attract the Arab and European audiences visiting Egypt in greater numbers. Her club soon became more than an ordinary cabaret, becoming Cairo's popular society hub, frequented by *le beau monde* and offering Muslim women a place to be seen in high society. It made local dance a respected art form. Traditional dancers were transported from their street-performing environments onto a large stage. Adopting props used in French shows and American films, Masabni's dancers used veils and sequined costumes, and expanded the traditional band of players accompanying the dancers into a formal classical orchestra. The larger orchestra meant more complex dance moves, and from this creative environment there emerged the two great dancers of the twentieth century, Tahiya Carioca and Samia Gamal. Hounded by tax collectors, Masabni left Cairo shortly before Egypt's 1952 revolution to set up a chicken farm in Chtoura in Lebanon. Her husband, actor Naguib Rihani, died in 1949.

REDA, MAHMOUD (B. 1930)

A pioneer of dance theater in Egypt, who in 1959 founded the Reda Dance Troupe, which preserves Egyptian folk dances and turns them into musical spectaculars that tour the world. Reda has been an actor, dancer, and choreographer in popular Egyptian films, and his troupe has performed in a number of Egyptian films, including the early 1960s musical *al-Hubb fi Karnak* (*Love in Karnak*). Reda represented Egypt in gymnastics at the 1952 Olympic Games in Helsinki, after taking a gold medal at the Arab championships in 1950. He also served in Egypt's ministry of culture during the 1980s.

ZAKI, SOHEIR (B. 1943)

Egyptian dancer born in the north Egyptian town of Mansoura, who epitomized the natural style of Egyptian belly dancing, though she was conservative in her dance and attire. She danced in traditional wedding parties in Mansoura and Alexandria until television producer Mohammed Salem discovered her. She failed an audition as a television presenter but went on to establish a glittering career as a dancer in the 1960s and 1970s, her heyday, when she danced for many politicians and visiting dignitaries. Anwar Sadat once called her "the Umm Kalthoum of dance," and American president Richard Nixon named her "Zagharit" when he learned that the word referred to an expression of joy. Her great rival was Nagwa Fouad, and each dancer's style offered a stark contrast: Fouad danced in cabaret spectaculars; Zaki's work was simple. She was the first dancer to interpret the revered songs of Umm Kalthoum—including *Inta Omri* (*You Are My Life*)—on a nightclub stage, and the singer's positive reaction to the performance helped spread Zaki's fame throughout the Arab world. She also danced at the weddings of each of the daughters of Gamal Abdel Nasser and Anwar Sadat. She retired in the 1980s during the period when society's view of dancing had turned negative, and the costumes were getting more conservative and less revealing. She teaches at the annual oriental dance school run in Cairo by Raqia Hassan.

Bibliography

Print Resources

Ali, Aisha. "The Dancers of Soliman: Adventures in Tunisia." *Habibi* 18, no. 2 (September 2000).

Alloula, Malek. *The Colonial Harem*. Trans. Myrna Godzich and Wlad Godzich. Minneapolis: University of Minneapolis Press, 1986.

al-Rawi, Rosina-Fawzia. *Belly Dancing: Unlock the Secret Power of an Ancient Dance*. New York: Interlink Books, 1999.

Amar, Paul. "Blame It on the Road." *Cairo Times*, 17–30 September 1998, vol. 2, no. 15.

Atia, Tarek. "Open Buffet." *al-Ahram Weekly*, 4–10 January 2001, no. 515.

"Beauty and the Beat." *al-Ahram Weekly*, 6 July 2000.

Bordieu, Pierre. *The Algerians*. Toronto: S. J. Reinauld Saunders, 1961.

Buonaventura, Wendy. *Serpent of the Nile: Women and Dance in the Arab World*. London: Saqi Books, 1994.

Campbell, Kay Hardy. "Loosening Their Tresses: Women's Dances of the Arabian Gulf and Saudi Arabia." *Habibi* 16, no. 3 (Fall 1997).

Capanzano, Vincent. *Tuhami: Portrait of a Moroccan*. Chicago: University of Chicago Press, 1980.

Darwish, Mustafa. *Dream Makers on the Nile*. Cairo: American University in Cairo Press, 1998.

Devichand, Mukul. "Foreign Moves." *al-Ahram Weekly*, 21–27 February 2002, no. 574.

Duff Gordon, Lucie. *Letters from Egypt*. London: Virago, 1986.

Ebers, Georg. *Egypt: Descriptive, Historical and Picturesque*. 2 vols. New York: Cassell, 1978–1979.

Father Anastis. "The Nawar or Gypsies of the East." *Journal of Gypsy Lore Society* (Edinburgh): 3, no. 4, 1913–1914.

Flaubert, Gustave. *Flaubert in Egypt*. Trans. Francis Steegmuller. London: Bodley Head, 1972.

Gellner, Ernest, and Charles Micaud, eds. *Arabs and Berbers: From Tribe to Nation in North Africa*. Lexington, Mass: D. C. Heath, 1972.

Geniesse, Jane Fletcher. *Passionate Nomad: The Life of Freya Stark*. New York: Random House, 1999.

Hassan, Fayza. "Beauty and the Beat." *al-Ahram Weekly*, 6–12 July 2000, no. 489.

Herodotus. *Histories, Book 2*.

Kearton, Cherry. *The Shifting Sands of Algeria*. London: Arrowsmith, 1924.

Klunzinger, C. B. *Upper Egypt: Its People and Its Products*. London: M. D. Blackie & Son, 1878.

Lane, Edward. *An Account of the Manners and Customs of the Modern Egyptians*. London: John Murray, 1860.

Mernissi, Fatima. *Dreams of Trespass: Tales of a Harem Girlhood*. New York: Perseus Publishing, 1993.

Morgan, Lawrence. *Flute of Sand: Experiences with the Mysterious Ouled Nail*. London: Odhams Press, 1956.

Nelson, Kristina. *The Art of Reciting the Qur'an*. Austin: University of Texas Press, 1985.

Olsen, Rovsing. *Chants et Danses de l'Atlas*. Arles: Actes Sud, 1999.

"Open Buffet." *al-Ahram Weekly*, 4–10 January 2001.

Penfield, Frederick Courtland. *Present-Day Egypt*. New York: Century, 1907.

Porch, Douglas. *The Conquest of Morocco*. New York: Fromm International, 1982.

Raafat, Samir. "From Badia to Abbas: Looking back on Giza's Riverside Drive." *Egyptian Mail*, November 18, 1995 (available at www.egy.com/landmarks).

Rakha, Youssef. "Dancing to the Rhythm of Time." *al-Ahram Weekly*, 23–29 September 1999, no. 448.

Richards, Tazz. *The Belly Dance Book: Rediscovering the Oldest Dance*. Concord, Calif.: Backbeat Press, 2000.

Rollow, Mardi. "The Tunisian Experience: Dress and Adornment in Tunisia." *Arabesque* 5, no. 1 (1979).

Ross, Heather Colyer. *The Art of Arabian Costume*. Fribourg: Arabesque-Commercial SA, 1981.

Saleh, Magda. "The Ghawazi of Egypt." *Arabesque* 19, no. 2 (1993).

Saud, Abeer Abu. *Qatari Women*. New York: Longman, 1984.

Smith, Donna L. "Morocco and Its Dances." *Arabesque* 8, nos. 3–4 (1982).

Soheir, Sami. "Nagwa Fouad: Hours of Glory." *al-Ahram Weekly*, 13–19 August 1998, no. 390.

St. John, Bayle. *Village Life in Egypt.* New York: Arno Press, 1973.

al-Torki, Soraya. *Women in Saudi Arabia.* New York: Columbia University Press, 1986.

van Nieuwkerk, Karin. *A Trade Like Any Other: Female Singers and Dancers in Egypt.* Cairo: American University in Cairo Press, 1996.

Warburton, Eliot. *Travels in Egypt and the Holy Land: The Crescent and the Cross.* Philadelphia: H. C. Peck & T. Bliss, 1859.

Weaver, Mary Anne. *A Portrait of Egypt: A Journey through the World of Militant Islam.* New York: Farrar, Straus and Giroux, 1999.

Westermarck, Edward. *Ritual and Belief in Morocco.* London: Macmillan, 1926.

Wilson, Albert. *Rambles in North Africa.* Boston: Little, Brown, 1926.

Zuhur, Sherifa, ed. *Images of Enchantment: Visual Performing Arts in the Middle East.* Cairo: American University in Cairo Press, 1998.

Web Sites

www.bdancer.com. Site run by a fan, with various tidbits and articles on belly dancing.

www.joyofbellydancing.com. "Yasmina's Belly Dance Page" offers useful information; site set up by an aficionado in Arizona.

www.belly-dance.org. "The Belly Dance Museum" site, which includes downloads of Gypsy dance music and photographs.

www.bellydance.org. The Web site of the International Academy of Middle Eastern Dance in California.

www.arab-esque.org. The Arab-Esque Dance Project, a German-based site with in-depth academic information on Middle East dance.

www.raqiahassan.net. Official site of the Cairo Oriental Dance Festival, run by Raqia Hassan.

www.discoverbellydance.com. A site where U.S. fans promote belly dancing in the States.

www.learn-to-belly-dance.com. U.S.-based site with good information on learning the dance and its history.

9

Consumerism

The Growth of Arab Consumer Cultures since the 1970s

In the past fifty years the Arab world has seen the increasing inroads of the Western model of mass consumer culture, to a degree that disturbs urban intellectuals. Egyptian historian Abdel-Wahhab al-Messiri told Abu Dhabi's *Mubdi'un* (*Creative People*) program that the West has become a monstrous consumer culture based on "Darwinist modernity which is against God, nature and the human being" (Abu Dhabi TV, June 2002). Writers argue that, as in the West, many aspects of life in the Arab world have been transformed into a commodity in today's market system and and globalization has only made this worse. Whether they are problematic land crossings, with cars overladen with clothes, electric appliances, and food, or airports with droves of air travelers, national borders see huge amounts of consumer goods transported for the sake of getting a bargain. Satellite television, shopping malls, the Internet—all have fed a consumer frenzy that shows no sign of letting up, even while economies shrink. The mobile phone has become the symbol of the new age, both glorified and lampooned in soap operas and TV ads as the ultimate sign of having made it in the merciless scramble to escape poverty and acquire the stuff of success. In some countries like Syria, security agencies were hesitant about introducing them at all, and Saudi Arabia's religious police are fretting that new digital camera technology in mobiles offers young people another means for surreptitious flirting in shopping malls. The dichotomies this accentuates are there for all to see: from the affluent Nile-side chic of Cairo's World Trade Center, Arcadia Mall, or glitzy new Conrad Hotel, one can look out onto the teeming, poor district of Bulaq al-Dakrour—scenes of wealth next to poverty that are repeated around the region, but at their starkest in Cairo. Poverty itself has been commodified. In Arabpop video clips, the poor are the backdrop for the shenanigans of the stars. In Egyptian singer Shaimaa Said's 2003 song *Khadny* (*He Took Me*), she and her boyfriend take a four-wheel drive to the desert outside Cairo. When he storms off after an argument, she returns on a donkey cart driven by an elderly peasant couple, lying among

Crowds in a Cairo market street. (Norbert Schiller/Focus MidEast)

the tomato crates in an elaborate dress and full makeup—a scenario that is almost impossible to imagine in real life.

Whole sections of Arab cities are monuments to a new consumer age. Dubai made an independent decision in the 1970s not only to Westernize but also to globalize; it invited nationals of the world to live and consume as they would at home, as long as they kept non-Islamic religious observance out of sight. The American military presence in the Gulf after the 1991 war, though largest in Saudi Arabia, had more of a social effect in Kuwait than anywhere else. Saudi Arabia was already a Westernized society with strong links to the United States and a well-entrenched consumer culture, where Western brand names were common. Kuwait also became Westernized when U.S. troops were in town, and their presence was all the more obvious in the

tiny state, while most Saudis hardly felt the presence of the military in their midst. Kuwait City looks like an American city, with American cafes and restaurants and, since just before the third Gulf war, a Virgin music store.

Beirut's downtown area, destroyed by the civil war, has been quickly revamped, but critics say the renewal lacks soul. What remained of elegant, European, colonial-era buildings and medieval souks was swept away, resulting in a spotless, reconstructed city center, where businesses relocate but where there is little warmth or surge of humanity except for overpriced boutiques, bars, and cafes that fill up in the evenings. What was a bustling city center gutted by war has become something akin to London's commercial district, the City. Beirutis even refer to the area as Solidere, the name of the company set up by Prime

Downtown Beirut. (Alison Wright/Corbis)

Minister Rafik Hariri to implement the project in 1992. According to Samir Khalaf in his 2002 study *Civil and Uncivil Violence in Lebanon*, the juxtaposition of neon restaurants and bars with empty-shell buildings, which invite speculators anticipating another boom, does no good for the psyche of a society recovering from war and disintegration, reinforcing a public mood of lethargy and disengagement. Urban redevelopment on a smaller scale is taking place in Cairo, where the commercial district in central Cairo has been pedestrianized with quaint period-piece lampposts, and plans are afoot to do the same to the heart of the original Islamic city of Cairo, the al-Azhar area, which is crammed with markets, artisans, mosques, cafes, and a labyrinth of alleyways. Property prices are expected to rocket as more businesses move in. Some are already

there, such as a fashionable interior design shop called al-Khatoun, which forms a model for the kind of aesthetically pleasing trendy business that the revamped district seeks to attract.

Many worry it could all go too far. Only a court order stopped Egypt's ministry of culture from allowing the construction of a five-star hotel inside the grounds of the Citadel. Critics, many of them foreign residents, say the underlying concept is to create a kind of voyeuristic timepiece for tourists to gawk at—something like the original London Crystal Palace Exhibition of 1850, except with real people living real lives. Ironically, from the nineteenth century up to the 1970s, sections of this large district were notorious as drug dens. Known as al-Batniya, it was immortalized as such in novels by Naguib Mahfouz. In the 1970s the film *al-Batniya*, which was

"Employing the Antiquities": "Pyramidiots" Beat Egypt at Its Own Game

Egypt's pyramids at Giza are the main attraction of its tourism industry and one of the country's key sources of revenue. (TRIP/Art Directors)

Egypt's ancient history adds up to big money, both for the state, which employs antiquities in its quest to derive tourist revenue, and for writers with newfangled ideas about their origins. Two authors have questioned conventional theory on the origins of the pyramids and ancient Egyptian civilization, enraging the Egyptology community around the world with best-selling books in Europe and America. Graham Hancock is the better known, via a string of titles that, as Britain's *The Guardian* newspaper says, have created a new literary genre of pop alternative history. The Scottish writer's "breakthrough to bestseller status," as his Web site (www.grahamhancock.com) says, came in 1992 with the publication of *The Sign and the Seal,* which tried to put flesh on the biblical story of the Ark of the Covenant. His foray into pyramidery began in 1995 with *Fingerprints of the Gods,* which has now sold more than three million copies.

Then in 1997 he put out in the United States *Keeper of Genesis: The Message of the Sphinx,* with coauthor Robert Bauval. Their central thesis is that Egyptology's consensus on the age of the Giza Pyramids is suspect and that the conventional figure of 4,500 years may be incorrect. "We are arguing that here are two scientific tools, astronomy and geology, against a rather dubious chronological system. As controversial as they may be, I'd rather look at these astronomical and geological arguments," Bauval said (interview with author, *Cairo Times,* 13 January 2000). Bauval realized that the positioning of Giza's three pyramids in a line and at an angle to the Nile River mirrors the three stars in the "belt" of the constellation Orion—as if ancients had consecrated the site according to the pattern of the night sky as they looked south toward Orion. But, according to star charts, that must have been 12,500 years ago. "When you investigate this site from an astronomical point of view, whether you like it or not, it spells out the date of 10,500 B.C.," Bauval said.

The pair have hinted at weirder things in their books, such as that there are unexplained pyramid-like structures on Mars and that the American space agency NASA has an "X-Files" determination to keep a lid on this fact (see *The Mars Mystery*). Zahi Hawass, an Egyptian Egyptologist and current head of the Supreme Council for Antiquities, has ferociously attacked Bauval, Hancock, and other alternative theorists as "pyramidiots." After much media scrutiny and academic criticism, they are now jettisoning the wackier stuff. "It was more an excursion into a different area of inquiry," Hancock said of the Mars idea. They may have been off the mark with some things, he argues, but they have succeeded in riling a secretive and elitist Egyptology community who are blocking new thinking on ancient Egypt. "Because of the overwhelming scientific ethic in Egyptology, we think the Egyptologists have blinded themselves to the true character of ancient Egyptian civilization. Because in our time people build gigantic structures to satisfy their own ego, because they're megalomaniacs, there's a feeling that the only reason why gigantic structures could have been built was to satisfy the egos of the pharaohs. But when you analyze this

The Pyramids of Giza in Cairo, Egypt. (Vanni Archive/Corbis)

closely, you find that it's simply an opinion on the part of Egyptologists, with nothing to substantiate it," Hancock said (interview with author, *Cairo Times*, 13 January 2000). Adds Bauval: "We have a problem. We start off in the Third and Fourth Dynasty with a fully blown culture, ready-made, with hieroglyphic texts, with the pyramids, with the knowledge and technology to raise monuments. Egyptologists will come and argue that there has been a process of development—which usually entails looking at the *mastaba* [stone-slab tomb] as a precursor to the pyramid. It's rubbish, I can tell you that. I'm a construction engineer, and you don't go from the *mastaba* to these kinds of monuments in a matter of one or two centuries. It makes more sense to see a much longer process of development than this simplistic view that is being given."

Graham Hancock (left) and Robert Bauval (right), the writers who popularized Egyptology with their books about the pyramids, but whom some experts attacked as "the pyramidiots." (Claude Stemmelin)

based on a Mahfouz novel, depicted the district in all its harshness, and as a result Sadat's wife Jihan launched a project to clean up the area. Restoration work in al-Batniya has stirred huge debate, with fears that the ministry of culture wants to turn old mosques into the Wahhabi-style, plain-marble structures of Saudi Arabia. The ministry thinks tourists prefer to see pristine, restored buildings rather than monuments that show their antiquity. It also argues that mosques should be fit for use as contemporary places of worship and not simply exist as historic buildings. Damascus has seen similar controversy over restoration work and the inexorable advance of concrete apartment blocks. Unlike in Cairo, most of Damascus's old buildings that once housed Turkish baths and caravanserai remain intact. The United Nations cultural organization UNESCO has named Damascus a world cultural heritage site, and in the 1970s Syria passed laws banning demolition inside the walls of the ancient city (though about two-thirds of historic buildings lie outside its walls).

Both new money and old money seek to separate themselves from the consuming masses through membership in elite groups and organizations, such as Algiers's Snobar Club and Egypt's Marina tourist area, both on the Mediterranean. Since the mid-1990s, Egypt has seen the sprouting of exclusive housing estates in empty, semidesert areas around the crowded capital, selling dreams of Americana with names like Beverly Hills, Palm Hills, and Dreamland. Even the holy month of Ramadan hasn't been saved. The traditional Ramadan lantern has been appropriated by rising commercialism as a symbol of the month-long festival of conspicuous consumption and festivity, in the same manner that the pine tree has come to represent the Western Christmas. Egypt has

Lovers steal a private moment by the Nile River. The river flows through Cairo, a dusty and overcrowded city. (Norbert Schiller/Focus MidEast)

led the way in commercializing Ramadan. Businessmen sponsor so-called mercy tables that offer free food at sunset to the poor or anyone else on the streets. Sometimes the food servers wear T-shirts with the name of the businessman who sponsored the meals. Some businessmen sponsor these meals to promote themselves in districts where they seek election in parliamentary polls. "Although the history of social responsibility in Egypt has always known a degree of conspicuous consumption and self-interest like this, it wasn't the predominant trend unlike today. Help from the privileged to the needy was done more in private than public, unlike what we see today in the Ramadan mercy tables," wrote political analyst Wahid Abdel-Meguid (*al-Hayat*, 3 December 2002). Governments have to stock up on sugar and wheat supplies in advance of the orgy of consumption that runs from dusk to dawn over twenty-eight days. Sales of dried fruit, nuts, and sweets skyrocket, as do hours of TV-watching. Advertising increases as consumerism adopts, molds, and expands the customs attached to the month. A barrage of television ads come before, during, and after prime-time soap operas, offering cash prizes for callers who correctly predict the outcome of the plots. The calls cost a fortune, and clerics have attacked the schemes as a form of gambling. Since the meltdown in Southeast Asia and political violence in the Middle East, many companies have invested heavily in spending on Ramadan. State-of-the-art, high-tech ads plug fancy hotel and tourist complexes, but they fail to mention where these hotels are, or that they are not yet built: the idea is to give banks an impression of success in order to secure loans. When Muslims break their daily fast during the holy month of Ramadan, dates are a part

Mount Sinai in Egypt, a tourist attraction in the wilderness of the Sinai where St. Catherine's Monastery is located. (TRIP/Art Directors)

of every *iftar* meal. Now dates come in myriad shapes and sizes and are sold with appealing names—the titles of classical Arabic songs, or even "Osama bin Laden," as in Cairo's markets in November 2001. Muslim tradition says the Prophet himself broke his fast with dates and water, so that's what millions of Arabs do. At the same time, Ramadan offers a chance for mass cultural reaffirmation in the face of the stream of foreign values perceived to be swamping Arab life during the rest of the year. Some state televisions take many foreign (non-Arab) pop videos and films off the air for the duration of the month.

The march of mass consumerism in the twentieth century has helped change the rural landscape: in countries with large

The Battle to Preserve the Past in Saudi Arabia

Saudi Arabia is struggling to preserve pockets of ancient architecture threatened by the relentless onslaught of modern construction. The rush to modernity has rendered old traditions in urban areas almost obsolete, such as in the Hejaz cities on the West Coast. Most of the country has been rebuilt after sudden oil wealth filled state coffers in the 1970s. In the face of that flood, the ancient Hejaz cities of Jeddah, Mecca, and Medina are struggling to save their unique heritage. In extreme cases, old towns built on ancient oases, such as Khaibar and al-Ula, with their labyrinthine alleys and mud-brick, palm-roofed homes, stand abandoned after residents moved to adjacent new communities in the 1970s. "It was a fashion to leave the old houses after the oil boom. People were moving all the way up to the late 1980s. Laborers moved into some [houses] as tenants, others were abandoned, and some fell down," said Sami Nawwar, the head of a government project to renovate Jeddah's old quarters (interview with author, April 2003).

Architecture in Jeddah is part of a tradition in the Red Sea region, which encompasses the Egyptian and Sudan coast on the west side and Yemen to the south of the Hejaz. Buildings lie in narrow alleys running north-south and east-west in order to utilize sea winds, but their walls along the alleyways jut out at angles to create shadows that lessen the effects of summer heat and sun. The houses are also constructed with large stone slabs to provide natural air-conditioning. Buildings have wooden balcony structures called *roshans,* with intricate woodwork (called *manqour* in the Hejaz and *mashrabiya* in Egypt), which gives mottled shade on the inside and protects the women from the view of outsiders. But no one is interested in this form of architecture anymore. It's expensive and doesn't meet the needs of a booming population, and developers are swamping Saudi cities with pristine apartment blocks and villas. "We

Traditional architecture stands among modern buildings in the Saudi coastal city of Jeddah where the kingdom's strict customs are more relaxed. (Scott Peterson/Liaison/ Getty Images)

eat from a freezer, we live in a freezer, we write in a freezer, we ride in a freezer," laments Jeddan architect Sami Angawi, who has built a stunning villa mixing old Hejazi and new styles (interview with author, Reuters, 22 April 2003). The house has an austere, well-protected view of a castle on the outside, giving way to an open interior where four stories of rooms surround a central courtyard flooded by natural light from a glass ceiling. "Islamic civilization is all about balance and we have to rediscover that. Architecture is a reflection of society and is its outer expression," he said.

Old buildings in Mecca are currently set for demolition as part of plans to increase the city's

A sign directing potential customers to an American fast-food restaurant competes for attention on the skyline with a local mosque in Amman, Jordan. (Norbert Schiller/Focus MidEast)

ability to absorb pilgrims in the hajj season, when some two million Muslims converge there. Previous renovations to expand the central mosque have resulted in the demolition of Mecca's old district, and American fast-food restaurants, commercial towers, and luxury hotels have taken their place. "Mecca and Medina are the most disturbed cities in the world in every sense. They are totally out of balance. New buildings are coming up and the skyline of Mecca will be like the skyline of New York," Angawi said (interview with author, Reuters, 22 April 2003). The key to understanding why the Saudi authorities engage in this activity, Angawi contends, is the tribal and fundamentalist ethos of the state. Ancient shrines are viewed with suspicion because ordinary folk come to venerate deceased holy figures. In Wahhabi ideology, this practice is tantamount to a perversion of the central, monotheistic message of Islam. Religious police have acted in tandem with the ministry of religious affairs to demolish places where locals believe the Prophet prayed, lived, or visited. Angawi claims to have excavated in the early 1990s what he thinks was the Prophet's home in Mecca. The authorities wanted to hush up the discovery to avoid a rush of pilgrims to the site, he said.

There is at least a national debate about these issues now. According to mainstream religious thinking, those lobbying for the preservation of religious sites were motivated by "devilish thoughts brought on by hopeless emotion," in the words of religious scholar Sheikh Saleh al-Haseen. Haseen wrote in a daily paper that "Islamic legal scholars have never talked about 'reviving monuments' in Mecca, except those God approved of: the Great Mosque and others which are part of pilgrimage rites. Neither the Prophet's companions nor anyone who came after them used to visit the alleged birthplace of the Prophet, because the Prophet didn't tell them to" (*al-Madina*, March 2003).

peasant populations, villagers in regular contact with big cities have accumulated and amassed goods. With nation-states groaning from population growth, manners are not what they used to be, simply because of the crush of people one has to deal with in everyday life. Today's Arab societies loudly proclaim the need to hold on to traditions in the face of an increasingly interconnected world that threatens to smother old, unique ways. In the last fifty years, these communities have gone through unprecedented change, more than at any other period in history and at a pace

A billboard advertises perfume. (Barry Iverson/Time Life Pictures/Getty Images)

that seems to have left society confused and running to catch up. Amman and Riyadh have been transformed from small Bedouin communities into expanding modern cities. Saudi novelist Abdel-Rahman Munif (who died in January 2004 in Damascus) even had his passport revoked for critiquing the country's overnight move from rough desert living to air-conditioned urban heaven in his series, *Cities of Salt*.

In Egypt, the biggest country, people are wondering, to quote the title of a recent book by economist Galal Amin, "whatever happened to the Egyptians?" (Amin 2001). Other Arabs marvel at the proportions of life in Egypt today. Viewed through the lens of Egypt's ubiquitous soap operas, people from Bahrain to Tripoli wonder how Cairenes manage to live in their choking

metropolis. Were it not for UNESCO intervention to stop a ring-road in their midst, the pyramids today would stand in the middle of a Cairo slum district. As it is, the sphinx faces fast-food restaurants, and the neighborhood of Nazlat al-Saman is only several dozen meters away. In a city whose population of at least 12 million rises to more than 16 million each working day due to commuters, a half million people live in an old tomb complex dubbed "the city of the dead," and one group of Christian migrants from the south live amidst the city's garbage, which they collect to make a living. Known as the *zabbaleen*, some of them are extremely wealthy despite appearances. Nearby, the elite resort community of Katamiya Heights is charging around $165 for a round of golf on reclaimed desert land. Cognizant of the changes wrought upon them, Egyptians today experience nostalgia, even for the not-so-distant time before the republic came into being in 1952. The old, landed gentry is still around, though in fewer numbers and with less visibility: one of the aims of Nasser's revolutionary government was to end their domination of Egyptian society. Dramas featuring fez-wearing pashas and courtly ladies in regal villas now fill the television screens, though the tradition of wearing a fez has yet to make a comeback. It is still worn by some men in Tunisia and Libya. Cairo's old elites—now a minority in a city originally built for three million but now swamped by rural migrants and their ways—fret over the changes in Egyptian life. "The Bedouin are being settled, the Nile bridged and dammed, and the ancient songs and stories are being forgotten," wrote Tori Haring-Smith in *Colors of Enchantment: Theater, Dance, Music, and the Visual Arts of the Middle East* (Zuhur

In a period of three decades Dubai has transformed itself into a modern city of skyscrapers. (Ludovic Maisant/Corbis)

2002). If it wasn't for Hassan Geretly's troupe, traditional theater would have died with its last practitioners. Similarly, realizing that an entire musical heritage is in danger of being lost, a few Egyptians are trying to recover old recordings stored by individuals and institutes in order to preserve dead forms that had lasted for centuries, such as the *zaffat al-arousa* wedding song (according to researcher Heba Farid, interview with author, June 2003).

Aware that the global context places a premium on local cultures, governments are offering up their countries as objects for consumption. Egypt and Tunisia heavily promote themselves as destinations for mass Western tourism, attempting to turn themselves into Gulf-style rentier states, but seeking rents from tourism instead of oil. Egypt and Morocco have been tradi-tional favorites for wealthy Saudis, with the royal family having a penchant for Morocco in particular. Syria, Lebanon, and Jordan are going more for the cultural tourism market. Wealthy Gulf states like Qatar and Dubai, and even Saudi Arabia, want to attract tourists too. Mecca now has an exclusive hotel called Burj Zamzam—towering over the central mosque and heavily advertised on al-Arabiya—where you pay the world for a view of the *Kaaba*. Dubai, already a major tourist and financial center, has embarked on a spree of hotel construction, and the barren peninsula of Qatar, trying to catch up with its savvy Gulf cousin, is promoting itself on CNN as "once seen, never forgotten" and "preserved for you." Luxury golf courses and other five-star sports facilities set the standard for the ambitions of these Gulf states.

A fourth tier of countries like Oman and Sudan are carefully planning to attract niche markets of tourists through marketing cultural diversity. "The world is developing an interest in Sudan. We have 580 tribes and 120 dialects, all intercommunicating in the Arabic language. This cultural diversity is an attraction," said minister of state for culture and tourism Siddiq Mujtaba (interview with author, Reuters, 22 August 2002). "But we want tourism with our own values. The government does not compromise between social values and economic objectives of the country: then you are losing because you are not marketing your nation or your heritage. Our country has its own traditions. There are millions of tourists per year in Iran, where they don't have wine or the other things of Western tourism—we don't want drunken tourists." The Arabic word for tourism, *siyaha*, has the connotation in Sudan of a traveling sheikh who spreads Islam through his piety. The country has a lot to offer: Sudan boasts one of the most stunning coral reefs in the world, off the east coast near the town of Port Sudan, as well as the unique Nubian culture of the north. Sudan is betting that an end to the civil war will bring in tourist money. Since September 11, when wealthy Gulf Arabs began to feel unwelcome in the West, inter-Arab tourism has picked up, and Egypt, Lebanon, Jordan, and Syria all hope for a new influx of Arab tourists.

The Growth of Arab Advertising since the 1990s

In terms of global standards, the advertising industry is still underdeveloped, but that doesn't mean there's not much advertising. On the contrary, in many countries advertisements bombard the consumer at every turn, with billboards, TV commercials, and soap operas that slip into ad breaks so that the viewer hardly notices. Despite the economic and political problems plaguing the region at present, advertising markets are set to grow in the coming years. Israel's total annual spending on advertising is over one billion dollars, which is only matched by Saudi Arabia's expenditures. Arab advertisers count all advertising spent on the pan-Arab satellite channels, such as al-Jazeera, al-Arabiya, and MBC, in the total annual spending figures for Saudi Arabia, since the vast majority of advertisers on these channels are aiming at the Saudi television audience, where there is about 70 percent satellite penetration among a population of over 20 million. This population has far higher per capita spending power than Egypt, where, despite a population three times larger than Saudi Arabia, per capita income is lower and annual spending on advertising is roughly half that of the kingdom. Alongside Saudi Arabia, the UAE and Lebanon are the most sophisticated advertising markets, with globalized promotion values and a style of execution that in Lebanon are generally not censored for political or sexual content. In Saudi Arabia, advertisers must blur human faces on billboards, because the religious establishment views that showing the human form is *haram*. There have been instances of banning images of tea being passed with the left hand, the hand traditionally reserved for the toilet (Karim Younes of Starcom, interview with author, April 2003). Yet in all three of these countries, the industry is left largely to its own devices. In socialist hangover states like Egypt and Syria, on the other hand, government bodies dominate the in-

Cigarettes Big in the Arab World

Hardly an Arabic film exists without a chain-smoking lead character, whose tobacco habit is presented as an intrinsic part of his or her attractiveness to the viewer. Directors argue that they are only reflecting real life, but antismoking campaigners say the movies are exaggerating, distorting, and encouraging the habit. In most countries television can't advertise cigarettes, while print media can, but the indirect advertising of films and soaps heavily undercuts these restrictions. Egypt has the region's largest number of smokers, at least 12 million smokers out of a population of 70 million. Campaigners consider that *shisha* (narghile, or flavored tobacco smoked through a water-filtered pipe) has become a new epidemic in the region, and one that is popular with middle-class young women in Cairo, Amman, Damascus, and Beirut. Traditionally, the most *shisha* a woman would smoke would be a few puffs to prepare the pipe for her husband. "Nowadays they'd smoke the whole lot," said World Health Organization official Fatima al-Awwa (interview with author, December 2001). Religious authorities in Saudi Arabia and Egypt have begun to speak out against smoking. In 2001 Saudi Arabia declared Mecca and Medina, sites of Islam's holiest shrines, as "tobacco-free zones." Hundreds of thousands of pilgrims will return home from these sites having seen antismoking messages. Egypt's highest religious authorities have issued fatwas saying smoking is Islamically forbidden. Governments are also acting, banning smoking in many public buildings, though Egypt's government is hampered by the fact that it owns the country's main tobacco manufacturer, whose virtual monopoly ensures regular profits.

dustry. Social customs that see everyone copying whatever is seen as successful have led to a whole generation in Egypt that sells products with dancing girls bopping to Arabpop jingles. This style has traveled to most other Arab television, creating what advertising moguls call a "jingle jungle." In Egypt during Ramadan, the viewer will see ad-industry guru Tarek Nour, whose Americana has dominated the sector for three decades, selling TVs, fridges, mobile phones, luxury flats, and fizzy drinks, plus asking viewers to donate money to kids with cancer, all within the space of ten minutes.

But the spread of satellites showing foreign ads means viewers are beginning to know and appreciate a good ad when they see one. Plus, multinational companies have moved into the region and have used expertise found mainly in Lebanon and the Gulf to bring advertising standards more in line with global norms. Up until a few years ago, ads in the Gulf were thought up by Lebanese, Pakistani, Indian, and Filipino expats, who might also star in them, and many ads were simply foreign versions with Arabic dubbing. Now you see men in dishdashas (white robe worn in the Gulf) and women in headscarves all the time as part of a trend of specialization in the Arab region. As trade barriers slowly come down, local services and industries that perhaps never advertised before are having to get in on the act to fight competition from abroad. In Egypt, mobile phone and cola wars are being fought with huge sums of money shelled out to pop stars and actors to plug products. The International Advertising Association held its annual conference of 2002 in Lebanon. But as a sign of the intellectual scorn that consumerism still provokes, Jordanian columnists last year attacked companies for the large amounts of money they spent on advertising during tough times for the economy. Advertisers retorted that this sort of commercial activity keeps the economy turning.

Rising anti-Americanism is also affecting advertising, but sparking creativity as much as smothering it. Egypt's Americana, set up in the 1970s after all things American became the rage with Sadat's opening up (*infitah*) to the West, now signs off its ads on television with the phrase "100 percent Arab." A whole host of products and services are being touted on different Arab television channels as possessing "Arab authenticity" (*al-asaala al-arabiyya*). British supermarket chain Sainsbury had to close down newly opened megastores in Egypt after persistent rumors throughout 2001 that it was "pro-Israeli," which affected sales. Throughout the region Coca-Cola, Pepsi, and McDonald's have suffered for their American identity (in Syria they are not present at all), and even Procter & Gamble was hit because its major product, Ariel, bears the same name as the Israeli prime minister elected in February 2001.

Traditional Weddings in the Consumerist Era

Weddings among the wealthy have become hugely expensive affairs for both Muslims and Christians, and costs have also become prohibitive for lower-income social groups. The trend among elites is to stage a lavish orgy of conspicuous consumption in a five-star hotel, with an entertainment list including singers famous and not so famous, per-haps more than one belly dancer, and a luxurious buffet. In fact, weddings are a major source of income for Arab singers, who command huge rates to turn up and may squeeze three or four weddings into an evening. In Damascus, expensive weddings—the subject of a social anthropological study by Nancy Lindisfarne Tapper—are an art form for affluent and influential families. In one example from 1995, a television director was hired to stage a wedding at the Sheraton Hotel in which the bride rode into the central procession, or *zaffa*, on a camel. Palestinian writer Edward Said bitterly criticized the conspicuous consumption at Palestinian elite weddings, especially among officials of the Palestinian Authority, under continuing Israeli occupation. Marriage has become so expensive in the United Arab Emirates that many men are marrying foreign women instead, usually Indians or Iranians. Costs have soared to around $100,000, despite 1998 laws that fine families for overly lavish weddings and restrict dowries to $10,000 maximum. A government fund was set up in 1992 to lend around $20,000 to men of limited means to help them get married and to discourage them from turning to foreign women. At the same time, Emirate women also turn to foreigners, fearing the strict social customs that men are likely to force on them, which could tie them to family life at an early stage before they have developed a career. The UAE's indigenous population numbers less than one million, around one-third of the total, and entire sections of its cities are built by and for foreign nationals, mainly Pakistanis, Indians, Filipinos, other Arabs, and Britons. So while the government wants to keep the foreigners to maintain the UAE's international status and affluence, it desperately wants to preserve Emirati purity and ensure it doesn't lose control of its own country.

In Egypt, weddings have always been loud and rambunctious affairs. In crowded lower-class districts, street weddings are usually the order of the day, involving belly dancers, singers with a traditional band pumping out *shaabi* music, and dancing in the streets. It will go on for hours into the night, and throughout it all the bride and groom will sit on two thronelike chairs on a platform, paraded before the crowds. More city customs include a nighttime ride by car through the city with horn-blowing to announce the marriage, before stopping on one of the road bridges over the Nile for a midnight souvenir photograph. In most Arab societies, social customs are demanding. First there is the engagement party, where the groom presents the bride with a wedding present of jewelry called the *shabka*, which can be anything from a ring

to a whole set of necklaces, earrings, and other accessories, forming part of the basic haggling a prospective groom must go through with the lady's family. The groom is also expected to provide a flat for the couple, though they usually share furniture costs. These days middle- and upper-class families film the entire proceedings, or even show footage of the bride and groom when they were younger. In Saudi Arabia, these wedding parties have become single-sex affairs, with the men in one room and the women in another. This is a modern religious innovation that runs counter to local customs in many areas, such as the more liberal west coast region of Saudi Arabia known as the Hejaz.

The visit to the hairdresser is crucial for women, and in many societies the bride has elaborate henna patterns painted on her arms and feet. Henna is a paste made from the leaves of the henna plant and used to

Moroccan women mixing henna before applying it in intricate designs to the hands and feet of a bride before a wedding. (Michelle Garrett/Corbis)

dye hair as well as to tattoo decorations on women. The patterns and mix of the henna vary from region to region. The Arab world mainly uses large floral patterns limited to hands and feet, while in India the entire arm can be covered in paisley patterns. Both use a reddish-brown color, while in sub-Saharan Africa black is the preferred color. Henna itself is a small shrub called *Lawsonia inermis* (also known as al-Khanna, Mehndi, and Egyptian privet), which grows throughout the middle zone of Africa and Asia, from Morocco through Malaysia. The leaves, flowers, and twigs of the plant are ground into a fine powder and then mixed with hot water. Leaves of other plants—indigo, tea, coffee, cloves, lemon—can be added to give different colors, plus sugar and oil to make sure the patterns don't immediately wash away. This powder mix is sieved through a nylon cloth, at which point industrial chemicals might also be added if it's for mass consumption and sale in shops.

The Internet's Slow Advance in the Arab Region

The huge space that the Internet has occupied in public consciousness is grossly disproportionate to the very weak penetration of the information and communication network in the Arab region. Governments and ruling elites fear that the Internet is a conduit for spreading political and moral subversion, and this fear has dominated the discourse on the use of the technology. The wicked power of the Internet was heavily present in the 1999 Yousef Chahine film *The Other* (*al-Akhar*), where actress Nabila Ebeid is presented as an American computer-whiz mom who uses cyber prowess to track her son's movements and his romantic attachments with women. According to the measure provided by *New York Times* columnist Thomas Friedman—that "the more installed bandwidth your country has, the greater its degree of connectivity"—the region scores badly (Friedman 1999). According to the UNDP's Arab Human Development Report, Arabs represent 0.5 percent of Internet users, but 5 percent of the world's population. In 2002 even Lebanon had only an estimated 90,000 Internet subscribers and 250,000 users. "The Arab region does not score too badly with respect to telephone lines and personal computers per thousand people, but it ranks last with respect to web sites and Internet users," the report said. Way ahead of any other Arab country in number of Web sites and users is the tiny United Arab Emirates, with its Dubai Internet City that has attracted leading international companies and provided Dubai with a sophisticated information network covering homes, schools, and businesses, but it is aimed primarily at foreign businesses. Egypt has up to 500,000 users, though the figure is set to reach over 2.5 million by 2006. Iraqis had only selective access to the Internet before the fall of the Baath regime in 2003, when it was hugely popular for offering a window on a closed world. Internet cafes are crammed with people reading newspapers online, finding out about new technologies, and following sports news.

But control mechanisms are never absent. The UAE allows only one service provider, which blocks access to sites deemed by the government to be socially, politically, or religiously unacceptable, but its filters can be rather arbitrary—a word-based search may prevent access to sites containing words like "Sussex," and while the user can enter the site of Israeli daily *Haaretz*, some of its pages won't open. Saudi Arabia is the strictest of all, blocking access to sites with criticism of the royal family. Many access Jordanian servers to get easy access to political information, pornography, and extremist Islamic Web sites. Oman, where fear of foreigners busting local values is equally strong, has a ban on all free e-mail sites like hotmail, forcing users to access them through illegal and very slow proxy servers. Tunisia and Egypt have prosecuted people for placing sexual and political information on the Net that governments didn't like. Egypt is one of the Arab countries that prides itself on its free Web access, choosing not to turn off the tap. But a special police task force apprehends men and women using the Web to seek or advertise sex. A lightweight site called *dabboor* ("hornet") was forced by its server to close down a section on insults in colloquial Arabic, and the son of celebrated Egyptian playwright and poet Naguib Sorour was given a one-year prison sentence in 2002 for publishing an infamous anti-regime poem that makes inventive use of colloquial Arabic swearwords—a no-no in print, television, and cinema. The poem was a passionate expression of the rage that gripped people after the 1967 defeat, aimed at a regime that demanded the sacrifice of civil liberties for nothing in return. Using Egyptian slang, it ripped into the "prostitution" of Sadat's pro-West policies and corrupt rule, as well as hypocrisy and nepotism in intellectual circles (themes repeated and expanded upon, albeit in higher language, by the late, celebrated Syrian poet Nizar Qabbani in his controversial poem *Mata Yu'linun Wafaat al-Arab?* or *When Will They Announce the Death of the Arabs?*, published in *al-Hayat* in 1994). Sorour himself was never hauled in over the poem, yet his son—who remains in self-imposed exile in Russia, where he has nationality—suffered two years after posting it on a Web site based in the United States. The site, www.wadada.net, now has audio files of the poem and English, French, and Russian translations. "Arab regimes are scared to death of the pan-Arab cyber-unity," Sorour's son Shohdy wrote in an e-mail contact with the *Cairo Times* (*Cairo Times*, 17 October 2002). "The Arabs have not yet known any efficient dissident movement and are on the verge of finding out that their regimes are helpless in the face of this new threat." Critics of this rigorous Internet policing say the obsession with maintaining a certain form of moral society is intimately linked to a sense of subjugation to the West, and a desire to claim superiority despite that fact. Acknowledging obscenity "might lead to the wicked suggestion that our cultural superiority to the West is essentially based in hypocrisy," leftist writer Hani Shukrallah wrote (*al-Ahram Weekly*, 29 August 2002). "Our region may be on the brink of disaster, our economy is in shambles, we've never been as maligned and humiliated, but, hey, we remain as chaste as the driven snow. The late Naguib Sorour, his voice echoing from the grave, begged to differ, rather graphically."

Government fears have proved to be something of a self-fulfilling prophecy. In reaction to the suppression, a subversive youth Internet culture is emerging. Web chatrooms in Arabic are a forum for saying all the nasty things about Arab rulers that can't be said in public (particularly political jokes concerning Tunisia and prewar Iraq). "With Arabic websites and Arab issues, the internet is important since it offers breathing space for freedoms in light of the blackout imposed on frank and open expression of opinion under the current authorities," wrote one writer in the *al-Hayat* newspaper (*al-Hayat*, 3 October 2002). The Internet is forming a minirevolution, a version of the wider one that took place with Arabic satellite television. All sorts of repressed, hidden debates and sociopolitical groups have been afforded space, from arguments over who built the pyramids to Islamist politics to belly dancing.

Islam has scored big through the Internet. There are numerous Islamic Web sites, and one of the biggest and most successful is www.IslamOnline.net (an English-language site, overseen by Sheikh Yousef al-Qaradawi and other scholars, it represents the Islamic mainstream), set up in Qatar and Cairo in 1999, and which now has around 2.8 million hits a day for news and religious views on Islam and Islamic countries. Islamist radical groups have also made use of Web sites, although there's no sign yet that the Internet will do for bin Laden what cassette tapes did for Ayatollah Khomeini in Iran. Radical Islamists who in 2003 launched an insurgency against the Saudi monarchy in the name of al-Qa'ida launched a parallel propaganda war on the Internet in 2004. They and their supporters filled the chatrooms of popular Islamic Web sites (islah.net, qal3ati.net, alsaha.net) with reports of the campaign against foreign forces and allied governments in Iraq, Afghanistan, and Saudi Arabia. The Saudi group launched a monthly Web magazine called *Sawt al-Jihad* (*Voice of the Holy War*), and groups in Iraq such as the Tawhid and Jihad Group (headed by Jordanian Abu Musab al-Zarqawi) joined the fray with their own Web site with postings carrying videotapes of the murder of foreign hostages and audiotapes of sermons by their leaders. The chatroom strings even carried links to Web pages with training manuals on bomb-making, weapons handling, and how to stage an assassination. The groups with their own sites have had to engage in a game of hide-and-seek with Internet providers, but there is too much space in the vastness of the World Wide Web to keep them down. On occasion they have been known to choose an innocuous chatroom of, say, an Arabic music site to announce a kidnapping or murder of a hostage, then simply wait for a sympathizer to find the statement and post it in the regular Islamist chatrooms for the world to see. In general, political Islam in the Arab world, led by educated professionals such as doctors, lawyers, and engineers, has quickly made use of modern technology. Egypt's Muslim Brotherhood, a bastion of modern Islamism, is the best example. When the government first began a new crackdown against them in 1995, Egypt's interior ministry would relay breathless reports to the state press listing the computer equipment uncovered among the allegedly radical pamphlets and books that police seized at the homes of Muslim Brothers during their meetings—showing paranoia over what one paper termed the "Cyber Brother" (*Middle East Times*, December 1995). Compared with the government, Islamists seem more attuned to the modern world, a continuing element of their appeal to young people.

Fashion, Waistlines, and Plastic Surgery

Fashion around the region diverges dramatically. Western and Islamic fashion exist side by side, and both have their hierarchies. The elites of Beirut, Cairo, Tunis, and Rabat are at the forefront of Western fashion. The Gulf excels in Islamic fashions for women, while Egypt is home to lower-class conservative dressing. Bedouin and rural fashions are becoming hip among educated classes throughout the region—usually with silver jewelry—in the same way that ethnic dressing is fashionable in the West. Lebanon has a number of respected designers, such as Ziad Nakad, Elie Saab, Robert Abi Nader, Georges Chakra (who dresses members of the Saudi royal family), Georges Hobeika, and Zuheir Murad, and some of them have established reputations in Paris; there is even a Saudi designer in Paris, Yehya al-Bashary. Actress Halle Berry accepted her Best Actress Academy Award (Oscar) in 2002 in a sweeping burgundy gown created by Lebanese designer Saab (although Lebanese fashion is often criticized internationally for an abundance of golden embroidery and flashy baubles). Women in entertainment operate in a diverse and complex environment, from liberal Lebanon to ultra-conservative Saudi Arabia where women must veil and cannot sing in public. In general, they must try to steer a middle course with their appearance between the choices presented by ascendant political Islam and the West. The well-dressed young presenters on Lebanon's Zein channel include a woman with short orange hair and earrings—prohibited elsewhere in the region. Lebanon has a recognized place in the Arab world as the testing ground for how the latest Western trends will be received in the region. Like anywhere else, pop stars and actors have become the setters of trends. Singers like Amr Diab, Nawal al-Zoghby, and Mohammed Mounir have sent millions of youth down a particular path of fashion, though the degree to which public figures become role models is obscured by a lack of statistical information and prejudice against youth culture. Syrian singer Asala, for example, presents a liberal aesthetic with conservative trimmings. "I've always tried to be moderate. I wear the same style of clothes of most girls in the Arab world and I don't wear a veil," she said ("Sultry Arab Singer Defends Self from Slurs," Reuters, 15 May 2004).

Women's attire has become highly politicized for Muslims since the 1970s, though there are many reasons for women donning the veil. A burgeoning young population means more men hassling women. Many institutions and communities will show more respect to a veiled woman than to an uncovered woman. State television in countries like Morocco, Algeria, Tunisia, Egypt, Syria, and Iraq promote unveiled women as a sign of modernity. The Hizbollah-run al-Manar TV station glories in women newscasters with white veils sharply formed in the shape of Israel/Palestine, and one can expect something similar if Jordan's Muslim Brotherhood succeeds in obtaining a TV license from the authorities in Amman. Veils are also big business, with shops specializing in Islamic attire all over the region. But in themselves they do not mean chastity. The veil has become a fashion accessory among elite urban youth in places like Cairo, worn above jeans and accompanied by makeup smuggled out of the house in handbags behind father's back but with mother's consent. The veil can provide a convenient cover for groups of girls to flirt on streets, in shopping malls, on sea promenades, or in any of the trendy middle-class *shisha* cafes in capitals like Beirut and Cairo. In Saudi Arabia women must appear in public with black cloaks and hoods (the *abeya*) and face the prospect of religious police hassling them to

A nightclub in the Egyptian tourist resort of Hurghada. (The Cover Story/Corbis)

cover up properly if they don't stick to the rules, but they still manage to surreptitiously exchange telephone numbers with men in shopping malls. Despite the strict rules on attire, fashion, clothes, jewelry, and makeup are major industries in Saudi Arabia. Retailers estimate that Kuwait, a sprawl of six-lane motorways, gleaming skyscrapers, and futuristic-looking towers without bars or nightclubs, is one of the biggest consumers of luxury items per person in the world, with women spending around $500 to $800 a month on perfume and beauty products alone. Competition among women in the fashion game is strong, and few Saudi women really complain about having to appear in public in black robes, which impose a kind of cease-fire in public space among women, rather like the theory often proffered by schools in the West for enforcing school uniforms. In Cairo, a shocked tabloid once revealed nefarious activities by veiled women in the

relative privacy of the backseats of air-conditioned public buses, while most poor folks cram into ramshackle, cheaper alternatives. "Unfortunately, young people of both sexes have exploited this aircondi-tioned bus for romantic trysts on the back seat. These youth love-seats are witnessing shocking and extremely inappropriate scenes that require the immediate interference of the morality police," *al-Khamis* said (7 September 2000). Jewelry is accorded great value in Arab culture, particularly gold. Bahrain has the region's biggest gold market, with close competition from Dubai. Gold has always been popular in the Gulf region and in Arab tribal society in general, and the preference has transferred to lower-class groups in urban Arab societies. Kilos of jewelry will be presented by men as gifts for a woman's hand in marriage. But urban elites and middle and upper classes in those urban societies, such as Beirut and Cairo, don't have the gold obsession. Men outside affluent Gulf society are also less inclined toward gold because of Islamic traditions that see silk and gold as inappropriate for men—they opt instead for silver or white-gold engagement and wedding rings. Silver isn't popular among men or women in the Gulf because it's seen as a poor second to more expensive gold, and diamonds and precious stones are only popular as a part of the gold jewelry. In North Africa, elaborate wedding dresses threaded with gold are made locally for weddings, while the upper classes in the Mashreq prefer to buy dresses from abroad. Perfumes are also hugely popular and involve ancient traditions. Apart from the modern manufactured versions imported from the West, men and women use an array of local perfumes, including sandalwood, amber, jasmine, rose, and fruit extracts.

Lebanon hosts numerous beauty pageants, even one for Miss Lebanon Abroad, tapping into the large expat community around the world, while Egypt tries to keep up with it, despite vocal opposition from Islamists in parliament and the press. In another era and another time, Egypt actually won Miss World in 1954: the lucky lady, Antigone Constanda, hailed from the country's Jewish and Greek communities and now lives in Athens. Fashion consciousness has been a feature of affluent Lebanese society for most of the twentieth century but it reached new heights after the civil war ended in 1990. Perhaps emerging from the fifteen-year experience with an emboldened desire to live for the moment, Lebanese women have made plastic surgery the norm in Lebanese society, even among teenage girls still at school. Beirut saw an art exhibition in 1999 featuring plaster casts of large, bulbous Lebanese noses

A stage show at the Babylon Festival in Iraq in the 1990s. (Norbert Schiller/Focus MidEast)

in an effort to defend what its organizers said was an endangered species amidst the craze for the perfect nose. In 1965, the Lebanese Society of Plastic, Reconstructive, and Aesthetic Surgery had six surgeons; today it has over forty. Other facial fashions of the moment in Lebanon include "face peeling" (il-peeling) to achieve a shiny white complexion; lifting the skin by the sides of the eyes to give a sexy, feline look; adding bone to cheeks and chins for additional felinity; hair implants; pumping up lips; and dyeing hair blonde to look European. This look has become the norm for television presenters, pop stars, and actresses. Tunisian presenter Kawthar al-Bishrawy, who walked out of al-Jazeera over the scant regard given to her cultural affairs show, has attacked the bimbo-presenter phenomenon in the Arabic press: "I'm shocked to the heart when I see the huge amount of female presenters compet-

ing to wear fashion which exposes themselves, colored contact lenses and dyed
hair. Worst of all is the kisses and winks"
(*Rose al-Yousef*, 20 December 2002). It's a
radical shift in tastes. A Levantine folk song
used to say: "Her lips are as fine as a cup's
rim / Her cheeks are red like a pomegran-
ate / There's nothing like her in all Syria."

Both Cairo and Beirut offer considerably
cheaper prices for cosmetic surgery than
Europe and the United States, attracting

business from around the Arab region and
abroad. There is hardly an actress in Egypt
or Lebanon who hasn't had something
done. When over-fifty actresses are con-
gratulated by TV interviewers on their new
look, what is usually meant is their new
facelift. Although somewhere close to age
seventy, Nadia al-Gindy and Nabila Ebeid
look twenty years younger. According to
the Arabic Web site albawaba.com, the
number of plastic surgery operations in the

Modernization Threatens Traditional Medicine in the Gulf

The United Arab Emirates is making an inten-
sive effort to save indigenous Bedouin medicines. Mazen Ali Naji, director of the Zayed
Complex for Herbal Research and Traditional
Medicine, located outside Abu Dhabi, said information that transferred through generations
of families is in danger of being lost in a rush
toward modernization—living in concrete city
blocks, eating at McDonald's, and relying on
modern drugstores. "We are trying to go out
and visit these people from Bedouin tribes, and
gather the information they pass on to their
sons but which has not been documented. Our
aim is to record," he said (interview with author,
August 2003). "Herbs growing in the desert are
very effective because they are concentrated
and grown naturally without human interference." These herbs have important uses.
Shweika was effective against hepatitis B; *al-
ashkhar* is for colon disturbance and irritable
bowel disease; *garadh* is for gastric ulcers; and
tartouth is a "sexual enhancer," as Naji puts it.
"We extract the active materials, but we keep
the whole concentrate rather than just taking
the active ingredient, which is what happens
with chemical-based medicines," Naji said (interview with author, August 2003). So far the
center has produced ten products that are offered for free to UAE nationals and for a small

cost to residents. Amazingly, so far the international drug companies are unaware of this gold
mine of plants in the Arabian Peninsula, and
the center has only just begun the process of
patenting its Viagra-like *tartouth,* which is produced in Britain. The UAE is part of a botanical
region of the Middle East renowned for unique
plant life. There are three regions: an African
one that includes Yemen and Saudi Arabia; a
Sindo-Arabian region that comprises North
Africa, the coastal areas of the Arabian Peninsula, and India; and the Iran/Turan area, which
includes the Persian Gulf countries of Iraq, Iran,
the UAE, and Oman. The key to uncovering this
knowledge is yearly visits to sites and traditional apothecaries in the still-undeveloped rural areas of the UAE, such as Ras al-Khaimah
and Fujeirah, which are worlds away from
Dubai and Abu Dhabi. "I don't want to [distin-
guish] between herbal and modern medicine—
acute cases should be treated in hospitals. But
while modern medicines used over the last fifty
years have side effects, herbal medicines have
been used for hundreds of years. However,
people became modern and adopted city living,
and the young generation is interested in pharmacy drugs and the apothecaries are old," Naji
said (interview with author, August 2003).

Arab world jumped to 650,000 operations in 2003 from 380,000 the year before, and in Egypt alone the figure jumped from 55,000 to 120,000. "The reason is that Arab women got frustrated from the continuous stress put by Arab husbands in comparing their wives with the female singers and actresses, especially those with very seducing music video clips," the Web site said, suggesting the explosion of seductive music videos also had something to do with a rise in divorce rates (17 January 2004). There was one noted case in 2003 of an Egyptian man who divorced his wife because he said she had wasted his savings to try to look like feline Lebanese pop singer Nancy Ajram; she filed a countersuit for divorce saying his adoration of Ajram amounted to infidelity. Prices for plastic surgery are relatively cheap, in global terms. The site reported that Ajram's new figure cost just over $1,000; the lips of Lebanese singer Elissa cost $500; Lebanese singer Haifa Wahby's breast operation cost $1,000; and Nawal al-Zoghby's nose cost just under $1,000. Said Cairo cosmetic surgeon Ali Muftah: "Even those actresses who veiled have had plastic surgery after they veiled, including those who wear the niqab (full face-covering veil).

Physique is one thing and religious behaviour is something else. Being covered is not an alternative to plastic surgery" (*Middle East Times*, February 1996). In Egypt, women undergoing breast operations increasingly want to make them firmer rather than bigger, a sign that Western concepts of breast beauty are making their mark on oriental tastes. Egypt's Pharaonic civilization had its own primitive form of plastic surgery, and it was an Egyptian doctor who in the 1970s pioneered the use of penile rods to deal with impotence. There

Nancy Ajram, the Lebanese singer who shot to fame with her coquettish style, popularized plastic surgery in the Arab world. (Ali Jarekji/Reuters/Corbis)

is even a brand of face cream on Lebanese and Egyptian television that claims to whiten the skin over a period of six weeks. Among men, before recent developments in hair transplant technology, toupees were extremely common in show business, and they're still proudly championed by famous actors Samir Ghanem, Adel Imam, and Samir Sabri. After nurturing a sexy, revolutionary image in the 1970s, Libya's Muammar Gaddafi was visibly suffering hair loss in the 1990s, but *al-Hayat* once revealed that Arab doctors in Brazil set things straight with transplants. During a visit to Cairo in 1996, Gaddafi railed against Western shampoos, saying they were full of chemicals that caused hair loss. "Real Arabs don't use shampoo," he declared in a meeting with university students.

In a study of British fashion in the swinging sixties, Shawn Levy noted that even physique was different then because postwar babies had wanted for food as they grew up—hence, the beautiful skinny people of the wanton era (Levy 2002). Over the last fifty years in general, concepts of feminine beauty in the West seem to have moved from the hourglass ideal, with large busts and hips, to a more androgynous figure and look (according to a *British Medical Journal* study published in December 2002). In the Arab world, fat has traditionally been considered a good thing, because it meant one was well fed, a sign of prosperity. Western conceptions of beauty have permeated mindsets to some degree. Gossip columns are full of news about cinema sex symbol Leila Elwi when she tries to shed some weight, while the public likes her large—rival star Yousra became more popular when she put more weight on her skinny frame. Up until now, being slim has implied a lack of nourishment. Advertising, fashion, music, cinema, and television are changing all that. But androgyny has yet to make a mark: large busts and a decidedly feminine face are very much "in," no matter what size a woman is.

Eating habits are also diversifying, though it's hard to say for good or ill. Western, chemical-filled, packaged food in supermarkets might be no better than fatty local foods, while Iraqi children have been malnourished by over a decade of United Nations sanctions, which now have been lifted. Arab women's summits offer interesting views on the state of women's fashion in the Arab world. Egypt's first lady, Suzanne Mubarak, offers the image of an older, Western-dressed women, while Jordan's Queen Rania and Syrian first lady Asma al-Assad are young and fashionably dressed like TV presenters. Ironically, Rania is not at all popular in Jordan, precisely because she strikes such a Western image in a country where most women, whether Palestinian or Bedouin, are conservatively dressed. Jordanians, however, were able to tolerate Western influence in their first lady when she was a foreigner: King Hussein's American wife Queen Noor was generally popular. The wives of some Gulf rulers usually take the podium at Arab gatherings in complete, head-covering veils, and television cameras draw back to make sure viewers don't clearly see those who show their faces. But moves are currently afoot in Qatar and Bahrain to present a new image, and the faces of the rulers' wives have begun appearing in newspapers as part of a new modernity drive.

Nightlife in the Arab Capitals

Drinking is still marginalized as a foible of working-class men, on the one hand, and elite Westernized youth, on the other, but consumption is rising. Young people are drinking more and smoking is rife, even among women, for whom *shisha*-pipes have become trendy in Egypt and the Levant. Western-style nightlife has gained a foothold in most capitals of the region. This nightlife is at its most developed in Beirut, where there is quick turnover of bars that need to repackage themselves to keep customers, and least prevalent in capitals like Riyadh (where *shisha* cafes are banished to the city limits), Kuwait City, and Khartoum, where even five-star hotels won't sell alcohol to foreigners. In Oman, the Emirates, Bahrain, and Qatar the rules are looser. Nothing quite matches nightlife in the Emirate of Dubai. Though alcohol is banned in the neighboring Emirate of Sharjah, Dubai excels in drinking holes of various types: English/Irish pubs that appeal to Western expats, Indian working men's clubs where women dance on stage to Indian pop, Lebanese bars oozing in affluent Arab chic, and cattle-market bars for prostitutes from all over the world.

Nightlife has taken off in Damascus since Hafez al-Assad was succeeded by his son Bashar, who encouraged hope of political and economic changes in the country. Although a poor cousin to Beirut, Damascus now has a number of bars, restaurants, and clubs catering to increasingly outgoing elites. Bashar has his favorites, and former Syrian defense minister mustafa Tlas can sometimes be found dancing in a nightclub called Iguana. In style, many of these places mix Arab/Ottoman décor and architecture with Western styles—such as the Omayyad Palace Restaurant and Piano Bar. Syrians are buying up traditional houses with secluded open-air courtyards, long abandoned by rich Damascene families in favor of modern flats, and converting them into cafes. At MarMar, a fashionable pub in the Christian quarter of Bab Touma, young men and women drink alcohol and dance all night to Western and Arabpop music. Nearby at Elissar, a mix of Syrians, Lebanese, and Europeans eat mezzes (traditional Middle Eastern appetizers like hummus and stuffed grape leaves) at tables set around a nineteenth-century courtyard fountain in a house decorated in marble with an elaborate painted wooden ceiling. Down the street is Oxygen, a late-night restaurant, which made headlines in April 2002 when its owner asked the American consul in Damascus to leave in protest over American support for Israel's crushing of the Palestinian uprising. In Aleppo,

houses that once belonged to rich Christian traders have been converted into charming hotels.

The redevelopment of the old city of Damascus, where some of these bars and restaurants are to be found, has been controversial. "Old" and "traditional" Damascus has become another element in the nouveau riche culture of consumerism, as people rush to preserve something of the past. Like other cities in the region, Damascus has been transformed by population growth and rural migration. Whole suburbs with tenement housing have sprung up; old two-story buildings have been replaced by high-rises, even in the old city itself; and Damascus's traditional elite families feel under threat from the newcomers. Damascenes complain that Syrians of the Alawi sect, which has dominated in the country since the Assad clan came to power in the 1960s, have taken over their city, dominating state positions and owning property, while Alawis say only a select few of them have been able to join in with the Damascene Muslim and Christian elites who still run the show. A body of nostalgia literature has emerged in the last twenty years, reminiscing over the pre-concrete city, such as *Dimashq al-Asrar* (*Damascus of Secrets*) by Nasreddin al-Bahra, published in 1992. A Society of Friends of Damascus set up in 1977 is still going strong among the old social elites.

The marketing of nostalgia in night culture has been slower to emerge in Cairo, but it's there all the same. A bar-restaurant called Abu Sid opened in 2000 in the fashionable Zamalek district, featuring Arabesque décor of elaborate chandeliers and posters of classical singer Umm Kalthoum, mixed with Louis Farouk furniture adopted from the French in the nineteenth century to become a standard of middle-class Egyptian culture (the flats of newlyweds of means must always have a Louis Farouk sofa and chairs for hosting guests). The music at Abu Sid is the latest Arabpop, and pop stars and actors can be seen huddled at tables in intimate tête-à-têtes. At the downtown Grillon, leftist artist and intellectuals hang out late into the night. A second Abu Sid opened in the affluent suburb of Dokki, and the Jordanian capital Amman also has a branch under the name Nai (meaning "reed flute"), with the same décor and attracting a similar moneyed crowd.

Amman has been transformed in recent years, with bars, fast cars, and fancy clothes a marked feature of a capital city once famed for its austerity and boredom. The change was partly due to Palestinian money that flowed into the country after Palestinians left Kuwait during and after the 1990–1991 Gulf War—an appropriate second wind, in that Palestinians flooded the country in 1948, giving Jordan its initial boost, and Amman is a city largely built by Palestinians. Unlike in Kuwait and Saudi Arabia, the Emirates has allowed a Western-style nightlife to develop that caters to its large expat population. Many countries have developed their own special tourist strips, mini–Sin Cities where Arabs can mingle with and behave like Westerners—Egypt's Sharm al-Sheikh, Tunisia's Hammamat, Lebanon's Jounieh. Some tourist areas have developed in Goa-like hippie colonies, such as Egypt's Dahab, Tunisia's Jerba Island, and numerous locations in Morocco, a key stopping point on the hippie trail since the 1960s. In places like this, local women find the freedom to walk around like Westerners, while in other resorts around the region, women in hejabs will take a dip in the water with their clothes on (these being the conservative majority that Egyptian singer Shereen Wagdy hoped to appeal to in a pop video from 2002 where she swam fully clothed in Thailand).

Some cities have it all. Marrakesh has a reputation for nightlife that covers modern discos to belly dancing, in ancient and modern settings. The medina, or the Islamic-era heart of the city, is alive with cafés, food stalls, and street entertainment, with everything revolving around the central square, or Jemaa al-Fna. Several of the hotels have rooftop cafes overlooking the square, while a number of old merchant houses known as *riyadhs* have been converted into upmarket restaurants offering an authentic Moroccan experience, including feasts, music, and dancing. There are some nightclubs, but unlike in Beirut, they tend to be geared toward tourists and are found mainly in hotels. Beirut is the only city in the region where discos are not the hunting ground of local prostitutes and young men looking for foreign women. Egypt, Lebanon, and Morocco have casinos that attract Gulf Arabs and Libyans, in whose countries casinos are banned because of Islamic mores. The prohibition of usury or interest is also the basic principle of Islamic banking, which outlaws investments in companies involved in gambling, alcohol, and pig farming. In Egypt it is illegal for Egyptians to play in these casinos, though the state taxes horse-betting—some religious figures have argued that it's not a sin to bet if one is sure of the result. Thus, in Saudi Arabia—as Islamically strict as it gets—punters write down their names and the names of the horses they think will win each race on a ballot paper that comes with the entrance fee and then put the papers in a designated ballot box. There is

The Jemaa al-Fna in the old Islamic city, or medina, of Marrakesh in Morocco. (TRIP/Art Directors)

The Jemaa comes alive with cafes, markets, and entertainment in the evening. (TRIP/Art Directors)

Egyptians, who have lived through the terms of three presidents since 1954, look down on punters in a Cairo coffee shop. (Norbert Schiller/Focus MidEast)

also a phone ballot system and the prizes are financed by the cost of the calls and the entrance receipts. Actor Omar Sharif was as famous for his gambling as for his film roles. Before the 1952 revolution, gambling was a favorite sport of Egypt's upper classes. One of the most controversial Arab casinos in the region was the Oasis Casino, set up with Palestinian Authority (PA) approval outside the ancient city of Jericho in the Jordan Valley—somewhere not too far from the biblical Sodom and Gomorrah. Attracting Israelis who can't gamble in Israel because of religious dictates, and staffed by Palestinians and foreign workers, the casino was set to bring significant tax revenue to the PA before the uprising forced its closure. It was the subject of considerable debate in both Palestinian and Israeli society. Jewish and Muslim religious bod-

ies said it was immoral, and Israeli right-wingers said the PA was sending suicide bombers to kill Israelis with money made from Israelis in the casino. Its closure has been a big loss to the PA coffers.

Shopping, Fast Food, and Eating Out

Except for the wealthy Gulf countries, eating out in restaurants is not as popular a pastime as it is in the West, but customs are changing. Western fast-food chains have become heavily present in the region over the last decade and have found a certain cachet among middle-class families. Taking the family to McDonald's, or ordering food for delivery, is a badge of membership in nouveau riche society. Many capitals in the region now have their fast-food strips, where the young and hip hang out in their cars and where Gulf tourists spend much of their summer. McDonald's even offers special takeaway Ramadan iftars that families can order for breaking daytime fasts. In fact, these restaurants are not really fast food at all, at least as the concept was originally conceived of in America. In Arab countries they are hip places for hanging out, wearing trendy clothes, and being seen. "Fast food" already existed, but according to an indigenous model: cheap takeaway cafes, often not that clean, offering shawarma, fava beans, falafel sandwiches, and so on for the masses. For these reasons those with money have avoided them, but in recent years this kind of food has developed its own cachet in response to the plethora of Western fast-food chains that have arrived. Now you can have a feast of cheap local food in clean local restaurants in many Arab capitals for the same price as one Big Mac meal. In the current anti-American climate, it's even seen as the patriotic choice to eat at local places. The elites of the big capitals have a choice of many expensive restaurants, offering French, Italian, and oriental cuisine. Chinese, Japanese, Mexican, and Indian foods are less popular, though all are found in most capitals. Of local cooking, Levantine/Lebanese food is popular throughout the region, and Moroccan is highly prized, though there are fewer Moroccan than Lebanese restaurants. Levantine women are seen as a big catch for Arab men because of their cooking talents.

Shopping mall culture has spread westward from the Gulf, where Western luxury goods have made inroads. The Faisaliya Center in Riyadh includes the prestigious British department store Harvey Nichols, and Hermes, Louis Vuitton, Calvin Klein, Christian Dior, and Chopard all have outlets in the Middle East. British department store Harrods, headed by Egyptian Mohammed al-Fayed, is set to expand in the Gulf with a series of shops. Saks Fifth Avenue, the German leather goods retailer Aigner, and Gianfranco Ferre are also competing in the developing consumer market. Dubai is the shopping capital of the Middle East. The most easygoing city in the region, Dubai has extensive duty-free shopping and an annual shopping festival, though really shopping is what you do in Dubai twelve months of the year. Dubai most likely has a higher number of shopping malls per square kilometer than any other city in the world, and perhaps the biggest number of restaurants too, including Indian, Iranian, Chinese, and various Arab cuisines. Beirut is another shopping magnet in the Middle East. On the weekends, Syria's elite classes head to Beirut in droves to shop in the upmarket Verdun district of West Beirut. They also bank with Lebanon's banks. Syria's banking sector is dire, while the Lebanese sector is highly developed.

In the Gulf itself there is no sign that the shopping industry is going to slow its pace. Dubai is planning massive expansion in the retail sector, and though the local market might seem saturated, developers have calculated they can bring in business for the new malls from outside the UAE by marketing Dubai as a shopping heaven fortuitously placed between the Middle East and south Asia. Dubai is just two hours' flight time away from major markets including Iran, India, Pakistan, and Arab countries, which together form a $1.5 billion strong market. Central to this extraordinary bid to attract the consumer tourist is the "shopping festival" concept that Dubai specializes in, even in the city's muggy summers. During the "Dubai Summer Surprises" campaign, hotels are encouraged to offer a range of bargain packages, with extra free nights and transfers offered for those visiting during the spree. The Emirate is on target to become not only the Middle East's major shopping center, but also one of the globe's, thus making retail the engine room for the rest of the service sector. "Companies specialising in everything from retail software and mannequins to cleaning firms and interior decorators will also benefit from the trickle-down effect," one report said (Oxford Business Group 2004).

Bearing all this in mind, Islamists may wonder that the stark vision of a valueless, capitalist world offered by Islamist radical Sayed Qutb in his seminal *Ma'alim Fil-Tareeq* (*Milestones*) is no less relevant than it was in the godless Arabist world of the 1960s when he wrote the hugely influential work. "The world now is in a 'state of ignorance' which is in no way eased by the formidable materialistic comforts of today . . . Arab society is one of the worst in terms of the distribution of wealth and justice. A small minority has wealth and business and increases its wealth through usury and the big majority has only hardship and hunger," Qutb wrote. "Yet we have something to give to mankind [Islam] which it does not have, something that isn't one of the 'products' of Western civilization or one of Eastern or Western European genius" (Qutb 1979, 8–25).

Bibliography

Print Resources

Amin, Galal. *Whatever Happened to the Egyptians?* Cairo: American University in Cairo Press, 2001.

Bauval, Robert. *The Secret Chamber.* London: Arrow Books, 2000.

Friedman, Thomas L. *The Lexus and the Olive Tree: Understanding Globalization.* New York: Anchor, 1999.

Golia, Maria. *Cairo: City of Sand.* Cairo: American University in Cairo Press, 2004.

Hancock, Graham. *Fingerprints of the Gods.* London: Heinemann, 1995.

Hancock, Graham, and Robert Bauval. *The Mars Mystery.* Post Falls, Idaho: Century Publishing, 1997.

———. *The Message of the Sphinx.* New York: Crown Publishing Group, 1997.

Khalaf, Samir. *Civil and Uncivil Violence in Lebanon: A History of the Internationalization of Communal Conflict in Lebanon.* New York: Columbia University Press, 2002.

Levy, Shawn. *Ready, Steady, Go!: Swinging London and the Invention of Cool.* London: Fourth Estate, 2002.

Nkrumah, Gamal. "No Question of Costume." *al-Ahram Weekly,* 12–18 September 2002, no. 603.

Oxford Business Group. "Online Briefing." 18 June 2004, Vol. 43.

Qutb, Sayed. *Ma'alim Fil-Tareeq* (*Milestones*). 1965. Reprint. Beirut: Dar al-Shurouq, 1979, pp. 8–25.

Salamandra, Christa. "Consuming Damascus: Public Culture and Construction of Social Identity." In *Mass Mediations: New Approaches to Popular Culture in the Middle East and Beyond,* ed. Walter Armbrust. Berkeley: University of California Press, 2000.

Tapper, Nancy Lindisfarne, and Bruce Ingham, eds. *Languages of Dress in the Middle East.* Richmond, UK: Curzon Press, 1997.

Tapper, Nancy Lindisfarne, and Mihai I. Spariosu, eds. *Dancing in Damascus.* Binghamton, N.Y.: SUNY Press, 2000.

Zuhur, Sherifa, ed. *Colors of Enchantment: Theater, Dance, Music, and the Visual Arts of the Middle East.* Cairo: American University in Cairo Press, 2002.

Web Sites

www.dabboor.com. Arabic humor Web site, sometimes difficult to access.

www.alhewar.org. The site of the Washington-based Center for Arab Dialogue.

http://i-cias.com. Site called the "Encyclopaedia of the Orient," featuring travel and general information on the Middle East.

www.wadada.net. A dissident Egyptian Web site dedicated to Naguib Sorour, a famous leftist poet.

www.IslamOnline.net. The most popular general Islamic Web site, run by clerics based in Qatar.

the_worst_government.tripod.com (also www.mubarak.veryweird.com). Site titled "The Underworld of Mubarak," run by a group of Egyptian dissidents who call themselves the Free Egyptians.

www.democracy-egypt.org. Site of Egyptian sociologist Saadeddin Ibrahim's Ibn Khaldoun Centre.

www.e-prism.org. Site of the Israel-based Project for the Research of Radical Islamism, which carries past issues of online radical Islamic magazines.

www.virtuallyislamic.com. UK-based site on radical Islamic groups.

www.MyTravel.com. Specialist travel Web site based in the Middle East and run by the Emirates Group.

10
Sport

Sports Become a Major Concern in the Arab World

Sports now occupy a hallowed place in the cultural life of the region. National pride and self-esteem are increasingly attached to the fortunes of sports teams, especially soccer. Lifestyle changes have meant people from all walks of life—women, wealthy elites, and the urban poor—seek a niche in a range of physical activities. In bureaucracy-obsessed Arab cultures, there are sports federations for nearly everything. In Saudi Arabia they are the preserve of the vast royal family; in Egypt their administration is usually awarded to retired members of the military elite. Debate has just begun about whether the federations are responsible for the ephemeral successes of their football teams, successes that they have sought to buy through hiring expensive foreign coaches. While Egyptians fret about football, there is little media awareness that Egypt is home to the world's top bodybuilders—a sign of a new populist direction in sports, with both affluent and poor Arab youth across the region heading for the gym. It was no major surprise to the Arab community that Egypt's five-medal performance in the 2004 Olympics in Athens came in wrestling, boxing, and tae kwon do. Interest in soccer is sure to soar even higher in the runup to the 2010 World Cup, which will be held in South Africa. Four Arab countries were among six African nations bidding to host the championship: Morocco, Tunisia/Libya (a co-host proposal), Egypt, Nigeria, and South Africa. Morocco was viewed as having the best chance of the Arab countries, due to its facilities and climate. Egypt's failure to garner even a single vote when the international soccer association FIFA made its decision was decried as a national disaster, and could be seen as symptomatic of the country's political and economic woes.

A new sports frenzy has gripped the Arab region in general in the wake of Olympic successes in Athens 2004. Arab countries fared well, taking more gold medals than ever before, though fewer than the total fourteen medals claimed at the Sydney Games in 2000. Morocco finished in thirty-sixth position (out of 202 total participating nations), with two golds for runner Hicham el-Guerrouj in the men's 1,500- and 5,000-meter races and

Morocco's Farid Talhaoui (center) clashes with Michael Umana of Costa Rica at a soccer match during the Athens Olympics in August 2004. (Nikos Papas/Reuters/Corbis)

a silver medal for Hasna Benhassi in the women's 800-meter race. Egypt shocked itself by winning five medals—a gold, a silver, and three bronze—and finishing forty-sixth overall. Egypt's last Olympic medal prior to Athens was a silver in judo in the 1984 Games in Los Angeles, and overall the 2004 games were the country's most successful since 1948. The Ministry of Youth had announced tax-free cash prizes for medal winners before the Olympics of up to one million Egyptian pounds (around US$170,000) for gold as an incentive, and President Mubarak's son Gamal and four government ministers met the Olympic team upon its return amid a state-media ballyhoo that aimed to make up for the bad

feeling toward the government after the costly failure to win the 2010 World Cup bid. Wrestler Karam Gaber won gold in the men's Greco-Roman 96-kilogram category; boxer Mohamed Ali Reda took the silver in the men's Super Heavy over-91-kilogram category; and bronze medals were won by Ahmed Ismail in the men's Light Heavy (81-kilogram) boxing, Mohamed al-Baz in the men's Heavy (91-kilogram) boxing, and Tamer Bayoumi in the men's under-58-kilogram tae kwon do competition. The United Arab Emirates won its first-ever Olympic medal when a member of the royal family in the Emirate of Dubai, Ahmed Al Maktoum, took the gold in the men's double trap shooting. Syrian Nasser

Middle East Is a Diving Mecca

Arab countries have a lot to offer divers. The Red Sea and the Gulf contain some of the world's most stunning coral reefs, and regional governments have had to juggle use of the reefs to foster tourism with the danger of destroying the reefs through exploitation. The classic example of crass, unplanned overuse of "coral-for-tourism" is the Egyptian resort of Hurghada. The Egyptians learned their lesson when they developed the Sinai resort of Sharm el-Sheikh and other locations on the Red Sea coast in the 1990s, taking pains to make sure that coral was preserved and tourism was sustainable. However, environmentalists say there are still problems and the coral has been badly depleted. The United Arab Emirates (UAE), awash with money, has ensured that the sector was developed to high standards. On the other hand, Sudan's Red Sea coastline around the area of Port Sudan is only now being developed, and divers are taking notice of this virgin territory. Diving for shipwrecks is another activity in the region, involving both amateurs and professionals. Amateurs can in-

The Red Sea is a major attraction for fans of diving and snorkeling. (Jeffrey L. Rotman/Corbis)

al-Shami won bronze in the men's heavyweight boxing (91-kilogram) category. But it was the Iraqi football team who attracted the most attention in the Arab and world media, with surprise wins over Portugal, Costa Rica, and Australia to reach the semifinals.

While soccer is a pan-Arab obsession, different countries excel in different sports. Basketball has taken off in Lebanon (La Sagesse/al-Hikma and al-Riyadi are the main teams), where it is the number-one sport and fastest-growing game, serviced by the Lebanese Basketball Federation, which was originally set up in 1949. The Federation was revamped in 1996 after the vestigate specially sunken ships off the coast-line of man-made, five-star islands off the coast of Dubai, while in Egypt French divers have made important historical discoveries on Alexandria's north coast.

Marine archaeologists are focusing new attention on the largely unexplored seabed of north Egypt, where the remains of a Greek city lie below the surface. In 1994 divers from the Centre d'Etudes Alexandrines, led by Frenchman Jean-Yves Empereur, located the remains of the ancient Pharos lighthouse, which was one of the seven wonders of the ancient world. In 1996 his team winched from the sea a colossal ancient statue of a pharaoh, one of the Ptolemaic rulers of Egypt. In addition, the team located dozens of sphinxes and over 2,000 architectural blocks and pillars. Another French explorer, Franck Goddio, head of the Paris-based European Institute of Marine Archaeology, has sought to match ancient descriptions of the city's royal quarter with identifiable underwater features. According to the Greek geographer Strabo, the main royal palace stood on a ledge that was submerged by tidal waves in the fourth century A.D. Goddio's team mapped an area of about one square kilometer, using GPS to fix within 30 centimeters the position of more than 1,000 artifacts and features including sphinxes, columns, and blocks inscribed with hieroglyphs. The city where Cleopatra walked and the things she saw in her lifetime are on display off the corniche of Alexandria.

In 2000 Goddio uncovered colossal statues, sunken ships, gold coins, and jewelry from another submerged ancient city not far from Alexandria, called Heracleion, which was likely destroyed by an earthquake. Ancient texts speak of the city as the port of entry to Egypt, which served as a major customs post on the Nile before Alexandria itself was founded in 331 B.C. on the western tributary of the Nile. The Greek historian Diodorus recounts how the god Heracles dammed a Nile flood in order to set the river back on its course. Local people built a temple to Heracles and called the town Heracleion. According to Herodotus, Helen of Troy and her lover Paris fled to Heracleion to escape Helen's husband Menelaus, but were rebuffed by Thonis, the watchman at the entrance to the Nile. No one was sure if Heracleion was myth or reality before Goddio's discovery. Among the most remarkable of Goddio's finds was an intact black granite stele, or inscribed slab, almost identical to one found in 1899 now in the Egyptian Museum in Cairo. Both feature an edict of Pharaoh Nektanebos the First (378–362 B.C.), imposing a 10 percent levy on Greek goods for a temple to the goddess Neith. The finds by Empereur and Goddio have opened up a whole new avenue of archaeological research and diving tourism in Egypt, with the realization that any point along Egypt's entire Mediterranean and Red Sea coasts could conceal such secrets. The same goes for the Red Sea coastal areas in Sudan and Saudi Arabia, and the Mediterranean littoral running along North Africa.

---

civil war was over, and by 2001 the national team had reached the World Cup. Lebanon regularly takes first place in Arab and African basketball championships. Egypt has succeeded in muscling into the international squash circuit with its annual Al-Ahram International Tournament, which is held every summer in spectactular, spe- cially constructed prefab squash courts at the foot of the pyramids. The fact that Egypt also had a world-class squash talent in Ahmed Barrada has also helped the profile of squash in the Middle East. But Barrada, who made it to number three in world rankings, retired in 2001, after a stabbing attack in Cairo by an unknown

Paris-Dakar Rally Puts North Africa in Spotlight

The Paris-Dakar rally features over 400 drivers in a grueling seventeen-day race over 6,500 miles, accompanied by great media fanfare. The competitors race a mixture of buggies, 4x4 vehicles, motorbikes, and quad bikes across the toughest terrain and conditions from North Africa to Egypt. "A challenge for those who go, a dream for those who stay behind. The Dakar is founded on two essential values: Courage and endurance. Both united in a grandiose setting—that of the most beautiful and mythical of all deserts—the Sahara," was how founder Hubert Auriol envisioned the rally when it began in 1978 (www.dakar.com, October 2003). Originally, the competitors began in Paris, racing across France, Spain, and Morocco before crossing Africa to finish in Dakar, Senegal. In 2000 organizers tried to renew interest in the rally by rerouting it as a cross-Sahara trip from Senegal to Egypt. In 1992 the course had also shifted from its traditional western Africa location by heading from Dakar all the way down to Cape Town, but the Egyptian experiment proved to be more successful. Organizers had the rally end at the pyramids in Cairo; recently the finishing post was moved to the Red Sea resort of Sharm al-Sheikh. The 2004 rally returned to the original Dakar ending, passing through Morocco and Mauritania.

assailant the previous year appeared to sap his confidence, and the temptations of women and movie parts took his attention. Squash is also highly developed in the United Arab Emirates, though mostly aimed at the majority expat community of Westerners and Asians. Handball is also big in Egypt, which hosted the World Cup in 1999 and reached the semifinals of the 2000 Olympics. The Maghrebis, on the other hand, usually shine in athletics, traditionally bringing in most of the medals Arabs get at Olympic finals.

Saudi Arabia, meanwhile, is to host the first Islamic Games of the Organization of the Islamic Conference (OIC) in 2005, featuring football, basketball, shooting, handball, and swimming. Iran will hold the next games in 2009, then Syria in 2013. While the United Arab Emirates doesn't have many world champions to boast of, it does have the most sports-friendly society. Dubai has built itself up as an oasis of five-star sports facilities for the international jet set. Since the city is home to few international sports stars or teams, the authorities bring in overseas teams for glamour and at major sporting events offer lucrative prizes to attract big-name stars. Tourists and expats are attracted by the sports that Dubai offers. Dubai's sports events include the PGA Dubai Desert Golf Classic held every February (www.dwtc.com), the Dubai Open Tennis Championship held every February (www.dubaitennischampionships.com), and the Dubai International Rugby Sevens held every December (www.dubairugby7s.com). There are even plans to build a Dubai ski resort and cricket stadium. Dubai hopes to have a spectacular "sports city" operating by 2007 ahead of a possible Gulf Olympic bid in 2016. At a cost of at least two billion dollars to build, the city will host the first Manchester United soccer school outside Europe, a golf course designed by South African Ernie Els, a David Lloyd tennis school, and a Butch Harmon golf academy, the first outside

North America. When the ferocious summer heat begins to decrease in autumn, the Emirates are ideal for athletes and outdoor enthusiasts, and almost every outdoor activity imaginable is being practiced somewhere within the boundaries of this small country. Summer sports like sailing, surfing, waterskiing, and kiteboarding are also popular. Yet intellectuals pine about the fact that the Arabs were too late in discovering modern sports. "We need to understand that the Arab person played sports for the sake of hunting and war, or as a sign of strength, but he was late in playing competitive sports by 500 years and late in playing soccer by 50 years," complained Hazem al-Mistikawy in the Egyptian literary monthly *Wughat Nazar* in July 2002. The popularity of Arab sports channels suggests they're doing their best to make up for it.

Arab Women in Sports

In the Arab world, as sports become victims of the unresolved debate between secularizers and Islamists, girls have tended to shy away from physical activities in public, concluding that it's not worth the hassle. When North African Arab soccer teams took part in the first women's African Nations Cup in Nigeria in 1998, Egypt made it to the finals—but instead of praising the players, local media either ignored the achievement, ridiculed it, or suggested the team wasn't worth the funding. Women are more encouraged to involve themselves in sports in the non-Arab Islamic republic of Iran, where there is a structure for encouraging women to play sports, albeit according to strict rules. Iran allowed women to play soccer in 1998 at indoor stadiums away from the glare of men. They can also take part in basketball, karate, riding, rowing, shooting, skiing, swimming, and volleyball. But there have been many Arab women who defied the odds and rose to the top, especially in athletics. Algerian athlete Hassiba Boulmerka, who won the 1,500-meter race at the 1992 Barcelona Olympics, has become a poster child for women's rights in Arab sports. Death threats during Algeria's Islamic insurgency of the 1990s forced her to live in Italy. "I am a danger to the fundamentalists. I am a symbol to the young that women don't have to live behind their chadors," she once said (Hargreaves 2001). Boulmerka dedicated her gold medal to Mohammed Boudiaf, the former president of Algeria assassinated in 1992. Many suspect he was killed by the army, who feared he would seek peace with the Islamist movement. Egypt has a women's weightlifting world champion (75-kilogram category) named Nahla Ramadan. "[Egyptian girls] are scared of trying out this sort of thing. I want to show them that the sport is not difficult for a girl and show what I can achieve with training, talent, and enthusiasm," she has said ("Egyptian Lifter Sees Herself as Role Model," Reuters, 10 March 2004).

As the commercialization of sport in the West puts women athletes on the pages of *Playboy* and has men leering over Web sites like www.sexyathletes.com, many Arab women have found an alternative in "Islamic sports." There are 500 million Muslim women in the world—one-quarter of the world's female population—many of whom cannot take part in Olympic competitions under existing conditions. Tehran was host to the first Women's World Islamic Games in 1993, where men were excluded at all times from venues so that women could wear sports gear. This is the only chance for women in some Gulf countries to participate in international sports, and for millions in other Arab countries it is a more comfortable option. Advocates of Islamic sports point to Islamic traditions that encourage sports for all Muslims. One tradition has it that the Prophet engaged in wrestling, racing, archery, and horse racing, as did his wife, Aisha, one of the main female figures from the age of the Prophet and the rise of Islam. Muslim scholars—both secular and Islamist—have written much about Aisha, seeing in her a strong and free-spirited heroine who is an example to Muslim women today. According to Hikmat Beiruty, an Islamist writer who typifies the views of women (and men) who advocate Islamic sports: "The restrictions on women participating in sport or physical activity is [sic] more than that of men. All Islamic observances must be followed, regardless of any school policies or social stigmas. Our obedience to our Creator cannot be given preference to a creature of Allah. When participating in sports, the clothing must be Islamically acceptable. This would therefore exclude shorts, t-shirts, leotards, swimming costumes etc. It is very important to ensure that there are no males watching. Mixing of sexes is forbidden in normal situations, except in special situations under certain conditions, let alone in a sporting arena or exercise facility. It also restricts your activities, and modesty would not allow this in any case" (www.zawaj.com, September 2004).

Women swimmers come in for particular problems. Many strict Muslims consider it wrong even to undress in front of female strangers or non-Muslim women in women-only public baths. Egypt had a top swimmer, Rania Elwany, but she retired and took the veil after failing to place in the 2000 Olympics. According to Beiruty: "Sports and exercise should be judged according to the level of modesty involved. Games such as netball played in a public arena is [sic] not befitting to the honour of a Muslim woman. No compromises can be made in terms of clothing or mixing. Public showers at female schools is [sic] totally forbidden. Many sisters will also apply deodorants after a work-out. What must be kept in mind is the Prophet's warning on fragrant perfumes: 'The woman who perfumes herself and passes through a gathering is an adulteress.' Some fragrant-free deodorants are available, otherwise apply enough so that the fragrance is not apparent. . . . Stadiums are not advisable places for Muslims in general, because of the language, drinking, and scenery. Allah has commanded the believing women to lower their gaze, and sport comes as no exception, especially with guys in shorts." She goes on: "To keep in line with today's excessive and unwarranted demands for women to have a 'supermodel' physique, many sisters will exercise for this sole purpose, only adding more stress and anguish to themselves. Keep it as a fun activity, involve your husband with it and make it an intimate part of your marriage life. Keep in mind that over-exercising can result in unrepairable tissue damage, and will turn you off it" (www.zawaj.com, September 2004).

Soccer Fanaticism among Arab Youth

The Arab world is as soccer-crazy as any other part of the globe. For millions of children throughout the region, *yalla nil'ab kora* ("let's play ball") means playing soccer, even with a bunch of socks tied together to substitute for soccer balls that might be expensive and out of reach. Although the sport has been around in the region for a long time—Egypt took part in the 1934 World Cup finals—it wasn't until the 1980s that the craze took off. It was around then that a number of Arab countries emerged with teams of reasonable quality, including Morocco, Tunisia, Egypt, and Saudi Arabia. Their success was largely based on hiring foreign managers, though only Saudi Arabia really had the money to afford them, and the foreign manager phenomenon has been a controversial issue in all of these countries. The Saudi national team has the support of the royal family, so there is no lack of money and facilities. Top players are given cars and houses and enjoy fame and fortune. In the 2002 World Cup finals both Tunisia and Saudi Arabia failed to make it to the second round, after a good run into the second round by Morocco four years earlier raised hopes that Arab soccer was going somewhere. The official rankings of FIFA (the sport's governing Federation Internationale de Football Association) as of September 2004 showed the big six still had a long way to go: Saudi Arabia 27, Morocco 33, Egypt 35, Tunisia 36, Jordan 37, Iraq 40. The rankings of other Arab countries are: Bahrain 44, Oman 50, Kuwait 55, Algeria 61, Qatar 61, Libya 73, United Arab Emirates 77, Syria 84, Sudan 108, Lebanon 110, Palestine 129, Yemen 139, Mauritania 174, Somalia 193 (Israel was 69, Turkey 13, Iran 21). Saudi Arabia has 118,000 players and Egypt has 50,000, while Japan, which has only been playing for about a decade, already has an estimated 3.5 million. But governments and their soccer federations are intent on pushing the game, and commentators haven't been blind to the possibility

that, as with the television entertainment overload that Arab governments inflict on their peoples, soccer is another means to numb the population's mind to politics and other heavy issues of state. No doubt with Arab countries in mind, Hassan al-Mistikawy wrote after the 2002 World Cup: "The more the poverty and political repression, the more important is the soccer. It's the alternative to absent parties in political life, in that belonging to a team makes up for belonging to a party. [Soccer] matches are also a chance to express an opinion on the economic situation with a scream against government or an inappropriate shout against a team, since stadiums are big enough to allow a bit of anger and letting go" (*Wughaat Nazar*, July 2002).

Prior to the 2002 World Cup debacle, the Saudi soccer federation was viewed as the best in the Arab world. Their coaches are almost all Brazilian, instilling in the players the famed South American flair. Officials also stick to the league schedules, hardly ever postponing games, and if an international fixture gets in the way, the clubs play on minus their internationals. In Egypt a season can be disrupted as many as a dozen times, and this chaos shows in the players' quixotic performances. The Saudi federation closely monitors its players and comes down on those who commit infractions, imposing heavy fines or long-term suspensions. And it shells out millions to churn out thousands of potential players. The result has been a sweep of virtually all major Gulf, Arab, and Asian championships at club and international levels in recent years. In soccer as in media, Egypt's dominance over Saudi Arabia and most of the Gulf is over, at least for the moment. But the Saudis did abysmally in the 2002 World Cup finals. They lost their first match with Germany 8–0, despite a declaration by the goalkeeper beforehand that they were bound to win because they had Islam on their side, and they failed to make the second round. Coach Nasser al-Johar, named Asian coach of the year in May 2002, was subsequently sacked, and a foreigner was brought in, Dutchman Gerard van der Lem—the thirty-fifth manager in the Saudi team's brief career and the second Dutchman. Saudi Arabia was traumatized by the debacle, not least because hopes had been high that the tournament would offer the country a chance to improve its self-respect after the September 11 attacks. The official Saudi Press Agency reported that "the national team has not developed to a level suitable to the fame of Saudi [soccer]" (June 2002). The eight unanswered goals Saudi Arabia leaked against Germany led to a number of caustic jokes on the streets of Riyadh, such as: "Saudi Arabia has banned the import of eight-cylinder German cars" and "Johar is hiding in Tora Bora" (the cave complex in Afghanistan where the U.S. military thought Osama bin Laden was in residence during the war to oust the Taliban in 2001). The normally reverential Saudi press ripped into the team and the football federation, and nepotism and favoritism were publicly outed as the cause of the failure in a country where nepotism and favoritism are central pillars of public life. "Our team returned from Japan with zero points and goals. What can I say? Absolutely nothing," wrote Adel Essameddin in the sports daily *Alam al-Riyada* (June 2002). "The federation is responsible for this scandal," one commentator said on the London-based satellite channel al-Mustaqilla, noting that the national team for some reason has nine players from the premier and most presti-

gious club in the country, the Riyadh-based al-Hilal. Another commentator said the sports ministry had "spent billions of riyals so the national team soils our reputation and makes us the laughing stock of the world. The media has fabricated cardboard stars who play without a soul, do not honour the national flag and think only of money" (al-Mustaqilla, June 2002). Commentator Elias Khoury wrote in the London-based pan-Arab daily *al-Quds al-Arabi* that Saudi Arabia's trouncing by Germany summed up the current state of the Arabs. "We understand, put up with, and grow accustomed to the inability of the Arab regimes to build armies, universities, research centers, and so on. But to be incapable of even putting together a football team?!" What this all means is that "when societies are ignored and their will is confiscated, they lose the ability to even amuse themselves with a ball" (*al-Quds al-Arabi*, 7 June 2002). Van der Lem was subsequently fired after Saudi Arabia lost the Asia Nations Cup to Iraq in July 2004. Egyptian writer Samir Ragab blatantly threatened Egypt's Under-17 team ahead of a 2001 match with Finland. "If they take it too easy and let us down we will not stand back and do nothing about it," he warned (*al-Gomhouriya*, 23 June 2001). "[Soccer] is about winning and losing, but this principle only applies to those who at least win sometimes. People who get used to exiting international tournaments in the first round ought to face a harsh reckoning. Success has a sweet taste, but failure has the curse of God upon it until Judgement Day."

If anyone knows about the price of failure, it's Egyptian coach Mahmoud al-Gohary. Gohary was the manager in 1988, when he took Egypt into the 1990 World

Cup, but he was fired after a 6–1 defeat to Greece. Only a year later he was reinstated, but when Egypt finished twelfth in the Africa Nations Cup in 1992, he was dumped again. He was reappointed in 1997 and hailed as a national hero on the streets when he steered Egypt to victory in the Africa Nations Cup held in Burkina Faso. On that occasion each member of the team was given a cash reward and a welcome at Cairo airport by President Mubarak. Youths ran through the streets carrying pictures of Coach Gohary, chanting his name—something that Egyptians wouldn't dare do over anyone other than a sportsman. But after a 5–1 defeat to Saudi Arabia in the Confederations Cup in Mexico in 1999, the sense of national humiliation was so great that it saw not only the resignation of Gohary but also the entire soccer federation board, which had sacked him twice. Then in 2000 Gohary was back at the helm again, replacing Frenchman Gerard Gili, who couldn't produce a good result in the Africa Nations Cup. Ultimately Gohary failed to get Egypt into the 2002 World Cup, though bad luck and bad attitude from the Algerians in a critical match in Ennaba had at least as much to do with it as his coaching abilities. Italian Marco Tardelli has been tasked with getting Egypt into the 2006 World Cup finals. The former Juventus midfielder was a member of the team that garnered Italy the World Cup in 1982, then went on to coach Inter-Milan, Bari, and Italy's Under-21 squad. Press reports in Egypt say he is now raking in $40,000 a month for his efforts.

According to foreigners who have tried to work with Arab teams, the main obstacle is egotistical players who play as individuals, not as team players. Local media in Arab countries snipe about the huge pay of these foreign managers, though soccer federations can't seem to resist dipping into their pockets to obtain a foreigner every time a local coach fails to produce the goods. With the shuffle from Gili to Gohary, Egypt's soccer federation moved from shelling out $35,000 a month to 45,000 Egyptian pounds (about $9,000), though 45,000 pounds still makes Gohary a superstar by Egyptian standards. This seesaw approach to soccer has been overseen for years by a soccer federation led by one man, former army officer al-Dahshouri Harb. Gili's verdict on the team was: "From what I've seen I can say that there is definitely talent in these players, but there is a lot of work to do. The league in Egypt is weak and cannot give birth to international players. Egyptian players have to work hard, especially on team play, techniques, tactics and physical fitness. They need to be trained in technical aspects in order to play as a team more than as individuals" (al-Ahram Weekly, 23 May 2001). Similarly, Tunisia's soccer association was all over the place in the runup to the 2002 World Cup. German Eckhard Krautzen steered Tunisia through the qualifying match but resigned because he thought the Tunisian association was interfering with his coaching. Frenchman Henri Michel replaced him, but he didn't last long amid accusations that he lacked passion. Ammar Souayah and Khemaies Laabidi were then named joint Tunisia coaches until after the World Cup, in which the team played dismally. Qatar even made a bold attempt to buy itself world-class status. It hoped to give citizenship to three prized Brazilian players who played in Germany so that they could play in the Qatari national squad, but FIFA ruled in March 2004 that players must have a "clear connection" to any country they want to play for other than their own. The rules now state a player must either have lived in a country for at least two years or have a parent or grandparent who was born there. Qatar national manager Philippe Troussier—a Frenchman who coached Japan in the 2002 World Cup—had been trying to naturalize overseas players overlooked by their national teams.

In Libya, Italian Franco Scoglio claimed he was sacked as national team coach in 2002 because he refused to select Gaddafi's son al-Saadi for the team and refused to train Libya's main club, al-Ittihad, which Saadi owns. Saadi also happens to head the Libyan football federation. "They sacked me because I wouldn't let him play," Scoglio said in widely published comments. "And I would never have let him play, even for a minute. As a [soccer player] he's worthless . . . I'm a [soccer] manager, not a puppet. With him in the squad we were losing. When he left we won" (Reuters, 19 September 2002). But Saadi moved on to better things—he joined the board of Italy's Juventus, after a Libyan company bought 7.5 percent of the club in 2001—a form of revenge, in Libyan eyes, for the Italian occupation that still takes much space in Libyan public consciousness, as well as a means of reestablishing Libya in Europe after years of isolation. Scoglio, who left to manage Italy's Napoli, was replaced by Abu Baker Bani, who was previously the coach of the second-division Libyan club Falouja. Iraq's national team became a political tool after Uday Saddam Hussein took over its management in 1979. Numerous human rights groups have reported that Uday used to torture members of the national team for losing games. With the threat of an invasion of their country, Iraq's top soccer players were quietly touring Italy in late 2002 in a trip sponsored by Italian companies. Sending the team abroad was likely a propaganda move to give Iraqis at home the sense that the world was with them and that it was only America that had a problem with Saddam Hussein's government. When the war was over, the national team made a fresh start, and began training for qualifying matches to reach the 2004 Olympic Games, despite the lack of funding or transport to make it into Baghdad, where the country's only international standard field is located. Worst of all, the team had to overcome years of abuse at the hands of Uday, which included chainings to walls, days bound up in contorted positions, dragging along pavements before being dunked in sewage to make sure the wounds became infected, beatings on the soles of the feet, and drubbings with iron bars. All of which might have made the likelihood of a better performance next time around all the more remote. But the Iraqi team got to the semifinals of the Olympic soccer event in Athens 2004, with a spirited performance that gave them surprise wins over Portugal, Costa Rica, and Australia. FIFA gave its fair play award to Iraq and Argentina for good conduct on and off the field and Iraq moved up FIFA's rankings to a respectable 40—quite an achievement considering everything the country and the team have been through.

The Egyptian sense of humiliation at the Saudi defeat belies a number of bitter rivalries in the region, and commentators are continually bemoaning the lack of cooperation. "Arab-Arab sensitivities will remain as long as there is this tragic Arab situation of political and ideological contradictions and socio-economic and behavioural crises," wrote sports columnist Mohammed Nabil Na'eem in *al-Hayat* (14 June 2003). "Unfor-

Iraq's national soccer team listens to their national anthem at a friendly match between Japan and Iraq in Tokyo, February 2003. (ISSEI KATO/Reuters/Corbis)

tunately, we find ourselves obliged to use these words today and sure that we'll be saying them again tomorrow." Sectarianism has crept into basketball in Lebanon, between two main teams—La Sagesse/al-Hikma, which is seen as Christian, and al-Riyadi, which is seen as Muslim. There was controversy in 2003 when their fans taunted each other with offensive chants. In Jordan, Wahdat is supported by the majority of Palestinians, while al-Faisaliya is the preserve of the East Bank Jordanians. Faisaliya fans habitually chant advice to King Abdullah to "divorce her," "her" being his Palestinian wife Rania. Inter-Arab defeats are the biggest blow to most Arab teams. The Algerians and Egyptians have a

particularly hostile history, which came to a head at a 2001 World Cup qualifier in the Algerian town of Ennaba. The match was stopped for fifteen minutes as Algerians threw water bottles on the field and burned the Egyptian flag, and the bus taking the Egyptian players away afterward was attacked by stone-throwing youths. The enmity has its roots in Egypt's domination of pan-Arab politics in the 1960s and its central role in Algeria's Arabization programs of the 1960s. For Algerians, Egypt represents a failed past. Soccer is often the arena for the region's political problems. Israeli crowds often shout "death to the Arabs," while riots have broken out at matches between Israeli-Jewish and

Israeli-Arab teams. Algeria has a few teams from the Kabyle region, such as Boulazdad, and star French soccer player Zinedine Zidane is feted in the Arab media because of his Algerian origins, oblivious to the fact that Zidane is a proud Kabyle who in France openly resents the designation "Arab." There were reports of pressure on the Iranian team to lose to Bahrain in the 2002 World Cup qualifying match with Bahrain, after ecstatic Iranians let their joy take them over red lines to shout slogans like "death to the Mullahs" in a previous match that Iran had won. Soccer is also the catalyst for healing wounds, of course. While the Intifada raged during the 2002 World Cup, Israeli Jews and Israeli Arabs were able to sit together in cafes and enjoy the spectacle. Israel has a model "peace community," called in Arabic *Waahat al-Salam* and in Hebrew *Neve Shalom*, where Jewish and Palestinian children grow up, go to school together, and play football.

Golf Becomes the Sport of Choice of the Affluent

Golf is flourishing in a region that is predominantly desert. The main center is the Gulf region, but Egypt has made a bid to put itself on the map, developing the sport as a choice past time for its new elites and catering to its large expat community. Golf in the Middle East is a unique experience. Oddities of the Gulf region include desert courses where you might play on "browns" rather than greens and play at night under floodlights to avoid soaring daytime temperatures. Peacocks, guinea fowl, and partridges freely roam many of the courses, which are of such good quality that Dubai hosts two championship tournaments rec-

ognized by the Professional Golfers Association (PGA), golf's ruling body. Dubai has the highest profile, with its highly developed tourist infrastructure and open-door policy to golfers, both amateur and professional. Highlights include the Doha Golf Club, where the Qatar Masters Championship is held—one expert's tip as the best golf course in the Gulf region—and the Dubai Creek, a masterpiece of architecture and landscaping, including a clubhouse in the shape of a traditional Arab ship or *dhow*. Bahrain's Riffa Golf Club is the Gulf's first PGA training academy for golf professionals, giving a boost to young golfers in the Gulf country, which currently has the best international team and produces qualified Arab trainers. To give an example of what's offered in the Gulf, the club has a 6,817-yard, par 72, 18-hole PGA golf course that includes floodlighting, grass, five lakes, more than 70 sand bunkers, over 500 date palms, and 400 specimen trees. It's managed by the Gleneagles Hotel in Scotland, one of the world's leading golf resorts. The academy employs three full-time PGA professionals and is equipped with a 30-bay floodlit driving range and air-conditioned swing studios that feature state-of-the-art video equipment for swing analysis.

Egypt might not be the first place you would associate with bunkers and bogeys, and for the majority of Egyptians it's an equally strange connection. But well-watered golf courses and tournaments have proliferated since 1997 on some two dozen sites catering to the country's emerging middle class, business tycoons, and the expatriate community. There is even a specialist magazine called *Golf in Egypt* to satisfy growing interest among wealthy Egyptians and foreigners. The craze began when developers built the Katameya Heights Golf and Tennis Resort, a 400-acre, exclusive pleasure complex with 280 villas and a 27-hole course next to a luxury new housing development overlooking the capital. The development sits next to run-down tenements of a low-class housing estate dating from an earlier era, when the government singled out Katameya as a place to build houses for the poor. With the current economic slide around the region, the golf courses aren't doing as well as expected. There are only around 1,500 players in Egypt, meaning most of the courses hardly see a few rounds a day. But Katameya is doing better than the others because of the luxury houses overlooking the course, which is a selling point for the villas, and also because Cairo expats have taken to it. Golf isn't new to Egypt. The British imported the game in 1886, creating a course at the Gezira Club, a British officers' hangout in central Cairo that is now patronized by the Egyptian elite. In the 1940s the Egyptian Open attracted some of Europe's finest professionals. There has been a golf course in the shadow of the 4,500-year-old Pyramids of Giza since the early twentieth century. Golf remained popular with Egypt's upper classes well after the 1952 military revolution sealed the departure of the British, but golfers had to pursue their sport more discreetly. By 1956 golf was smarting from the populist ethos of President Gamal Abdel Nasser's socialist-style government. The Gezira Club was divided and a new, less exclusive club was created. The temperate winter months, ideal for golfers escaping harsher northern climates, are the peak period for sun-seeking tourists from Europe, Japan, and North America.

Camel Racing Survives in Bedouin Societies

Camels are raced in virtually every Arab country, and the sport has even migrated to the desert expanses of Australia and the United States. It was originally staged at formal settings in Bedouin communities, such as weddings or special festivals, but now it's the prestige spectator event of sheikhs, princes, and kings in societies transformed by the wealth of oil and gas, where the four-wheel drive has ironically put camels out of a job. In the Gulf customized tracks feature races every weekend from October to April, attracting huge crowds and fans who speed along the track in fancy cars, cheering the camels on. Prizes can reach as high as $100,000, with numerous flashy cars thrown in to boot. A fast camel might sell for as much as half a milion dollars. It's no surprise then that the sport has spawned its own industries of camel breeding and camel training. Early in 1990 the Transfer Research Center for Racing Camels produced the world's first embryo-transfer calves from racing camels. Camels produce up to thirty embryos at a time, which can be transferred immediately to waiting recipients or stored indefinitely in liquid nitrogen. In February 1995 the world's first baby camel was born from a frozen embryo-transfer. The UAE's al-Ain Center remains dedicated to improving reproductive knowledge and efficiency of the camel in the quest for faster ships in the desert. One of the big races is the Dubai King's Cup.

Camels are to Bedouins what cows are to the Nuer tribes in south Sudan and the Hindus in India. For the Bedouin, camels are transport, companion, hair to make tents and clothes, and providers of meat, milk,

Young camel jockeys from the United Arab Emirates and other Gulf countries in the three-kilometer Heritage Surprises 2000 camel race at Nad al-Sheba in Dubai, August 2000. (Reuters/Corbis)

and dung (for fuel). Bedouins will talk for hours about breeds of camel, their fine-colored hair, elegant looks, and sturdy frame. Lighter camels tend to come from the north of Arabia, where camels are larger than in the south of the peninsula. The finest breed is said to be the *batiniya* from Oman, with exquisitely small heads, long ears, and large eyes. The breed also has extraordinary stamina. A camel can locate water in the desert, and because it loses body liquids slowly and builds up a large hump of fat, it can go for days without water. At the end of a fast a camel can gulp up to 100 liters of water in the space of 15 minutes. Bedouins brand camels, not horses, and if they have to move on and leave a load because their camel has died in the desert, they will mark the load with the brand sign. Any other desert travelers will leave the load untouched if they come across it, understanding the mark of respect. In racing the camel is steered via a nose string, which is attached to a peg in a small hole in the camel's nose, and young boys are tied down to the racing saddle known as the *khurj* so that they don't fall off—an early initiation. Stirrups aren't used in racing.

Horse Racing Popular in Gulf States Today

Horse racing offers even more money than camel racing, especially in Saudi Arabia and the Emirates. The Dubai World Cup, organized by the Dubai Racing Club in March, has become the world's richest horse racing event, with $15 million in prize money. Dubai also hosts the annual Emirates Championship Cup, a 130-kilometer (80-mile) endurance horse race through the shifting sands of the desert. The Emirates boasts the 1,600-meter Abu Dhabi International Championship race, featuring three-year-old, purebred Arabian horses, and the 1,000-meter UAE Equestrian and Racing Federation Rous Stakes, which attracts purebred Arabian horses aged three years and above. The UAE Equestrian and Racing Federation is on a drive to raise and enhance the status of purebred Arabian horses at the international level and to dispel the belief that the purebred Arabian horses are not fit for flat racing. Saudi Arabia had a recent addition to its race circuit when the King Abdul-Aziz Racecourse near Riyadh was opened in 2002, holding the first Japan Cup. The state-of-the-art course was designed over three years by a Hong Kong company, then built over four years for a sum of $210 million—a fairly small amount because the land is owned by the royal family, labor costs are low in Saudi Arabia, and the cost of foundation work is low due to the absence of earthquakes in the kingdom. The course's vital statistics are impressive. The racecourse has an all-weather, counterclockwise, 2,000-meter red-clay dirt course with a width of 25 meters; an 1,800-meter training course with a width of 20 meters; and a trotting ring. The track is built so that the height of the surface of the back stretch is 5 meters higher than that of the home stretch. As a result even the spectators standing at the rail on the grandstand side can watch the horses on the back stretch and wherever else they are running on the track. It also boasts a huge 5x5-meter video matrix screen in the infield, with electronic information boards on both sides of the screen. The track and the six-story, 3,500-seat grandstand are surrounded by lighting facilities for night racing—men sit on the left, women sit on the right, and the royal family has a special area at the front.

The Arabian horse is unchallenged in the endurance marathons, a discipline in which Arabian horses have 95 percent of the top rankings. The international race circuit for Arabian horses includes Morocco, Algeria, Tunisia, Egypt, Qatar, Saudi Arabia, Oman, and the Emirates. Today's racehorses in the West are thought to be descendants of Arabian stallions brought from the Middle East during the Crusades in the eleventh through the fourteenth centuries and bred with the sturdy mares of England to produce faster horses that could carry weight over greater distances. So horse racing was a sport developed in Europe with Arab input. It became popular for knights and royalty to wager on races between two horses over a private course or an open field. King Charles II of England (1660–1685) was an early supporter, originating the nickname "the sport of kings." This sparked interest in breeding, and ultimately the thoroughbred lines known today can trace their male lines all the way back to three Arabian stallions from the seventeenth and eighteenth centuries, one from Tunisia, one from Syria, and one taken from the Turks in Hungary. The pure Arab horse is considered the most beautiful and elegant of breeds, and today it's Arabs who are at the forefront of horse racing. Famous breeders in the Arab world include Sheikh Mohammed bin Rashid Al Maktoum of Dubai in the UAE and Saudi Crown Prince Abdullah. The horses of

Horse-riding on the pyramids plateau at Giza in Cairo. (Norbert Schiller/Focus MidEast)

Sheikh Mansour bin Zayed Al Nahyan and Sheikh Ahmed bin Rashid Al Maktoum—both Emirates royalty—have a strong presence in Britain's racing circuit, including the prestigious Newmarket course, the headquarters of racing for over 300 years.

Falconry Still Popular among Bedouins

The ancient sport of falconry (*al-qanas*) is still popular in Bedouin communities and among Gulf royal families. The UAE has the Abu Dhabi Falcon Research Hospital, one of the only facilities in the world dedicated solely to medical care and research for falcons. The hospital has an examination room, a surgery, a pharmacy, and a research laboratory, as well as wards for housing sick birds and a necropsy where the vets can perform autopsies on dead birds. Vets have equipment to deal with routine procedures such as vaccinations and X-rays or the more complicated endoscopy—a process where a tiny camera is placed inside the bird to allow the vet to look at its internal organs. Traditionally, the birds were used for food, augmenting the desert's pickings of dates, milk, and bread, but today the birds are admired for their loyalty, beauty, and mastery of the hunt, and they symbolize bravery to the Arabs. Falcons have eyes that can spot the movement of prey more than a mile away. They range from fifteen to nineteen inches in size and can live for fifteen years or more if well cared for. And they are expensive to buy, from $330 to $330,000, depending on strength, age, eyesight, and speed. The females are bigger and stronger and make better hunters. The Bedouins catch wild falcons during autumn migration and

Falconry is popular in the United Arab Emirates and all over the Gulf region. (Caroline Penn/Corbis)

train them for the hunting season, which begins in early November and lasts until March or April. A trainer spends a month getting acquainted with a bird, patiently holding it on his arm, stroking it, talking to it, feeding it from the hand, and getting it used to a soft leather hood called a *burqu'* (also the name of the women's veil that leaves only the eyes showing). Once the falcon has adjusted to its handler, the leather hood is removed so eye contact can be developed. When it can jump from the trainer's hand to a wooden perch, it is considered to be tamed. Then the bird is encouraged to attack lures just a few meters away while still on a leash, before being unleashed to attack live pigeons at short distances. Hunting parties cook their game over an open fire in the desert in the evening, with each falconer bragging about the skill and courage of his falcons. That's

the romantic part, but hunting has come to be considered a problem in some Arab countries. It is an uphill struggle to enforce rules against trade in rare falcons and other animals upon wealthy visitors from the Gulf region. In Egypt, falcons and dogs are brought in especially by hunting parties to hunt down animals in the Sinai Peninsula and Red Sea mountains, where special environmental zones have been set up to protect species including deer and mountain rabbits. Egypt's Environmental Affairs Agency has over fifty rangers who work with Bedouin guards to monitor these areas and hand out fines to violators.

The New Cult of Bodybuilding

With the spread of gymnasiums and health clubs, "violent chic"—a fascination with bodybuilding and martial arts, or combat-ready sports—has become hugely popular all over the Arab world in the last decade. Sports that focus on individual invincibility and success are muscling their way onto the scene alongside traditional team sports like soccer. They offer a means to self-empowerment and self-respect in societies whose political systems strip so many people of those qualities. Depression about the political situation adds to the individual's sense of worthlessness. Legal steroids and protein powders are brazenly advertised in pharmacy windows, and action films (*aflaam akshun*) are a big favorite in video stores and all-night coffee shops, where the rock-bottom poor watch Indian films, Jean-Claude Van Damme, or Jackie Chan. Even karate classes for girls have become common. Egypt has its own action-movie star, Shahat Mabrouk, who started out as a poor kid doing shoeshines before becoming the Arnold Schwarzenegger of Arab cinema. In Cairo's *shaabi*—the sprawling, poor districts—a successful bodybuilder will be the talk of the neighborhood, and someone who can make a living as a bodyguard at a club or fancy villa, or even set up his own gym, is ironically seen as securing the frontier between the rich and the poor. Most of them pray and fast during Ramadan, having put behind them emaciated bodies, bad tempers, addictions, or an interest in Islamic militancy.

Though there is a debate in the press about the phenonemon, which coincides with a higher level of violent crime in society, less connection is made between violent film and violent behavior. Most of the violent crime has involved wealthy people hiring poor musclemen to beat people up for them, in the knowledge that legal systems are too cramped or compromised to deal with all the litigation already going on in society. Egyptian bodybuilders—around 50,000—dominate Arab and African bodybuilding championships, and they made it to first place in international competitions in 1995, 1996, and 1998. The Egyptian Bodybuilding Federation has poured all its resources into training two bodybuilders in each weight category, making sure they compete in as many international competitions as possible to get maximum experience. Shahat Mabrouk even came out of retirement in 1994 to take part in the 1998 world championships in the light-middleweight competition. "Unfortunately most of the young bodybuilders take one look in the mirror and forget competition. They see catwalk models. They start thinking about looking for a job as a bodyguard which can allow them to pick up chicks in their free time. Or they think of Shahat Mabrouk, who stopped representing Egypt in the international competitions and is now satisfied with showing off his muscles on TV," Federation head Adel Fahim—also head of the African federation—once said (*Middle East Times*, 22 November 1998). Egypt's bodybuilding team also placed first in the first intercontinental championship, held in Assiut in May 2001 in south Egypt (a backwater rural area renowned for its religious conservatism and a focus of fighting between the government and Islamic insurgents in the 1990s), winning four gold medals, while Saudi Arabia came in third. The list of countries that fielded teams makes for interesting reading: fourteen nations from three continents participated, with a huge Arab presence of ten countries and flimsy European interest. They were Egypt, Sudan, Libya, Tunisia, Algeria, the UAE, Syria, Lebanon, Saudi Arabia, Yemen, Japan,

Italy, Portugal, and Poland. "Assiut made us proud to host the inaugural edition of the event which was Egypt's idea in the first place," Fahim told the media afterwards (*al-Ahram Weekly*, 31 May 2001).

If it's poverty that drives bodybuilding in Egypt, it's affluence that motivates it in the UAE. In recent years, a slew of fitness centers have sprung up in the Emirates, catering to the growing number of health and fitness buffs in the country. The country has witnessed the proliferation of a broad range of fitness centers, including everything from bodybuilding and aerobics to yoga and karate. Young UAE men have turned up in hordes at state-of-the-art gymnasiums, where they mostly take up bodybuilding. Most apartment complexes also have fitness rooms and saunas. Leisure activities in Dubai extend to beauty salons, bridge, chess, health spas, massage, meditation, reiki, yoga, and dancing, to name just a few.

A-to-Z:
Key People and Terms

ABDULLAH, MAJED (B. 1958)
Saudi soccer player seen as Saudi's best-ever striker. He joined the Riyadh team al-Nasr in 1977 and was part of the Saudi national team that won the Asian Nations Cup for the first time in 1984 and again in 1988. He was also in the Saudi squad that qualified for the Olympics for the first time in 1984 and the World Cup finals for the first time in 1994. Abdullah led al-Nasr to eleven national, regional, and Asian titles, and he was on every Saudi national team that played between 1977 and 1994. His career spanned the coming-of-age period of

Saudi soccer and he became a force on the international scene. He retired in 1998.

AL-AHLY
One of Egypt's (and Africa's) two leading soccer teams (the other being Ahly's traditional Egyptian rival, Zamalek), based in Cairo. The African Soccer Federation chose it in 2000 as Africa's "team of the century." In 2001 the team surprised its own fans by beating Real Madrid in a friendly showcase that cost the Cairo team $1.5 million to host. The club, which plays in the red color of the old Egyptian flag, was set up in 1907 by Egyptian aristocrats in the plush neighborhood of Zamalek, but the team went on to acquire a reputation as the "people's side," as opposed to the more sophisticated image radiated by Zamalek (actually based in another district of Cairo). The team's fortunes have slumped since the death of President Saleh Selim in 2002, and Zamalek has the upper hand in Egypt and Africa as a whole. Their main player is striker Mahmoud al-Khatib, nicknamed Bibo, who has resisted European interest. Rivalry between Ahly and Zamalek is so intense that foreign referees have to be brought in to handle their derby matches, always held at Cairo's National Stadium.

BARRADA, AHMED (B. 1977)
Egyptian squash star and pinup celebrity who was one of the world's top ten players until he decided to quit after a stabbing attack against him in a Cairo neighborhood in 2001. His convalescence after the mysterious attack took longer than expected, and in the meantime he received offers to appear in Egyptian movies. In 2004 he married Egyptian actress Halla Sheeha and be-

gan a film career. He was ranked world number two in 1998 and once famously said: "I have one simple aim—to become champion of the world." The attack, the pressures of the media at home, and the attractions of his superstar status seem to have stymied that ambition.

BOULMERKA, HASSIBA (B. 1968)

The first African woman and Arab competitor to win a World Championship title. She finished first in the African Championship 800-meter and 1,500-meter races in 1988 and again in 1989. Boulmerka's performance at the Tokyo World Championships in August 1991 established her as a runner of international standing when she took

Algerian champion Hassiba Boulmerka, whose success challenged traditional views on women in sport. (Gray Mortimore/Getty Images)

the gold medal in the 1,500-meter race. Boulmerka became the first Algerian to win an Olympic Gold medal when she won the 1,500-meter race in the 1992 Barcelona Games. She won another gold for the same race in the Gothenburg World Championships in 1995. Her success on the track has been met with a mixed response in Algeria. She has been simultaneously hailed as a national hero and awarded state medals and castigated and threatened by Islamic militants for running in immodest attire. She dedicated her 1992 Olympic medal to the assassinated Algerian president Mohammed Boudiaf and criticized militant Islamists for repression of women and manipulation of Islamic cultural norms for political gain.

ESPERANCE (TARAJJI)

Tunisia's prime soccer team, founded in 1919. Their main player is striker Ali Zitouni, who is seen as one of Tunisia's brightest talents. Esperance plays in probably the most competitive league in Africa. Esperance, Club Africain, and CSFX have all won the African Cup, but Esperance is the team with the most prestige and history behind it. They won the African Cup in 1994 and were runners-up in 1999 and 2000.

GADDAFI, AL-SAADI (B. 1973)

Son of Libyan leader Muammar Gaddafi who has led Libyan "soccer diplomacy" in ending Libya's isolation in Europe. He is vice president of the Libyan football association, owner of Libya's al-Ittihad club, player on the Libyan national team, player with Italian team Perugia, and former member of the board of legendary Italian club Juventus. In October 2003 he failed a drug test, resulting in a surprisingly lax three-month playing ban. Saadi, one of Gaddafi's four sons, was trained in 1999 in Libya by Canadian sprinter Ben Johnson, who was stripped of his 1988 Olympic gold in the 100-meter after he tested positive for steroids at the Seoul Olympics. Saadi made a bid to run for the presidency of the African soccer association in January 2004 and fronted Libya's bid to co-host the 2010 World Cup with Tunisia. Italian Franco Scoglio left his position on Libya's national team in 2002 on bad terms, saying he refused to field the stylish Saadi, who analysts say Gaddafi is grooming to succeed him, because he was no good.

EL-GUERROUJ, HICHAM (B. 1975)

Moroccan runner who was crowned Male Athlete of the Year for the third year running in 2003 at the World Athletics Final in Monaco. The 1,500-meter world record holder, he broke the previous record when he chopped off a second over the previous 3:27:37 record set by Algerian Noureddine Morceli in Nice in 1995. Known for his Islamic piety and dedication, he has often said: "Hicham is my only enemy and only the clock can beat me." As expected, he won gold in the men's 1,500- and 5,000-meter in the Athens Olympics in 2004.

HASSAN, HOSSAM (B. 1966)

Egyptian soccer player seen as Egypt's best ever. In May 2001 he broke the record for most international games played with 157 caps. He is remembered for scoring Egypt's goal, a dramatic header against Algeria, which took the country into the 1990 World Cup. Hassan has an Egyptian high of sixty goals in international games, placing him eighth on the all-time list. He and his twin brother, player Ibrahim, have infamous tempers, making them the bad boys of Egyptian soccer. Hossam Hassan made a controversial decision to quit al-Ahly in 2001 for its archrival, Zamalek, citing problems with the team's French manager.

AL-HILAL

One of the two dominant teams in Saudi Arabia (along with al-Ittihad), the new arrival on the Arab soccer scene. Founded in 1957 in Riyadh by Sheikh Abdel-Rahman bin Said, it was the first team to win the Asian Football Federation championships since 1992 and supplies much of the talent for the Saudi national team. It won the Arab Club championship in 1994 and 1995. Popular players include Badr al-Khorashy and Saleh al-Hoti

IMAM, HAMADA (B. N.A.)

Famous Egyptian striker know as "The Fox" for his impeccable nose and killer instinct for goals. He scored a famed hat trick in a 5–1 win over English League winners West Ham United, who had come to Cairo in 1966 with English World Cup–winning heroes Bobby Moore and Geoffrey Hurst. Imam is now vice president of the Egyptian soccer association and host of a popular TV phone-in soccer show on Egyptian state television. Another famed striker is Mahmoud al-Khatib, an Egyptian al-Ahly player from 1972 to 1988 who was named Arab Sportsman of the Twentieth Century.

MABROUK, SHAHAT (B. 1961)

The Arab world's Jackie Chan. Winner of

Arabs Make It in Athletics

North Africans have excelled in athletics. Morocco has been the envy of Arab countries since it first rose to world prominence in athletics in 1984 when Nawal al-Moutawakel and Said Oueita won two gold medals in the Los Angeles Olympic Games, Oueita in the men's 5,000-meter and Moutawakel in the women's 400-meter hurdles. In Atlanta in 1996, Morocco took three bronze medals and a silver, and in Sydney in 2000 it won a silver and four bronzes. At the Sydney Olympics in 2000, Algeria claimed five medals, including the region's sole gold for Nouria Merah-Benida in the 1,500-meter race, following her compatriot Hassiba Boulmerka, who won the 1,500-meter race in Barcelona in 1992. "This was a victory for Arab women. Europeans have sponsorship and facilities but we have courage and heart," Merah-Benida said after the victory (Hargreaves 2001). Algerian Ali Saidi-Seif took the silver medal in the 5,000-meter race and Algerian Aissa Djabir Said-Guerni won a bronze in the men's 800-meter race. Abdel-Rahman Hammad won the bronze in the high jump and Mohamed Allalou won a light-welterweight bronze medal in boxing. Algerian middle-distance runner Noureddine Morceli previously set world records for the mile (1993), the 3,000-meter race (1994), the 1,500-meter race (1995), and the 2,000-meter race (1995), and he set indoor records for the 1,000-meter and 1,500-meter races. In Sydney Hicham el-Guerrouj of Morocco, the two-time 1,500-meter world champion, won silver in the men's 1,500-meter race. Countryman Ali Ezzine won a bronze medal in the men's 3,000-meter hurdles, becoming the first Arab to win a medal in an event usually dominated by Kenyans. Moroccan Nouzha Bidouane took bronze in the women's 400-meter hurdles, compatriot Brahim Lahlafi took the bronze in the men's 5,000-meter race, and Moroccan boxer Taher Tamsamani won the bronze medal as a losing semifinalist in the 57-kilogram category. Saudi Arabia took a silver in athletics and a bronze in show jumping. Hadi Souan Somayli became the first Saudi to win an Olympic medal when he clinched the silver medal in the men's 400-meter hurdles. Saudi national Khaled al-Eid emerged with a bronze medal in a three-way jump-off in the final equestrian event at the Games. (Also in Sydney, army officer Fehaid al-Dihani grabbed a first-ever Olympic medal for Kuwait on the fifth day of the sixteen-day-long event when he won the bronze medal in the men's shooting double trap event. Qatar's Assad Said Seif grabbed the bronze medal in weightlifting in the 105-kilogram category.) At the 2004 Athens Games, Morocco won two of the three golds won by Arab states with Hicham el-Guerrouj's victories in the men's 1,500- and 5,000-meter. Moroccan Hasna Benhassi won the silver medal in the women's 800-meter. Egyptian wrestler Karam Gaber won the third Arab gold, making Athens the most successful ever for Arabs in terms of gold medals (taking ten medals in all).

the Under–80-kg category at the first intercontinental bodybuilding championship in Egypt in 2001, before which he had already won five world bodybuilding championships and used his fame to build a film career in Egyptian action films. A shoemaker as a youngster, he won the world championship in his first stab at it in 1987, and followed that with his first film, *The Guide*. He is a cult hero among young men in poor neighborhoods, where they crowd into coffee shops late at night to watch his "violent chic" films and fill the local gyms by day to get a body like his.

MERAH-BENIDA, NOURIA (B. 1970)

Algerian runner who won the Arab world's only gold at the Sydney Olympics in 2000, taking the women's 1,500-meter title. "This was a victory for Arab women," she said. "Europeans have sponsorship and facilities but we have courage and heart."

MORCELI, NOUREDDINE (B. 1970)

Algerian middle-distance runner who won three World Championships in the 1,500-meter category and the 1996 Olympics 1,500-meter race. At one point, he held all outdoor records from 1,500-meter to 3,000-meter, as well as the indoor 1,000-meter and 1,500-meter. He has been superseded in men's middle-distance running by Moroccan athlete Hicham el-Guerrouj.

STANGE, BERND (B. 1948)

German manager of Iraq's national soccer team who caused an uproar by accepting the post in November 2002 when Saddam Hussein's regime was still in power. But during 2003 he managed to take Iraq to its highest FIFA (Federation Internationale de Football Association) ranking in fifteen years, moving 30 places up the list from 74 to 44, higher than countries like Scotland, Wales, and Austria. The team reached the Asian championships and is aiming for the World Cup finals in Germany in 2006. Stange, along with Iraqi soccer association chief Mohammed Hussein Said and team captain Naji Hossam, received an FIFA award in late 2003 for his efforts to resuscitate Iraqi soccer, especially since he did it without any wages for most of the year. Stange previously coached communist East Germany from 1983 to 1988 and later Bundesliga team Hertha Berlin. Iraq's main sta-

dium was badly damaged in the 2003 war and twelve major players moved to play abroad. Efforts to revive the national league got nowhere because of crowd violence. Stange's driver was shot and he has funded his team partly from his own pocket. He was replaced by Adnan Hamad before the 2004 Olympics.

TARDELLI, MARCO (B. 1954)

Egypt's current national soccer coach, appointed in April 2004 after Egypt's poor performance in the Africa Nations Cup in Tunisia in January 2004 led previous incumbent Mohsen Saleh to resign (clearly jumping before he was pushed). Tardelli, a former Juventus midfielder who went to coach Inter-Milan and Bari, is tasked with getting Egypt to the 2006 World Cup finals. Perhaps no man has enjoyed scoring in a World Cup final as much as Marco Tardelli. The latest of a stream of Europeans to lead Egypt, he is reportedly getting $40,000 per month from the Egyptian soccer association. He brought with him fellow Italian player Gannini Luca as his assistant coach.

TROUSSIER, PHILIPPE (B. 1955)

Frenchman who signed a two-year deal to coach Qatar's national team after the World Cup in 2002, during which his previous charge, Japan, gave its best-ever performance at the World Cup finals. He is aiming to get Qatar, which has no professional soccer league but big hopes, into the World Cup finals in 2006, but with Doha staging the 2006 Asian Games, he also faces the challenge of producing a team good enough to impress at the prestigious continental event. The Frenchman coached Nigeria, South Africa, Burkina Faso, and the Ivory Coast before becoming Japan's most successful manager by taking them to the last sixteen of the World Cup finals. Troussier replaced another Frenchman, Pierre Lechantre, in a job pressured by Qatar's impatience to make it big in soccer in record time. He said on accepting the job that Qatari soccer officials were practical about what they expected of him. "If I had gone to Saudi Arabia they would have straightaway asked me to get the World Cup," he joked. "But I think there is just one Qatari playing in Europe. Only when you have 30 to 40 players playing in big European clubs, you can say Qatar [soccer] is of some class."

VAN DER LEM, GERARD (B. 1952)

Dutch manager of the Saudi national team. He moved to Riyadh from his position as reserve team coach of Ajax Amsterdam in the Netherlands in mid-2002 after Saudi Arabia sacked Nasser al-Johar over the team's poor showing during the 2002 World Cup finals. He suffered a heart attack in December 2002. The team was once coached by Hungarian ace Ferenc Puskas.

ZAMALEK

One of Egypt's two major teams (the other is archrival al-Ahly) and one of Africa's most successful clubs. Founded in 1911, it currently has the upper hand in Egypt and the continent as a whole, a situation that came about after a humiliating 6–1 defeat to al-Ahly in 2001. They bounced back, winning the Egyptian Cup 2002, Egyptian Super Cup 2002, African Champions League 2002 (for the fifth time), African Super Cup 2003 (for the third time), and the Egyptian League title for 2002/2003. In 2003

they won the Arab Club Championship. In Egypt the team has the image of being the thinking man's team, as opposed to al-Ahly's more populist, working-man image. Zamalek plays in white shirts. Their main player is Hossam Hassan, though Zamalek supplies most of the national team.

ZIDANE, ZINEDINE (B. 1972)

Real Madrid soccer star from the Algerian immigrant suburbs of Marseilles in France, where he was born to Berber Algerian parents. The FIFA ranked him the best player in the world in 1998, the year he shone for France when it won the World Cup, and in 2000. He played for Italian giant Juventus for most of the 1990s before heading in 2001 to Real Madrid, which was in the process of putting together what it regarded as one of the strongest teams in the world, including English midfielder David Beckham and Portuguese star Luis Figo. Signed by Cannes at age 14, he moved to Bordeaux before getting the lucrative Juventus signing in 1996.

Bibliography

Print Resources

Al-Mistikawy, Hassan. "The Republic of Football." *Wughat Nazar* 4, no. 42 (July 2002).

Amar, Paul. "Show of Strength." *Cairo Times*, 9–22 July 1998.

Beiruty, Hikmat. "Muslim Women in Sport." In *Nida'ul Islam Magazine* (www.islam.org.au; reprinted on www.zawaj.com, a site about Muslim marital issues).

"Egyptian Lifter Sees Herself as Role Model." Reuters, 10 March 2004.

Hargreaves, Jennifer. *Heroines of Sport: The Politics of Difference and Identity.* London: Routledge, 2001.

Mazhar, Inas. "Don't Look Now." *al-Ahram Weekly*, 24–30 May 2001.

Naim, Mohammed Nabil. "A New Setback for Arab Football." *al-Hayat*, 14 June 2003.

Shahine, Alaa. "What Bodies!" *al-Ahram Weekly*, 31 May–6 June 2001.

Thabet, Nagy. "Women's Soccer Arrives All over Middle East." *Middle East Times*, no. 18 (1998).

Web Sites

www.ziyara.com. Arabic site about sport and recreation.

www.fifa.com. The official site of soccer's governing body, FIFA.

www.dubaisports.com. UAE site dedicated to sports in the high-tech fitness heaven of Dubai.

www.ifyougolf.com. A site with information on where to golf in the Middle East.

www.middleeastfootball.com. Site concerning soccer in the Middle East.

www.typecamelracing.com. Web site about the sport of camel racing.

www.allcamels.com. Site about camels in general.

www.austcamel.com.au. Site concerning the Australian and international camel trade.

www.ifahr.net Site of the International Federation of Arabian Horse Racing Authorities.

www.arabians-international.com. Site dedicated to racing with Arabian horses.

www.dubaiworldcup.com. Official site of Dubai's premier horse-racing tournament.

www.alzaeem.com. Saudi-based site about Arab sports, with a focus on soccer.

www.dakar.com. The official site of the Paris-Dakar (sometimes called the Dakar-Sharm) rally.

http://darwish.sytes.net/bid/index.php?task= tournaments. An unofficial Web site concerning Egypt's bid for the 2010 World Cup.

www.egyptiansoccer.com. Egyptian site with up-to-date information on Egyptian soccer.

www.sport4ever.net. Global sports news in Arabic.

www.egyptsport.com. Site with information on soccer and major competitive sports in Egypt.

www.egyptianfootball.net. Soccer site set up by Egyptian plastic surgeon Tarek Said.

www.efa.com.eg. Official site. of the Egyptian Football [Soccer] Association.

www.egypt-2010.com. The official Web site of Egypt's ill-fated 2010 World Cup bid.

www.mido-online.com. Popular site for fans of heartthrob Egyptian soccer star Ahmed Hossam, aka Mido.

11

The Arabic Language

Arabization's 1,400-Year Struggle Continues Today

The new realities in the Arab region over the last fifty years have in-flicted more changes upon the Arabic language than any other period since the Arab tribes united the Middle East and North Africa in the sev-enth century and their language interacted with the conquered peoples' tongues. Arab intellectual and cultural elites display a fair amount of paranoia about the health of the language and the Arab identity it pre-serves. This is partly because of the large minorities in the Arab world who still have their own languages (or remember that they once had their own languages) and partly because of a historical awareness of how the fortunes of civilizations tend to ebb and flow, and the ancestors of most of today's Arabs once belonged to the non-Arabic-speaking *'ajam*. The Arab intelligentsia are also acutely aware that bits of the Ara-bic language have been lopped off by foreigners before, from Andalusia 500 years ago to Palestine and Iskanderun 50 years ago.

The battle to Arabize the region continues today as it always has done since the time of the conquests. But much of the anxiety of intellectuals and academics over the deterioration of the classical language—and the vitality of dialects and inroads of foreign tongues—is misplaced. The re-ality is that the language, in all its forms, is unifying the region as it never has done previously. Modern communications, entertainment, media, politics, and business have facilitated more linguistic unity and mutual understanding than ever before. Arabic dialects are being standardized within individual Arab countries based on the prestigious dialects of their capital cities, and these national dialects are in turn being affected by other dialects and formal Arabic through the unifying power of mass media and communications. Cairene Arabic first played this role during the Arab nationalist period and continues to do so via Egyptian televi-sion's huge reach—you can watch Egyptian soaps in Mauritania in the west and Oman in the east—but today Levantine and Gulf dialects com-pete with Egyptian for public space. Even dialects in the Maghreb, which have always been receivers of linguistic culture from the Mashreq, are now better understood in the Arab East. Both formal and colloquial Arabic are interacting in popular culture and politics in the Arab world today in a manner critical to the final victory of the Arabs over the world they called "Arab."

Sudan and the North African countries have seen critical moves to complete this process of Arabization. The Atlas Mountains, Kabylia, and the Aures Mountains in North Africa, as well as Jebel Marra in west Sudan, the Red Sea Hills in east Sudan, Mount Lebanon, north Iraq, and the mountains in the south of the Arabian Peninsula—all have been strongholds against the Arabization that more easily swept the rest of the region. While some of these outposts maintain their separate languages today, only the most remote Atlas mountain villages retain true non-Arabic speakers.

These minorities are regarded to varying degrees as threats. Sudan's Islamic government has succeeded in making Arabic the lingua franca of southerners, overtaking English. Linguist Amin Abu Manqa estimates that 65 percent of Sudanese today speak only Arabic, compared with 51 percent in 1956 at independence. Government zeal to establish Arabic has been successful, to the extent that many smaller languages are threatened with extinction. "The smaller languages should be recorded because they are endangered," Abu Manqa said (interview with author, Reuters, 22 August 2002). "If we stamp them out we deprive ourselves and the world of their richness." The dialects of the Nubians, the indigenous ethnic group along the Nile in north Sudan, are also losing ground to Arabic, said Nubia specialist Khidir Abdelkarim (interview with author, August 2002). Modern Nubians, like the modern Egyptians, consider

themselves to be an integral part of the Arab world, but unlike Egyptians most of them retain their pre-Arabic language. In fact, the Nubian Mahas dialect, and the Beja language in the east, have been the key indigenous influences behind Sudan's mainstream Arabic dialect, Abu Manqa says. Though there is no official public usage of Beja or Nubian dialects, only a minority of intellectuals in these groups feel threatened by Arabic. The Nuba Mountain people (who have no connection to the Nubians) are caught in the maelstrom, because they are non-Arabic-speaking Muslims of clear non-Arab ethnicity on the border between "north" and "south" Sudan. Arabic is now threatening their own Nyimang language, and as nominal "northerners" (because they are Muslim) they are not in a strong position to resist. "Any language has an ideology but with Arabic it is systematic," said Ismail Ali Saadeldin, state minister for Nuba Mountain affairs (interview with author, August 2002), who rails against the ideological spread of Arabism through the Arabic language. "It's now a psychological problem, because we feel inferior while they think that being Arab makes them superior. The first step is a political agreement to build our confidence about who we are. That's the base line. It'll take a generation to change people who now think they are Arab." In another example of the ideology of Arabism in action, Sudan has Hausa-speaking tribes, a legacy of Sudan's place on the traditional pilgrimage route to Mecca from West Africa. But the authorities list them in censuses as "Nigerian," as if they were somehow less Sudanese than other ethnic groups who speak Arabic. As part of these efforts by post-independence governments to promote Arabic and Muslim-Arab identity as the

The Great "Origins of Arabic" Debate

If one includes "non-Arab" countries with Arabic-speaking minorities, Arabic is spoken in all of the following countries: Afghanistan, Algeria, Bahrain, Chad, Cyprus, Djibouti, Egypt, Eritrea, Iran, Iraq, Israel, Jordan, Kenya, Kuwait, Lebanon, Libya, Mali, Mauritania, Morocco, Niger, Oman, Palestinian West Bank and Gaza, Qatar, Saudi Arabia, Sudan, Syria, Tajikistan, Tanzania, Tunisia, Turkey, United Arab Emirates (UAE), Uzbekistan, and Yemen. Arabic has about thirty main dialects, the largest of which are, in descending order of number of speakers: Egyptian, Algerian, Maghrebi (Moroccan), Sudanese, Saidi (Upper Egyptian), North Levantine, Mesopotamian (Iraqi), and Najdi (Saudi). Other languagues using the Arabic script are Hausa, Kashmiri, Kazak, Kurdish, Kyrghyz, Pashto, Persian/Farsi, Sindhi, Turkish, Uyghur, and Urdu. There are also, of course, diaspora communities speaking the language around the world (there are one million North Levantine speakers in Argentina, for example; see www.ethnologue.com). Scholars have traditionally held that Semitic languages (sometimes referred to as Afro-Asiatic) evolved in the Arabian Peninsula, but thinking is changing, with many now arguing that these languages began in the Levant and from there penetrated into the Peninsula. Arabic in a form of Aramaic script is found scattered across the Levant, in the Negev, Dead Sea, Petra, Hauran in Syria, and Egypt's eastern desert, all dating from the few centuries before the Arab conquests. There are also examples of pure classical Arabic from the same period in other Semitic scripts. The Nabataeans, a confederation of tribes in modern Jordan and northwest Saudi Arabia, appeared to have spoken some mixture of Arabic and Aramaic and to write Aramaic in a script seen as a precursor to the Arabic that emerged after the conquests. How much Aramaic and Arabic languages should be viewed as connoting separate peoples or ethnicities is open to question: Arab nationalists tend to be wary of interpretations of the Nabataeans or any other Semitic group in the Peninsula and Fertile Crescent that place them outside the Arab sphere, and there is a natural tendency in the Arab region to equate "Semitic" with "Arab." It is usually claimed that the earliest text to have survived in a language identifiable as Arabic is the famous tomb inscription of Imru al-Qays from Namara (southeast of Damascus), dated to A.D. 328, but it's written in a variant of the Nabataean/Aramaic script and some scholars deny that the language can be usefully analyzed in any way as Arabic. The mystery is how and where, over some 600 years, the mix of Aramaic and Arabic spoken and written in this vast area was united to produce the Arab conquests and the Arabic language and dialects that we know today. The Islamic tradition says this development was the work of the Qureish tribe of Mecca, which, via the mission of the Prophet, imposed its Arabic

great unifier, the regime of Jaafar al-Nimeiri even issued different types of passports, one valid only for Arab countries and a more difficult-to-obtain "international" passport for movement elsewhere.

Algeria's Berber activism since 1980 comes at a time when Berber language and identity are at a historic low point vis-à-vis its 1,300-year-old relationship with Arabic and Arabism. The language and the identity are on the point of extinction in Tunisia and Libya. Of Algeria's four main Berber groupings, only the Kabyles are fighting back. In Morocco, numerical strength is

A first-century C.E. burial box with an Aramaic inscription that reads "James, son of Joseph, brother of Jesus." Archaeologists say this box possibly held the remains of James, the brother of Jesus of Nazareth. Aramaic in various dialects was the major language of the Levant and Mesopotamia until the advent of Arabic, a sister language of both Aramaic and Hebrew. (Biblical Archaeology Society of Washington, D.C./Getty Images)

as the standard for the united peoples and tribes of the Middle East. The dialects, the argument goes, were a corruption from that pure form accepted by all. Others, from within Islamic tradition, as well as Westerners, identify classical Arabic with a nonspoken, or at least formal, literary language used by various tribes for the composition of poetry. The huge variation in today's dialects in the Peninsula and Fertile Crescent may support this latter view: classical Arabic was an amalgamation of most of the extant Semitic tongues, and only the Aramaic speakers in the Fertile Crescent were required to engage in what might be termed a language switch of major proportions once they came under the rule of the Arab conquerors. Some Aramaic-speaking communities remain, mainly Christians in north Iraq, and speakers of ancient Semitic languages/dialects (debate rages) have remained outside the Arabic circle in mountainous regions of the far south of the Peninsula, like the Jibali speakers of Dhofar in south Oman.

compromised by cultural and geographic diversity. For political reasons, the Moroccan royal family often marries Berber women, just as the Abbasid caliphs in Baghdad often married the daughters of important Persian families. All Moroccan primary school pupils in Morocco will be required to learn some Berber language by 2008. In the midst of continued violent protests, Algeria began moves in 2001 to give the Kabyle Berber dialect official status. The Arabizers also have French to deal with. Though the battle has been tough, Arabic is essentially winning out in the

Lebanese singer Majida al-Roumy is one among many regional stars who usually sing in classical Arabic. (Norbert Schiller/Focus MidEast)

struggle with Francophone elites—many of them Berbers—to impose French. When in 1987 Zein al-Abidine Ben Ali removed Habib Bourguiba, who had always been reticent about bringing formal Arabic back to Tunisia after the French experience, the government began a decisive wave of Arabization in public life, though secondary-school instruction in many subjects is still conducted in French. Daily newspapers now appear in colloquial Tunisian Arabic—something once seen by purists as anathema, but now regarded as strengthening Arab identity because the reference point for colloquial language is correctly recognized as the classical Arabic language, the "other" without which it wouldn't exist.

This doesn't negate the fact that French has entered the fabric of colloquial speech in North Africa more than anywhere else in the Arab world, but in an Arabized form (for example, in Algeria, one will hear ordinary people saying *watanique* for "patriotic" instead of the Arabic *watani*). Once, linguists and politicians cared greatly about these matters; now few assign it much significance in the wider scheme of things. Classical Arabic is still hip. Some of today's biggest singers, such as Majida al-Roumy and Kazem al-Saher, and newer pop stars such as Yuri Mrakadi (Muraqqadi), have made their names singing in the classical language. Many of the world's Muslims learn Arabic as a second language. "The United States is actively turning the globalization trend into an Americanization process, seeking world hegemony and domination and forcing its values and criteria worldwide," Lebanese Arabic-language expert Sheikh Abdel-Nasser al-Jabri said

Colloquial Arabic Today

Colloquial Arabic language is obviously in use everywhere, but public recognition of its status has been problematic. Language in any culture often plays a role in exploitative social and political situations: control of the formal expression can mean one has access to knowledge and power, and an inability to manipulate formal language can leave one disenfranchised and weak. Egyptian director Khaled Yousef hinted at this when one character in his 2001 comedy film *Gawaz bi Qarar Gumhouri* (*Marriage by Presidential Decree*) had difficulty pronouncing the big political statements uttered by her son, a poor boy expecting to meet the president of the republic. Arab leaders have attained respect through their mastery of the formal language; others have won ridicule for their failure to do so. But in a sign of how classical Arabic is being knocked off its pedestal, leaders no longer see the need to demonstrate erudition, and will even make a virtue of their lack of it. There are newspapers in many Arab countries that make liberal use of colloquial language as a means of boosting sales, as they search for new appeals to readers in cutthroat press wars. Attitudes toward language have loosened, perhaps because colloquial language is now seen as less of a threat to Arab unity, on both the cultural and political levels. The interrelated experience of postindependence pan-Arabism, culminating in the satellite revolution, has meant there's also more awareness around the region of different dialects. "All these [Arab] nationalities come together, especially on the lighter programs. It's bringing people together. All the issues and problems are the same—women, religion, freedoms. The same divide exists in each country between liberals and conservatives," said Jordanian rights activist Sa'eda Kilani, who is preparing a study on the effects of satellite channels on the Arab world (interview with author, June 2002). "People are even getting to know the accents. We wouldn't know what North Africans were saying before." Hazem al-Oulabi, director of the Damascus Institute for Teaching Arabic to Foreigners, agrees. "The satellite channels bring the local dialects closer, increase the ability for mutual understanding between different Arab countries, and increase the ability to understand local cultures," he said (interview with author, December 2002). In the 1970s Morocco had to offer translations of Syrian drama; today, pan-Arab satellite channel al-Jazeera will only occasionally feel it has to offer formal Arabic translations of Moroccan speakers. Yet the differences between Maghrebi and Mashreqi dialects are stark, and they catch many off guard and lead to amusing misunderstandings. The Egyptian colloquial word "to look at" in Tunisia means "to give wind," but the Egyptian understanding is the one that has traveled around the entire Mashreq, so it's Tunisians who are at a disadvantage. While the contemporary barriers over colloquial language came down long ago in Egypt, through vernacular poets like Bairam al-Tunsi, Salah Jahine, and Ahmed Fouad Negm, they have yet to be breached in Saudi Arabia. Anthropologist Saad Sowayan's work on colloquial poetry has met with a cold reception in Saudi Arabia. "People think I'm hired by the colonialists to divide and undermine the Arabs because I write about colloquial poetry," he said (interview with author, April 2003).

(*The Daily Star*, 23 April 2003). But, he went on: "In facing this challenge, the Arabic language becomes instrumental in preserving our cultural hemisphere and protecting our heritage, religion and values."

Efforts Today to Simplify the Classical Language

Today's confidence among linguists over the status of the language is the end product of a difficult century when things weren't always looking up. The first half of the twentieth century saw Turkey under Kemal Ataturk swap the Arabic script for the Latin alphabet, while the French authorities in Algeria declared French to be the country's official language. An Egyptian movement called for elevating colloquial dialect to the status of formal language in an attempt to debunk classical Arabic and fix Egypt in the European constellation alongside Turkey. Maronite Lebanon celebrated French over Arabic in public life, only 51 percent of Sudanese spoke Arabic, and probably less than half the population of the Maghreb countries, excluding Egypt, were native Arabic speakers. All this was going on in the world we have come to call "Arab."

Unlike Hebrew, which was reinvented, standardized, and simplified for a clear purpose, Arabic, with its immense, rich, and diverse vocabulary and grammatical possibilities, remains an uncontrollable beast. That makes it a problem for Arabs themselves to learn. After decades of arguments over the supposedly evil influence of colloquial speech, the elders of the Arabic linguistic heritage have concluded that Arab cultural unity today requires that the formal language be made easier for Arabs

to learn. Arabs face a far more complex situation than speakers of most other languages. Each era of Arab history has had its own vocabulary, which usually involved the same words developing new meanings and usages. A writer today could pluck out any one of them for use in an article, essay, or novel. Those steeped in the classical tradition will frequently throw an archaic phrase from the past into a newspaper article, or suddenly toss in a rhetoric flourish or an ancient reference, to spice up the text and display much-respected erudition in the Arabic language. For English speakers, this would be the equivalent of language appearing in an op-ed column not only from the time of Shakespeare but also from Chaucer, William the Conqueror, and Queen Victoria, all in one go. During the Iraq war, Iraqi minister of information Mohammed Said al-Sahhaf bamboozled everyone in the Arab world with his description of the invading forces as "'*uluuj* of colonialism." A debate raged throughout the Arab press about what '*uluuj* meant—most concluded it was an archaic term for "bloodsucking insect" or "parasite" ("It's not mine or his [Saddam's]; it's from Caliph Omar Ibn al-Khattab," Sahhaf said when asked about the origin of the word on Abu Dhabi TV in August 2003). It's this complexity that journalists and other writers have been tackling for decades, and language academies are finally admitting that this complexity actually promotes disunity rather than unity.

The new aim of educators and linguistic experts for the coming generation is to focus on a set of grammatical essentials that all Arabic speakers should grasp, cutting out more elaborate phrasings and at the same time ironing out divergences that have appeared in formal Arabic used in the

An example of the Arabic script from a book of hadiths, or sayings of the Prophet. (Claude Stemmelin)

Maghreb and Mashreq. Now a process of homogenization is in place between Arab East and Arab West, in formal and everyday speech. The aim is to match this with modern teaching methods (Arabic learning at school is a notoriously unpleasant experience). The grammatical mistakes on Egyptian television are legion, and even in Saudi Arabia—the Bedouin heartland—there is a sense that the level of Arabic competence is deteriorating, as families push their children to learn English. Knowledge of English is for the most part poor. The definite article is much overused, and even the United Nations Development Program's Arab Human Development Report talks repeatedly of "the Arab civilization," while in Egypt Bobby Ewing in the U.S. soap *Dallas* was translated in Egypt with the classical Arabic word for "puppy dog" (*jarw*) because state television translators misheard "Bobby" as "Puppy." Now state-run televisions in numerous Arab countries carry educational programs asking questions, such as Why do people have problems learning classical Arabic? Should Arabic be shorn of its grammatical flourishes and simplified for Arabs to learn it more easily? "Experts now see the need to simplify the teaching of Arabic grammar, especially in the early stages of teaching, via relying on the essentials and not going into complex side issues. We cannot ask a child to learn Arabic as the early grammarians used it. We need to be objective in teaching grammar. It used to be an end in itself, but now it is seen as a means to enable the student to talk in an easy and expressive way," said Hazem al-Oulabi, director of the Damascus Institute for Teaching Arabic to Foreigners. "The language is the biggest element in

Arab unity" (interview with author, December 2002).

This new approach means that forms of Arabic that were once considered enemies of unity are now being reappraised as "weapons" in cementing Arab identity over the last fifty years. Journalism, for example, has played a pioneering role in simplifying classical Arabic for modern usage. Newspapers in some Arab countries use colloquial speech not only in cartoon captions but also in editorial content. Up to now, experts at the many Arabic-language academies in the region have worried over the spread of foreign concepts and errors in grammar, spelling, morphology, and logical sequence of ideas. Now journalese is being recognized as having gone some way to rejuvenate and elevate formal Arabic and make it expressive like other world languages. Governments are using the media to help in teaching this pared-down formal language, Oulabi said, pointing to the Arabic version of *Sesame Street* and the Spacetoon cartoon channel. "There has been a rise in the level of spoken language so that the gap between formal and spoken has been reduced. Children's programs on television are mainly in formal Arabic and this is supporting the spread of formal language among children," Oulabi said. "Within a few years we will have enabled the Arab child to use formal Arabic in a better way than he did last century" (interview with author, December 2002). Though local terminology for administrative and public offices and institutions varies throughout the region, the normalized journalistic style is remarkably uniform. "The service that the media have rendered the Arabic language is sometimes put on a par with the contributions of the Arabic Language Academy [in Cairo]," academic Nabil

Abdelfattah wrote in a 1996 essay on journalese in Egypt (Elgibali 1996). "This language genre could serve as a model for further changes in Modern Standard Arabic (MSA), making it more communicative, rather than purely academic." Writers are also breaking conventions. According to columnist Abdo Wazen in *al-Hayat*, today's novelists "want to write as they talk, with complete spontaneity, surpassing the censorship imposed by the language itself and all the other censorships out there" (*al-Hayat*, 8 October 2002). In fact, well-established writers like Naguib Mahfouz, Elias Khoury, Maroun Abboud, Youssef Habashy al-Ashqar, and Yousef al-Qa'id led the way in using colloquial language for dialogue in

Arabic script, as it appears in this passage from the Quran. (Claude Stemmelin)

their novels. They pioneered the modern challenge to the linguistic order. As Syrian poet Mohammed Maghout once famously said: "With my foot I kick the dictionary and the conventions" (*al-Hayat*, 8 October 2002).

The Arabic-language academies are a strong presence in the Arab world. Algeria recently added its own academy to the list, which began with the Damascus Academy in 1920. The most prestigious is in Cairo, home to a Federation of Arabic Language Academies since the early 1990s, where members from around the region attempt to unify their fatwas on new words and concepts entering the language. Their purist theory continues to demand that foreign loanwords be replaced with pure Arabic forms. But they have had only limited

An example of Quranic script. (Claude Stemmelin)

success, and the result has been a multiplicity of words for one idea. Egyptian President Anwar Sadat, in a visionary speech, once promised that every Egyptian would own his very own *electrona*, an on-the-spot coinage for "computer." His innovation didn't last, as purists settled on *al-haasib al-aali* ("the mechanical calculator"), which today vies in newsprint with the transliteration for "computer," *kumbyutir*. "Plastic" suffers from similar confusion, with some uneducated rural dwellers in Egypt even pronouncing it *bulushtiki*, in an apparent conflation with the word "ballistic." The Damascus Language Academy famously invented the *haatif* for the word "telephone" (from a formal Arabic word meaning "to call or shout out") and the term has won acceptance in most of the Arab world, although the Egyptian media often prefer the transliteration *tilifone*. The Cairo Academy's *mahmoul* ("carried") and Damascus's *khalawi* ("cellular") are still battling it out as the formal Arabic version of "mobile" phone. Political terms like "Islamist" and "fundamentalist" are as controversial in Arabic as they are in English. Many writers don't like the word *islami* for "Islamist" because they argue it implies that these politicians are more Muslim than others and thus is in itself a concession to the Islamist agenda. They might prefer *islamawi* (Islamicist), or even the more clearly pejorative *muta'aslim*, meaning "trying/claiming to be Islamic."

Only today are linguists and sociologists coming to grips with the idea of Arabic as a dynamic and changing language. New thinking on the origins of the language has spilled over into other fields of study. One of the reasons formal Arabic is difficult to master is that, as linguist Alaa Elgibali argues, it is possibly a composite language, not a natural language like any of its dialects (Elgibali 1996). As a vast amalgamation of Semitic dialects, it is a repository for words from other Semitic dialects/languages that died out and others that survive. Canaanite, Aramaic, and Arabic appear to be the three dominant dialects of one original proto-Semitic language. (Hebrew is close to Aramaic, as is the extant Jibali language of Oman.) Whether the classical language already existed at the time of the conquests or was put together by post-conquest grammarians, these self-appointed guardians of the language "believed in its supremacy over all other languages, equated their grammar books with native intuition, and resisted the slightest reform to its description or even orthography" (Elgibali 1996). They also set Quranic diction and pre-Islamic poetry as the only pure forms of the language.

The result is that, for centuries, the language has been seen as immune to change, and the new ideas, findings, and approaches of modern linguistics have been routinely dismissed as irrelevant. Egyptian man-of-letters Taha Hussein was famously tried over his investigations into whether pre-Islamic poetry was truly pre-Islamic: he suggested that the classical grammarians propagated the poetry as pre-Islamic to back up the idea of the Arab tribes as the bearers of the pure Arabic used in the Quran. In recent decades scholars of early Islamic history have realized that linguistic research can explain some of the mysteries surrounding the early development of Arab-Islamic civilization. Christoph Luxenberg, a scholar of Semitic languages in Germany (writing under a pseudonym), has argued that the term *houri*, which medieval Muslim scholars of the Quran took to mean "young virginal

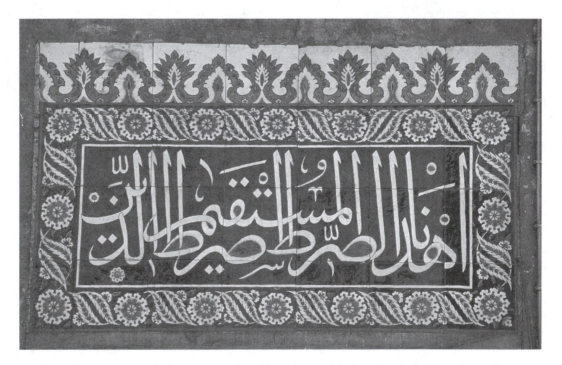

Arabic script on patterned blue ceramic tiles. The tiles are displayed in the Calligraphy Galleries at the Topkapi Palace in Istanbul, Turkey. (Adam Woolfitt/Corbis)

maidens," could derive from an Aramaic word for white raisins (Luxenberg 2000). Similarly, Lebanese scholar Kamal Salibi has argued that Arabic can be used to shed light on the meaning of obscure Hebrew biblical texts. None of this is surprising, considering that Arabic is so vast and ancient that it even contains words of Sumerian and Pharaonic origin—the two oldest (and incidentally non-Semitic) languages in the Middle East. One example is *haikal*, meaning "structure, framework, or temple" in Arabic, but which started life as *a-gal*, a Sumerian word meaning "house of worship," which can be traced in variant pronunciations through all the Semitic languages in the Mashreq until it reached today's still-extant Hebrew and Arabic. Donny Youkhanna, director of Baghdad's Antiquities Research and Studies Department, argues that a significant portion of the dialect of the dwellers of Iraq's southern marshes use vocabulary that has origins in the Sumerian language of their ancient ancestors (interview with author, May 2002).

Although the Arabic language is normally referred to as diglossic, meaning it has two distinct formal and informal forms, like German or Greek, the picture is quite a bit more complicated. Egyptian linguist el-Said Badawi was first to expose this complexity in his theory of five levels of speech, ranging from the absolutely colloquial to the absolutely formal language of the Quran, which speakers continually slip in and out of. Badawi says modern television ads provide the clearest example of this polyglossic system (Elgibali 1996). The highest level is used only in admonitory commercials promoting water conservation or sexual chastity to combat AIDS, and the language is invariably Quranic. The next level down is employed as the male "voice of reason"

or scientific voice, which often appears as voice-overs to banking or car advertisments. At the middle level things are a bit more intimate: a family doctor talks to the camera, lecturing on the quasi-scientific properties of a brand of toothpaste, the protective quality of a baby diaper, or the curative powers of a certain medicine. But most ads on Arab national television are delivered on the next level, the "standard colloquial," of each region, which is reserved for objects of indulgence such as food and fancy clothes. A small number of commercials use the pure, "mother-tongue" colloquial language for goods aimed at the lowest stratum of society.

A comparison with Latin can help put the proportions of the Arabic language in perspective. Latin spawned a number of derivatives, including Italian, Spanish, French, and Romanian, which developed into separate languages partly because Latin, despite its hallowed status, was not a holy Christian language. Arabic, on the other hand, was theorized as being God's chosen language and those who spoke it were considered to be among God's chosen people. Not only that, the elevation of the Quranic text to a concept of divine linguistic perfection created an imperative to maintain the use of that formal language. So colloquial Arabic never evolved into separate written languages in the way of the Romance languages. Shorn of the Quran, formal Arabic, and Islam, the Maltese did just that—today's "Malti" is the Egyptian, Tunisian, and Iraqi languages that never were. Indeed, some linguists prefer to consider some Arabic dialects as separate languages, by which reckoning "Egyptian" is the fourteenth most widely spoken language in the world. Modern pan-Arabism has provided an additional push

Malta: The Dialect That Got Away

In Malta's experience, colloquial Arabic speech has been elevated into a neat, compact formal language. The Maltese case shows how an Arabic dialect evolved into an official language, something that has never happened in the mainstream Arab-Islamic culture. Modern Maltese is a mesh of medieval Sicilian, Italian, and English verbs integrated into a basic Arabic structure. The Maltese like to say that they gained from the Romans their Christianity, from the Knights of St. John their sense of national identity, and from the British their good governance. But it's from the Arabs that they got their language, despite the brief period of Arab-Muslim rule from 870 to 1090 C.E. The names of virtually all Maltese towns, except the capital Valletta, are Arabic: Marfa, Ghadira, Mgarr, Zebbiegh, Dwejra, Bahriya, Mdina, Rabat, Qawra, Gharghur, Sleima, Mqabba, Zejtun, Ghaxaq, Zurrieq, and Hamrun. The language lost all connection to formal classical Arabic after the Maltese entered the Christian fold and shelved the Arabic script. When they first took Malta as their home, the Knights of St. John, who had come in flight from the Ottoman Turks after Suleiman the Magnificent chased them out of Rhodes, found the islands' inhabitants jabbering in an Arabic dialect. When they surprised themselves by repelling an Ottoman invasion in 1565, the Knights celebrated by building the capital city of Valletta, named after Jean de la Vallette, the ingenious military leader who held off Suleiman's massive assault. Valletta was built as a European city, based on European architectural tastes, that glorified European cultural values. The new city and the developing towns and harbor areas bustled to the cadences of Italian and Sicilian traders, and over 20 percent of the entries in a four-volume manuscript dictionary compiled in 1755 are of Sicilian or Italian origin. So how did Arabic survive? Maltese historians wonder whether Malta's early Phoenician settlers from Lebanon and Tunisia, whose Punic language was Semitic, laid the foundation for the successful adoption of Arabic. According to linguistic historian Joe Felice Pace, the dialect of the inhabitants was little affected by short periods of French (the Angevins) and Spanish (the Aragonese) rule before the Knights took over in 1530. At the

for promotion of classical Arabic. Lebanese Christians played a major role in the late nineteenth century in perpetuating the idea that classical Arabic was a standard that should be maintained for all Arabic speakers and in codifying the classical language (as Modern Standard Arabic).

Badawi and a British scholar of early Islam, Martin Hinds, were responsible for a monumental study of colloquial Egyptian Arabic in the 1970s, the first and only work of its kind and a testament to the creative development of the language in the new urban settings where it is spoken. Three decades and over 20 million people later,

the situation has changed even further, with more words coming into the language from outside and being invented from within. Linguists have noted that Egyptian Arabic is even producing inventive expansions of the verb system. The *Egyptian Arabic Dictionary* was an immense scholarly effort and an academic landmark that legitimated study of colloquial speech. "Arab societies are using new words all the time, our vocabularies have become incredibly rich now, and I don't know at all how many words we have. The problem is that none of this is being documented. Nasser's era had its own vocabulary and none of it is

Malta's European capital of Valletta was built after the end of Arab rule, but the Arabic language survived and is still spoken there today. (Johnathan Smith; Cordaiy Photo Library Ltd./Corbis)

same time, studies of documentary evidence have shown that in Sicily and probably Malta the local Arabic was influenced by the Latin dialects spoken before the Arabs came. The Malti language of Malta is most closely related to the dialects of neighboring Tunisia and Algeria. Bukhara in Central Asia offers a similar tale. A community of Arabic speakers continues today, descendants of north Iraqi soldiers who settled there in Abbasid times.

recorded, and we wouldn't understand it now—Mahfouz isn't understood now. Translators need our dictionary," Badawi said (interview with author, September 1996). "Various Arab societies are in danger of having no links at all between them. Dr. Johnson compiled the first important dictionary in the history of the English language—before him it was in a state of flux. People now realize that what he did was to make the language mutually intelligible. He gathered the language together and documented it in one book, so that people could understand each other. Our young people in universities and schools will soon have to guess at it." Education systems have encouraged students to use Arabic dictionaries that are old and irrelevant to the twentieth century. The Arabic Language Academy has been working on one for over twenty years but they are years away from completing it, Badawi said.

Arabization in North Africa since Independence

Arabization in administration and education in Algeria has faced strong opposition from ruling elites and bureaucracies, as well as from Kabyle Berbers. There is still no complete enforcement of a 1991 law stating that virtually all official contacts and documents in public life should be in Arabic, including those on television. At independence in 1952 Algeria had an educated minority elite in French, and 85 percent of its population was illiterate. But bit by bit the Arabization laws are being implemented. On state television Arabic prevails, and guests—even government ministers—who respond in French to questions on discussion programs will find that their interviewers stick doggedly to Arabic, evidence that French is being slowly squeezed out. With the spread of the Internet, young people are increasingly turning to English as a way out of the language wars—a tactic that is also being adopted to some degree in neighboring Tunisia. The moves to complete Arabization during the 1990s have likely owed much to the political ascendancy of Islamist groups in a repeat of the phenomenon seen around the region whereby governments have successfully resisted Islamist insurgencies but adopted elements of the Islamist discourse to maintain their grip on power. The banned Islamic Salvation Front (FIS)—which the authorities banned after elections in 1992 that it was set to win, thus setting Algeria on the course of a bloody civil war—argued that English offers a larger window on the world than French. The view of the pro-French lobby, on the other hand, is that Algeria's nationalist governments were bent on a policy of social engineering to create a "new man" versed in a dead classical language—Arabic—at the expense of their Arabic-French or Berber-French mother tongue, inhibiting their intellectual development and stifling creativity. "The domination of school history teaching by the 'ulama [religious scholars] has obscured Algeria's real history and promoted a preoccupation with the Arab Mashreq at the expense of an understanding of Algeria itself. Thus, the acculturation promoted by French colonialism has been succeeded by a second acculturation, with disastrous effects. In vivid contrast to this, the spontaneous and informal development of rai music in western Algeria since the early 1980s testifies to the creative impulses of Algerian youth and demonstrates the potential of cultural forms rooted in Algeria's own linguistic and artistic traditions," wrote Mohamed Benrabah in an essay, "Arabisation and Creativity in Algeria" (Benrabah 2002). Islamists and pro-France writers like Benrabah represent two extremes, one imagining a return to an authentic state before the colonial encounter and the other imagining it was possible for postindependence Algeria to simply pick up the pieces after the brutal 132-year experience and consider France as just the latest in a series of bit-part contributors to its national identity.

Arabization policies by the Ben Ali government adopted in Tunisia since 1987, which aim to reverse the domination of French in public life, have succeeded in creating a new middle class and lower class, for whom formal Arabic is their first language of education. Previously, Tunisians whose mother tongue was colloquial Tunisian Arabic found it easier to use French to articulate anything more complex than everyday matters. English is slowly making inroads, and *L'Economiste* supplements in English have proven a big success in recent years, but there are as yet no major English-language publications. The market share of the French-language press is ever shrinking, and observers reckon that within a decade there will be few French publications. "I don't think the French market has a future. In 10 years' time Arabic will dominate," said Hedi Mechri, editor of *L'Economiste Maghrebien* (interview with author, February 2003). "We are at a crossroads. My education was all French in primary and secondary school and Arabic had a minor role: now it's the other way round." The state's attempts to squeeze out French have also reflected official displeasure with criticisms of the country in the French media: renewed zeal for Arabization in various sectors of public life have coincided with periods of tension with France. North African scholars writing in English have consistently used the term "Arabization" rather than "Arabicization," because the policy and its implementation have not been limited to promoting the Arabic language as a linguistic phenomenon (language use in education and the wider environment, corpus planning, and literacy), but have involved the reassertion of Arab-Muslim identity. Arabization continues to be used as a means to counter the former colonial power's interference in national affairs.

There are factors hindering further Arabization of education, though. Mohamed Daoud of the Institut Supérieur des Langues de Tunis in Carthage wrote: "Arabization may continue in the administration of government and in certain areas of the ambient environment that the government can control (e.g., billboards, signs), but it seems to have run its course in education. French will remain the medium of instruction for science, technology and business subjects in secondary and tertiary education in the foreseeable future. Another factor working against Arabization is the lack of a coherent pan-Arab policy and (if one existed) the will to implement it and factor it into the economic activity in the Arab World, taking the issue out of Tunisia's hands" (Daoud 2001). He noted that "Arabization cannot achieve ultimate success if it produces a generation of unemployable people"—figures on Tunisian trade with the Middle East News Agency's region were at the meager rate of 3 percent of imports and 12 percent of exports in 1998. Fearing the spread of English in science and business, France spends some $20 million a year on promoting language, cultural, and educational activities in Tunisia alone, way beyond the less than $1 million a year the United States and Britain each spend, according to former Fulbright senior lecturer John Battenburg (1997/1998). But the Arabs are playing the money game too—in Morocco King Hassan II and King Fahd of Saudi Arabia provided the funding for the country's first Anglophone university, al-Akhawayn ("the two brothers"). English is also gaining prominence over French in Lebanon, where Muslims are challenging the traditional domination of the Francophone Maronite elite through promotion of English. Both economic interests and ideology are players in these wars. While Tunisians and Lebanese shift from French to English in the field of business and science, minority communities have ditched or are in the process of ditching once-majority indigenous languages in favor of Arabic. Tunisia has only a handful of villages left that are entirely Berber-speaking. "We are the original people of Tunisia, but our culture is disappearing," said Abouda Bahry, from the mountain village of Matmata (interview with author, February 2002). Bahry's effort to save what's left has been to build a hotel in the old architectural style of the southern mountain villages, where Berbers sought refuge from what he calls "the Arab encroachment" since the seventh century.

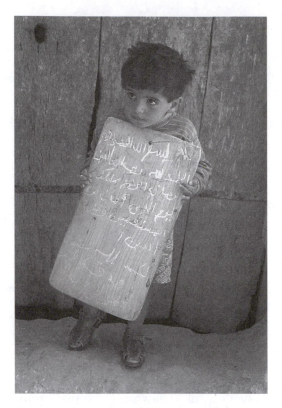

Belgacem Snini holds a Quranic board in Matmata, Tunisia, 1995. (Margaret Courtney-Clarke/Corbis)

"Here in Matmata children are not speaking the language anymore. They are starting to forget. There are only three villages where people still really speak the language." It is not known if there are any native Aramaic speakers left on Mount Lebanon, but at least one village remains in Syria (Maaloula) and there is still a thriving native community in northern Iraq.

Arabic Literature Struggles to Find Arab Audience

Though Arabic is one of the world's oldest and richest extant languages, few Arabs are reading modern literature in Arabic. With literacy rates varying between 40 per-cent for Mauritania and a high of 85 percent in Lebanon, roughly 40 percent of the Arab region of 280 million people lack the ability to read in the first place. And this in a literary culture that has at its center a religious text whose first word is an order to "read!" out loud. The United Nations Arab Human Development Report depicted a barren literary landscape. "Many indicators suggest a severe shortage of writing; a large share of the market consists of religious books and educational publications that are limited in their creative content," said the report, which has provoked much debate (AHDR 2002, 78). "The figures for translated books are also discouraging. The Arab world translates about 330 books annually, one-fifth of the number that Greece translates. The cumulative total of translated books since the Caliph Ma'moun's time [ninth century A.D.] is about 100,000, almost the average that Spain translates in one year." In the aftermath of the report, a translation movement has begun in the Levant via new publishing projects, such as the Beirut-based Arab Organization for Translation and the Syrian publishers Dar Emar and Dar al-Mada.

Underlying this trend is a deterioration in the value writers themselves assign to their own language. "Most novelists and political analysts want to get into English and many will write sloppy Arabic because they don't care about that audience, while those who do care about their writing in Arabic don't have much of an audience anyway since few people read that much in the Arab world. You will find work by a respected Arab researcher in English which is tightly argued and worded and the same work in Arabic full of repetition, chaos and lack of clarity," columnist Dalal al-Bizry wrote in *al-Hayat* (2 June 2002). "The majority of writers have the feeling that what they write has no value unless it's translated into a foreign language. Readers sense this, so they only read essential things and migrate to Arab satellite channel culture." Said top Egyptian novelist Sonallah Ibrahim, "There is always movement towards the stronger economic center, and this center imposes its music, its ideas, its language, by force of its economic strength. The Arabic language is not protected by an economic power . . . because it [the Arab region] was exposed to continuous invasions and continuous sapping of its ability to accumulate knowledge and wealth—from the Turks, the French, the English [and] the Italians. So you get to a situation where the language has no one to protect it. The language is under threat, of course, but I think this threat won't succeed" (interview with author, October 2002). Palestinian American intellectual Edward Said pointed to political reasons behind concerted attacks on the Arabic language. "In a paper he wrote a few years ago Francis Fukuyama, the right-wing pontificator and philosopher who was briefly celebrated for his preposterous 'end of history' idea, said that the State Department was well rid of its Arabists and Arabic speakers because by learning that language they also learned the 'delusions' of the Arabs," he wrote (al-Ahram Weekly, 21 August 2003). "One of the basic themes of all Orientalist discourse since the mid-19th century is that the Arabic language and the Arabs are afflicted with both a mentality and a language that has no use for reality. Many Arabs have come to believe this racist drivel, as if whole national languages like Arabic, Chinese, or English directly represent the minds of their users."

State media around the region barely ac-knowledge that the Arabic novel exists—Egyptian television has no arts show that discusses literature and there are no best-seller lists, though it was Egypt that produced the Arab world's only Nobel laureate up to now, the 1988 literature prize-winner Naguib Mahfouz. The leading presenter of "cultural television" has been Tunisian Kawthar al-Bishrawy, via programs on MBC, before a move to al-Jazeera that ended acrimoniously in 2002 with accusations that the station's bosses didn't care about culture and dealt undemocratically with staff. "All Arab channels consider cultural programs as an embarrassment to be hidden away, so they don't show interest in these programs or air them at appropriate times. What they care about is 'who will win the million,'" Bishrawy told Egyptian magazine Rose al-Yousef (20 December 2002). The novel is another victim of the same attitude. "Up to now there is no best-seller list in the Arab world. The bestsellers are political books—if you publish a novel, no one will talk about it," said Ibrahim Moallem, head of the Arab Publishers Federation (interview with author, The Middle East, January 2003). Egypt has the largest population in the region, with 68 million, but it produced no more than 12,000 books in 2001, which comprised around 37 percent of the total annual output of the Arab world, Moallem said. In Egypt, less than 50 percent of those titles were new publications, and religious and school-textbook material took up the lion's share, with a smattering of political tracts and novels. The consistent best-seller in recent years, reflecting Arab-Israeli tensions, has been Mohammed Hassanein Heikal, the right-hand man of former president Gamal Abdel Nasser, whose political analyses are accorded huge respect in the Arab world.

One Heikal book will sell 50,000 copies in Egypt alone. Novels of note invariably touch on the political, social, and economic climate in their countries in one way or another, providing a disincentive for authoritarian regimes to fete them, and if the authorities think modern literature is suspect politically, Islamists think it's suspect morally. Both the rise of religious conservatism since the 1970s in Arab societies and protests against writing seen as blasphemous or immoral have created a climate inimical to literary output. Syrian writer Haider Haider's *A Banquet for Seaweed* (*Walima li a'Shab al-Bahr*) provoked mass protests by religious students in Cairo when the government published it in 2000.

Despite the disdain, the small community of Arabic-language novelists have made great strides since the halcyon days when Mahfouz put the Arabic novel on the global literary map. Ibrahim scored a critical success in 2001 with *Warda*, which mixed fiction with the true story of a rebel movement in south Oman in the early 1970s, a time when utopian leftists thought traditional Arab societies were ripe for revolutionary change. Following the leftist Arab nationalist writers of the 1960s, personified by Sonallah Ibrahim, a new generation of young writers has emerged, mainly in Egypt, who put the psychology of individuals, often women and marginalized youth, at the center of their work. Algerian writer Ahlam Mosteghanemi made waves with her 1993 *Dhakirat al-Jasad* (*Memory in the Flesh*), the first Arabic novel by an Algerian woman in a local literary culture still dominated by the language of former colonial master France (the counterpoint to which is Malika al-Muqaddem's novel *al-Muhajirun al-Abadiyun*, originally written in French and published in Arabic in

2002, which was met with critical disgust in *al-Hayat* because of its more positive portrayal of the French occupation). Today it is possible to talk about Gulf literature, Palestinian literature, and Moroccan or North African literature, whereas before, none of these genres existed. But the best-known and best-selling novelist throughout the region is probably still Mahfouz, according to Moallem—Mahfouz who initially made his mark writing in and about pre-1952 Egypt. "People say no one reads any more, but no one read in the first place," Moallem said. Which at least suggests things can only get better.

The few Aramaic speakers remaining in the Levant include the residents of the Syrian village Maaloula and Assyrian émigres from northern Iraq in Lebanon.

The Great Quran Debate, Pre– and Post–September 11

As classical Arabic can be seen as a melting pot of different tongues, the Quran itself can be seen as a composite of different texts, incorporating earlier material written in Arabic and Aramaic. The idea is out there, but it's highly controversial. Millions of people refer to the text in their daily lives. If it had not been for the idea of *i'jaaz*, the Arabic term for the perfection of the Quran, a concept developed in Abbasid times that effectively blocked any movement to translate the text into other languages, the Arabs today might not be the Arabs. And translating the Quran is no easy task: for example, the grammar at times can seem nonsensical, with dramatic shifts in style, voice, and subject matter from verse to verse; it assumes a familiarity with language, stories, and events that were often lost on the early Muslim exegetes (hence the body of *tafsir* literature); and God may be referred to in the first and third persons in apparently the same sentence. The temptation is to see in this work not evidence of an incomprehensible and divine origin, but a mélange of different texts, a problem that has been addressed by scholars only in recent decades. Scholars also point to divergent versions of the same story that are repeated at different points in the text, and note that injunctions mentioned in different parts of the text can seem to contradict one another. The revelation also seeks to answer in its own textual flow the polemical charges from non-Muslims that it is not an authentic book of divine origin, as if it is part of a wider debate of the time. The Quranic inscriptions on the Dome of the Rock in Jerusalem, built at the Temple Mount/al-Aqsa Mosque compound and completed in 691 C.E., show variations from the standard versions of the text, suggesting a still-evolving text. Classic Islamic tradition, as with the poetry presented as pre-Islamic, says that the text of the Quran was revealed to the Prophet during his lifetime, that a final version of the text was completed in writing in the time of the Caliph Uthman, who died in 656 C.E., and that all other versions of the text were destroyed. Some scholars think that a more likely explanation for the familiarity with the monotheistic tradition of Judaism and Christianity shown in the Quran, as well as the presence of words of Aramaic, Greek, Persian, and Egyptian origins, is that the text was composed in the conquered territories after the Arabs took control of them, and not in Mecca. In this light, the Mecca/Medina origins are cast, in the manner of religious and other traditions, as a foundation myth.

The seminal work in this field was John Wansbrough's 1977 book *Quranic Studies*, in which the scholar, who died in 2002, concluded that the text of the Quran had been finalized some 200 years after the death of the Prophet in 632 C.E. He argued that it appeared in its final form, defined as the word of God, at the time when the written sources for the early history of Islam were also first appearing. The conclusion was that the Quran, like the Jewish and Christian Bible, was the product of a long period of composition, which is at variance with Muslim belief and its accepted corollary, that it was a text that dated from the time of Mohammed as the foundation of the religion he preached. In *The Sectarian Milieu* (1978), Wansbrough went further and argued that the composition of the Quran was part of a long polemic in which the followers of the Prophet elaborated their faith in opposition to Judaism and Christianity, the older religions in the tradition of Semitic monotheism.

The result was a distinctive version of that tradition (whose key characteristic was the use of the Arabic language), on the same historical and theological footing as its predecessors, and entitled to the same measure of respect as well as criticism. While attempting to show how this had been intellectually achieved, Wansbrough refused to go beyond the material to a reconstruction of the underlying events, which he regarded as out of the question. More recently, the German scholar Luxenberg argued that the Quranic passages on paradise are based on a fourth-century Aramaic Christian text called *Hymns of Paradise* (Luxenberg 2000). Luxenberg argues that *janna*, the Arabic term for "paradise," is of Aramaic origin, where the term specifically meant "garden." Standard interpretations of the early Quranic text said the word *hur* meant *huri*, or "virgin," giving rise to the now-widespread belief in Islam that a paradise of virgins awaits the believing Muslim male in death. But in Aramaic where the word has its origin, Luxenberg said, *hur* meant "white raisin," and there is some evidence that the word was used directly in Arabic, in the Levant, with the same meaning. Early Arabic was written without diacritical marks, which can be essential to establishing the meaning of written words. Thus, the classical interpreters of the early Quran also noted some verbs that could mean "to fight" as well as "to kill." Interestingly, Luxenberg accepts the historicity of the Quran offered by Islamic tradition, unlike Wansbrough. (He also argues that the Arabic word *jaww*, which today means "the air/climate/atmosphere" but is used colloquially to mean "inside," arises from a misunderstanding by early Quranic redactors of a phrase taken from Aramaic, in which the word means only "inside.")

Other scholars have pointed to earlier Arabic texts that could also form the basis for what became standardized Quranic verse. In 1971 a "paper grave" of Quranic manuscripts was uncovered in the Great Mosque of Sanaa in Yemen, and subsequent work suggests these texts could date from the seventh and eight centuries, making them possibly the earliest Qurans in existence. What's striking about them is that the text diverges from that of the official versions, with unconventional verse orderings, some textual variations, and rare styles of orthography and artistic embellishment. Research by Gerd-R. Puin, a specialist in Arabic calligraphy and Quranic paleography at Saarland University in Germany, showed that some bits of text had been overwritten, with discernible signs on the manuscripts of earlier versions underneath, all of which suggested an evolving text, and not one presented in its entirety

to the Prophet. While to Christians Christ is the word of God made flesh, the Quran is the word of God made text, but these documents suggest that wasn't always the case. Gerd-R. Puin told the *Atlantic Monthly:* "My idea is that the Quran is a kind of cocktail of texts that were not all understood even at the time of Mohammed. Many of them may even be a hundred years older than Islam itself. Even within the Islamic traditions there is a huge body of contradictory information, including a significant Christian substrate; one can derive a whole Islamic *anti-history* from them if one wants" (January 1999).

Post–September 11, these theories are gaining more currency in public space, especially in the United States, where up to that date they had been largely ignored or attacked in academia as anti-Islamic and—at least at that time—not politically correct. Some scholars, as the Luxenberg examples suggest, have apparently been tailoring their research and interpretations to meet the parameters of the great debate today about Islam as "politics, faith, and terrorism." Luxenberg's theories were given a positive airing in a *Newsweek* article, "Challenging the Qur'an" (28 July 2003). According to journalist Alexander Stille in the *New York Times*, the revisionist scholars' work "might lead to a more tolerant brand of Islam, as well as one that is more conscious of its close ties to both Judaism and Christianity" (2 March 2002). This would result in what Egyptian scholar Abdel-Wahhab al-Messiri derides as *al-islam al-sihayi,* or "tourist Islam" (a play on the Arabic phrase *al-islam al-siyasi,* "political Islam"), that is, the kind of Islam that suits politicians in the West.

This final subjection of Islam to the same scholarly indignities that have already been visited upon Christianity, Judaism, and other religions could threaten to secularize and pull apart the one major world cultural bloc that, as Ernst Gellner argued, is best equipped to remain intact in the future because, while it has modernity, it will still have faith. Christendom killed its own belief in God; Islam stands out as set on keeping God alive and well. Some writers in the West openly tout using Quranic research as a means to deal a blow to Islamic society's rock-solid faith in God. A former Muslim in the United States called Ibn Warraq, of Iranian origin, who runs the Institute for the Secularization of Islamic Society, has published books with that aim, such as *The Origins of the Koran* and *The Quest for the Historical Muhammad.* Inside the Islamic world, though, there is as yet little knowledge of the details of Western scholarship and these arguments; however, there is a widespread sense among Arab intellectuals, politicians, and preachers that the West wants to shake the faith of Muslims, perhaps in order to rebuild its own lost sense of faith. Scholar Nasr Abu Zeid, who was declared an apostate by a Cairo court over his teaching that much of the Quranic text should be interpreted metaphorically and not literally, said before fleeing Egypt in 1996 that he was not aware of Wansbrough's theories, though he may have been dissembling to avoid more controversy and may have become aware of Wansbrough's writings since leaving for Europe in 1996 (interview with author, May 1995). Maverick writer Sayed al-Qimany, who argues publicly that the Arab invasion was a disaster for Egypt, was entirely unaware of these avenues of modern research (interview with author, August 1997). Their views tend to fall within the bracket of now-démodé arguments about the motives

and meanings of the Prophet and other key personalities (such as French scholar Maxime Rodinson's attempt at a pychological analysis of the Prophet as a secular explanation of his revelations). In other words, they do not question the fundamental historicity of the text, or any other events surrounding the received wisdom on the origins of the religion. Other Arab scholars, such as Sheikh Khalil Abdel-Karim, a Muslim Brother who became a leftist, argued that institutions like Egypt's al-Azhar have maintained a centuries-long monopoly on interpretation of the Quran and other aspects of Islamic tradition, which were subject to quite a bit of debate and divergent opinion in the early centuries of Islam. But he would be shocked at what the Western academics are saying today. In an attempt to accommodate this range of views and breadth of debate, a group of professors of Islamic studies (with Nasr Abu Zeid as a member of the group's advisory board) have compiled the first-ever *Encyclopaedia of the Quran.*

Muslim scholars who have responded to these specific points of revisionism argue that the Quran is subject to an "Orientalist assault." S. Parvez Manzoor, a Muslim scholar and critic based in Sweden, has written that the aims of these scholars is as follows: "In order to rid the West forever of the 'problem' of Islam . . . Muslim consciousness must be made to despair of the cognitive certainty of the Divine message revealed to the Prophet. Only a Muslim confounded of the historical authenticity or doctrinal autonomy of the Quranic revelation would abdicate his universal mission and hence pose no challenge to the global domination of the West. Such, at least, seems to have been the tacit, if not the explicit, rationale of the Orientalist assault on the Quran" (*Muslim World Book Review* 7, no. 4 [summer 1987]). Hatoun al-Fassi, a Saudi historian of Semitic peoples in the Arabian Peninsula, said: "They want to break our faith rather than understand our culture as we understand it. They are not going to change the way most of us think" (interview with author, April 2003). Many scholars in the West and the Arab and Muslim world have also pointed out that the text is primarily intended as an aural experience of recitation and it is here that its power lies.

The attempt to defang Islam and find allies for the job in the Islamic world, then, is undoubtedly a risky one; it could simply provoke a bigger backlash against America and the West. There are a considerable number of verses in the Quran that talk of jihad; any endeavor to conceal them in religious education would be difficult, and an effort to give them a pacifist spin is easily exposed as politically motivated. The classical exegetes never denied that jihad could take on many forms, and former Tunisian President Habib Bourguiba famously drank orange juice on state television during Ramadan to ram home his point that the country was on an economic jihad that required maximum effort from all for a full twelve months of the year, including the holy month. Secular intellectuals in the region argue that there is no shortage of ideologies people can die for, and the Islamic tide is symptom not cause. But as far as the world of ideas is concerned at least, the *Atlantic Monthly*'s Toby Lester is surely right in his conclusion that the study of the Quran "promises in the years ahead to be at least as contentious, fascinating, and important as the study of the Bible has been in this [the twentieth] century" (January 1998).

Bibliography

Print Resources

Abu Zeid, Nasr. *The Concept of the Text*. Cairo: 1990.

Badawi, S., and M. Hinds. *Dictionary of Egyptian Arabic*. Cairo: American University Press in Cairo, 1986.

Battenburg, John. "A Fulbrighter's Experience with English Language Teaching in Tunisia: The Land of Mosaics." *CATESOL Journal* 10, no. 1 (1997/1998): 113–120.

———. "The Gradual Death of the Berber Language in Tunisia." *International Journal of the Sociology of Language* 137 (1999).

Benrabah, Mohamed. "Arabisation and Creativity in Algeria." *Journal of Algerian Studies*, nos. 4 and 5 (February 2002).

Brett, Michael. "Obituary for John Wansbrough." *The Independent* (London), 28 June 2002.

Cook, Michael. *Muhammad*. Oxford: Oxford University Press, 1983.

Daoud, Mohamed. "The Language Situation in Tunisia." *Current Issues in Language Planning* 2, no. 1 (2001).

Donner, Fred M. *Narratives of Islamic Origins: The Beginnings of Islamic Historical Writing*. Princeton, N.J.: Darwin Press, 2000.

Elgibali, Alaa, ed. *Understanding Arabic: Essays in Contemporary Arabic Linguistics*. Cairo: American University in Cairo Press, 1996.

Gilliot, C., W. Graham, and J. McAuliffe, eds. *Encyclopaedia of the Qur'an*. Leiden: Brill Academic Publishers, 2002.

Hoyland, Robert. *Arabia and the Arabs*. London and New York: Routledge, 2001.

Ibn Warraq, ed. *The Origins of the Koran: Classic Essays on Islam's Holy Book*. New York: Prometheus Books, 1998.

Lester, Toby. "What Is the Koran?" *Atlantic Monthly*, January 1998.

Luxenberg, Christoph. *The Syro-Aramaic Reading of the Koran: A Contribution to Deciphering the Qur'ânic Language*. 1st ed. Berlin: Das Arabische Buch, 2000.

Manzour, S. Parvez. "Method against Truth: Orientalism and Qur'anic Studies." *Muslim World Book Review* 7, no. 4 (Summer 1987).

———. "Antidote to Modern Nihilism: The Qur'anic Perception of Time." www.Islamonline.net/english/Contemporary/2003/10/ (October 2003).

Phenix, R., and C. Horn. "Book Review: Christoph Luxenberg." *Hugoye: Journal of Syriac Studies* 6, no. 1 (January 2003).

Rodinson, Maxime. *Muhammad.* 1961 (in French). Reprint. London: I. B. Tauris, 2002.

Sakkut, Hamdi. *The Arabic Novel: Bibliography and Critical Introduction 1865–1995.* Cairo: American University in Cairo Press, 2001.

Sowayan, Saad. *Nabati Poetry: The Oral Poetry of Arabia.* Berkeley: University of California Press, 1985.

Stille, Alexander. "Scholars Are Quietly Offering New Theories of the Koran." *New York Times Literary Supplement,* 2 March 2002.

Wansbrough, John. *Quranic Studies: Sources and Methods of Scriptural Interpretation.* Oxford: Oxford University Press, 1977.

———. *The Sectarian Milieu: Content and Composition of Islamic Salvation History.* Oxford: Oxford University Press, 1978.

Youssef, Ahmad Abdel-Hamid. *From Pharaoh's Lips: Ancient Egyptian Language in the Arabic of Today.* Cairo: American University in Cairo Press, 2003.

Zaman, Shibli. "Hur(un) 'Een: Clear Raisins or Just Sour Grapes?" http://www.atrueword.com/index.php/article/author/view/1 (October 2003).

Web Sites

www.ethnologue.com. Linguistics site run by SIL International, with details on all languages of the world.

www.omniglot.com. An online guide to writing systems.

www.almisbar.com. Arabic-English dictionary and translation site.

tarjim.ajeeb.com/ajeeb. Translation site.

www.diwan.com Arabic-language and multilingual software.

www.arabic2000.com. Arabic software, lessons, directory, Internet services, and more.

www.rosettaproject.org. A global collaboration of language specialists and native speakers working to develop a contemporary version of the historic Rosetta Stone via a meaningful survey and near permanent archive of 1,000 languages.

www.angelfire.com/darkside/franco. Site run by a group of Andalusian Spaniards calling themselves el-Asbiyya, who have taken Arabic names and converted to Islam.

http://saif_w.tripod.com/explore/stereo/orientalism_misinformation_islam.htm. Islamic site with articles rebutting Orientalist theories on the origins of Arabic and Islam.

http://maaber.50megs.com. Syrian literary and intellectual site that also promotes translation into Arabic.

Glossary

Abbasid   The name of the second major dynasty of Islam, which established itself in Iraq in 750 C.E. and lasted until the Mongols sacked Baghdad in 1258 (though a branch survived in Cairo until 1517, when the Ottoman Turks took Egypt).

al-Ahram   One of the oldest and most prestigious newspapers in the Arab world, now the Egyptian government's flagship daily. The name means "the pyramids" and the paper's trademark symbol is three red pyramids.

al-Andalus   The last of the Arab-Islamic provinces of the Iberian Peninsula to fall to the Spaniards, in 1492. Often used as a reference point for the loss of Palestine to the Israeli state.

al-futuhaat   The Arabic name for the conquests of the region in the seventh century C.E., which brought the new religion of Islam.

Ali Baba   Famous figure from *The 1,001 Nights*, who, along with his forty thieves, robbed the caliphal riches of Baghdad. He and the forty thieves are often mentioned in popular culture today, in the press, television, theater, and everyday speech.

'awlama   The Arabic name coined for today's process of "globalization."

Berbers   The main ethnic group in North Africa before the Arab conquests. Berber rights activists today prefer the Berber-language term *Amazigh* when discussing the Berber issue in English, French, or Arabic.

caliph   The name of the figure designated by Muslims to rule over the community of believers in the Prophet Mohammed's stead. These rulers termed themselves the "successor/vice-regent of the prophet of God" (*khalifat rasul allah*), though there is debate over whether some of them presented themselves as "the vice-regents of God" (*khalifat allah*) in the manner of the Shi'ite imams.

Fatimid   The third great caliphate of the Islamic world, established in

Cairo in 969 C.E. Unlike the other other two (Umayyad and Abbasid), it was Shi'ite.

fundamentalist   Term used to refer to the current of political thought that favors a return to the way of early Muslims in all forms of life, institutional and individual, public and private.

hajj   The three- to five-day Muslim pilgrimage to Mecca, which takes place in the twelfth month of the Islamic lunar calendar each year.

haram   Religious term referring to that which is forbidden according to Islamic precepts (the opposite being *halal*), but used in a much lighter sense in colloquial Arabic as a term of rebuke or censure.

Haroun al-Rashid   One of the most famous of the early Baghdad caliphs, who presided over the Islamic lands at the height of his power. He also figures prominently in *The 1,001 Nights*.

al-Hayat   The most respected pan-Arab newspaper. Originally Lebanese, but now Saudi-owned, it is based in London.

hejab   The hair-covering veil worn by many Muslim women, which Islamists argue is a clear obligation in Islam, not for discussion or interpretation.

hijra (sometimes written *hegira*)   The Prophet's flight or emigration in 622 C.E. from Mecca to Medina, where he set up the first Islamic state. This marks the beginning of the Muslim era, whose dates are designated AH.

Hizbollah   Lebanese Shi'ite group that fought the Israeli occupation of south Lebanon and remains a powerful political and paramilitary force.

Ibadism   Puritanical sect of early Islam (part of the Kharijite movement) whose emphasis on religion (and not Arab ethnicity) made it appealing to Berbers in North Africa as well as remote tribal regions in the mountains of Oman. Ibadi communities survive in both areas today, where their reputation is now of extreme moderation.

Ibn Khaldoun   Historian of Spanish-Arab origin who wrote *Kitab al-'Ibar* (*The Book of Exemplary Information*, sometimes called *The Universal History*) and also *al-Muqaddima*, its preface on the rise and fall of Arab-Islamic dynasties. The book itself focused on the history of North Africa and the Berbers. Born in Tunis in 1332, he died in Cairo in 1406. Egyptian rights activist Saadeddin Ibrahim runs the Ibn Khaldoun Centre for Development Studies, invoking his name for the civil rights struggle in the Arab world today.

ijtihad   The name given to any act of personal initiative, but also a term from Islamic law, which means that in the absence of clear direction from the Quran or the Sunna, clerics can issue religious opinions for the community based on their own intellectual endeavor and analogy with other Islamic teachings.

Islamist   Term used to refer to the movement of political Islam.

jihad   Any effort, including holy war, made for the sake of the Islamic community—something akin to the English term "crusade."

jinn   Collective name for the spirits.

Joha   Figure of Arab lore who seems stupid but possesses unexpected wisdom and lateral thinking. Often referred to in popular culture, newspaper articles, television soaps, and everyday speech.

Kaaba Structure at the centre of the mosque in Mecca, housing a mystical black stone. Muslims all over the world pray in the direction of the *Kaaba*, where Islamic tradition says God's presence is most felt on Earth.

Kabyle The Berbers who hail from the mountainous Kabyle area, east of Algiers.

Levant The geographical area comprising Israel, the Palestinian territories, Jordan, Syria, and Lebanon.

Maghreb The Arabic term for the western part of the Arab world, as well as for Morocco specifically. It also refers to the setting of the sun and prayers that take place at that time.

Mahdi A messianic figure ("the rightly guided one") in Muslim eschatology who will appear at the end of time to right the wrongs of the age. A mainly Shi'ite idea, it can refer specifically to the last of the Shi'ite leaders (imams) who disappeared in the nineth century C.E. and whose return is awaited. The concept has inspired a number of political movements, from those of the Fatimid Caliphate to Iraqi cleric Muqtada al-Sadr.

maqam The term for a musical scale in Arabic music, as well as for states of being in Sufism.

Maronites The main Christian sect in Lebanon.

Mashreq The Arabic term for the eastern part of the Arab world.

moulid Celebration of the birth of a holy figure.

mufti A religious scholar charged with issuing religious opinions, or fatwas.

muraabit *(marabout)* Deceased holy men in North Africa and the general term for the Muslims who pushed the frontiers of Islam in the area in the early centuries of Islam.

Muslim Brotherhood The first group of political Islam in the Arab world, set up in Egypt in 1928. It is viewed as the most influential Islamist organization today, though it is officially banned in Egypt.

nakba The Arabic term, meaning "the catastrophe," for the dispossession of up to one million Palestinians in the fighting that saw the establishment of the State of Israel in 1948.

naksa The Arabic term, meaning "the setback," often used to refer to the Arab defeat to Israel in the 1967 war.

Nasserism Term for the strident nationalism—fascist in some of its methods and symbols—followed by charismatic Egyptian president Gamal Abdel Nasser. Huge debate continues today over its legacy for Egypt and the Arab world.

niqab The full face-covering veil, worn by many women in Gulf states.

normalization Term used to mean the setting up of normal relations with Israel, beyond political relations at the level of the state, that is, trade relations, tourism, cultural exchange, academic mingling, and so forth.

Nubian An ethnic group in north Sudan and the far south of Egypt, with various dialects spoken in conjunction with Arabic.

Orientalism Term popularized by Palestinian American scholar Edward Said, in his study of the same name, to refer to a European intellectual tradition with its roots in colonialism that tended to belittle the non-Western world, in particular Arab-Islamic culture.

political Islam   Term referring to the political movement in Islamic societies calling for the Islamization of public life as well as private life, inasmuch as Islamic customs concern individual behavior, usually through the implementation of Islamic law.

Prophet   Islam theorizes that God's final revelation, completing the message of the prophets of Christians and Jews, came through his final prophet, Mohammed (or Muhammad in strict transliteration).

pyramidiots   Term coined by Zahi Hawass, Egypt's director of antiquities at the pyramids plateau (as well as overall head of the Supreme Council for Antiquities), for New Agers and other alternative theorists on the origin and meaning of the pyramids.

al-Qa'ida   Loose radical Islamist network headed by Saudi dissident Osama bin Laden and formed in the cauldron of post-Soviet Afghanistan, which has dedicated itself to fighting the U.S. presence in the Islamic world, as well as Israel.

al-Quds   The Arabic term for Jerusalem, with an inherent religious connotation for Muslims: the word means "the sacred" or "the holy" and is only used to refer to the city.

Quran   In Islam, God's final revelation came in a text referred to as *al-Qur'an*, meaning "the reading" or "the recitation." The term is flexible since Islamic tradition says God revealed the word to Mohammed

via asking him to recite the words out loud, but at some stage in early Islam this oral text was codified in book form.

rai   The Algerian pop-rock music that became popular in France in the 1980s and 1990s and went on to achieve worldwide renown.

Ramadan   A month of the Islamic lunar calendar when Muslims fast from dawn to dusk.

Salafist   Another term used to refer to Islamists. Islamic movements, both moderate and those that advocate use of violence, usually refer to themselves as Salafist, meaning that they seek to return to the ways of the early Muslims.

Saudi   The Bedouin family from the Nejd area, which united the territories of the Arabian Peninsula known today as Saudi Arabia.

sa'wada   The effort to replace foreign workers in Saudi Arabia with Saudi nationals, in order to reduce the reliance on a huge expat population and combat unemployment among Saudis.

secular-nationalist   Arab nationalists have for the most part been secularists. Intellectuals in the media say that only in recent years, when Islamic groups like Hamas have been in the ascendancy over the Palestinian Authority, have they felt that Islamism is winning more hearts and minds over secular Arab nationalism. In general, Arab nationalism and political Islam have stood in historical opposition to each other.

shaabi   Urban working-class music in Arab countries, the Egyptian version of which has found a niche market in the Arabpop music scene.

Sharia General term connoting the whole of Islamic law, itself a vast and changing corpus; often used as a rallying cry for creating a more moral, ordered society.

sheikh Term of respect for older men (fem., Sheikha), referring to people of wisdom or religious knowledge. Only rarely is it a formal title (such as when referring to the head of Egypt's religious educational network al-Azhar).

Six Day War The phrase often used to refer to the 1967 war between Israel and several Arab states, since it lasted only six days.

takfir Term associated with radical Islamist groups who declared certain sections of society in Arab countries to have strayed from Islam to such a degree that they should no longer be considered Muslims and have become infidels (*kafara* or *kuffaar*). These groups have made war on government and society in a number of countries since the 1970s, killing officials, tourists, and ordinary citizens. Al-Qa'ida is an extension of these radical Islamic fundamentalist groups, though al-Qa'ida does not declare ordinary Arabs to be infidels.

tarab The sense of pleasure engendered by the power of music, involving instruments, human voice, and words.

ulama Generic term for the class of religious scholars in Arab societies (sing.,

'aalim). The name derives from the word "knowledge" (*'ilm*), which is the same word used today to refer to science. Knowledge in Islamic civilization was inherently religious.

Umayyad The first dynasty in early Islam, named after the Bani Umayya family and based in Damascus, Syria, from 661 to 750 C.E.

al-'uruuba Political term meaning "Arabness" and the sense of Arab identity.

Wahhabism Saudi Arabia's particular version of Sunni Islam, which is rigorously enforced throughout the country, is often termed by outsiders as Wahhabism, in reference to Mohamed Ibn Abdel-Wahhab, an eighteenth-century religious reformer whose ideas on purifying Islam inspire the Saudi state.

Zionism The dominant ideology among Jewish settlers in Palestine since the late nineteenth century, which holds that Palestine (the West Bank of the Jordan River, Galilee, and the coastal plain) is a birthright for all Jews and where they succeeded in setting up a state of their own. Zionist views have differed on the extent of the territory that should return to Jews, with some arguing for bits of the East Bank of the Jordan River and others eyeing the Sinai. They also vary on what to do about the territory's indigenous inhabitants, who numbered over one million before Israel came into existence.

Selected Bibliography

The following is a general list of recommended books and Web sites in English that cover the subjects of politics, culture, and pop culture discussed in this book. Most book titles chosen are themselves general works.

Books

Ahmed, Laila. *Women and Gender in Islam.* New Haven, Conn.: Yale University Press, 1992. An examination of the place and role of women in Islamic societies, which is regarded as one of the more insightful and sensitive forays in the topic.

Armbrust, Walter, ed. *Mass Mediations: New Approaches to Popular Culture in the Middle East and Beyond.* Berkeley: University of California Press, 2000. A collection of studies offering a broad perspective on how popular culture is produced, expressed, and reflected in modern mass media.

Brett, M., and E. Fentress. *The Berbers.* Oxford: Blackwell Publishers, 1996. An excellent summary of how Berber North Africa became Arab North Africa from the Islamic conquests to the present day.

Crone, Patricia, and Michael Cook. *Hagarism: The Making of the Islamic World.* Cambridge: Cambridge University Press, 1977. A hugely controversial work of historical revisionism that shook up the study of the emergence of Arab-Islamic civilization.

Eickelman, Dale. *The Middle East and Central Asia: An Anthropological Approach.* Princeton, N.J.: Prentice Hall, 2001. A wide-ranging cultural profile of the region that has become a standard in Middle East anthropology.

Elgibali, Alaa, ed. *Understanding Arabic: Essays in Contemporary Arabic Linguistics.* Cairo: American University in Cairo Press, 1996. This collection of studies provides insight into ongoing debates in linguistic circles about the origins and future of the Arabic language.

Gilsenan, Michael. *Recognizing Islam: Religion and Society in the Modern World.* New York: Pantheon Books, 1983. Introductory anthropological study by a non-Muslim that describes the diversity of popular Islamic culture, without veering into the pejorative.

Halliday, Fred. *Islam and the Myth of Confrontation.* London: I. B. Tauris, 2003. One of the best of a rash of studies in recent years that try to analyze the phenomenon of political Islam.

Hancock, Graham, and Robert Bauval. *The Message of the Sphinx.* New York: Crown Publishing Group, 1997. A pop-culture classic and best-seller that irked the Egyptology community, helped bring tourists to Egypt, and demonstrated the huge pull that ancient civilizations have on popular imagination in the West.

Hourani, Albert. *Arabic Thought in the Liberal Age 1798–1939*. Cambridge: Cambridge University Press, 1993. A study that dominates its field on how thinkers in the region wrestled with and developed new ideas on politics and society.

Huntington, Samuel P. *The Clash of Civilizations and the Remaking of the World Order*. London: Simon & Schuster, 1996. An essay on what the author sees as a developing clash between Western values and those of other cultural and political groupings, foremost among them Islamic, which has come to define Arab-Muslim fears of U.S. misunderstanding of and predatory desires toward the Middle East.

Jayyusi, Salma, and Roger Allen, eds. *Modern Arabic Drama: An Anthology*. Bloomington: Indiana University Press, 1995. Rare general tome on Arabic drama as it developed throughout the last century.

Kepel, Gilles. *Muslim Extremism in Egypt: The Prophet and Pharaoh*. Berkeley: University of California Press, 1985. One of the best analyses of Islamist thought, which in one particular context, that of 1970s Egypt, precisely examines its meaning and origins.

Lewis, Bernard. *What Went Wrong?: The Clash between Islam and Modernity in the Middle East*. London: Phoenix, 2002. Controversial work that for some accurately summarizes the origins and nature of "the problem" of the Arab world and Islam today, but that for others is deeply flawed and a prime example of the intellectual assault on the region by many Western "Orientalist" writers.

Macfie, A. L. *Orientalism: A Reader*. Cairo: American University in Cairo Press, 2000. An excellent reader on the huge debate over Western approaches to culture, politics, and history in the Middle East.

Owen, Roger. *State, Power and Politics in the Making of the Modern Middle East*. London: Routledge, 1992. One of the best general introductions to the region, written from a political science perspective.

Pappe, Ilan. *The Israel/Palestine Question*. London: Routledge, 1999. An excellent collection of essays that show recent scholarly debates and new thinking on the conflict that is key to the region's future.

Qutb, Sayed. *Ma'alim Fil-Tareeq* (Milestones). 1965. Reprint. Beirut: Dar al-Shurouq, 1979. The seminal work in modern Islamic radical thinking, whose ideas have been the inspiration for groups denouncing society as apostate and un-Islamic from the 1970s to today.

Ruthven, Malise. *Islam in the World*. London: Penguin, 2000. One of the most arresting studies by a non-Muslim of Islam and the interaction between Islamic faith and Islamist politics today.

Said, Edward. *Orientalism*. Princeton, N.J.: Princeton University Press, 1979. The seminal assault on the tradition of Western writing about the Arab and Islamic worlds, which has had huge ramifications in numerous fields of scholarship.

Sakkut, Hamdi. *The Arabic Novel: Bibliography and Critical Introduction 1865–1995*. Cairo: American University in Cairo Press, 2001. Rare comprehensive study in English on the development of the Arabic novel.

Shafik, Viola. *Arab Cinema: History and Cultural Identity*. Cairo: American University in Cairo Press, 1998. Comprehensive study of the emergence of the cinema industry across the Arab world and its role in the postcolonial search for identity and independence.

van Nieuwkerk, Karin. *A Trade Like Any Other: Female Singers and Dancers in Egypt*. Cairo: American University in Cairo Press, 1996. Famed anthropological study of belly dancing in Egypt, offering one of the most comprehensive insights into the subject.

Yapp, M. E. *The Near East since the First World War.* New York: Longman, 1991. A straightforward general history of the region as it moved from colonial control into the era of Arab nationalism.

Zuhur, Sherifa, ed. *Colors of Enchantment: Theater, Dance, Music and the Visual Arts of the Middle East.* Cairo: American University Press in Cairo, 2002. Series of essays shedding light on some of the more marginalized elements of cultural life in the Arab region.

The following media Web sites in English are valuable forums for public debate in the Arab world and offer the best insight into how the Arabs see themselves.

Web Sites

www.english.aljazeera.net. Qatar's pan-Arab al-Jazeera television station.

http://english.daralhayat.com. The London-based pan-Arab daily paper *al-Hayat.*

www.dailystar.com.lb. The Beirut-based paper *Daily Star.*

www.albawaba.com. The most prominent Arab Internet news service, covering politics, sports, and entertainment (see also www.elaph.com, which is only in Arabic).

www.Islamonline.net. The most popular and comprehensive Islamic Web site.

www.haaretzdaily.com. Israel and the Arabs through Israeli eyes in Israel's premier daily.

Index

A

H

About the Author

Andrew Hammond is a journalist who has written extensively on political and cultural issues in the Middle East. Based in the region, he has been a commentator on the Arab media in publications and seminars and is currently a correspondent for Reuters news agency. Any comments on this book are welcome at: arabpopculture@hotmail.com.